P9-DEP-213

University Textbook Series

Especially Designed for Collateral Reading

HARRY W. JONES
Directing Editor
Professor of Law, Columbia University

ADMIRALTY
Grant Gilmore, Professor of Law, University of Chicago.
Charles L. Black, Jr., Professor of Law, Yale University.

ADMIRALTY AND FEDERALISM
David W. Robertson, Professor of Law, University of Texas.

CIVIL PROCEDURE, BASIC
Milton D. Green, Professor of Law, University of California, Hastings College of the Law.

COMMERCIAL TRANSACTIONS—Selected Statutes, Fourth Edition
Robert Braucher, Professor of Law, Harvard University.
Arthur E. Sutherland, Jr., Professor of Law, Harvard University.

CONFLICT OF LAWS, Third Edition
The late George W. Stumberg, Professor of Law, University of Texas.

CONFLICT OF LAWS, COMMENTARY ON THE
Russell J. Weintraub, Professor of Law, University of Texas.

CORPORATIONS, Second Edition
Norman D. Lattin, Professor of Law, University of California, Hastings College of the Law.

CRIMINAL LAW, Second Edition
Rollin M. Perkins, Professor of Law, University of California, Hastings College of the Law.

ESTATES IN LAND & FUTURE INTERESTS, PREFACE TO
Thomas F. Bergin, Professor of Law, University of Virginia.
Paul G. Haskell, Professor of Law, Case Western Reserve University.

EVIDENCE: COMMON SENSE AND COMMON LAW
John M. Maguire, Professor of Law, Harvard University.

EVIDENCE, STUDENTS' TEXT ON THE LAW OF
John Henry Wigmore.

JURISPRUDENCE: MEN AND IDEAS OF THE LAW
The late Edwin W. Patterson, Cardozo Professor of Jurisprudence, Columbia University.

LEGAL RESEARCH, FUNDAMENTALS OF, Third Edition, with 1970 Assignments Pamphlet
Ervin H. Pollack, Professor of Law, The Ohio State University.

THE PROFESSION OF LAW
L. Ray Patterson, Professor of Law, Vanderbilt University.
Elliott E. Cheatham, Professor of Law, Vanderbilt University.

PROPERTY
John E. Cribbet, Dean of the Law School, University of Illinois.

TORTS
Clarence Morris, Professor of Law, University of Pennsylvania.

TRUSTS, Second Edition
Ralph A. Newman, Professor of Law, University of California, Hastings College of the Law.

TRUSTS AND WILLS, THE PLANNING AND DRAFTING OF
Thomas L. Shaffer, Dean of the Law School, University of Notre Dame.

BASIC CIVIL PROCEDURE

MILTON D. GREEN
Professor of Law
University of California
Hastings College of the Law

Mineola, New York
The Foundation Press, Inc.
1972

COPYRIGHT © 1972

By

THE FOUNDATION PRESS, INC.

Library of Congress Catalog Card Number: 76–190042

Green, Basic Civ.Proc. UTB

PREFACE

This book is designed as an aid for first year law students. It makes no pretense of being a comprehensive treatise. Its purpose is to assist the student along the thorny pathways of procedure by providing an over-view and by serving as a compact interpretive ally in helping him to understand the cases and the classroom discussions. An earnest effort has been made to adapt it to the leading casebooks in current use.

In planning this book, I have tried to chart a course between an outline and a tome, hoping to come up with an uncomplicated statement of a very complicated subject. An essence only. The challenge always was, how much do I dare leave out and still cover the essentials of an intricate subject? To masters in the field, it may seem too simplistic; to students, too complex. My hope is that it may clarify without confusing.

My debts and acknowledgments go back over many years and to many people: to my excellent teachers on the faculties of the University of Michigan and Columbia University, who instilled in me a love of the law and who bludgeoned me into a realization of the need for never-ending research; to my many dedicated colleagues—practitioners, judges, academicians—whose writings, contributions and crusades keep a lively current of creative thought constantly moving through the law; to my hundreds of former students, from whom I learned so much as I sought to teach them; and to my wife, Jerry, to whom I owe the most.

To all of these, this book is dedicated.

MILTON D. GREEN

San Francisco, California
March, 1972

*

v

SUMMARY OF CONTENTS

*

TABLE OF CONTENTS

†

BASIC CIVIL PROCEDURE

*

CHAPTER I. A PRELIMINARY SURVEY

Courts are the instrumentalities established by government for the settlement of disputes. Each state is free, within constitutional limitations, to fashion its own court system, its own substantive law, and the rules of procedure which will be used in its courts. The same thing is true of our federal government. We therefore have fifty-one court systems, no two of which are exactly alike, each operating under its own procedural rules.[1] Stated in its simplest terms, civil procedure is that portion of the law which is concerned with the establishment and operation of these instrumentalities, the ground rules laid down by our legislatures and the courts for the settlement of civil disputes—the machinery of justice.

Courts, and court systems, are part of the apparatus of government. They exercise the judicial power of the state and they obtain that power by a grant from the sovereign, usually found in the state constitution, but sometimes spelled out in further detail by the legislature. For instance, in the federal government, the judicial power of the United States is defined in the constitution and, except in the case of the original jurisdiction of the Supreme Court, the constitution delegates to Congress the duty of establishing the lower federal courts and defining the judicial power each may exercise.[2] Some courts are invested with broad authority to handle all types of cases. They are known as courts of general jurisdiction. Other courts are invested with judicial power which is restricted to the handling of particular types of cases, or cases arising in particular geographical areas, or cases which fall within certain minimum or maximum monitary amounts. They are known as courts of limited jurisdiction. Trial courts are said to be courts of original jurisdiction, because the case originates in them, as distinguished from appellate courts which are courts of review. The problem of the jurisdiction of courts, the power or authority which they may exercise, is one of the most important and complex problems of civil procedure. The judgment of a court which has not been invested with authority to handle the type of case to which the particular case belongs is a nullity. The books are full of cases which have been

---

1. Pound, Organization of Courts (1940); Joiner, The Judicial System of Michigan, 38 U.Det.L.J. 505 (1961); Symposium, The Judicial System of Illinois, 1952 U.Ill.L.F. 461; Ames, The Origin and Jurisdiction of the Municipal Courts in California, 21 Cal.L.Rev. 117 (1933); H. Jones, The Courts, the Public and the Law Explosion, Ch. 1 (1965).

2. U.S.Const. art. III.

tried and won in a lower court only to be reversed and dismissed on appeal because the court which rendered the judgment had no authority to do so. Thus, it is of paramount importance for an attorney to bring his suit in a court which has been invested with authority to handle it. Such power is known as *subject matter jurisdiction.*

In order to render a valid judgment a court must not only possess subject matter jurisdiction, it must also have jurisdiction over the parties to the dispute. This is known as *in personam jurisdiction.* There is rarely any problem with regard to the plaintiff since he submits himself to the jurisdiction of the court when he files suit. Defendants, however, are generally unwilling suitors who come to court only as the result of some compulsion. In an earlier age the court acquired jurisdiction over the defendant by having him arrested. Today, all that is required is the service of a summons upon him, which sounds easy, but which often presents perplexing problems. In some cases the ownership or status of property is involved, and, when a court undertakes to decide such an issue, it is said to be exercising *in rem jurisdiction.*

It often happens that a plaintiff who desires to bring a suit may have a choice of forums. In other words, there may be more than one court which has subject matter jurisdiction and which is in a position to acquire in personam jurisdiction over the parties. For example, let us assume that a plaintiff, who lives in Los Angeles, is seriously injured when a defective color tube of his television set explodes. The defendant, who made the set, is a Michigan corporation, but sells its product in California. Here the plaintiff would have a choice of suing in a California state court, a Michigan state court, or a federal court in either California or Michigan because the case is between citizens of different states, one of the traditional grounds of federal jurisdiction.[3] Would the result be different if the plaintiff chose one forum rather than another? Before an answer to that question can be given it is necessary to consider: (1) the distinction between substance and procedure, and (2) the law to be applied by a federal court.

All law can be classified as either substantive law or procedural law. Substantive law is the law which defines the rights and duties of individuals toward each other and toward the state, and prescribes the rules of conduct to promote the welfare of the social group. Most of it is to be found in our common law, or case law, which has evolved over the centuries to meet changing needs.

3. U.S.C.A. § 1332.

It is supplemented by statutory law, passed by the legislature, to alter common law rules or to supplement them. Procedural law, or adjective law, furnishes the means by which the substantive law is enforced. It does not define rights or duties, but merely implements them. The distinction between the two types of law is important in several situations, but in none has it received more attention than in relation to the law to be applied in the federal courts.

Prior to 1938 the procedure in common law actions in the federal courts was governed by the Conformity Act [4] which provided that a federal court should follow "as near as may be" the procedure of the courts of the state in which it sat. Since there were great variations in the procedures in the different states, this meant that there was no uniform procedure for the federal courts. Another act of Congress provided that, except where federal law was involved, "the laws of the several States" shall apply.[5] This latter statute dealt with substantive law, but it was interpreted to mean that only the statutory law of the state was meant by the word "laws", leaving the federal courts free to fashion their own version of what the common law was.[6] Under this interpretation, a large body of "federal common law" was developed by the cases which a federal court would apply even if it conflicted with the common law of the state. In summary, prior to 1938, there was uniformity in the federal courts as to substantive common law, but not as to procedure. In 1938 two events occurred, which completely changed the picture, and which make 1938 a landmark year: (1) the Supreme Court promulgated uniform rules of practice and procedure for the federal courts, and (2) it decided the case of Erie Railroad Co. v. Tompkins.[7]

The federal rules were the result of a long campaign for reform of federal procedure which finally culminated in the passage by Congress of an enabling act delegating to the Supreme Court the authority to make rules of procedure for the federal district courts.[8] The statute provided, however, that the rules should not affect the substantive rights of any litigant. This delegated power was exercised by the Supreme Court by the promulgation of the uniform rules. From time to time one of the rules has been attacked as invading substantive rights and thus going beyond

4. 17 Stat. 196 (1872).

5. Fed.Judiciary Act of 1789 § 34, 1 Stat. 92.

6. Swift v. Tyson, 41 U.S. (16 Peters) 1, 10 L.Ed. 865 (1842).

7. 304 U.S. 64, 58 S.Ct. 817, 82 L. Ed. 1188 (1938).

8. 28 U.S.C.A. § 2072.

the grant of power in the enabling act,[9] but to date the Supreme Court has not invalidated any rule on this ground. The rules stand as one of the great landmarks in procedural reform because they made uniform the procedure in the federal courts, because they simplified and modernized the procedure, and because they served as a model for reform in many states.

Erie, decided at the same term of court, made equally revolutionary changes in the substantive law in the federal courts. It overruled nearly 100 years of precedent and held that, in diversity of citizenship cases, there was no federal common law and that the federal court must apply the common law of the state. The logic of Erie may be summarized as follows: the diversity jurisdiction of the federal courts was not granted because any federal law was involved, but to furnish an impartial forum where the litigants were citizens of different states; in such cases the litigants were relying upon state substantive law; that when, in such a case, a federal court applied federal common law it was unconstitutionally invading rights reserved to the states. The essence of Erie was that, as far as substantive law is concerned, a federal court must apply the same law that a state court would apply.[10] It remained for later cases to make it clear that the state law which the federal court must apply was the law of the state in which it sat, including that state's conflict of laws rules,[11] and its notions of public policy.[12] In our hypothetical case of the defective television, if the case were tried in a California state court, it would apply the California rule on the liability of a manufacturer for defective products. If the case were tried in a Michigan state court, it would apply its own rule in products liability cases, which might differ from the California rule.[13]

---

9. In Sibbach v. Wilson & Co., 312 U.S. 1, 61 S.Ct. 422, 85 L.Ed. 479 (1941), Rule 35 (providing for physical and mental examinations of parties whose condition is in issue) was attacked as involving substantive rights, but the rule was sustained by a 5–4 decision. The rule was again sustained in Schlagenhauf v. Holder, 379 U.S. 104, 85 S.Ct. 234, 13 L.Ed.2d 152 (1964).

10. In Ford Motor Co. v. Mathis, 322 F.2d 267, 269 (5th Cir. 1963), Judge Brown said, "Writing with an Erie-Texas pen, it might be that, as of old, the Moving Finger writes, and having writ, moves on. But it may be that having written, what we write is soon erased. This is not the last word, only the latest. And before the slug drops in a St. Paul linotype, the first writing Texas court may melt down the lead to so much dross. Such are the perils of diversity jurisdiction."

11. Klaxon Co. v. Stentor Elec. Mfg. Co., 313 U.S. 487, 61 S.Ct. 1020, 85 L.Ed. 1477 (1941).

12. Griffin v. McCoach, 313 U.S. 498, 61 S.Ct. 1023, 85 L.Ed. 1481 (1941).

13. It is possible that, under its conflict of laws rule relating to torts involving products liability, that a Michigan court would apply the substantive law of California. See generally, Weintraub, Commentary

If the case were tried in a federal court sitting either in California or in Michigan, it would be required, under Erie, to apply the substantive law of the state in which it sat and not some notion of its own as to products liability.[14] It could, however, use its own procedure since the new rules established uniform procedure for all federal courts.

If the distinction between substance and procedure were clear-cut, the rule of the Erie case might be easy to apply. The distinction, however, is not clear-cut. There is a gray area. Any procedural point could, conceivably, affect substantive rights. Some obviously do. The statute of limitations,[15] usually regarded as procedural, cuts off a substantive right if suit is not filed in time. The burden of proof, generally regarded as procedure, will tip the scales when the evidence is evenly balanced.[16] The mode of trial, whether to a judge or jury,[17] or to an arbitrator,[18] normally considered a procedural matter, may vitally affect the decision. Under the rule of Erie the accident of diversity of citizenship should not affect the substantive rights of the litigants. The Supreme Court, therefore, in a series of subsequent cases, decided that a point of state law, although normally regarded as procedural, should be applied by a federal court in a diversity case if it would, or could, vitally affect the outcome of the case.[19] This is the famous "outcome-determinative" test: for the purposes of the Erie doctrine, a point of state law, usually considered procedural, will be characterized as substantive and applied by a federal court if it would or could determine the outcome of the case. This exception to the Erie doctrine proved too much. Carried to its logical extreme it would require a federal court, in a diversity case, to apply not only state substantive law but also state procedure. Sensitive to the dilemma in which it found itself the Supreme Court sharply limited the outcome-determinative exception. In Byrd v. Blue Ridge Rural Electrical Coopera-

on the Conflict of Laws, 253–59 (1971).

14. Nor could it choose the better of the two rules if the Michigan and California rules differed. Klaxon, supra n. 11.

15. Guaranty Trust Co. v. York, 326 U.S. 99, 65 S.Ct. 1464, 89 L.Ed. 2079 (1945); Keaton v. Crayton, 326 F.Supp. 1155 (W.D.Mo.1969).

16. Sampson v. Channell, 110 F.2d 754 (1st Cir. 1940).

17. Byrd v. Blue Ridge Rural Elec. Cooperative, 356 U.S. 525, 78 S. Ct. 893, 2 L.Ed.2d 953 (1958).

18. Bernhardt v. Polygraphic Co. of America, 350 U.S. 198, 76 S.Ct. 273, 100 L.Ed. 199 (1956).

19. The test was first articulated in the case of Guaranty Trust Co. v. York, supra n. 15.

tive,[20] a case involving the right to jury trial on a particular point, the Supreme Court held that, notwithstanding the fact that the outcome of the case might be influenced by the mode of trial, federal law must be applied because of the strong countervailing influence of the federal preference for trial by jury. In Hanna v. Plumer,[21] a case involving the mode of service of process, which in the particular case might have been outcome-determinative in view of the statute of limitations, the court said that where a point of law is *specifically* covered by one of the federal rules, the federal rule must be applied unless it can be said that the rule cuts so deeply into substance as to go beyond the power of the Supreme Court to promulgate it under the enabling act. Hanna does not entirely eliminate the outcome-determinative exception to Erie, but it reduces its dimensions to an extent which only future cases can define.[22]

The lesson to be learned from the age-old struggle to distinguish between substance and procedure is that the advocate must be thoroughly conversant with both branches of the law: the branch which defines the rights and duties of his client, and the branch which defines the means by which those rights and duties may be implemented. The scope of the present volume is limited to the latter.

Our hypothetical case, in which the plaintiff had a choice of suing in either a state or a federal court, suggests another problem: the delicate balance between federal and state jurisdiction. The general rule is that when a court acquires jurisdiction over a case it may exercise that jurisdiction to a conclusion, resulting in a final judgment, without interference by some other court. A state has no power to limit the jurisdiction of a federal court,[23] nor may it enjoin parties from suing in a federal court.[24] The converse of that proposition is not true. The federal courts do possess limited power to interfere in state court proceedings. As we shall see later, in certain situations, upon the petition of

20. Supra n. 17.

21. 380 U.S. 460, 85 S.Ct. 1136, 14 L.Ed.2d 8 (1965).

22. On the Erie doctrine, in general, see: Friendly, In Praise of Erie— and of the New Federal Common Law, 39 N.Y.U.L.Rev. 383 (1964); Clark, State Law in the Federal Courts: The Brooding Omnipresence of Erie v. Tompkins, 55 Yale L.J. 267 (1946); McCoid, Hanna v. Plumer: The Erie Doctrine Changes Shape, 51 Va.L.Rev. 884 (1965); Stason, Choice of Law Within the Federal System: Erie v. Hanna, 52 Cornell L.Q. 377 (1967); Comment, Choice of Procedure in Diversity Cases, 75 Yale L.J. 477 (1966).

23. Chicago & N. W. R. R. v. Whitton's Adm'r, 80 U.S. (13 Wall.) 270, 20 L.Ed. 571 (1871).

24. Donovan v. City of Dallas, 377 U.S. 408, 84 S.Ct. 1579, 12 L.Ed.2d 409 (1964).

the defendant, a case may be removed from the state to a federal court. Congress has also invested the federal courts with power, in certain situations, to enjoin state court proceedings.[25] However, the general rule, as expressed in the Federal Judicial Code, prohibits federal interference with state court action "except as expressly authorized by Act of Congress, or where necessary in aid of its jurisdiction, or to protect or effectuate its judgments."[26] The interpretation of this statute has not always been uniform, but at present it is being narrowly construed.[27] A federal court may enjoin a state official from violating rights protected by the United States Constitution.[28] However, to prevent abuse of this power, Congress has provided that such actions, seeking injunctive relief against state action, must be brought in a specially convened three-judge district court.[29] In diversity actions in the federal courts, where the substantive state law is unclear the federal court may dismiss or suspend action in the case until the state courts have cleared up the point. This is known as the doctrine of abstention.[30] Full treatment of such federal-state relationships lies within the domain of constitutional law and federal jurisdiction and is consequently beyond the scope of the present volume.[31]

abstention

The book follows a chronological order. The first subject treated, and perhaps the most difficult, is *jurisdiction*, over the subject matter and over the parties. It is followed by *venue*, the place where that jurisdiction should be exercised. Next comes the size of the law suit, which is traditionally treated under the heading of joinder of parties and joinder of causes of actions, but which is here combined under the heading of *claims and claimants*. All parties must file with the court their respective con-

25. The extent of this power is discussed in Toucey v. New York Life Ins. Co., 314 U.S. 118, 62 S.Ct. 139, 86 L.Ed. 100 (1941).

26. 28 U.S.C.A. § 2283.

27. Atlantic Coast Line R. R. v. Brotherhood of Locomotive Eng'rs, 398 U.S. 281, 287, 90 S.Ct. 1739, 1743, 26 L.Ed.2d 234, 241 (1970) in which the court said that ". . . any injunction against state court proceedings otherwise proper under general equitable principles must be based on one of the specific statutory exceptions to § 2283 if it is to be upheld."

28. Ex parte Young, 209 U.S. 123, 28 S.Ct. 441, 52 L.Ed. 714 (1908).

29. 28 U.S.C.A. § 2281. For an excellent historical study of the three-judge system, how it has operated, and the present movement to amend or eliminate it, see Ammerman, Three-Judge Courts: See How They Run! 52 F.R.D. 293 (1971). For recent representative cases see Gold v. Lomenzo, 425 F. 2d 959 (2d Cir. 1970); Bistrick v. University of So. Carolina, 319 F. Supp. 193 (D.So.Car.1970).

30. Warren v. Government Nat'l Mortgage Ass'n, 443 F.2d 624 (8th Cir. 1971).

31. For a full treatment of the subject see Wright, Law of Federal Courts (1970), Ch. 8.

tentions regarding the controversy. These are the *pleadings* which, if properly drawn, should disclose the nature of the case and the points of disagreement between the parties. *Pretrial discovery* devices are available to all parties so that they can fully inform themselves of the facts of the case, thus avoiding surprise at the trial. The *trial*, with or without a jury, depending upon the nature of the case, allows each party an opportunity to present his evidence, to cross-examine his opponent's witnesses, and to argue his case to the court or jury. The *judgment*, pronounced by the court, is the final determination of the controversy, which precludes the parties from ever relitigating the matter (res judicata), but the losing party has his right to *appeal* to a higher court which will review the record to determine whether prejudicial error was committed in the court below.

CHAPTER II. JURISDICTION

SECTION 1. IN GENERAL

Jurisdiction is something which must be explained, rather than defined. In essence it is quite simple: the power, or authority, of a court to decide a case or controversy. In practice, it may become quite complicated because there are so many different kinds of courts, state and federal, and there are so many different kinds of cases, involving so many different kinds of parties, residing in so many different possible places, and perhaps having interests in so many different kinds of property which may become involved in the litigation. Consequently, in order to answer the question whether a court has jurisdiction to decide a particular case, one must have some knowledge of the jurisdictional rules which have been developed over the centuries. These rules can be grouped under several headings: (1) whether the court, in the particular case, has been granted authority to decide this type of case, (2) whether the court, in the particular case, has authority over the individuals involved, (3) whether the court has given adequate notice to the parties, and (4) whether the court has acquired jurisdiction over the property involved. In discussing these four subjects, there is a complication: in this country we have two sets of courts, state and federal. In regard to the first subject there is a substantial difference between state and federal courts—consequently, they will be discussed in separate sections; in regard to the other three, there is little difference between state and federal courts, hence they will be discussed together.

SECTION 2. STATE COURTS—JURISDICTION OVER THE SUBJECT MATTER

Under the Tenth Amendment each state is free to establish its own judicial system, and to distribute its judicial power among the courts which it creates. Some state judicial systems are simple, some are complex. Some states have established special courts with limited jurisdiction over probate, domestic relations, and criminal law, and most established minor courts with pecuniary or geographical limits. All states have courts of so-called general jurisdiction which are empowered to handle all types of cases which are not pre-empted by one of the special courts. In all states the subject matter jurisdiction is defined by the organic act which created the court, whether that be in the state

11

constitution, in the state statutes, or in the cases interpreting the constitutional and statutory provisions.

A court is said to have jurisdiction over the subject matter of an action when it has been invested by the sovereign with the power to decide the type of case to which the instant case belongs. Where the jurisdictional lines are clearly drawn, serious questions regarding subject matter jurisdiction are unlikely to arise. However, the apparent clarity of statutory language may be deceptive. For example, where a trial court was invested with power to try all "actions at law and suits in equity" it was held that the court had no divorce jurisdiction since neither the common law courts nor the equity courts possessed such power.[1]

A state trial court can not handle cases belonging to a type over which the federal courts have been given exclusive jurisdiction.[2] For the most part the limitations on the subject matter jurisdiction of state courts have been cast in the form of monetary or geographical restrictions. Justice of the peace courts and municipal courts have monetary ceilings on their jurisdiction which give rise to three sorts of problems: (1) may a plaintiff with a claim over the jurisdictional amount split it up into several smaller suits so as to keep within the jurisdiction of the inferior court?[3] (2) may several plaintiffs, each with a claim below the jurisdictional limit of a higher trial court, lump their claims so as to make the jurisdictional amount?[4] and (3) where a plaintiff brings a suit within the limits of an inferior court and the defendant interposes a counterclaim for an amount beyond the jurisdictional limit, may the court retain and decide the whole case?[5] Geographical limits also pose problems. It is not unusual for the jurisdictional grant of an inferior court to restrict its power to causes of action arising within the geographical limits of the area served by the court: precinct, county, or municipal-

---

1. Kenyon v. Kenyon, 3 Utah 431, 24 P. 829 (1861).

2. C. J. Hendry Co. v. Moore, 318 U.S. 133, 63 S.Ct. 499, 87 L.Ed. 663 (1943).

3. The general rule is that a plaintiff may not split his cause of action: Kruce v. Lakeside Biscuit Co., 198 Mich. 736, 165 N.W. 609 (1917).

4. To the effect that such aggregation is not permissible see Winer v. Bank of Blytheville, 89 Ark. 435, 117 S.W. 232 (1909). Compare Hammell v. Superior Court, 217

Cal. 5, 17 P.2d 101 (1932) where all claims were assigned to one plaintiff and the court held the aggregate amount could be used.

5. There is a split of authority on this point. Weinick v. I. G. S. Pants Co., 189 Misc. 516, 72 N.Y. S.2d 380 (1947) held the counterclaim would be scaled down to the jurisdictional limit. Dyett v. Harney, 53 Colo. 381, 127 P. 226 (1912) held that the court should take jurisdiction of plaintiff's claim and dismiss the counterclaim. The West's Ann.Cal.Code Civ.Proc. § 396 provides the case shall be transferred to a higher court.

ity. It may be convenient for all of the parties to bring the action in a particular court because they live in the area, but the cause of action arose elsewhere. This they cannot do because subject matter jurisdiction cannot be conferred by consent of the parties.[6] There is another type of geographical limitation which is troublesome because it applies to all types of trial courts: the rule that the courts of a state have no power to try suits for damages for a trespass to real property which is situated beyond the borders of the state.[7] This limitation is a carryover from the English distinction between "transitory" and "local" actions. At one time in England all actions were local—they had to be tried in the county where the event occurred. At that time jurors were chosen because they had knowledge of what had happened. When, at a much later date, the jury became a body of disinterested persons chosen because of their lack of knowledge of the case, the necessity of tying the trial down to a particular locality ceased, nearly all actions became transitory, and could be tried in any competent court. There remained, however, one type of case which the British insisted was local. That was an action affecting real property. It had to be tried in the county where the land was located. This made sense when the purpose of the action was to try the title to the land or to recover the possession of it because only the court where the land was located could afford the necessary relief. It did not make sense where the only relief asked was for damages—money—which any court was competent to give. Nevertheless, the English rule in regard to trespass to foreign land remained, and we inherited it. The rule has been severely criticized, and a few bold states have disavowed it, but it still remains the law in a majority of the states.[8]

SECTION 3.   FEDERAL COURTS—JURISDICTION OVER THE SUBJECT MATTER

In general. Jurisdiction over the subject matter is of vital importance in the federal court system because all federal courts are courts of limited jurisdiction.[9] The framers of the consti-

---

6. Werner v. Illinois Cent. R. R., 379 Ill. 559, 42 N.E.2d 82 (1942).

7. Ellenwood v. Marietta Chair Co., 158 U.S. 105, 15 S.Ct. 771, 39 L.Ed. 913 (1895).

8. The rule has been repudiated in Minnesota: Little v. Chicago, St. Paul, M. & O. R. R., 65 Minn. 48, 67 N.W. 846 (1896); and in Arkan-

sas: Reasor-Hill Corp. v. Harrison, 220 Ark. 521, 249 S.W.2d 994 (1952). See Stumberg, Conflict of Laws (1963) 173–74.

9. The judicial power of the United States is defined by the constitution as extending to "all Cases, in Law and Equity." U.S.Const. art. III, § 2. It does not extend to matters which were historically han-

tution recognized the need for a federal judicial system but they wished to restrict its power in order not to encroach upon states' rights. Consequently, in the judicial article they sharply limited the judicial power and vested it "in one Supreme Court, and in such inferior Courts as the Congress may from time to time ordain and establish." [10] Pursuant to this constitutional authority Congress created the district courts giving them exclusive jurisdiction in admiralty, bankruptcy, patents, copyrights and trademarks, and concurrent jurisdiction (with the state courts) in federal question cases and diversity of citizenship cases.[11] The latter two categories comprise the bulk of the work of the district courts.

Federal question jurisdiction. The Congressional act provides: "The district courts shall have original jurisdiction of all civil actions wherein the matter in controversy exceeds the sum or value of $10,000, exclusive of interest and costs, and *arises under the Constitution, laws, or treaties of the United States.*" [12] (Emphasis supplied). The language of the statute

dled by the Ecclesiastical Courts, such as divorce, Blank v. Blank, 320 F.Supp. 1389 (W.D.Pa.1971), or probate, Davis v. Hunter, 323 F. Supp. 976 (D.Conn.1970).

10. U.S.Const. art. III, § 1.

11. 28 U.S.C.A. §§ 1331–61. The present code is the result of numerous amendments, over the years, many of them on an ad hoc basis. In 1959, Chief Justice Warren, in his annual address to the American Law Institute, suggested that the time had come for a detailed study of the "proper jurisdictional balance between the Federal and State court systems." Responding to this suggestion, the Institute embarked upon such a study, and ten years later presented a proposal for a complete revision of the federal judicial code. It is a truly monumental document, consisting of a proposed new draft of the statutes (comprising 98 pages) and over 400 pages of explanatory comment. It will hereinafter be referred to as the ALI Study. A summary of the proposals, prepared by Professor Field, the Chief Reporter, may be found in 46 F.R.D. 141 (1969). An excellent explanation of the proposed

changes may be found in Wright, Restructuring Federal Jurisdiction: The American Law Institute Proposals, XXVI Wash. & Lee L.Rev. 185 (1969), which is reviewed by Professor Keeffe in 56 A.B.A.J. 286 (1970). The proposals of the ALI Study undertake to place federal jurisdiction on a more rational and workable basis, and in so doing they propose to restrict federal jurisdiction in some respects, to expand it in others, to correct defects in the current statutes, and to clarify existing law. Some of the proposals are highly controversial. Many of them would result in obvious improvements in the law. To what extent the proposals will be adopted by Congress remains to be seen.

12. 28 U.S.C.A. § 1331. The ALI Study proposes to abolish the $10,-000 minimum in most cases where jurisdiction is based on a federal question, in the interest of preserving uniformity in federal law "and to protect litigants relying on federal law from the danger that state courts will not properly apply that law, either through misunderstanding or lack of sympathy." ALI Study, 4.

seems clear, but it has required a great deal of judicial interpretation.

One of the leading cases involved the question of whether the passage of the Interstate Commerce Act by Congress disabled a railroad company from carrying out its contract to issue free yearly passes to the plaintiffs who had been injured in a wreck and who had accepted the contract in settlement of their claim against the railroad.[13] When the railroad stopped issuing passes the plaintiffs sued in a federal court alleging the Interstate Commerce Act did not apply to their case, and if it did it was unconstitutional. Although neither party raised the question of the jurisdiction of the court, which granted relief to the plaintiffs, the Supreme Court reversed and dismissed. It said that a case "arises" under the Constitution, laws, or treaties of the United States only when the plaintiff's statement of claim shows that his right is based on such. It is not enough that the defendant may interject a federal question in the case by way of defense.[14]

In Gully v. First National Bank,[15] the defendant was the assignee of the assets of a former bank and had agreed to pay all valid debts of the former bank. The plaintiff, a state tax collector, sued to collect taxes which he alleged were one of the valid debts. The defendant argued that the taxes (involving a national bank) were not a valid debt unless lawfully imposed and this depended on a federal statute, which raised a federal question. In dismissing for want of jurisdiction, the court held that to come within the statute the federal right or immunity must be an *essential* element of plaintiff's case. Mr. Justice Cardozo, writing for the court, said that it is not enough that a question of federal law "is lurking in the background." [16]

As the above cases indicate, the Supreme Court has taken a strict and narrow view as to what constitutes a federal question for jurisdictional purposes. However, if a plaintiff in his complaint squarely bases his claim on a federally created right—derived from the federal constitution or statutes—even though

13. Louisville & Nashville R. R. v. Mottley, 211 U.S. 149, 29 S.Ct. 42, 53 L.Ed. 126 (1908). The ALI Study would change the rule in the Mottley case by not requiring the "federal question" to appear on the face of the complaint. " . . . [T]he need for a federal forum is as great for the defendant who relies on federal law to defeat a state-created claim as it is for the plaintiff whose claim is derived from federal law." ALI Study, 4.

14. Accord: Brough v. United Steelworkers of America, 437 F.2d 748 (1st Cir. 1971).

15. 299 U.S. 109, 57 S.Ct. 96, 81 L. Ed. 70 (1936).

16. Id. at 117, 57 S.Ct. at 100, 81 L. Ed. at 74.

it appears that his claim is debatable, he has passed the jurisdictional hurdle unless the court considers his claim not only debatable but frivolous.[17] If, during the course of the proceedings, it appears from the facts that his alleged claim does not in fact "arise" out of the constitution or federal law, the case will then be dismissed for want of jurisdiction.[18]

Diversity jurisdiction. The second principal ground of jurisdiction in the federal courts is diversity of citizenship which is satisfied when the action is between "(1) citizens of different States; (2) citizens of a State, and foreign states or citizens or subjects thereof; and (3) citizens of different States and in which foreign states or citizens or subjects thereof are additional parties." [19]

17. Bell v. Hood, 327 U.S. 678, 66 S.Ct. 773, 90 L.Ed. 939 (1946).

In Bivens v. Six Unknown Named Agents, 403 U.S. 388, 91 S.Ct. 1999, 29 L.Ed.2d 619 (1971), relying on Bell v. Hood, the Court holds a violation of the 4th Amendment (search and seizure) gives rise to a federal cause of action, even without an implementing act of Congress. The court split 6–3. The case is noted in 57 A.B.A.J. 1025 (1971).

18. Wheeldin v. Wheeler, 373 U.S. 647, 83 S.Ct. 1441, 10 L.Ed.2d 605 (1963). Textile Workers Union of America v. Lincoln Mills of Ala., 353 U.S. 448, 77 S.Ct. 912, 1 L.Ed. 2d 972 (1957) held that a suit seeking enforcement of arbitration under § 301 of the Labor Management Relations Act of 1947 "arises" under federal law, and is removable from a state to a federal court. However, in Clairol, Inc. v. Suburban Cosmetics & Beauty Supply, Inc., 278 F.Supp. 859 (N.D.Ill.1968) it was held that an unfair competition case brought in a state court could not be removed to a federal court because the plaintiff did not rely upon the Federal Food, Drug & Cosmetic Act. In Ivy Broadcasting Co. v. American Tel. & Tel. Co., 391 F.2d 486 (2d Cir. 1968) it was held that the plaintiff's claim need not arise from a federal statutory source; that it is sufficient if it arises out of federal common law. The question of how much federal common

law is left after the decision of Erie R. R. v. Tompkins is considered supra, in Chapter I.

19. 28 U.S.C.A. § 1332. Whether or not mere diversity of citizenship should be a valid ground for federal jurisdiction has been a subject of controversy over the years, especially in view of the congested dockets of the federal courts. The ALI Study takes the position that it is a valid ground. It states: "[The] basic principle is that the function of the jurisdiction is to assure a high level of justice to the traveler or visitor from another state . . . " ALI Study, 2. The ALI proposals therefore retain diversity jurisdiction but, in line with their basic premise that its justification is to overcome prejudice, they restrict it in three ways: (1) they bar a plaintiff from suing in a federal court in his home state, (2) they bar a corporation or other business enterprise from suing in a federal court in a district in which it has maintained a "local establishment" for more than two years, and (3) they bar a commuter from suing in a federal court in the state in which he works. The proposals increase diversity jurisdiction in two areas: (1) where all necessary parties are not amenable to the process of a state court, and (2) they treat partnerships, unions and unincorporated associations the same as corporations in regard to determining diversity.

The first point to be noted is that, although based upon the citizenship of the parties, diversity jurisdiction is subject matter jurisdiction. It is one of the types of cases the federal courts are empowered to entertain. The basic reason for it is to furnish an impartial forum for the traveler who is away from home. If no diversity exists (and there is no federal question involved) then the court is without power to hear the case. This will be true even if the parties appear and "consent" to the jurisdiction because the parties cannot supply a power which the court does not possess.[20]

Since such an important part of federal subject matter jurisdiction is based upon citizenship, it seems desirable to define the term. The Constitution provides that "All persons born or naturalized in the United States . . . are citizens of the United States and of the State wherein they reside." [21] Residence is synonomous with domicile.[22] Domicile is the state where a person has his home.[23] One may change his domicile by acquiring a new one. This is accomplished by (1) his physical presence in the new place, and (2) his intention to make it his home.[24] His motive for changing his domicile is immaterial if there was a bona fide change.[25] It follows that a person who lives abroad may be a United States citizen but not a citizen of any state. Whether such a person be a plaintiff [26] or a defendant [27] his lack of state citizenship will defeat federal jurisdiction where it is

20. The earliest case on the point is Capron v. VanNoorden, 6 U.S. (2 Cranch) 126, 2 L.Ed. 229 (1804), in which the plaintiff brought the suit in federal court, lost and appealed on the ground that the court lacked jurisdiction. The court sustained his point and reversed the case, since diversity did not appear, even though the plaintiff was the one who chose the court and started the suit and the defendant did not object. That the ancient rule is still very much alive is demonstrated by the recent case of Knee v. Chemical Leaman Tank Lines, Inc., 293 F.Supp. 1094 (E.D.Pa. 1968). In that case the plaintiff, a citizen of Pennsylvania, sued the defendant, a Delaware corporation, who participated in pretrial procedures until after the statute of limitations had run, and then raised the question of lack of jurisdiction because its principal place of business was in Pennsylvania (which made it a citizen for diversity purposes: 28 U.S.C.A. § 1332(c)). The

plaintiff loudly protested that this was unfair, but the court nevertheless dismissed because jurisdiction cannot be conferred by consent.

21. U.S.Const. amend. XIV.

22. Janzen v. Goos, 302 F.2d 421 (8th Cir. 1962).

23. Stumberg, Conflict of Laws (1963) Ch. II.

24. Baker v. Keck, 13 F.Supp. 486 (E.D.Ill.1936).

25. Williamson v. Osenton, 232 U.S. 619, 34 S.Ct. 442, 58 L.Ed. 758 (1914); Janzen v. Goos, supra n. 22; Napletana v. Hillsdale College, 385 F.2d 871 (6th Cir. 1967).

26. Pemberton v. Colonna, 189 F. Supp. 430 (E.D.Pa.1960).

27. Hammerstein v. Lyne, 200 F. 165 (W.D.Mo.1912).

based solely upon diversity. Is one who lives in the District of Columbia a citizen of a "state" within the meaning of the diversity jurisdiction? Congress has given an affirmative answer by defining "states" to include the District.[28] The constitutionality of this act was upheld by a sharply divided Supreme Court in one of the strangest cases on record.[29]

Although not mentioned in the Constitution, corporations have been held to be citizens for the purpose of diversity jurisdiction.[30] Some corporations are chartered in more than one state and thus have dual or multiple citizenship. Where this is true the courts are in disagreement as to what it does to diversity jurisdiction. In the early case of Strawbridge v. Curtiss [31] the rule was established that there must be complete diversity. This means that where there are multiple plaintiffs or defendants, if any plaintiff is of the same citizenship as any defendant, the diversity is not complete and no jurisdiction attaches.[32] In the case of the corporation with dual citizenship, should both be considered? Jacobson v. New York, New Haven & Hartford Ry.[33] represents one line of authority, and holds yes, reasoning that federal jurisdiction should be restricted, not expanded. In that case a Massachusetts plaintiff sued a corporation which was chartered by both Massachusetts and Connecticut; the court held there was not complete diversity, and dismissed. The other line of authority is represented by Hudak v. Port Authority Trans-Hudson Corp.[34] which applied the "forum" theory, i. e., where a corpora-

[handwritten margin notes: "Complete diversity", "Corp. problems", "split"]

28. 28 U.S.C.A. § 1332(d).

29. National Mut. Ins. Co. v. Tidewater Transfer Co., 337 U.S. 582, 69 S.Ct. 1173, 93 L.Ed. 1556 (1949). All of the justices of the Court agreed that the validity of the act would depend upon whether it could be supported by Art. I, or Art. III. On the question of the validity of the act under Art. I the vote was Yes—3, No—6. On the question of the validity of the act under Art. III the vote was Yes—2, No—7. Thus, a majority of the Court held the act invalid under both articles, but a differently constituted minority of 5 held the act valid under one or the other, but were in disagreement as to which one.

30. Marshall v. Baltimore & O. R. R., 57 U.S. (16 How.) 314, 14 L.Ed. 953 (1853).

31. 7 U.S. (3 Cranch) 267, 2 L.Ed. 435 (1806).

32. Some states have "direct action" statutes under which one who is injured by a tortfeasor who is covered by liability insurance may sue the insurer direct without joining the insured. However, 28 U.S.C.A. § 1332(c) provides that the insurer shall be deemed a citizen of the same state as the insured. This means that even though there is diversity between the injured plaintiff and the company, if the tortfeasor and the plaintiff are citizens of the same state there is no diversity jurisdiction. Narvaez v. British Am. Ins. Co., 324 F.Supp. 1324 (D. Puerto Rico 1971).

33. 206 F.2d 153 (1st Cir. 1953), aff'd per cur. 347 U.S. 909, 74 S.Ct. 474, 98 L.Ed. 1067 (1954).

34. 238 F.Supp. 790 (S.D.N.Y.1965).

tion is sued in a state in which it is incorporated it is, for that suit, a corporation of that state. In that case a New Jersey plaintiff sued the defendant corporation in a New York federal court. The corporation was incorporated in both New York and New Jersey, but the court sustained the federal jurisdiction by considering only the New York citizenship. In 1958 Congress amended the Judicial Code to provide that for jurisdictional purposes a corporation will be deemed to be a citizen of "any State by which it has been incorporated and of the State where it has its principal place of business." [35] The purpose of the amendment was to prevent a corporation, sued in the state of its principal business, from removing the case to the federal court on the ground of diversity.[36] The new provision has caused some difficulty in its application because, in the case of the large national companies, it is sometimes far from clear where the principal place of business is located.[37]

Unincorporated associations, such as labor unions, have been assuming an increasingly important role in modern society, but have not yet achieved "citizenship" for diversity purposes.[38]

There is a provision in the Judicial Code that "A district court shall not have jurisdiction . . . in which any party, by assignment or otherwise, has been improperly or collusively made or joined to invoke the jurisdiction of such court." [39] In Kramer v. Caribbean Mills, Inc.,[40] this section was invoked to invalidate jurisdiction in a case in which there was an assignment of the claim to create diversity, the assignee agreeing to repay to the assignor 95% of the net recovery. In Lester v. McFaddon,[41] it was also invoked to invalidate jurisdiction, in a

35. 28 U.S.C.A. § 1332(c).

36. Supra n. 34.

37. Kelly v. United States Steel Corp., 284 F.2d 850 (3d Cir. 1960), wherein the court refers to the "nerve center" of the corporation; Celanese Corp. of America v. Vandalia Warehouse Corp., 424 F.2d 1176 (7th Cir. 1970), wherein the court refers to the "center of corporate activity"; Mahoney v. Northwestern Bell Tel. Co., 258 F. Supp. 500 (D.Neb.1966), wherein the court says both theories are largely linguistic, and each case must be decided on its own facts.

38. United Steelworkers of America v. R. H. Bouligny, Inc., 382 U.S. 145, 86 S.Ct. 272, 15 L.Ed.2d 217 (1965).

39. 28 U.S.C.A. § 1359.

40. 394 U.S. 823, 89 S.Ct. 1487, 23 L.Ed.2d 9 (1969).

41. 415 F.2d 1101 (4th Cir. 1969). Accord: McSparran v. Weist, 402 F.2d 867 (3d Cir. 1968); Groh v. Brooks, 421 F.2d 589 (3d Cir. 1970); O'Brien v. Avco Corp., 425 F.2d 1030 (2d Cir. 1969). However, where there are bona fide reasons for appointing the nonresident (apart from creating diversity) the jurisdiction will be sustained: Joyce v. Seigel, 429 F.2d 128 (3d Cir. 1970); Green v. Hale, 433 F.2d 324 (5th Cir. 1970).

wrongful death case, where a nonresident administrator plaintiff had been appointed to create diversity.

In a class action, where the named parties represent the members of a class, diversity is determined by the citizenship of the named parties. If diversity exists as to them it will not be defeated by the intervention of other class members having the same citizenship of parties on the opposite side of the suit.[42]

Removal jurisdiction. So far we have been discussing the *original* jurisdiction of the United States District Court, that is, the competency of the court to try actions originally brought in it. One of the reasons justifying diversity jurisdiction is to avoid possible local prejudice. The need for an impartial court is even more pressing when a defendant is sued away from home. To take care of this situation Congress has provided that any case which could originally have been brought in a federal court may be removed from a state court to a federal court on the petition of the defendant.[43] The right to remove extends to both types of cases, those involving a federal question and diversity cases, but in respect to the latter the defendant may remove only if he is a nonresident of the state in which the suit was brought.[44]

The situation becomes complicated when the case involves multiple parties and multiple claims. Suppose a plaintiff brings suit in a state court against two defendants, one of whom is a citizen of the state and the other is a nonresident; does the latter lose his right to remove the case to the federal court because the plaintiff has joined a local defendant with him? If so it would mean that a knowledgeable plaintiff could effectively destroy a defendant's right to remove in a diversity case. Congress has struggled with the problem. Prior to 1948 the statute provided for removal by the nonresident defendant in such a situation if the case against him was a "separable controversy." This phrase

42. Supreme Tribe of Ben-Hur v. Cauble, 255 U.S. 356, 41 S.Ct. 338, 65 L.Ed. 673 (1921).

43. 28 U.S.C.A. § 1441(a). The bulk of removed cases involve diversity of citizenship or a federal question. These are spelled out in §§ 1331, 1332, and are subject to the $10,000 jurisdictional amount. There are other sections of the Code conferring original jurisdiction on the district courts which are not subject to that restriction. These are also generally removable. An example is Avco Corp. v. Aero Lodge No. 735, Int'l Assn. of Machinists, 390 U.S. 557, 88 S.Ct. 1235, 20 L.

Ed.2d 126 (1968). In that case suit was brought in a state court to enforce the no-strike clause in a collective bargaining agreement. The court held the case was governed by § 301 of the Labor Management Relations Act, and was removable under 28 U.S.C.A. § 1337. It should also be noted that certain types of actions which may be brought in the federal courts are specifically made nonremovable by § 1445. The principal ones are Federal Employers Liability and Workmen's Compensation cases.

44. 28 U.S.C.A. § 1441(b).

caused trouble and was replaced when the Judicial Code was revised in 1948 [45] to provide: "Whenever a separate and independent claim or cause of action, which would be removable if sued on alone, is joined with one or more otherwise non-removable claims or causes of action, the entire case may be removed and the district court may determine all issues therein, or, in its discretion, may remand all matters not otherwise within its original jurisdiction." [46]

This statute was interpreted in American Fire & Casualty Insurance Co. v. Finn.[47] In that case the plaintiff had instructed his insurance broker to obtain fire insurance on his warehouse. Later there was a fire loss and the plaintiff brought suit in a state court against two foreign insurance companies and the broker, who was a local man. His theory against the companies was that an oral contract of insurance had been made. His alternate theory against the broker was that if no insurance contracts had been made, the broker was liable for his negligence. The companies removed the case to a federal court, but the Supreme Court reversed, holding that the case was not removable by the companies because there was no "separate and independent claim or cause of action." To reach this result it adopted a broad definition of a cause of action, emphasizing that there had been but a single wrong to the plaintiff.[48]

The motion picture Cleopatra served as the occasion for another interpretation of the statute.[49] Twentieth Century-Fox Film Corp. brought suit in a New York state court against Elizabeth Taylor and Richard Burton for breach of their separate contracts, for inducing each other to break their contracts, and in tort for the damage they caused the company by their behavior during the shooting of the film. Burton removed the case to the federal court and the plaintiff moved to remand to the state court. The plaintiff was a Delaware corporation with its principal place of business in New York; Miss Taylor was a United States citizen, but not a citizen of any state; Burton was a Brit-

---

45. For a history of this section see Wright, Law of Federal Courts (2d ed. 1970) [Hereinafter cited as Wright] 136 et seq.

46. 28 U.S.C.A. § 1441(c).

47. 341 U.S. 6, 71 S.Ct. 534, 95 L.Ed. 702 (1951).

48. In Frontier Enterprises, Inc. v. ICA Corp., 319 F.Supp. 1156, 1159–60 (D.Minn.1970), after quoting extensively from the Finn case, the court said: "A single wrong is not parlayed into separate and independent causes of action by multiplying the legal theories upon which relief is sought or by multiplying defendants against whom a remedy is sought for the same injury." Accord: Smith v. General Motors Acceptance Corp., 324 F. Supp. 105 (W.D.Mo.1970).

49. Twentieth Century-Fox Film Corp. v. Taylor, 239 F.Supp. 913 (S.D.N.Y.1965).

ish subject. Had Burton been sole defendant he could have removed the case without question, and had Miss Taylor been sole defendant the case would have been clearly non-removable. The court distinguished the Finn case, where the plaintiff had suffered a single wrong. Here, said the court, there were two separate contracts of employment, made on different dates, and for different periods of time. They did not "coalesce" into a single contract. The allegations of conduct amounting to a joint tort "do not destroy the independent character of the cause of action against Burton for breach of his individual agreement . . . . In sum, plaintiff here charges more than a single wrong." [50] The court held the case was removable.

The statute gives the right to remove only to defendants, since, if the plaintiff had wanted to sue in the federal court, he could have brought the case there in the first place. But what of the situation where a plaintiff sues in a state court (because his claim is below the jurisdictional limit of the federal court) and the defendant files a counterclaim seeking damages well above the federal limit? May the plaintiff remove on the theory that as to the counterclaim he is really a defendant? The Supreme Court has held not.[51] There was a time, as the court points out, from 1875 to 1887, when Congress gave the right to either party, but since then it has been restricted to defendants, which is in line with the Congressional purpose to restrict rather than expand the jurisdiction of the federal courts.

Jurisdictional amount. No pecuniary jurisdictional limits have been imposed on the federal courts in relation to admiralty, bankruptcy, commerce and antitrust regulations, and patent, copyright and trade-mark cases.[52] However, where the jurisdiction is based upon a federal question, or diversity of citizenship, the statute provides that the amount in controversy must exceed the sum of $10,000, exclusive of interest and costs.[53] This arbi-

50. Id. at 917–18.

51. Shamrock Oil & Gas Co. v. Sheets, 313 U.S. 100, 61 S.Ct. 868, 85 L.Ed. 1214 (1941).

52. 28 U.S.C.A. §§ 1333, 1334, 1337, 1338. In interpleader the minimum is lowered to $500. § 1335.

53. 28 U.S.C.A. §§ 1331, 1332. When the statute says "exclusive of interest and costs" it means "penalty" interest. Interest which was bargained for, as in a promissory note, may be included: Brain-

in v. Melikian, 396 F.2d 153 (3d Cir. 1968). A plaintiff may aggregate his claims against a defendant to make up the jurisdictional amount, but he may not aggregate claims against several defendants unless they derive from a common nucleus of operative fact: Stone v. Stone, 405 F.2d 94 (4th Cir. 1968). However, two or more plaintiffs, who have separate and distinct claims but who have joined in the same suit for convenience, cannot aggregate their claims to make up the jurisdictional amount. Georgia Ass'n of Independent Ins. Agents,

trary figure, which has been increased from time to time by Congress in response to inflationary pressures, represents an attempt to restrict access to the federal courts and limit the courts' jurisdiction to cases of some importance.[54] A plaintiff cannot circumvent the restriction by arbitrarily demanding a sum in excess of $10,000 when his actual claim falls below that amount.[55] The courts have said the amount asked for will be more closely scrutinized in a case originally brought in the federal court than when the case is removed there by the defendant, the reason being that a plaintiff suing in a state court would have no motive to exaggerate his claim above the federal limit.[56] It is the amount which the plaintiff in good faith claims which governs, and this cannot be augmented or enlarged by any counterclaim of the defendant.[57] Assuming the plaintiff's claim to have been made in good faith, the jurisdiction is not lost because he ultimately fails to recover an amount above the jurisdictional limit. However, the 1958 amendment to the Judicial Code included a section which authorized the district court, in its discretion, to "deny costs to the plaintiff and, in addition, . . . impose costs on the plaintiff" where the amount finally adjudged the plaintiff is below the $10,000 limit.[58]

Ancillary and pendent jurisdiction. As a general rule the Supreme Court has rather rigidly held the district courts to the jurisdiction which Congress has explicitly granted to them. In two situations, however, the court has recognized a small margin

Inc. v. Travelers Indem. Co., 313 F.Supp. 841 (N.D.Ga.1970); Ciaramitaro v. Woods, 324 F.Supp. 1388 (E.D.Mich.1971). This rule places a significant limitation on the utility of class actions. See Snyder v. Harris, 394 U.S. 332, 89 S.Ct. 1053, 22 L.Ed.2d 319 (1969).

54. Wright, supra n. 45, 107 et seq.

55. Arnold v. Troccoli, 344 F.2d 842 (2d Cir. 1965).

56. St. Paul Mercury Indem. Co. v. Red Cab Co., 303 U.S. 283, 58 S.Ct. 586, 82 L.Ed. 845 (1938).

57. The above statement in the text needs qualification. It is submitted that on principle it is the correct rule because jurisdiction is normally considered a threshold matter, to be determined at the beginning of the case. This means that it must be determined from the plaintiff's complaint. The cases seemed to support this rule until 1961 when the Supreme Court decided Horton v. Liberty Mut. Ins. Co., 367 U.S. 348, 81 S.Ct. 1570, 6 L.Ed.2d 890 (1961). Horton filed a workmen's compensation claim for $14,035, but was awarded only $1,050. Liberty sued in federal court to set aside the award and Horton counterclaimed for the full amount. The Supreme Court, in a 5–4 decision, sustained the federal jurisdiction. The vigorous dissent by Mr. Justice Clark said the case upsets a quarter century of case law, that the sum claimed by the plaintiff governs. Professor Wright refers to the case as "baffling." For a full discussion of the topic see Wright, supra n. 45, 124 et seq.

58. 28 U.S.C.A. §§ 1331(b), 1332(b).

of extra jurisdiction by pure implication. The first is in what
is called ancillary jurisdiction. A leading case is Moore v. New
York Cotton Exchange,[59] in which the plaintiff sued in a federal
court seeking an injunction against the defendant for violations
of the antitrust laws. Since the right sprang from a federal statute this was federal question jurisdiction. The defendant filed
a counterclaim against the plaintiff which arose out of the transactions mentioned in the complaint, but it had nothing to do with
the antitrust act. The trial court dismissed plaintiff's claim and
granted defendant's counterclaim. On appeal the plaintiff argued
that since there was no independent ground of jurisdiction for
the counterclaim, the court was without authority to hear it after
it had dismissed the plaintiff's claim. The Supreme Court held
otherwise. It said that since the counterclaim was a compulsory
one (arising out of the same transaction) the district court had
ancillary jurisdiction to handle it; that jurisdiction was a threshold matter and did not cease with the disposition of the plaintiff's claim. It indicated that an independent ground of jurisdiction would be necessary in the case of a permissive counterclaim.[60] Since the Moore case the Federal Rules of Civil Procedure have become effective. They expand the permissible scope
of a lawsuit on the theory it is good judicial economy to settle as
many matters as possible in the same suit. Hence, they permit
one defendant to file a cross-claim against a codefendant,[61] and
they permit a defendant to bring in a third party against whom
he would have a claim of indemnity in case he is held responsible
to the plaintiff.[62] Both of these situations have been held to be
appropriate occasions for the exercise of ancillary jurisdiction.[63]

Pendent jurisdiction, so-called, is closely akin to ancillary. It
permits an expansion of the lawsuit, but it views the matter from
the plaintiff's perspective, rather than the defendant's. The
leading case is Hurn v. Oursler [64] which held that where a plaintiff has suffered injury resulting from a single wrongful act of
the defendant (in this case infringement of a copyrighted play)
he has a single cause of action which can be supported on two

59. 270 U.S. 593, 46 S.Ct. 367, 70 L.Ed. 750 (1926).

60. It is now well settled that a compulsory counterclaim requires no independent ground of jurisdiction, while a permissive one does. United States v. Heyward-Robinson Co., 430 F.2d 1077 (2d Cir. 1970); Revere Copper & Brass, Inc. v. Aetna Cas. & Sur. Co., 426 F.2d 709 (5th Cir. 1970).

61. Fed.Rules Civ.Proc. 13(g).

62. Fed.Rules Civ.Proc. 14.

63. Cross-claim: R. M. Smythe & Co. v. Chase Nat'l Bank, 291 F.2d 721 (2d Cir. 1961); Childress v. Cook, 245 F.2d 798 (5th Cir. 1957). Third party claim: Dery v. Wyer, 265 F.2d 804 (2d Cir. 1959).

64. 289 U.S. 238, 53 S.Ct. 586, 77 L.Ed. 1148 (1933).

grounds: violation of the federal copyright statute, or violation of the common law prohibition against unfair competition. Since federal question jurisdiction existed as to the first, the court held the plaintiff could include the second under the pendent jurisdiction doctrine. The reasoning: there was really only one cause of action and the court could, in the interest of completeness, also handle the state-created right along with the federal. Congress codified the Hurn case in its revision of 1948 by providing: "The district courts shall have original jurisdiction of any civil action asserting a claim of unfair competition when joined with a substantial and related claim under the copyright, patent or trademark laws." [65] In United Mine Workers v. Gibbs [66] the Supreme Court revisited the problem and found the approach in Hurn "unnecessarily grudging" (requiring the two claims to comprise but one cause of action). The new test, as stated by Mr. Justice Brennan, is: "The state and federal claims must derive from a common nucleus of operative fact. But if, considered without regard to their federal or state character, a plaintiff's claims are such that he would ordinarily be expected to try them all in one judicial proceeding, then, assuming substantiality of the federal issues, there is *power* in federal courts to hear the whole," [67] a power, he adds, which the district court may or may not exercise, depending on the circumstances of the case.

Ecological litigation. The grave social problems caused by the increasing pollution of our environment include many legal problems, one of which involves judicial jurisdiction. What courts have power to enjoin interstate polluters? In Ohio v. Wyandotte Chemicals Corp.,[68] the state of Ohio sought to invoke the original jurisdiction of the United States Supreme Court to abate a nuisance caused by Michigan, Delaware and Canadian corporations which, it was alleged, were dumping mercury into Lake Erie and polluting its waters, and contaminating its fish and wildlife. The Court admitted that the case fell within its original jurisdiction, as defined by the Constitution, but declined to exercise it due to the fact that it was not as well equipped as a regular trial court to handle the very complex evidential problems involved, and that to entertain such cases would divert it from performing its primary appellate duty. That the federal district courts are open to such suits is illustrated by the case of Texas v. Pankey,[69]

---

65. 28 U.S.C.A. § 1338(b).

66. 383 U.S. 715, 86 S.Ct. 1130, 16 L.Ed.2d 218 (1966).

67. Id. at 725, 86 S.Ct. at 1138, 16 L.Ed.2d at 228.

68. 401 U.S. 493, 91 S.Ct. 1005, 28 L.Ed.2d 256 (1971).

69. 441 F.2d 236 (10th Cir. 1971).

another interstate pollution case, which the district court had dismissed, but which the Court of Appeals reversed. It held that the fact that the Supreme Court also had original jurisdiction in such cases did not deprive it from exercising its own, and that the case was one arising under the Constitution and laws of the United States within the meaning of the judicial code

SECTION 4. JURISDICTION OVER THE PARTIES

In general. A justiciable controversy involves at least two parties. In this section we are assuming that a particular court has subject matter jurisdiction: that it has been invested with power to try this particular type of case. The question is whether it can *exercise* that jurisdiction over the parties to the particular dispute. The plaintiff presents no problem. He comes into court voluntarily and asks for its help. By doing so he submits himself to the court's jurisdiction. Not so with the defendant. As a general rule he comes into court reluctantly and only because of compulsion. The question is the extent of the court's power to compel his attendance.[70] In the early days of the common law the court acquired jurisdiction over the person of the defendant by having the sheriff arrest him. He was then kept in the dungeon pending the outcome of the case. This was the "physical power" theory of jurisdiction at its worst. Such unfair treatment of defendants, especially when they finally prevailed in the suit, gave way to a more enlightened and humane procedure. Instead of arresting the defendant the sheriff merely served him with a summons to appear and defend.[71] Such service, plus the sheriff's certificate that he had "duly executed the writ" was sufficient to give the court jurisdiction. A sheriff's authority did not extend beyond the territorial limits of the court of which he was an officer. Hence, the presence of the defendant within the jurisdiction, plus service while there, were the indispensable ingredients for the acquisition of jurisdiction over the person of the defendant. This was the common law tradition, which we inherited from England. It still remains the basic method of acquiring jurisdiction over the defendant.[72] It matters not how

---

70. The leading case in this country is Pennoyer v. Neff, 95 U.S. 714, 722, 24 L.Ed. 565, 568 (1877), in which the Court, speaking through Mr. Justice Field, said: "Every state possesses exclusive jurisdiction and sovereignty over persons and property within its territory . . . and no state can exercise direct jurisdiction and authority over persons or property without its territory."

71. This satisfied the physical power theory since the sheriff could have arrested the defendant instead of merely handing him a summons.

72. Hanson v. Denckla, 357 U.S. 235, 78 S.Ct. 1228, 2 L.Ed.2d 1283

transient the presence of the defendant is, if he is served within the jurisdiction.[73] One case has held that service on a defendant while he was in an airplane passing over a state was sufficient.[74] However, as our modern society has changed from the patterns of rural England, so has our procedure in regard to obtaining in personam jurisdiction over defendants. We now turn to those other methods. Before we do so, note should be taken of the fact that a voluntary appearance by the defendant would suffice *O.K.* to give the court jurisdiction over him. This was ancient law, and it is still valid.[75] The only question is what constitutes an appearance, which is discussed infra, in Section 7.

Citizenship, domicile and residence. In Blackmer v. United States [76] the Supreme Court held that citizenship was a sufficient basis for in personam jurisdiction, even permitting service of process abroad, provided there was a specific act of Congress authorizing it, and providing that the notice requirements of due process were met. In Millikin v. Meyer,[77] building on Blackmer, the Supreme Court held that domicile was a sufficient basis for in personam jurisdiction in state courts, provided there was a statute authorizing out of state service, and providing that due process requirements were met. Blackmer has had little impact because Congress has restricted most federal process to the continental United States, but Millikin has opened the door for states to provide for out of state service on their domiciliaries. The Restatement has taken the position that mere residence is a sufficient basis for in personam jurisdiction "unless the individu-

(1958); Developments in the Law—State-Court Jurisdiction, 73 Harv. L.Rev. 909 (1960); Hazard, A General Theory of State Court Jurisdiction, 1965 Sup.Ct.Rev. 241; Ehrenzweig, The Transient Rule of Personal Jurisdiction: The "Power" Myth and Forum Conveniens, 65 Yale L.J. 289 (1956).

73. Smith v. Gibson, 83 Ala. 284, 3 So. 321 (1887); Darrah v. Watson, 36 Iowa 116 (1872); Barrell v. Benjamin, 15 Mass. 354 (1819).

74. Grace v. McArthur, 170 F.Supp. 442 (E.D.Ark.1959).

75. An interesting case arose in California when a nonresident plaintiff sued, and the defendant filed a cross-action (not a counterclaim growing out of the plaintiff's original case) and served the attorney for the plaintiff. The plaintiff defaulted and the defendant was awarded judgment on his cross-action which Texas refused to enforce. The Supreme Court reversed, saying there was nothing in the 14th Amendment to prevent California from providing for such service on the attorney of a nonresident who had invoked the jurisdiction of the court. Adam v. Saenger, 303 U.S. 59, 58 S.Ct. 454, 82 L.Ed. 649 (1938).

76. 284 U.S. 421, 52 S.Ct. 252, 76 L.Ed. 375 (1932).

77. 311 U.S. 457, 61 S.Ct. 339, 85 L.Ed. 278 (1940).

al's relationship to the state is so attenuated as to make the exercise of such jurisdiction unreasonable." [78]

Consent, actual and implied. There is no reason why a person may not consent to the jurisdiction of a court.[79] Indeed, that is what he does when he files a general appearance. In this situation he is consenting to become a party to a lawsuit which is in progress. May he consent in advance to the jurisdiction of a court in the event that a lawsuit arises? It has been held that he may do so in cases involving contracts, especially negotiable instruments.[80] All courts are not agreed upon the validity of such clauses, and there is a growing tendency of courts to find no true consent existed if the agreement was an adhesion contract.[81]

Consent in advance may also be accomplished by appointing an agent in the state upon whom process may be served. This device is commonly employed in the case of foreign corporations seeking to do business in a state. In order to qualify under the law the corporation must designate such an agent. This is an actual consent.[82] Some corporations do business in a state without qualifying. As to such, a state statute frequently says they will be deemed to have appointed the secretary of state as their agent upon whom process may be served. This is an implied—fictional—consent, but has been upheld on the ground that a corporation is not protected by the privileges and immunities clause of the Constitution, and hence the state may exclude the corporation entirely, or admit it on condition.[83] This fictional

78. Restatement, Second, Conflict of Laws (1971) § 30. The United States Supreme Court has not gone this far, but there is a California case which upheld out of state service on one who had been domiciled in the state when the suit was filed but had changed his domicile to Oregon at the time of the service. Allen v. Superior Court, 41 Cal.2d 306, 259 P.2d 905 (1953).

79. Restatement, Second, Conflict of Laws (1971) § 32.

80. See Hopson, Cognovit Judgments: An Ignored Problem of Due Process and Full Faith and Credit, 29 U.Chi.L.Rev. 111 (1961); Schuchman, Confession of Judgment as a Conflict of Laws Problem, 36 Notre Dame Law 461 (1961).

81. See National Equip. Rental, Ltd. v. Szukhent, 375 U.S. 311, 84 S.Ct. 411, 11 L.Ed.2d 354 (1964) (dissenting opinions); Seigelman v. Cunard White Star, Ltd., 221 F.2d 189 (2d Cir. 1955) (Frank, J., dissenting); Atlas Credit Corp. v. Ezrine, 25 N.Y.2d 219, 303 N.Y.S.2d 382, 250 N.E.2d 474 (1969); Arthur Schlanger & Sons v. Beaumont Factors, 205 Misc. 943, 129 N.Y.S. 2d 784 (1954). There are valuable notes in 70 Colum.L.Rev. 118 (1970); 42 U.Colo.L.Rev. 173 (1970); 45 N.Y.U.L.Rev. 367 (1970).

82. Bagdon v. Philadelphia & Reading Coal & Iron Co., 217 N.Y. 432, 111 N.E. 1075 (1916).

83. Old Wayne Mut. Life Ass'n v. McDonough, 204 U.S. 8, 27 S.Ct. 236, 51 L.Ed. 345 (1907); Simon v. Southern Ry., 236 U.S. 115, 35 S.

consent cannot, however, be invoked against individuals because a state has no power to exclude them.[84]

This seemed to be the law in 1923, and it was against this background that Massachusetts passed a statute which provided that nonresident motorists were deemed to have appointed the registrar of motor vehicles as their agent for service of process in cases "growing out of any accident or collision in which said nonresident may be involved." [85]   In the famous case of Hess v. Pawloski [86] the United States Supreme Court upheld the statute against constitutional attack, chiefly on the ground that the implied consent was not unreasonable in the light of the state's police power to regulate the use of its highways.   Other states were not slow in seizing upon Hess to pass similar nonresident motorist statutes and thus provide their citizens with local forums for injuries caused by nonresident motorists.[87]   Indeed, some went further and passed statutes subjecting nonresident boat owners and airplane owners to local forums.[88]   Under the reasoning of Hess it was thought that in order to subject the nonresident to local jurisdiction the activity engaged in must be one subject to state regulation under the police power.[89]   Consequently the first

Ct. 255, 59 L.Ed. 492 (1915); Pennsylvania Fire Ins. Co. v. Gold Issue Mining Co., 243 U.S. 93, 37 S.Ct. 344, 61 L.Ed. 610 (1917).

84. Flexner v. Farson, 248 U.S. 289, 39 S.Ct. 97, 63 L.Ed. 250 (1919).

85. Mass.Gen.Laws, ch. 90, as amended by Stat.1923, ch. 431, § 2.

86. 274 U.S. 352, 47 S.Ct. 632, 71 L.Ed. 1091 (1927).

87. See generally Culp, Process in Actions Against Non-resident Motorists, 32 Mich.L.Rev. 325 (1934); Culp, Recent Developments in Actions Against Non-resident Motorists, 37 Mich.L.Rev. 58 (1938); Scott, Jurisdiction Over Non-resident Motorists, 39 Harv.L.Rev. 563 (1926); Scott, Hess and Pawloski Carry On, 64 Harv.L.Rev. 98 (1950).   In Wuchter v. Pizzutti, 276 U.S. 13, 48 S.Ct. 259, 72 L.Ed. 446 (1928) the Supreme Court held the New Jersey nonresident motorist statute unconstitutional because it did not contain a provision (as the Massachusetts act did) reasonably calculated to give actual notice to the nonresident.

88. See Tardiff v. Bank Line Ltd., 127 F.Supp. 945 (E.D.La.1954); Note, Constitutional Aspects of a Statute Imposing In Personam Jurisdiction Over a Foreign Corporation Operating Aircraft Within a State, 41 Iowa L.Rev. 662 (1956); Note, Recent Legislation Asserting Jurisdiction Over Non-resident Tort-Feasors, 54 Mich.L.Rev. 1026 (1956); Note, Jurisdiction Over Nonresident Aircraft Operators by Substituted Service of Process, 29 Notre Dame Law 640 (1954).

89. When Hess was first decided there was some doubt as to the precise basis upon which it rested. It soon became apparent that the fictional consent theory was at variance with the actual facts. This was made clear by Mr. Justice Frankfurter, in a later opinion in which he said, "In point of fact, however, jurisdiction in the cases does not rest on consent at all . . .. The potentialities of damage by a motorist, in a population as mobile as ours, are such that those whom he injures must have opportunities of redress against him provided only that he is afforded an opportunity to de-

extensions of the Hess principle were to such situations as the sale of securities, an industry subject to a high degree of regulation,[90] and the ownership of local real estate.[91] It never became necessary to determine how far the implied consent theory could be stretched and still remain within constitutional limits because the Supreme Court announced a new theory of jurisdiction when it decided International Shoe Co. v. Washington.[92]

The minimum contacts theory. International Shoe was a corporation case, blazing a new trail in the quest for a better rationalization for a state to exert in personam jurisdiction over foreign corporations. The early view regarded corporations as creatures of the state which created them, having no legal existence outside that state, and consequently not subject to suit elsewhere.[93] When, in an expanding economy, it became clear that corporations were in fact carrying on their activities in many states, the courts sought theoretical justification for subjecting "foreign" corporations to the jurisdiction of the courts of the states in which they operated. In so doing, they used various rationalizations.[94] One line of cases stretched the presence theory to hold that a corporation which was doing business in a state was present in that state.[95] Other courts justified the exercise of jurisdiction on the theory of consent, actual or implied.[96] Some courts, less conscious of the need for theoretical justification, held that doing business was in itself a sufficient basis for jurisdiction.[97] It was against this background that International Shoe was decided. The point involved was due process. Had the State of Washington violated the foreign corporation's constitutional rights by exercising in personam jurisdiction over it? Instead of resorting to one of the older theories (which probably would have sufficed) the court announced a new test. Although the case dealt with a foreign corporation, in articulating the new

fend himself."   Olberding v. Illinois Cent. R. R., 346 U.S. 338, 341, 74 S.Ct. 83, 85, 98 L.Ed. 39, 43 (1953).

90. Henry L. Doherty & Co. v. Goodman, 294 U.S. 623, 55 S.Ct. 553, 79 L.Ed. 1097 (1935).

91. Dubin v. City of Philadelphia, 34 Pa.D. & C. 61 (C.P., Philadelphia Cty.1938).

92. 326 U.S. 310, 66 S.Ct. 154, 90 L.Ed. 95 (1945).

93. See Bank of Augusta v. Earle, 38 U.S. (13 Pet.) 519, 10 L.Ed. 274 (1839).

94. The various theories antedating International Shoe are examined in R. Leflar, American Conflicts Law (1968) 56–58.

95. Barrow S. S. Co. v. Kane, 170 U.S. 100, 18 S.Ct. 526, 42 L.Ed. 964 (1898).

96. See cases supra nn. 82, 83.

97. See generally R. Leflar, supra n. 94 at 57–58.

test, the Court spoke not in terms of corporations, but of *defendants.* It said that

> due process requires only that in order to subject a de-
> fendant to a judgment in personam, if he be not present
> within the territory of the forum, he have certain mini-
> mum contacts with it such that the maintenance of the
> suit does not offend "traditional notions of fair play
> and substantial justice."[98]

The trend which began with Hess was quickened by International Shoe. States began to enact so-called "long-arm" statutes. Illinois was the first in 1955. It provided that a nonresident would be subject to the jurisdiction of its courts as to any
cause of action arising from the doing of any of the following:

(a) The transaction of any business within this State;

(b) The commission of a tortious act within this State;

(c) The ownership, use, or possession of any real estate
situated in this State;

(d) Contracting to insure any person, property or risk
located within this State.[99]

New York patterned its statute after Illinois.[100] The Montana statute is more explicit,[101] the Wisconsin statute is more detailed,[102] but none has exceeded California in its economy of
words.[103]

The primary purpose of these statutes is to provide local forums
for local plaintiffs on locally generated causes of action. International Shoe authorizes such expanded jurisdiction if the contacts of the nonresident defendant with the forum are such that
the exercise of jurisdiction does not offend our traditional notions of fair play and substantial justice. "Fair play and substantial justice" is an attractive phrase which is emotionally sat-
isfying, but is it a good yardstick to measure jurisdiction? What
does it mean? How minimum may the contacts be without becoming constitutionally offensive? Three cases shed some light

98. 326 U.S. 310, 316, 66 S.Ct. 154,
158, 90 L.Ed. 95, 102 (1945).

99. S.H.A. ch. 110, § 17.

100. McKinney's N.Y. CPLR § 302.

101. Mont.Rev.C.Ann. Rule 4 (1947).

102. W.S.A. 262.05.

103. The California statute, which
went into effect in 1970, reads:
"A court of this state may exercise jurisdiction on any basis not
inconsistent with the Constitution
of this state or of the United
States." West's Ann.Cal.Code Civ.
Proc., § 410.10. See Green, Jurisdictional Reform in California, 21
Hast.L.J. 1219 (1970).

on the problem. Perkins v. Benguet Consolidated Mining Co.,[104] decided in 1952, spoke in terms of general fairness to the foreign corporation. It noted that in International Shoe the cause of action arose in the forum, whereas in Perkins it arose abroad. Nevertheless, the court said the record showed enough contacts with the forum to justify the assumption of jurisdiction, but it intimated that more contacts were necessary where the cause of action sued on did not arise from the activity of the defendant within the territorial limits of the forum.[105] The second case, McGee v. International Life Insurance Co.,[106] decided in 1957, involved a Texas insurance company which issued a life insurance policy to a California resident, and as far as the record shows this was the only business the company had done in California. When the policyholder died the company refused to pay on the ground the deceased had committed suicide. The beneficiary sued in a California court, serving the defendant by registered mail pursuant to a California statute. The plaintiff recovered a judgment which the defendant attacked on due process grounds. The Supreme Court upheld the judgment, and in so doing spelled out the following California contacts: the policy was delivered in California, the premiums were mailed from there, the deceased was a California resident, as was the plaintiff, the witnesses on the suicide issue resided there, and California had an interest in providing effective means of redress for its citizens. The third case, Hanson v. Denckla,[107] decided in 1958, involved the attempt by a Florida court to obtain in personam jurisdiction over a Delaware trustee who had been administering a trust created by the testatrix when she was domiciled in Pennsylvania, but who later moved to Florida. Notwithstanding the considerable business correspondence which flowed between the testatrix and the trustee the court held the contacts were insufficient to satisfy due process requirements. On a purely quantitative basis the contacts in Hanson may have been as great as those in McGee. The crucial distinction between the two cases seems to be that in McGee the contacts, such as they were, were initiated by the defendant, whereas in Hanson they were not.[108] Hanson served warning that state boundaries

---

104. 342 U.S. 437, 72 S.Ct. 413, 96 L.Ed. 485 (1952).

105. Accord, Fisher Governor Co. v. Superior Court, 53 Cal.2d 222, 347 P.2d 1 (1959).

106. 355 U.S. 220, 78 S.Ct. 199, 2 L.Ed.2d 223 (1957).

107. 357 U.S. 235, 78 S.Ct. 1228, 2 L.Ed.2d 1283 (1958).

108. "The unilateral activity of those who claim some relationship with a nonresident defendant cannot satisfy the requirement of contact with the forum State. The application of that rule will vary

still mean something, and there are constitutional limits to the reach of long-arm statutes.[109] One must await further clarification by the Supreme Court for a more precise definition of those limits. Meanwhile, state and federal courts must continue to decide cases as they arise and attempt to anticipate the lines which will ultimately be drawn. We turn to those cases.

One of the most widely cited state court cases is Gray v. American Radiator Co.[110] It involved the following situation: Titan, an Ohio corporation, manufactured valves which it sold to American Radiator, a Pennsylvania corporation, which incorporated them into furnaces which it manufactured. One of the furnaces was sold to the plaintiff in Illinois. It exploded and injured him and he sued both companies in an Illinois court, seeking to obtain jurisdiction by virtue of the long-arm statute. No point was made in regard to the Illinois contacts of American Radiator, which were apparently substantial. Titan, however, argued that even if the defective valves had been negligently produced, the "tortious act" would have occurred in Ohio, and thus did not come within the scope of the Illinois statute. The Illinois Supreme Court held, however, that, for the purposes of the statute, a "tortious act" is committed where the resultant damage occurs. Finding no constitutional impediment, the court upheld jurisdiction. On substantially similar facts, the New York Court of Appeals refused to give a similar interpretation to its statute, intimating that such a liberal construction would present constitutional questions.[111] Two cases from the ninth

with the quality and nature of the defendant's activity, but it is essential in each case that there be some act by which the defendant purposefully avails itself of the privilege of conducting activities within the forum State, thus invoking the benefits and protections of its laws." Id. at 253, 78 S.Ct. at 1239, 2 L.Ed.2d at 1298.

109. In Duple Motor Bodies, Ltd. v. Hollingsworth, 417 F.2d 231 (9th Cir. 1969) a British company was subjected to jurisdiction by Hawaii's long-arm statute. This was challenged in a dissenting opinion, which stated, in part: "The extension of Hawaii's 'long-arm' statute so that it reaches halfway around the world to grab the alien appellant brings to mind a caricature of Blind Justice with arms of rubber!" Id. at 236. See provocative note on Duple in 22 Hast.L.J. 856 (1971).

In Rosenblatt v. American Cyanamid Co., 86 S.Ct. 1, 15 L.Ed.2d 39 (1965), an application was made by the defendant to Mr. Justice Goldberg for a stay pending an appeal on constitutional grounds. The case involved a conspiracy in Italy to steal trade secrets from plaintiff in furtherance of which one of the defendants flew to New York to obtain some of Plaintiff's product; jurisdiction was attempted under the New York long-arm statute. In denying the stay Mr. Justice Goldberg said that if a single negligent tort will support jurisdiction (Hess), an intentional one will.

110. 22 Ill.2d 432, 176 N.E.2d 761 (1961). See also Nelson v. Miller, 11 Ill.2d 378, 143 N.E.2d 673 (1957).

111. Feathers v. McLucas, 15 N.Y. 2d 443, 261 N.Y.S.2d 8, 209 N.E.2d

circuit indicate the different results which may flow from slightly different fact patterns. In Duple Motor Bodies, Ltd. v. Hollingsworth,[112] a passenger sued in Hawaii for injuries he received in a bus accident. One of the defendants was a British corporation which manufactured bus bodies that it sold to another British corporation, which in turn filled the Hawaiian order for busses. The court upheld jurisdiction under the long-arm statute because the bodies were produced with knowledge that they were destined for Hawaii. The other case, Taylor v. Portland Paramount Corp.,[113] was a suit by the corporation against Miss Taylor for damages due to loss of patronage for the film Cleopatra allegedly resulting from her misconduct with Richard Burton which caused many persons to boycott the film. Relying heavily on Denckla, the court said Miss Taylor's contacts with the state were too insubstantial. In Erlanger Mills, Inc. v. Cohoes Fibre Mills,[114] long-arm jurisdiction was denied in a case against a New York firm which sold yarn to be shipped to the forum state. This the court said was too minimum.[115] Curtis Publishing Co. v. Birdsong,[116] was another case in which long-arm jurisdiction was denied. That was a suit in a federal court in Alabama for libel brought by the commander of the Mississippi Highway Patrol on behalf of himself and other members

68 (1965). The following year the legislature, less impressed with constitutional complications, "overruled" Feathers by amending its long-arm statute to cover the situation of a nonresident defendant who "commits a tortious act without the state causing injury to person or property within the state" (with certain qualifications). N.Y. Sess.Laws 1966, ch. 590.

See Buckeye Boiler Co. v. Superior Court, 71 Cal.2d 893, 80 Cal.Rptr. 113, 458 P.2d 57 (1969), a products liability case similar to Gray, in which the court upheld jurisdiction. The court said that if the constitutional requirements are met, then the question is one of balancing conveniences to the parties. "A balancing of inconvenience to the defendant against the interests of the state and the plaintiff in having the present litigation in California strongly favors the local jurisdiction." Id. at 907, 458 P.2d at 67.

112. 417 F.2d 231 (9th Cir. 1969). The Duple principle was applied in the later case of Jones Enterprises,

Inc. v. Atlas Serv. Corp., 442 F.2d 1136 (9th Cir. 1971) in which a subsubcontractor who, outside of Alaska, prepared architectural drawings for a building to be constructed in Alaska, was held to be subject to the reach of Alaska's long-arm statute when the building collapsed due to alleged defects in structural design.

113. 383 F.2d 634 (9th Cir. 1967).

114. 239 F.2d 502 (4th Cir. 1956).

115. "To illustrate the logical and not too improbable extension of the problem, let us consider the hesitancy a California dealer might feel if asked to sell a set of tires to a tourist with Pennsylvania license plates, knowing that he might be required to defend in the courts of Pennsylvania a suit for refund of the purchase price or for heavy damages in case of accident attributed to a defect in the tires." Id. at 507.

116. 360 F.2d 344 (5th Cir. 1966).

of the patrol, against the publishers of the Saturday Evening Post for publishing an article reporting the Meredith affair in Mississippi which referred to the highway patrol as "those bastards." Although the Post had considerable circulation in Alabama, the court held the contact was insufficient since the incident which stimulated the article took place in Mississippi and the article was written in New York.[117]

The chief barrier to an undue extension of long-arm jurisdiction is the fourteenth amendment.[118] It is reinforced by the first amendment in libel suits where free speech and free press is involved. Thus a greater showing of contact with the forum is required.[119]

One further comment is in order. In the states which do not have long-arm statutes, resort must be had to the traditional bases of jurisdiction. Even in the states which do have long-arm statutes they are usually drafted to cover only certain situations, and in all other areas traditional bases are required.[120]

---

117. On long-arm statutes in general see: D. Currie, The Growth of the Long Arm: Eight Years of Extended Jurisdiction in Illinois, 1963 U.Ill.Law F. 533; Homburger, The Reach of New York's Long-Arm Statute; Today and Tomorrow, 15 Buffalo L.Rev. 61 (1965); Comment, Long-Arm and Quasi in Rem Jurisdiction and the Fundamental Test of Fairness, 69 Mich. L.R. 300 (1970); Comment, In Personam Jurisdiction Over Nonresident Manufacturers in Product Liability Actions, 63 Mich.L.Rev. 1028 (1965); 27 A.L.R.3d 397 (1969); 24 A.L.R.3d 532 (1969); 19 A.L.R.3d 171 (1968); 19 A.L.R.3d 138 (1968).

118. Another possible constitutional limitation, which has received scant attention, is the commerce clause. See Scanapico v. Richmond Fredericksburgh & Potomac R. R., 439 F.2d 17 (2d Cir. 1970) where the New York contacts upon which long-arm jurisdiction were based were required of the foreign railroad by ICC regulations. The majority opinion upheld jurisdiction and rejected the commerce clause argument because the plaintiff was a resident of New York. Judge Lumbard dissented on the ground that the majority view would virtually subject every

railroad to New York jurisdiction, which would be a burden on interstate commerce.

119. New York Times Co. v. Connor, 365 F.2d 567, 572 (5th Cir. 1966), "First Amendment considerations surrounding the law of libel require a greater showing of contact to satisfy the due process clause than is necessary in asserting jurisdiction over other types of tortious activity." Buckley v. New York Post, 373 F.2d 175, 182 (2d Cir. 1967): "the only normative principle we can extract from the opinions is that jurisdiction over an action against an out-of-state newspaper for circulating a libel within the state, even when brought by a resident, cannot be asserted consistently with due process 'where the size of his circulation does not balance the danger of this liability.'" See Comment, Long-Arm Jurisdiction Over Publishers: To Chill a Mocking Word, 67 Colum.L.Rev. 342 (1967); Comment, Constitutional Limitations to Long-Arm Jurisdiction in Newpaper Libel Cases, 34 U.Chi. L.Rev. 436 (1967).

120. The New York statute does not cover injuries received beyond the borders of the state. Bryant **v.**

In the federal courts. The above discussion in this section has been directed to the acquisition of jurisdiction over the parties in state courts. What has been said is applicable, with slight modification, to the federal courts. In the federal court system the United States is divided into federal districts, with at least one federal district in each state, and in the more populous states there may be several. Summons from any district court may be served upon the defendant "anywhere within the territorial limits of the state in which the district court is held." [121] This is the basic common law provision for service within the territorial limits of the court. There is another provision in the federal rule which permits the court to utilize local state court procedure for acquiring jurisdiction, which would include a long-arm statute.[122] In a few special situations Congress has provided that process from a federal court may be served anywhere within the United States.

SECTION 5. JURISDICTION OVER PROPERTY

In general. Under the physical power theory of jurisdiction it was axiomatic that a state, through its courts, could exercise jurisdiction over all property which was present within the territorial boundaries of the state. The converse was also true: a state could not exercise jurisdiction over property located beyond its borders. These rules were easy to apply in the early days of the common law since most property consisted of land or tangible chattels whose physical location was readily discernable. They are not so easy to apply today when much of the wealth of the world is represented by intangibles: debts, claims, and choses in action, which have no physical location in space and whose "situs" is largely fictional.

A court which exercised jurisdiction over property was said to be proceeding *in rem.* If the action was a true proceeding in

Finnish Nat'l Airlines, 15 N.Y.2d 426, 260 N.Y.S.2d 625 (1965) (injury in Paris); Gelfand v. Tanner Motor Tours, Ltd., 385 F.2d 116 (2d Cir. 1967) (injury in Arizona). As to such cases the old "doing business" test is applied and, if the case is in the federal court on the basis of diversity, the federal court must use the state standard as to what constitutes doing business. Arrowsmith v. United Press Int'l, 320 F.2d 219 (2d Cir. 1963), overruling Jaftex Corp. v. Randolph Mills, Inc., 282 F.2d 508 (2d Cir. 1960). A recent case following Arrowsmith is Litvak Meat Co. v. Baker, 446 F.2d 329 (10th Cir. 1971).

121. Fed.Rules Civ.Proc. 4(f).

122. Fed.Rules Civ.Proc. 4(e). For an interesting discussion of this "borrowing" provision in the rule see Marra v. Shea, 321 F.Supp. 1140 (N.D.Cal.1971).

rem, the judgment which fixed the status of the thing was binding on all persons everywhere, whether they had actual notice
of the action or not. It was said to be binding on the whole world.
True in rem actions are relatively rare. The most common examples are proceedings in admiralty to libel a ship, condemnation
proceedings,[123] registrations of land titles under a Torrens system,[124] proceedings in probate, and proceedings for the forfeiture
of things involved in violation of the criminal or revenue laws.[125]
If the purpose of the proceeding was merely to determine the
status of the property as between the named parties to the suit,
the action was said to be *quasi in rem.* A judgment in such a
proceeding was not binding on one who was not a party to the
action and had received no notice of it. The most common examples of quasi in rem proceedings are attachment and garnishment.

Attachment. Attachment is a statutory proceeding, unknown
to the common law, by which a creditor may subject the tangible
property of his debtor to the payment of the debt even though
he is unable to obtain in personam jurisdiction over the debtor.[126]
For example, A owes B $5,000 which he refuses to pay, and B is
unable to bring an ordinary action against A because he is a nonresident or because he is in hiding to avoid service of process.
If B discovers that A has property within the state (a piece of
land, a truck, etc.) B can have the property seized and sold and
the proceeds applied toward payment of the debt. The mechanics
differ slightly from state to state, but B usually must prepare
and file his complaint, stating his cause of action against A, prepare and file an affidavit of attachment alleging one of the statutory grounds (nonresidence of the defendant is usually a sufficient ground), execute and file a surety bond guaranteeing the
payment of damages in case it turns out the attachment was unwarranted or illegal, and pay the required docket fee. The writ
of attachment will then issue. The sheriff will thereupon execute
it by seizing the property.[127] Statutory notice must be given to

123. Walker v. City of Hutchinson,
352 U.S. 112, 77 S.Ct. 200, 1 L.Ed.
2d 178 (1956).

124. Tyler v. Judges of the Court of
Registration, 175 Mass. 71, 55 N.E.
812 (1900).

125. Restatement, Judgments § 32,
comment (a) at 128 (1942).

126. Restatement, Judgments § 34
(1942).

127. Tangible personal property, for
example, an automobile, may be
physically seized by the sheriff and
taken to the county garage; in the
case of real property the "seizure"
is necessarily constructive and usually consists of posting a notice on
the property and filing a document
with the clerk and recorder stating
that the property has been attached. See West's Ann.Cal.Code Civ.
Proc. § 542.

A.   If all of these steps are properly taken the court has acquired quasi in rem jurisdiction over the property.

Garnishment.   The chief difference between garnishment and attachment is in the type of property which is being seized.[128] Garnishment deals with intangibles—debts—which have no actual situs.[129]   How then may a debt be seized?   The Supreme Court answered this question in the famous case of Harris v. Balk.[130]   It held that, for the purposes of garnishment, a debt clung to a debtor and followed him wherever he went.   Therefore, quasi in rem jurisdiction could be obtained over the debt by personal service of process on the debtor.   The concrete facts of the case were these: Harris and Balk were both residents of North Carolina; Harris owed Balk $180; and Balk owed money to Epstein, a resident of Maryland.   While Harris was temporarily in Maryland, Epstein brought suit there and had Harris served with a garnishee summons, which attached the debt, and the court applied it to pay the debt which Balk owed Epstein.   Later, when Balk sued Harris in North Carolina, Harris pleaded the Maryland judgment as a defense.   The state court disallowed it, but the United States Supreme Court reversed, holding that the debt which Harris owed Balk was property which Harris carried with him when he went to Maryland, so that the Maryland court could exercise quasi in rem jurisdiction over it.   It further held that since Balk had notice of the Maryland suit, he was concluded by it and this protected Harris from double payment.   This result was required by the Full Faith and Credit clause of the Constitution which obligated North Carolina to respect the Maryland judgment.[131]   Would the situation have been any different if

128.   The Restatement describes garnishment as follows: "A court by proper service of process may acquire jurisdiction to apply to the satisfaction of a claim an obligation owing to the person against whom the claim is asserted, if the court has jurisdiction over the obligor, although it has not [sic] jurisdiction over the person against whom the claim is asserted."   Restatement, Judgments § 36 (1942).

129.   There is difficulty in ascribing a situs to an intangible.   "Under various circumstances, situs has been found at the residence of the obligor, the residence of the obligee, the location of a written instrument in which the intangible is incorporated, or wherever the obligor was present; and some decisions have refused to discuss the situs at all and have refused to exercise jurisdiction in the absence of valid personal service on the persons affected."   Note, Jurisdiction: Quasi in Rem: A New Basis for Jurisdiction Over Intangibles in California, 46 Cal.L.Rev. 637 (1958); see Andrews, Situs of Intangibles in Suits Against Nonresident Claimants, 49 Yale L.J. 241 (1939).

130.   198 U.S. 215, 25 S.Ct. 625, 49 L.Ed. 1023 (1905).

131.   "The 14th Amendment did not, in guarantying due process of law, abridge the jurisdiction which a state possessed over property within its borders, regardless of the residence or presence of the owner.   That jurisdiction extends alike

Balk had sued Harris in another country rather than in another state? The question was raised in Weitzel v. Weitzel,[132] in which the plaintiff had a judgment for alimony against her husband who was working in Mexico for the Southern Pacific Railroad. She served a garnishee summons on the railroad in Arizona to reach the debt it owed him for wages earned in Mexico. While admitting that under Harris the situs of the debt follows the garnishee, it declined to allow the garnishment for the reason that the garnishee was a mere stakeholder who should not have to pay twice and that under Mexican law it was probable that the courts there would not respect the quasi in rem judgment of the Arizona court. The Weitzel case suggests another problem. In Harris the garnishee was an individual who, though he carried the debt on his back, could only be in one place at a time. In Weitzel the garnishee was a corporation which could be sued in many states, which gives rise to the possibility that the device of garnishment may be used oppressively. In Morris Plan Industrial Bank of New York v. Gunning,[133] the defendant worked for the Pennsylvania Railroad in Pennsylvania, but his wages were garnisheed in New York. The Railroad argued that the situs of the debt was in Pennsylvania. It lost on that point, but the court applied the New York exemption statute under which only ten percent of his wages were attachable.

In both attachment and garnishment the property of the defendant may be seized before any hearing on the merits of the plaintiff's claim against the defendant. This has been traditional practice and was assumed to be good because the court was proceeding against the property, in rem, and the defendant, who had to be notified, could have his hearing afterwards and obtain the return of the property if the plaintiff's claim proved to be groundless. In the meantime, however, the defendant would be deprived of the use of his property. In the recent case of Sniadach v. Family Finance Co.,[134] the Supreme Court cast a serious constitutional doubt over the validity of such prehearing seizures. That case held that the Wisconsin statute permitting prejudgment garnishment of an employee's wages, violated the due process clause

to tangible and to intangible property. Indebtedness due from a resident to a nonresident—of which bank deposits are an example—is property within the state . . . .. It is, indeed, the species of property which courts of the several states have most frequently applied in satisfaction of the obligations of absent debtors." Pennington v. Fourth Nat'l Bank, 243 U.S. 269, 271, 37 S.Ct. 282, 61 L.Ed. 713, 714 (1917).

132. 27 Ariz. 117, 230 P. 1106 (1924).

133. 295 N.Y. 324, 67 N.E.2d 510 (1946).

134. 395 U.S. 337, 89 S.Ct. 1820, 23 L.Ed.2d 349 (1969).

of the fourteenth amendment. The actual holding only involved garnishment of wages,[135] but the principle upon which it was based—that the deprivation of a party of the use of his property before a hearing violates his constitutional rights—might very well apply to other summary proceedings. Indeed, some state courts, under the supposed compulsion of Sniadach, have held the constitutional inhibition applies also to attachment and replevin.[136]

The quasi in rem jurisdiction of the New York courts was greatly expanded by the case of Seider v. Roth.[137] The plaintiff, a New York resident, was injured in an automobile accident in Vermont. The driver of the other car was a Canadian who had a policy of liability insurance with the Hartford Accident and Indemnity Co. The plaintiff sued for damages in New York, garnisheeing Hartford on the theory that the obligations which Hartford assumed under its policy (to investigate, to defend, and to pay any judgment within the policy limits) constituted a debt which could be proceeded against in rem. The basic issue was whether these policy obligations which Hartford owed the non-resident constituted a "debt" within the meaning of Harris v. Balk.[138] Hartford argued that no debt was created because the obligations were conditional and contingent. The plaintiff, on the other hand, argued that the obligation to defend, which was assumed under the policy, could be enforced wherever the insurer could be found. A divided Court of Appeals agreed with the plaintiff. In Simpson v. Loehmann,[139] on similar facts, the court adhered to the position it had taken in Seider.[140] The constitu-

---

135. The actual holding of Sniadach, that ex parte garnishment of wages, without a hearing, is unconstitutional, is binding on the states: Termplan, Inc. v. Superior Court, 105 Ariz. 270, 463 P.2d 68 (1969); McCallop v. Carberry, 1 Cal.3d 903, 464 P.2d 122 (1970).

136. Randone v. Appellate Dept. of Superior Ct. of Sacramento City, 5 Cal.3d 536, 488 P.2d 13, 96 Cal. Rptr. 709 (1971) (attachment); Blair v. Pitchess, 5 Cal.3d 258, 486 P.2d 1242, 93 Cal.Rptr. 42 (1971) (claim and delivery, which is the California name for replevin). See Moran, Garnishment Restrictions Under Federal Law, 56 A.B.A.J. 678 (1970); P. Albert, Attachment in California: A New Look at an Old Writ, 22 Stan.L.R. 1254 (1970); Note, Some Implications of Sniadach, 70 Colum.L.R. 942 (1970).

137. 17 N.Y.2d 111, 216 N.E.2d 312, 269 N.Y.S.2d 99 (1966).

138. Supra n. 130.

139. 21 N.Y.2d 305, 287 N.Y.S.2d 633, 234 N.E.2d 669 (1967).

140. Breitel, J., concurred, but "only on constraint of Seider", Id. at 314, 234 N.E.2d at 674, 287 N.Y. S.2d at 640. Two passages illustrate his view and are worthy of quotation: "It is the most tenuous of nominalist thinking that accords the status of an asset, leviable and attachable, to a contingent liability to defend and indemnify under a public liability insurance policy." (Id.) "As for the effect of the rule, the practical consequences are highly undesirable. This State, and particularly its chief city, is the mecca for those seeking high

tional issue was whether such expanded jurisdiction offended "traditional notions of fair play and substantial justice" under the rule of International Shoe.[141] The New York court held it did not, but the issue was raised in another case in the federal court which had been removed on the basis of diversity of citizenship. In that case, Podolsky v. Devinney,[142] the federal court disagreed. It said the policy obligations of Hartford did not constitute a "debt" within the meaning of Harris v. Balk.[143] This was a district court case. The United States Court of Appeals has, however, grudgingly approved the Seider doctrine as applied to New York plaintiffs.[144]

The Supreme Court has made a distinction between garnishment and interpleader. In the former the plaintiff initiates the proceeding and seeks to attach a debt owing by the garnishee. In the latter the debtor initiates the proceeding and seeks to be

[handwritten margin note: garnish v. interpleader]

---

verdicts in personal injury cases. On the basis of the rule in the Seider case, it will be the rare plaintiff who cannot invoke the jurisdiction of New York courts, even though only quasi in rem, since it will be a very small insurance company that does not have a palpable contact with this State." Id. at 316, 234 N.E.2d at 675, 287 N.Y.S.2d at 641. See LaBrum, The Fruits of Babcock and Seider: Injustice, Uncertainty and Forum Shopping, 54 A.B.A.J. 747 (1968).

141. Supra n. 92.

142. 281 F.Supp. 488 (S.D.N.Y.1968).

143. "Although the duty to defend is unquestionably a benefit accruing to an insured by reason of a liability insurance contract, this duty cannot arise until jurisdiction is obtained over the insured. Nor can the obligation to indemnify arise until a judgment has been entered against the insured." Id. at 494.

144. Minichiello v. Rosenberg, 410 F.2d 106, 121 (2d Cir. 1969). A dissenting opinion distinguished Harris on two grounds: (1) It involved a simple debt, not a complex "package of rights and duties," and (2) in Harris the garnishee was a natural person who could be physically present in only one state at a time; "therefore, although the situs of the debt might change, there could never exist more than one quasi in rem jurisdictional situs at any given time."

Farrell v. Piedmont Aviation, Inc., 411 F.2d 812 (2d Cir. 1969) involved an airplane crash in North Carolina. Wrongful death actions were brought in New York by New York personal representatives of decedents, all of whom were residents of states other than New York. The Court of Appeals affirmed the District Court in dismissing the action because it thought the New York courts would restrict the Seider doctrine to cases involving New York plaintiffs, and that the appointment of local administrators was a subterfuge.

Other states have rejected the Seider doctrine on the ground the obligations of the insurer under a liability policy are not a debt within the meaning of Harris v. Balk: State ex rel. Government Employees Ins. Co. v. Lasky, 454 S.W.2d 942 (Mo. App.1970); DeRentiis v. Lewis, 258 A.2d 464 (R.I.1969); Howard v. Allen, 254 S.C. 455, 176 S.E.2d 127 (1970); Housley v. Anaconda Co., 19 Utah 2d 124, 427 P.2d 390 (1967). See R. Carpenter, New York's Expanding Empire in Tort Jurisdiction: Quo Vadis? 22 Hast. L.J. 1173 (1971).

[handwritten margin note: other juris.]

discharged from his liability. A debtor may do this when he knows he owes the debt but is uncertain as to which of two or more claimants is entitled to it. In the case of New York Life Insurance Co. v. Dunlevy,[145] there were rival claimants to the cash surrender value of a policy. The company brought an interpleader action in Pennsylvania, paying the amount into court, and asking the court to decide to whom it was owed. One of the claimants lived in Pennsylvania, the other in California. The court found for the Pennsylvania claimant. In a later suit in California by the other claimant, the court found for her. On appeal to the Supreme Court it held that the Pennsylvania court had no jurisdiction to pass on the rights of the California claimant. In other words, there was no in rem jurisdiction. If the Pennsylvania court had found that the company owed the California claimant, there would have been a "debt" within the state, but when the court found the money belonged to the local claimant there was nothing belonging to the nonresident for the court to act upon. The result was that the company had to pay twice. It was this type of unfair consequence which led to the passage of the federal interpleader act, which affords relief to persons in the position of the insurance company, at least where the amount involved exceeds five hundred dollars.[146]

The situs of a debt is, of course, a fiction. For the purposes of garnishment it has been ascribed a fictitious situs where the debtor may be found. For other purposes the fictitious situs may be elsewhere. This is graphically illustrated in the escheat cases. Where property is abandoned or where there are no legal heirs, property escheats to the state. With tangible property there is little difficulty. How about a debt? To what state does it escheat? In Western Union Telegraph Co. v. Pennsylvania,[147] suit was brought by Pennsylvania against the company to escheat funds unclaimed for seven years. The funds arose from the company's money order business in its Pennsylvania offices. In the thousands of money order transactions carried on by the company, it sometimes happens that it can neither make payment to the payee or make a refund, and occasionally people fail to cash money orders. It was the sums which accumulated from these transactions which Pennsylvania sought to escheat. The state of New York intervened, claiming the funds since it was the home office of the company. The Pennsylvania court declared the escheat and the company appealed, claiming the judg-

---

145. 241 U.S. 518, 36 S.Ct. 613, 60 L.Ed. 1140 (1916).

146. 28 U.S.C.A. § 2361.

147. 368 U.S. 71, 82 S.Ct. 199, 7 L. Ed.2d 139 (1961).

ment would not protect it from multiple liability. The Supreme Court agreed with the company and said the case should have been dismissed and suggested that an original suit in the Supreme Court might be the answer. In Texas v. New Jersey,[148] the Supreme Court took original jurisdiction in a dispute involving New Jersey, Texas, Florida, and Pennsylvania over the power to escheat intangibles (unclaimed credits on the books of the Sun Oil Co.). Each state had a theory as to why it should win (major contacts, state of incorporation, principal place of business) but the court adopted Florida's, "the state of the creditor's last known address as shown by the debtor's books and records." [149]

SECTION 6. SERVICE OF PROCESS AND NOTICE

A plaintiff puts the judicial machinery into motion by filing suit and having the defendant served with a summons. The summons is obtained from the clerk of the court, upon payment of a fee, ordering the defendant to appear and defend or judgment by default will be taken against him. The form of the summons is prescribed by statute or court rule. The usual requirements are that it contain the names of the parties, the name of the court in which the action is being brought, a short statement of the plaintiff's claim (or a copy of his complaint) and the number of days within which the defendant must appear. When a sheriff serves the summons upon the defendant he endorses his "return" on the back of it which describes the time, place and manner of service. When the summons is served by an unofficial process server he must file an affidavit including the same information. The original summons, with its "return" or affidavit of service, is then filed with the court. The above described procedure accomplishes two purposes: (1) it gives the defendant notice of the suit so that he may come in and defend, and (2) it "invokes" the jurisdiction of the court, investing it with authority to proceed with the case.

There are three methods of service of process. The basic common law method was *personal service* which consisted of personally handing to the defendant a copy of the summons and explaining to him what it was. Today, in this country, we have added two other methods. *Substituted service* which consists of personally handing a copy of the summons to someone on behalf of the defendant. That someone must be closely related to the

---

148. 379 U.S. 674, 85 S.Ct. 626, 13 L.Ed.2d 596 (1965).

149. Id. at 682, 85 S.Ct. at 631, 13 L.Ed.2d at 601.

defendant, by blood or otherwise, so that there is a high probability that the defendant will receive actual notice. Obviously substituted service has shortcomings but it is provided for by statute or rule to take care of situations in which the defendant is temporarily absent from the state, or is hiding, or cannot be found. The third method is *constructive service*, by mailing the summons to the defendant or publishing notice of the lawsuit in a newspaper, which is obviously the least satisfactory method since such notices are usually published in legal newspapers with very limited circulation. Constructive service is restricted by statute to limited situations, usually involving land, estates, or status.[150]

Each method of service has generated its own problems. In personal service the sheriff may have been unable to make sufficient contact with the defendant to constitute a delivery,[151] he may have mistaken someone for the defendant and served the wrong person,[152] or his "return" may have been erroneous or even false.[153] In substituted service the statute commonly requires the service to be upon someone of "suitable age" residing at the dwelling house of the defendant or his "usual place of abode." [154] All of these concepts are sufficiently ambiguous as to have provoked litigation.[155]

---

150. Where substituted or constructive service is used, there must be strict compliance with the requisite statutory procedures. Bond v. Golden, 273 F.2d 265 (10th Cir. 1959); Stamps v. Superior Court, 14 Cal.App.3d 108, 92 Cal.Rptr. 151 (1971).

151. In Trujillo v. Trujillo, 71 Cal. App.2d 257, 162 P.2d 640 (1945), as the sheriff approached, the defendant jumped in his car, rolled up the windows, and locked the doors. When the sheriff put the summons under the windshield wiper, the defendant drove away. The court held the service was good.

152. See Martz v. Miller Bros., 244 F.Supp. 246 (D.Del.1965) where the court draws a distinction between a misnomer (which can be corrected by an amendment) and serving the wrong person (which cannot).

153. The common law rule was that the sheriff's "return" was conclusive and could not be controverted. The defendant's remedy was to sue the sheriff on his bond. Vaughn v. Love, 324 Pa. 276, 188 A. 299 (1936). The majority modern rule is that the sheriff's return may be challenged: Swartzwelder v. Freeport Coal Co., 131 W.Va. 276, 46 S.E.2d 813 (1948). One reason for the change is that we now permit substituted service which, unlike personal service, makes mistakes easier, and we now permit unofficial process servers who are not under bond. Crosby v. Farmer, 39 Minn. 305, 40 N.W. 71 (1888).

154. Fed.Rules Civ.Proc. 4(d) (1).

155. See Nowell v. Nowell, 384 F.2d 951, 953–54 (5th Cir. 1967) in which the court says "The appropriate construction of Rule 4(d) (1) varies according to whether the defendant received notice of the suit." See also Rovinski v. Rowe, 131 F.2d 687 (6th Cir. 1942); Skidmore v. Green, 33 F.Supp. 529 (S. D.N.Y.1940).

[handwritten: sheriff stops at state]

It should be noted that a sheriff's authority stops at the state line. So does the authority of a United States Marshal, in regard to his power to serve civil process.[156] This does not mean that a court may not acquire in personam jurisdiction over one beyond its borders if there exists a nonresident motorist or long-arm statute.

There is an additional problem when the case is brought in the federal court on the basis of diversity of citizenship, and there is a difference between the state statute on substituted service and the one provided for in the federal rule. The question of which takes precedence was settled in the case of Hanna v. Plumer,[157] which held that the federal rule applied. Substituted service is permitted on the assumption that the defendant will receive actual notice of the suit. Suppose he does not? The cases seem to hold that if the case was one appropriate for substituted service and if the statute was strictly complied with, then the service is good even though the defendant did not receive actual notice.[158] Service by publication was the traditional means of notifying out-of-state defendants in proceedings in rem, and for many years it was thought to be sufficient.[159] However, in recent years the line between in personam and in rem jurisdiction has become blurred, and stress has been placed upon the due process requirement of fairness.[160] Hence, today, even in proceedings

[handwritten margin note: federal prevails]

[handwritten margin note: notice]

156. Under Fed.Rules Civ.Proc. 4(f) process may be served anywhere within the state in which the district court sits. This rule was unsuccessfully attacked as going beyond the rule-making power granted by Congress in Mississippi Pub. Co. v. Murphree, 326 U.S. 438, 66 S.Ct. 242, 90 L.Ed. 185 (1946). In a few exceptional cases, such as interpleader, federal process runs throughout the United States. 28 U.S.C.A. § 1335.

157. 380 U.S. 460, 85 S.Ct. 1136, 14 L.Ed.2d 8 (1965).

158. Smith v. Kincaid, 249 F.2d 243 (6th Cir. 1957).

159. Arndt v. Griggs, 134 U.S. 316, 10 S.Ct. 557, 33 L.Ed. 918 (1890); Closson v. Chase, 158 Wis. 346, 149 N.W. 26 (1914).

160. Mullane v. Central Hanover Bank & Trust Co., 339 U.S. 306, 70 S.Ct. 652, 94 L.Ed. 865 (1950). Mullane upheld notice by publica-
tion where it was impractical to give better notice but struck it down as a violation of due process where the names and addresses of parties were known and a better method could be used. Mullane built on McDonald v. Mabee, 243 U.S. 90, 92, 37 S.Ct. 343, 344, 61 L.Ed. 608, 610 (1917), in which Mr. Justice Holmes said that where personal service is dispensed with "the substitute that is most likely to reach the defendant is the least that ought to be required if substantial justice is to be done." The softening of the hard line of distinction between in personam and in rem jurisdiction is also seen in such cases as Atkinson v. Superior Court, 49 Cal.2d 338, 316 P.2d 960 (1957). In commenting on that case the author of a note says, "But by abandoning use of a situs to justify quasi in rem jurisdiction and replacing it with a standard indistinguishable from the rules for personal jurisdiction the court has really raised the question whether quasi in rem jurisdiction over in-

in rem, publication is regarded as constitutionally deficient if there is a better way to notify the defendant.[161] Earlier in this chapter we have seen the modern tendency to expand the in personam jurisdiction of courts over nonresidents, as long as the expanded jurisdiction did not offend our traditional notions of fair play and substantial justice. Perhaps as a safeguard to this trend, the Supreme Court has tightened up its conception as to the constitutional sufficiency of notice under the due process clause.[162]

There are two situations in which the court will decline to exercise jurisdiction over a defendant even though he has been properly served with process. The first is where he was induced to come into the state by the fraud or trickery of the plaintiff.[163] In that situation it is sometimes said that no jurisdiction was acquired over the defendant because of the fraud.[164] This is not strictly accurate because the defendant was personally served while within the territorial boundaries of the court, and if the fraud were not called to the attention of the court it could proceed with the case. The more accurate analysis is that, upon proof of the fraud, the court will decline to exercise jurisdiction.[165] The second situation is where the defendant has come into the state solely for the purpose of attending a judicial proceeding as a witness or as a party. Here again, service of process on the defendant would invest the court with jurisdiction, but the court would decline to exercise it because the defendant enjoyed an immunity from service during the necessary time he

tangibles ought not simply to be merged into the expanded modern rules for personal jurisdiction," 46 Cal.L.Rev. 637, 639 (1958).

161. Schroeder v. City of New York, 371 U.S. 208, 83 S.Ct. 279, 9 L.Ed. 2d 255 (1962).

162. See cases cited supra n. 160; see also Walker v. City of Hutchinson, supra n. 123.

In addition to the notice requirement, due process requires a reasonable time for the defendant to appear. In Roller v. Holly, 176 U.S. 398, 20 S.Ct. 410, 44 L.Ed. 520 (1900) the defendant was served in Virginia on December 30, with a summons requiring him to appear in a suit in Texas on January 5 which the court held to be so unreasonably short a time as to contravene due process. In Robins v. Robert Lawrence Electronics Corp., 84 N.Y.S.

2d 99, 100 (Cty.Ct., 1948) the court said, "Means of communication have improved, to be sure, but there is a certain absolute minimum in any given case, and a six-day period in which to respond from Minnesota falls below that minimum."

163. Sawyer v. LaFlamme, 123 Vt. 229, 185 A.2d 466 (1962).

164. Wyman v. Newhouse, 93 F.2d 313 (2d Cir. 1937).

165. Tickle v. Barton, 142 W.Va. 188, 95 S.E.2d 427 (1956). The fraud must have induced the defendant to come into the state. If he was already there, but avoiding service, a little deception on the part of the process server is tolerated. Gumperz v. Hofmann, 245 App.Div. 622, 283 N.Y.S. 823, aff'd 271 N.Y. 544 (1935).

was in the state for the purpose of attending the judicial proceeding.[166] The immunity is granted as a matter of public policy to encourage the attendance of witnesses and thus develop the full facts in a case.[167]

SECTION 7.   CHALLENGES TO THE JURISDICTION

A defendant who has been sued may believe that the court has no jurisdiction over him. How may he challenge it? The obvious answer would seem to be to file a motion with the court asking that the case be dismissed for want of jurisdiction. May he do this without submitting to the court's authority? Most states have allowed him to do so if he makes only what is known as a "special appearance."[168] If he asks for any other relief he is, by implication, admitting that the court has power to grant it, and he is thus making a general appearance.[169] If his special appearance is overruled, may he litigate the case on the merits without waiving the issue as to jurisdiction? The courts are not agreed on this. One line of authority holds that he must choose between two courses: (1) withdraw from the case, allow judgment to go against him by default, and appeal from that judgment, or (2) abandon his jurisdictional point and litigate the case on the merits. It is a Hobson's choice since he must abandon one line of defense in any event. Other courts are less rigorous. They permit him to litigate on the merits without waiving his jurisdictional point, and if he loses, then he may urge both grounds on appeal.[170] Although the federal rules have abolished

---

166. Although the authorities are not uniform, perhaps the general rule is that the immunity extends to witnesses, parties, and perhaps attorneys during the necessary time required to attend the court proceeding: I. C. C. v. St. Paul Transp. Co., 39 F.R.D. 309 (D.Minn. 1966); Franklin v. Superior Court, 98 Cal.App.2d 292, 220 P.2d 8 (1950) (controlling purpose of trip must be the suitor's attendance at court); cf. Zumsteg v. American Food Club, 166 Ohio St. 439, 143 N.E.2d 701 (1957). Contra: Wangler v. Harvey, 41 N.J. 277, 196 A. 2d 513 (1963), in which the court feels that none of the historical reasons for the immunity are valid today, and that the problem is best disposed of by the application of the doctrine of forum non conveniens.

167. Cooper v. Wyman, 122 N.C. 784, 29 S.E. 947 (1898); State ex rel. Sivnksty v. Duffield, 137 W. Va. 112, 71 S.E.2d 113 (1952).

168. Harkness v. Hyde, 98 U.S. 476, 26 L.Ed. 237 (1878); Yaffe v. Bank of Chelsea, 271 P.2d 365 (Okl.1954).

169. Milstein v. Ogden, 84 Cal.App. 2d 229, 190 P.2d 312 (1948); Mack Constr. Co. v. Quonset Real Estate Corp., 84 R.I. 190, 122 A.2d 163 (1956); Ozaukee Fin. Co. v. Cedarburg Lime Co., 268 Wis. 20, 66 N.W.2d 686 (1954).

170. Union Bond & Mtge. Co. v. Brown, 64 S.D. 600, 269 N.W. 474 (1936); Sunderland, Preserving a Special Appearance, 9 Mich.L.Rev. 396 (1911).

federal rules.

special appearances, they have, in effect, adopted the latter rule since they allow a defendant to challenge jurisdiction and plead to the merits at the same time.[171]

A similar problem is involved when the defendant is a non-resident owner of land in the forum state which is attached by the plaintiff. May he appear specially and fight the attachment without subjecting himself to the in personam jurisdiction of the court? In Salmon Falls Manufacturing Co. v. Midland Tire and Rubber Co.,[172] the court held that he could. In that case the attached property was worth $2,000 but the trial court rendered a $30,000 judgment against the defendant on the ground that by contesting the plaintiff's claim, the defendant had made a general appearance. The Court of Appeals reversed, saying that the defendant could insist that no personal jurisdiction was acquired over him and still, without being inconsistent, protect his property by contesting the plaintiff's claim.[173] This means that the plaintiff has recovered $2,000 on his $30,000 claim and he can still pursue the defendant to collect the balance in a court which can obtain in personam jurisdiction over him.[174] However, in that suit for the balance, may the defendant again fight the case on its merits? There is authority that he may not; that having litigated the issue of liability in the first case and lost, the matter is now res judicata.[175] This has led some courts to hold that the Salmon Falls rule was wrong; that the defendant should be held to in personam liability if he comes in to contest the merits of the claim to protect his property.[176] As Judge Clark explained: "a rule against personal jurisdiction will only bring on further

171. Fed.Rules Civ.Proc. 12(b); Orange Theatre Corp. v. Rayherstz Amusement Corp., 139 F.2d 871 (3d Cir. 1944). However, if the jurisdictional point is not made in apt time, either by motion or answer, it will be deemed waived. Wyrough & Loser, Inc. v. Pelmor Labs, Inc., 376 F.2d 543 (3d Cir. 1967); C. S. Foreman Co. v. H. B. Zachry Co., 127 F.Supp. 901 (W. D.Mo.1955). For many years no special appearance was allowed in Texas. York v. Texas, 137 U.S. 15, 11 S.Ct. 9, 34 L.Ed. 604 (1890). The rule was changed in 1962 permitting a special appearance to contest jurisdiction, but it is rather strictly construed. Cuellar v. Cuellar, 406 S.W.2d 510 (Tex.Civ.App. 1966).

172. 285 F. 214 (6th Cir. 1922).

173. Accord: Dry Clime Lamp Corp. v. Edwards, 389 F.2d 590 (5th Cir. 1968).

174. Strand v. Halverson, 220 Iowa 1276, 264 N.W. 266 (1935); Riverview State Bank v. Dreyer, 188 Kan. 270, 362 P.2d 55 (1961); Oil Well Supply Co. v. Koen, 64 Ohio St. 422, 60 N.E. 603 (1901); Carrington, The Modern Utility of Quasi In Rem Jurisdiction, 76 Harv. L.Rev. 303 (1962).

175. Harnischfeger Sales Co. v. Sternberg Co., 189 Miss. 73, 191 S. 94 (1939). Contra: Cheshire Nat'l Bank v. Jaynes, 224 Mass. 14, 112 N.E. 500 (1916).

176. United States v. Balanovski, 236 F.2d 298 (2d Cir. 1956).

litigation, which the taxpayers [defendants] will lose on the merits by collateral estoppel or stare decisis." [177]

According to Anglo-American tradition every man is entitled to his day in court, but this means one day, not several. The doctrine of res judicata is based on the idea that where an issue has once been litigated to a final judgment, that should end it. This principle has been applied to questions of jurisdiction. In the leading case of Baldwin v. Iowa State Traveling Men's Association,[178] the defendant had objected to the court's jurisdiction over it, litigated the matter, lost, and then withdrew from the case. The plaintiff proceeded to obtain judgment. Later, when he sought to enforce it in another state, the defendant objected on the same jurisdictional grounds urged before. The court held the matter was res judicata. The same principle has been applied when the challenge to the jurisdiction was over the subject matter.[179] The moral from these cases seems quite clear: one who challenges the jurisdiction of a court must be prepared to stay in that court and fight, and appeal if he loses, because he has had his day in court and cannot raise the jurisdictional point at another time in another court.

177. Id. at 302.

178. 283 U.S. 522, 51 S.Ct. 517, 75 L.Ed. 1244 (1931).

179. Stoll v. Gottlieb, 305 U.S. 165, 59 S.Ct. 134, 83 L.Ed. 104 (1938);

Chicot County Drainage Dist. v. Baxter State Bank, 308 U.S. 371, 60 S.Ct. 317, 84 L.Ed. 329 (1940); Treinies v. Sunshine Mining Co., 308 U.S. 66, 60 S.Ct. 44, 84 L.Ed. 85 (1939).

CHAPTER III. VENUE

The distinction between jurisdiction and venue is an elusive one which sometimes causes trouble, even to appellate courts. The reason is that both deal with the problem of the proper court in which an action should be brought. The fundamental difference beween the two is that jurisdiction addresses itself to the power or authority of a court to entertain a case whereas venue addresses itself to the criteria for choosing a particular court among several which are jurisdictionally possible.

SECTION 1. CHOOSING A FORUM

One of the first problems confronting a plaintiff's lawyer is where to bring suit, the choice of a forum. It frequently happens that a number of choices are open to him. Let us suppose our prospective litigant is a resident of San Francisco who, while visiting in San Diego, is run over and seriously injured by a nonresident motorist who resides in Chicago. We know that any superior court in California would have subject matter jurisdiction since the amount involved is over $5,000.[1] We know that the state may obtain in personam jurisdiction over the defendant via the state long-arm statute.[2] Consequently, if the only problem were jurisdiction, the plaintiff could sue in a superior court in any one of the state's 58 counties. Which one he would choose would depend upon many practical considerations, such as his own convenience, the convenience of the witnesses to the accident, or the relative size of possible jury verdicts in San Diego, San Francisco, or elsewhere. Or, the plaintiff might want to sue in a federal court, for there is diversity of citizenship and the amount involved exceeds $10,000, so the federal courts would have subject matter jurisdiction.[3] Also the federal courts in either California or Illinois could obtain in personam jurisdiction over the defendant.[4] The plaintiff's problem is complicated, however, by the venue statutes of the state of California and of the United States. If the plaintiff desired to sue in the California courts, he would find that his choice of county was unlimited because the defendant was a nonresident.[5] Should the plaintiff desire to sue

---

1. Cal.Const. art. VI, § 10; West's Ann.Cal.Code Civ.Proc. §§ 82, 89.

2. West's Ann.Cal.Code Civ.Proc. § 410.10.

3. 28 U.S.C.A. § 1332.

4. Fed.Rules Civ.Proc. 4(e), 4(f).

5. West's Ann.Cal.Code Civ.Proc. § 395, which, in personal injury cases provides for venue in the county where the injury occurs or in the county of defendant's residence;

50

in a federal court he would find that his choice is limited to the district where he resides, the district where the defendant resides, or the district in which the injury occurred.[6]

The above hypothetical situation illustrates the difference between jurisdiction and venue.[7] Jurisdiction deals with the authority of a court to exercise judicial power. Venue deals with the place where that power should be exercised. Jurisdiction over the subject matter cannot be conferred by the parties, and the lack thereof may not be waived.[8] Venue, on the other hand, is bottomed on convenience, and improper venue may be waived.[9]

There was a time in the early common law when the problem did not arise, because all actions were required to be tried in the county where the event occurred.[10] At a much later date the common law developed the concept of a transitory cause of action, one which could be sued on anywhere if jurisdiction could be obtained over the defendant. Today most actions are regarded as transitory which has led legislatures, in the interest of fairness, to tie them down to certain specified places. The venue statutes vary widely from state to state.[11] Most agree that actions affecting land must be tried in the county in which the land is situated.[12] Other than that there is great variety. The most

but if the defendant is a nonresident "the action may be tried in any county which the plaintiff may designate in his complaint."

6. 28 U.S.C.A. § 1391(a).

7. Neirbo v. Bethlehem Shipbuilding Co., 308 U.S. 165, 60 S.Ct. 153, 84 L.Ed. 167 (1939). "The jurisdiction of the federal courts—their power to adjudicate—is a grant of authority to them by Congress and thus beyond the scope of the litigants to confer. But the locality of a lawsuit—the place where judicial authority may be exercised—though defined by legislation relates to the convenience of litigants and as such is subject to their disposition . . . ." Id. at 167, 60 S.Ct. at 154, 84 L.Ed. at 170.

8. Id.

9. Id. Denver & Rio Grande W. R. R. v. Brotherhood of R. R. Trainmen, 387 U.S. 556, 87 S.Ct. 1746, 18 L.Ed.2d 954 (1967); Altman v. Liberty Equities Corp., 322 F.Supp. 377 (S.D.N.Y.1971). Fed.R.Civ.P. 12(h) (1). By bringing the suit the plaintiff waives any question of improper venue in advance in regard to any counterclaims, even permissive ones: General Elec. Co. v. Marvel Rare Metals Co., 287 U.S. 430, 53 S.Ct. 202, 77 L.Ed. 408 (1932).

10. Hardenburgh v. Hardenburgh, 115 Mont. 469, 146 P.2d 151 (1944).

11. The most comprehensive study on the subject is Stevens, Venue Statutes: Diagnosis and Proposed Cure, 49 Mich.L.Rev. 307 (1951).

12. Where the land involved in the suit is situated in several counties, the suit may be brought in any one of them: Murphy v. Superior Court, 138 Cal. 69, 70 P. 1070 (1902); where several forms of relief are sought it is the chief one which determines whether the action is local or not: Hammon v. American Exploration & Mining Co., 203 Cal.App.2d 306, 21 Cal. Rptr. 409 (1962); some courts hold that suit in the county of the situs

common provision is that the venue must be at the residence of the defendant.[13] Other bases for venue are: where the plaintiff resides, where the cause of action arose,[14] where the defendant is doing business or has an office, or where the defendant may be found.[15] The answer to a venue problem will usually be found in the appropriate code or statute. This statutory language, however, is not always clear, and even when it appears to be clear it is subject to judicial interpretation. It is therefore important to consult the cases as well as the statutes. The point is graphically illustrated by the federal cases.

SECTION 2. VENUE IN THE FEDERAL COURTS

The problems respecting venue are substantially the same in the state courts and in the federal courts except that in a state court system we are dealing with counties and in the federal system we are dealing with federal judicial districts. Congress has divided the United States into 89 judicial districts. Each state has at least one, but states with large populations may have as many as four. In the state court systems venue is defined in terms of the proper county. In the federal system it is defined in terms of the proper judicial district.

The federal judicial code has specific venue provisions covering diversity cases,[16] federal question cases,[17] cases against aliens,[18] cases against federal officers,[19] fine, penalty and forfeiture cases,[20] tax cases,[21] interstate commerce cases,[22] patent and copyright cases,[23] and cases removed from state to federal courts.[24] The one that has created the least trouble is the last.[25] The one

of the land is a matter of jurisdiction and not venue, but that if the suit is brought in the proper county it may be moved by a change of venue: Cugini v. Apex Mercury Mining Co., 24 Wash.2d 401, 165 P.2d 82 (1946); actions for replevin are often held to be local and must be brought in the county where the goods are detained: Central Maine Power Co. v. Maine Cent. R. R., 113 Me. 103, 93 A. 41 (1915).

13. Hoag v. Superior Court, 207 Cal. App.2d 611, 24 Cal.Rptr. 659 (1962); Hardenburgh v. Hardenburgh, supra n. 10.

14. Bergin v. Temple, 111 Mont. 539, 111 P.2d 286 (1941).

15. See Stevens, supra n. 11.

16. 28 U.S.C.A. § 1391(a).

17. 28 U.S.C.A. § 1391(b).

18. 28 U.S.C.A. § 1391(d).

19. 28 U.S.C.A. § 1391(e).

20. 28 U.S.C.A. § 1395.

21. 28 U.S.C.A. § 1396.

22. 28 U.S.C.A. § 1398.

23. 28 U.S.C.A. § 1400.

24. 28 U.S.C.A. § 1441(a).

25. The obvious reason is that the case was already pending in a state court, and the removal is to

which has caused the most trouble is the first, diversity jurisdiction.

The earliest venue statute spoke in terms of the district in which the defendant is an "inhabitant" or where he can be "found".[26] This was later changed to the district in which "all plaintiffs or all defendants reside." [27] The Congressional language was in terms of persons, not corporations. Where does a corporation reside? May it be sued in a state other than the place of its creation? In Neirbo v. Bethlehem Shipbuilding Co.[28] the question was raised but avoided because the foreign corporation had appointed a local agent upon whom process could be served. The court held that this constituted not only a consent to jurisdiction, but a waiver of improper venue. The point arose again in Olberding v. Illinois Central Railway,[29] a case in which an Indiana defendant caused damage to a bridge in Kentucky belonging to the plaintiff, an Illinois corporation. The plaintiff, suing in the Kentucky federal court, obtained jurisdiction over the defendant by virtue of the nonresident motorist statute. The court held that the "implied consent" under the nonresident motorist statute was a fiction which did not waive improper venue. It distinguished Neirbo, where there was actual consent. Subsequent to Olberding, Congress amended the venue statute and broadened it by permitting suit in the district "in which the claim arose." [30] That would have taken care of the situation in Olberding. But Congress went further; it added a subsection providing that a corporation may be sued in any district "in which it is incorporated or licensed to do business or is doing business, and such judicial district shall be regarded as the residence of such corporation for venue purposes." [31] It should be noted that

the federal district court "embracing the place where such action is pending." Id.

26. 1 Stat. 79, § 11 (1789); 18 Stat. 470 (1875); interpreted in Ex Parte Schollenberger, 96 U.S. 369, 24 L. Ed. 853 (1878).

27. 28 U.S.C.A. § 1391(a).

28. Supra n. 7.

29. 346 U.S. 338, 74 S.Ct. 83, 98 L.Ed. 39 (1953).

30. After Olberding, in 1963 Congress added a subsection (f) to permit venue in the district where the accident happened, but in 1966 this was repealed and a final clause was added to § 1391(a) permitting suit in the district "in which the claim arose."

31. 28 U.S.C.A. § 1391(c). This amendment greatly enlarged the number of districts in which a corporation could be sued. Did it also expand the venue for the corporate plaintiff? In Robert E. Lee & Co. v. Veatch, 301 F.2d 434 (4th Cir. 1961) the court held that it did not. See Note, Federal Venue and the Corporate Plaintiff: Judicial Code Section 1391(c), 28 Ind.L.J. 256 (1953); Comment, The Corporate Plaintiff and Venue Under Section 1391(c) of the Judicial Code, 28 U. Chi.L.Rev. 112 (1960). See Pure

the venue provision regarding corporations is much more liberal than the jurisdictional provision which only deems a corporation is a citizen of the district in which it has its principal place of business, in addition, of course, to the place in which it was incorporated.[32] If the jurisdictional provision were as broad as the venue provision, the diversity jurisdiction would be virtually withdrawn from the large national corporations. What of the unincorporated associations, such as the labor unions? The statute is silent as to them. Do they "reside" where they do business, as the corporations do, at least for venue purposes? The question was not answered until 1967 when the Supreme Court analogized them to corporations and held they may be sued in any district in which they are doing business.[33]

SECTION 3.   FORUM NON CONVENIENS

In selecting a forum a plaintiff will naturally try to choose the one most favorable to him. In doing so he may choose the one most inconvenient for the defendant. Indeed, he may do this deliberately to harass the defendant in order to force a settlement. During recent decades the courts in some states have reacted to this situation by developing and applying a doctrine known as *forum non conveniens*.[34] The gist of the doctrine is that a court may, in its discretion, refuse to entertain a case even though jurisdictional and venue requirements have been met, if it feels there is no legitimate reason for the case to be brought in that court. In exercising its discretion the court will consider the relative inconvenience to both parties and witnesses, the con-

Oil Co. v. Suarez, 384 U.S. 202, 86 S.Ct. 1394, 16 L.Ed.2d 474 (1966) in which the court held § 1391(c) applicable to a Jones Act case in spite of the fact the Jones Act has a special venue provision. The broad language of the section is duplicated in some state venue statutes; see State ex rel. Verd v. Superior Court, 31 Wash.2d 625, 198 P.2d 663 (1948).

32. 28 U.S.C.A. § 1332(c).

33. Denver & Rio Grande W. R. R. v. Brotherhood of R. R. Trainmen, supra n. 9.

34. One of the earliest cases was Collard v. Beach, 81 App.Div. 582, 586, 81 N.Y.S. 619, 622 (1903), in which a Connecticut plaintiff sued in New York for an injury received in Connecticut; the court dismissed, saying "it is against the settled policy of the State to permit our courts to be used by nonresidents for the redress of personal injuries received in the State of their domicile." The doctrine may be applied in a contract as well as a tort action: Bata v. Bata, 304 N.Y. 51, 105 N.E.2d 623 (1952); Plum v. Tampax, Inc., 402 Pa. 616, 168 A.2d 315 (1961). The doctrine will seldom be applied when the plaintiff is a resident of the forum state, Thomson v. Continental Ins. Co., 66 Cal.2d 738, 59 Cal.Rptr. 101, 427 P.2d 765 (1967). See Dainow, The Inappropriate Forum, 29 Ill.L.Rev. 867 (1934); also, extensive annotation in 90 A.L.R.2d 1109 (1961).

tacts which the case has with the forum, whether the case is to be governed by local or foreign law, the expense to the government in trying "imported" litigation, and the backlog of cases awaiting trial on the court's calendar. The court will not dismiss the case under the doctrine unless the plaintiff has another forum open to him. In Gulf Oil Corp. v. Gilbert,[35] decided in 1947, the Supreme Court sanctioned the use of the doctrine by a federal district court. Mr. Justice Black wrote a strong dissent in which he contended that, unlike a court of equity which had a discretionary power to refuse a case, a court of law had a mandatory duty to exercise the jurisdiction with which it had been invested. "Never until today," he said, "has this court held, in actions for money damages for violations of common law or statutory rights, that a district court can abdicate its statutory duty to exercise its jurisdiction for the convenience of the defendant to a lawsuit." [36] He said it was for Congress, not this court, to decide whether the district courts should be entrusted with such discretion. The following year Congress amended the judicial code and added the following:

> § 1404(a) For the convenience of parties and witnesses, in the interest of justice, a district court may transfer any civil action to any other district or division where it might have been brought.[37]

SECTION 4. CHANGE OF VENUE IN THE FEDERAL COURTS

The new provision stimulated a rash of interpretative litigation. Shortly after its passage a plaintiff sued in a New York federal court and then moved to transfer the case to a California federal court on the theory the case could have been "brought" there by the mere filing of a complaint.[38] In disallowing the transfer the court said the final clause of the statute, "where it might have been brought," referred not merely to filing a complaint, but also to acquiring jurisdiction over the defendant by service of process.[39] This was a case where the plaintiff was seeking the trans-

---

35. 330 U.S. 501, 67 S.Ct. 839, 91 L.Ed. 1055 (1947).

36. Id. at 513, 67 S.Ct. at 845, 91 L.Ed. at 1065.

37. 28 U.S.C.A. § 1404(a).

38. Foster-Milburn Co. v. Knight, 181 F.2d 949 (2d Cir. 1950).

39. The case raises some nice questions as to when an action is "brought." Under Rule 3 of the Fed.Rules Civ.Proc., "A civil action is commenced by filing a complaint with the court." Does "commenced" in the rule mean the same as "brought" in the statute? Judge Learned Hand, in the Foster-Milburn case, held that it does not.

fer and the defendant was resisting it. In the later case of Hoffman v. Blaski [40] the Supreme Court had before it a situation in which the defendant, who was seeking the transfer, was willing to waive venue and submit to personal jurisdiction in the transferee district. This, the court held, was not sufficient. The transferee court must have been one in which the plaintiff could have satisfied the jurisdictional and venue requirements without any waivers by the defendant. "We do not think the § 1404(a) phrase 'where it might have been brought' can be interpreted to mean, as petitioners' theory would require, 'where it may now be re-brought, with defendants' consent.' " [41] The case was the subject of a considerable amount of critical comment on the ground that the court's narrow interpretation violated the Congressional purpose in permitting the district courts to exercise discretion in transferring cases to the most convenient forum.[42] The phrase came before the Supreme Court again in Van Dusen

---

A contrary holding would mean that a plaintiff could dispense with service on the defendant in the district where the case was to be tried, bring the case in the defendant's district, serve him there, and then have the case transferred to a forum 3000 miles away to a district where the defendant does not live and perhaps never set foot. Since the plaintiff has the choice of forum in the first place, a strong argument can be made that § 1404 (a) is not available to plaintiffs: see notes in 63 Harv.L.Rev. 708 (1950); 48 Mich.L.Rev. 1032 (1950); 28 Tex.L.Rev. 872 (1950). The question of what constitutes the commencement of an action is also important in determining whether an action has been brought within the period of time allowed by the applicable statute of limitations. As noted above, under the federal rule an action is commenced by the filing of a complaint. Under state codes there are a variety of answers: when the complaint is filed, when the defendant is served, when the complaint is filed and service is made, and when the complaint is filed and put in the sheriff's hands for service. For a case dealing with a conflict on the point between federal law and state law, see Ragan v. Merchants Transfer & Warehouse Co.,

337 U.S. 530, 69 S.Ct. 1233, 93 L.Ed. 1520 (1949). Ragan was a case brought in the federal court because of diversity of citizenship, and although it was filed before the two-year statute of limitations had run, the defendant was not served until afterward. Under the federal rule filing was enough, but under the Kansas statute of limitations, service must have been made within the statutory period. The court held that the Kansas statute applied and the case was barred. The authority of Ragan has been weakened, or destroyed, by the later case of Hanna v. Plumer, 380 U.S. 460, 85 S.Ct. 1136, 14 L.Ed.2d 8 (1965), which seems to hold that, in a diversity case, if the point is explicitly covered in one of the federal rules, it takes precedence over a conflicting state rule.

40. 363 U.S. 335, 80 S.Ct. 1084, 4 L.Ed.2d 1254 (1960).

41. Id. at 342, 80 S.Ct. at 1089, 4 L.Ed.2d at 1261.

42. See notes in the following law reviews: 1961 Duke L.J. 349; 49 Geo.L.J. 765 (1961); 45 Minn.L.Rev. 680 (1961); 35 St. John's L.Rev. 169 (1960); 14 Van.L.Rev. 646 (1961).

v. Barrack [43] and received gentler treatment.　The case involved the crash of a Philadelphia bound plane during its takeoff from Boston.　As a result, over 150 actions for personal injuries and wrongful death were filed.　More than 100 of these were in the federal court in Massachusetts and 45 were in the federal court in Pennsylvania.　The defendants moved to transfer the Pennsylvania cases to the District of Massachusetts.　The District Court granted the transfer but was reversed by the Court of Appeals on the authority of Hoffman.　It held the plaintiffs (Pennsylvania executors and administrators) were not qualified to sue in Massachusetts and therefore suits could not have been brought there.　The Supreme Court reversed, noting that, unlike Hoffman, the transferee court was one in which both jurisdiction and venue were proper.　In short, it held that "might have been brought" refers to the suability of the defendant and not to the capacity of the plaintiff. [44]

In passing on a motion for transfer under § 1404(a) the court may exercise a wide discretion. [45]　It will normally give great weight to plaintiff's choice of forum, [46] and the defendant carries a heavy burden, [47] but where the court feels that the balance of inconvenience strongly favors the defendant, a transfer will be ordered. [48]　A defendant who has removed the case from a state to a federal court may then ask for a transfer under the section. [49] Notwithstanding the availability of the section there are occasions when a court may apply the doctrine of forum non conveniens and dismiss.　This will be true in cases in which there are practically no contacts with the forum and the only other available forum is a court in a foreign country. [50]

Hoffman and Van Dusen dealt with the situation in which the plaintiff brought his case in a district in which venue was proper, but inconvenient to the defendant.　What if the plaintiff

43. 376 U.S. 612, 84 S.Ct. 805, 11 L.Ed.2d 945 (1964).

44. "We cannot agree that the final clause of § 1404(a) was intended to restrict the availability of convenient federal forums by referring to state-law rules, such as those concerning capacity to sue, which would have applied if the action had originally been instituted in the transferee federal court." Id. at 621, 84 S.Ct. at 812, 11 L.Ed.2d at 953.

45. Vinita Broadcasting Co. v. Colby, 320 F.Supp. 902 (N.D.Okla. 1971).

46. Triangle Indus., Inc. v. Kennecott Copper Corp., 325 F.Supp. 150 (E.D.Pa.1971).

47. Id.

48. Transcontinental Serv. Corp. v. True Temper Corp., 319 F.Supp. 920 (S.D.N.Y.1970).

49. McGraw-Edison Co. v. United States Fidelity & Guar. Co., 322 F. Supp. 1049 (E.D.Wis.1971).

50. McCarthy v. Canadian Nat'l Rys., 322 F.Supp. 1197 (D.Mass. 1971).

sues in a district of improper venue? Another section of the Code provides that, in such event, the court may dismiss the case or transfer it to any district "in which it could have been brought." [51] Notwithstanding the similarity in language in the concluding phrase, the Supreme Court has given it quite a different interpretation. In Goldlawr, Inc. v. Heiman,[52] the court held that such a case could be transferred even before the transferor court had acquired jurisdiction of the persons of some of the defendants. This curious holding sparked the following comment from Mr. Justice Harlan in his dissenting opinion:

> The notion that a District Court may deal with an in personam action in such a way as possibly to affect a defendant's substantive rights without first acquiring jurisdiction over him is not a familiar one in federal jurisprudence.[53]

51. 28 U.S.C.A. § 1406(a).

52. 369 U.S. 463, 82 S.Ct. 913, 8 L.Ed.2d 39 (1962).

53. Id. at 467, 82 S.Ct. at 916, 8 L.Ed.2d at 43.

CHAPTER IV. CLAIMS AND CLAIMANTS

SECTION 1. IN GENERAL

A law suit, in its simplest form, consists of a controversy between one plaintiff and one defendant which the court is asked to decide. Many suits, however, do not fit into this simple pattern. A plaintiff may have more than one claim against a defendant. May he join them in the same suit? A plaintiff may have separate claims against several defendants. May he join them in one suit? Several plaintiffs may have similar claims against a single defendant. May they join in suing him in a single action? Several plaintiffs may have several claims against several defendants. May they all be joined in one suit? All of these questions deal with the problem of *permissive* joinder of claims, or parties, or both. There is a related problem which deals with *compulsory* joinder. Must a plaintiff assert all the claims he has against a defendant in the same suit? Must plaintiffs with similar claims against a defendant join in asserting them? Must a plaintiff sue all defendants who may be liable to him? Or, may he pick and choose? And if he may, is it possible for those who have been left out to join the suit later by intervening or by being forced to do so at the insistence of another party?

Answers to the foregoing questions have varied according to the time in history under review. In the days of the common law the size of a law suit was sharply restricted, due largely to the rigidity of the writ system.[1] Joinder of causes or of parties as a matter of convenience or for reasons of judicial economy was unknown. Equity, on the other hand, was more liberal. Its very reason for existence was to relieve against the rigor of the common law and, where justice required, to furnish a remedy when the common law provided for none. It recognized causes of action which were not cognizable at law and, under its maxim that "equity delights to do justice and not by halves," it expanded the scope of a suit by permitting the joinder of parties whose interests would be affected by the controversy between the main litigants. The code reform of 1848 represented a compromise. Its greatest achievement was the merger of law and equity, thus eliminating the necessity for two sets of courts and two bodies of jurisprudence. This was accomplished by borrowing from both

1. Harris v. Avery, 5 Kan. 146 (1869).

systems. The framers of the first code did not consider the permissible size of a law suit as one problem. Rather, they felt they were attacking two problems: (1) the problem of joinder of causes of action, and (2) the problem of joinder of parties. For a solution to the first they looked primarily to the common law system; for a solution to the second they looked primarily to equity.[2] As a result, the code sections on joinder have caused trouble. They have been amended from time to time by the legislatures of states under the code system, with good results, but it was not until the federal rules appeared in 1938 that a synchronized approach was used.[3] The philosophy of the federal rules was one of practically unlimited joinder of both claims and parties subject only to limitations based upon trial convenience. It was thought to be socially desirable to settle all cognate controversies in one law suit, rather than many, if it could be done without undue hardship or injustice to the parties. The federal rules were far superior to the original codes, but they were not perfect, and they too have been amended from time to time.

SECTION 2. UNDER THE CODES

Joinder of causes. The original New York code served as a model for procedural reform in more than half of the states. Although there was some variation in wording from state to state, the usual section relating to joinder of causes tended to follow a uniform pattern consisting of a list of the causes of action which a plaintiff could unite in the same complaint. It was reminiscent of the old forms of action at common law. The usual code provision listed eight categories or types of action which could be joined, but it expressly said that all causes so united must belong to only one of those classes. The usual classes, according to Judge Clark, were: "(1) contracts, express or implied; (2) injuries to the person; (3) injuries to the character; (4) injuries to property; (5) actions to recover real property with or without damages; (6) actions to recover chattels with or without damages; (7) claims against a trustee by virtue of a contract or operation of law; (8) actions arising out of the same transaction or transactions connected with the same subject of action." [4] The usual code provision contained the additional restriction that

2. For a comprehensive treatment see Clark, Code Pleading (2d ed. 1947) [Hereinafter referred to as Clark], Chapters 6, 7.

3. For a review of the evolution of the problems of joinder under the common law, the codes and the federal rules see the opinion of Judge Foster in Adams v. Allstate Ins. Co., 58 Wash.2d 659, 364 P.2d 804 (1961).

4. Clark, supra n. 2 at 441.

the causes so united "must affect all the parties to the action, and not require different places of trial." [5] This is the only place in the section which intimates that there may be multiple parties and, as we shall see, it has caused difficulties.

In Fielder v. Ohio Edison Co.[6] the decedent was electrocuted by one of the defendant's hot wires; his administrator sued: (1) for pain and suffering under a survival statute, and (2) for damages under the wrongful death statute. The court held there had been a misjoinder since the plaintiff was suing in two capacities, that on the first cause of action any recovery would go to the estate, that on the second cause of action it would go to him as trustee for the beneficiaries named in the statute, and that therefore the causes of action did not affect him in both capacities. In Ryder v. Jefferson Hotel Co.[7] a husband and wife were ejected from defendant's hotel at midnight on the assumption they were not husband and wife. They joined in suing the hotel, she claiming damages for inconvenience, embarrassment and injury to her reputation, he claiming damages for loss of custom in his business. The court held there was a misjoinder since the several causes of action did not affect "all of the parties." In other words, she was entitled to her damages, and he to his. In Ader v. Blau [8] a wrongful death action was brought against two defendants, one cause of action sounding in negligence for maintaining an attractive nuisance (a picket fence upon which the decedent was impaled) and the other sounding in malpractice against the physician who treated the boy. Although there were common questions of fact (cause of death, proximate cause, etc.) the court held there was a misjoinder of causes and parties because the causes did not affect "all of the parties" and the causes did not arise out of the same transaction or subject of action.

Real party in interest. Before proceeding to the problem of joinder of parties brief mention should be made of another contribution of the codes, the requirement that suit must be brought in the name of the real party in interest.[9] Today this would seem self-evident but in 1848 it was an innovation. That was because, at that time certain rights were characterized as "legal" and others as "equitable," and the characterization largely determined

---

5. Quoted from West's Cal.Code Civ.Proc. § 427.

6. 158 Ohio St. 375, 109 N.E.2d 855 (1952).

7. 121 S.C. 72, 113 S.E. 474 (1922).

8. 241 N.Y. 7, 148 N.E. 771 (1925).

9. The original New York code made an exception in the case of "an executor or administrator, or a trustee of an express trust, or a person expressly authorized by statute" who could sue "without joining with him the person for whose benefit the action is prosecuted." Clark, supra n. 2 at 158.

the court in which they could be enforced. In the long struggle for supremacy between the law courts and the equity courts many fictions were developed to avoid sharp jurisdictional distinctions. One of these was that, although the law did not recognize assignments of choses in action, it would entertain an action to enforce an assignment (against the obligor) providing suit was brought in the name of the assignor. With the merger of law and equity the code provided, very simply, that suit should be brought by the real party in interest, which was interpreted to mean the one to whom the substantive law gave the right.[10] The clause has, however, provoked some controversy among courts as to its true meaning.[11] For instance, insurance policies covering fire losses and property damage customarily contain subrogation clauses under which, upon being paid the amount of the loss, the policyholder assigns to the insurance company his cause of action against the tortfeasor who caused the loss. It is generally believed that many juries have prejudices against insurance companies. May an insurance company, suing on such a subrogation claim, overcome this prejudice by bringing the suit in the name of the policyholder? The courts are divided on an answer to this question [12] with perhaps the prevailing view that the code requires the company to sue in its own name.[13]

Compulsory joinder of parties. Practically all codes contain provisions requiring parties who are united in interest to be joined as plaintiffs or defendants.[14] Such provisions have raised difficult problems of interpretation which have plagued the courts from the beginning. The leading case on the subject is Shields v. Barrow,[15] decided by the United States Supreme Court

---

10. The framers of the code explained the clause as follows: "The true rule undoubtedly is, that which prevails in the courts of equity, that he who has the right, is the person to pursue the remedy. We have adopted that rule." First Rep.Comm'rs. on Prac. & Pl., N.Y. 1848, 124; Clark & Hutchins, The Real Party in Interest, 34 Yale L.J. 259 (1925).

11. For a thorough discussion of the real party in interest rule see Clark, supra n. 2 at 155–209.

12. In Anheuser-Busch, Inc. v. Starley, 28 Cal.2d 347, 170 P.2d 448 (1946) the court held the policyholder could sue, Justice Traynor dissenting. In Ellis Canning Co. v.

International Harvester Co., 174 Kan. 357, 255 P.2d 658 (1953) the court held the insurance company was the real party in interest and only it could sue.

13. See Spencer v. Standard Chem. & Metals Corp., 237 N.Y. 479, 480, 143 N.E. 651, 652 (1924): "If, as between the assignor and assignee, the transfer is complete, so that the former is divested of all control and right to the cause of action, and the latter is entitled to control it and receive its fruits, the assignee is the real party in interest."

14. Clark, supra n. 2 at 358, 380.

15. 17 How. 130, 15 L.Ed. 158 (1854).

in 1854. Curiously, the court was not interpreting a code provision, but was deciding whether a federal court had the power to proceed with a case in the absence of an "indispensable" party. The plaintiff was suing to rescind a contract which had been signed by a number of persons. He had invoked the jurisdiction of the federal court on the basis of diversity of citizenship and had omitted to join as defendants some of the signers whose presence in the case would have destroyed the diversity. The court held the omitted parties were indispensable and dismissed the suit. In so doing it defined three categories of parties: (1) formal parties, who may be dispensed with when they cannot be reached, (2) necessary parties, those having an interest in the controversy who should be included in order to do complete justice, but whose interests are so separable that the court may proceed to decide the case as to the parties before it without affecting the rights of the absentees, and (3) indispensable parties, "Persons who not only have an interest in the controversy, but an interest of such a nature that a final decree cannot be made without either affecting that interest, or leaving the controversy in such a condition that its final termination may be wholly inconsistent with equity and good conscience." [16] Although these definitions were enunciated for the purpose of determining a question of federal jurisdiction, they have served as guide-lines for deciding questions of compulsory joinder under the codes.[17]

Permissive joinder of parties. The original codes permitted persons to join as plaintiffs in one action if they had "an interest in the subject of the action and in obtaining the relief demanded." [18] Unfortunately the use of the word "and" led some courts to interpret the clause as setting up a double-barreled requirement.[19] Thus, in Thigpen v. Kinston Cotton Mills, [20] the plaintiff, a minor, sued for damages for personal injuries and his father sought to join to recover for loss of the son's services, but the court held there was a misjoinder since neither plaintiff had any interest in the cause of action of the other. The original codes

16. Id. at 139, 15 L.Ed. at 160.

17. For cases applying the Shields v. Barrow definitions see: *Necessary parties*: Bank of Cal. v. Superior Court, 16 Cal.2d 516, 106 P.2d 879 (1940); Keene v. Chambers, 271 N.Y. 326, 3 N.E.2d 443 (1936); Castle v. City of Madison, 113 Wis. 346, 89 N.W. 156 (1902). *Indispensable parties*: Thomson v. Talbert Drainage Dist., 168 Cal. App.2d 687, 336 P.2d 174 (1959); Cunningham v. Brewer, 144 Neb. 211, 16 N.W.2d 533 (1944). Nonjoinder of an indispensable party is a matter of jurisdiction which may be raised at any time, even by the appellate court on its own motion: Peerless Ins. Co. v. Superior Court, 6 Cal.App.3d 358, 85 Cal.Rptr. 679 (1970).

18. Clark, supra n. 2 at 365.

19. Id.

20. 151 N.C. 97, 65 S.E. 750 (1909).

also provided for joinder of persons as defendants who "claim an interest in the controversy adverse to the plaintiff." [21] Such provisions were likewise narrowly interpreted, as illustrated by the case of Ader v. Blau discussed above. That case advanced another reason why the code provisions regarding permissive joinder could not be given a liberal interpretation: such clauses must be read with the code provision relating to joinder of causes of action which contained the restrictive clause that the causes so joined must affect all of the parties.

It was inevitable that such decisions would lead to amendments to the codes, widening the permissible scope of a law suit to handle all cognate claims. The California amendments, which are typical, and which were borrowed from the English practice,[22] provide that all persons may join as plaintiffs "who have an interest in the subject of the action or in whom any right to relief is alleged to exist, whether jointly, severally or in the alternative, where if such persons brought separate actions any question of law or fact would arise which are common to all the parties to the action". [23] A companion amendment provided for permissive joinder of defendants "against whom the right to any relief is alleged to exist, whether jointly, severally, or in the alternative." [24] It is regrettable that the legislature which adopted these amendments as to parties did not amend the old provision regarding joinder of causes by removing the restrictive clause requiring the causes to "affect all of the parties." This oversight was not fatal, however, since the California Supreme Court held the restrictive clause was repealed or amended by implication.[25] The modern codes, as amended, are producing good results.[26]

21. Clark, supra n. 2 at 382.

22. Clark, supra n. 2 at 369.

23. West's Ann.Cal.Code Civ.Proc., § 378.

24. West's Ann.Cal.Code Civ.Proc., § 379.

25. Kraft v. Smith, 24 Cal.2d 124, 148 P.2d 23 (1944).

26. In Lambert v. Southern Counties Gas Co., 52 Cal.2d 347, 340 P.2d 608 (1959) the plaintiff loaned his bulldozer to the defendant to bulldoze a field, and the machine was destroyed by fire when it hit a gas pipe which was too near the surface; the court held plaintiff could join the bailee and the Gas Co. as defendants, each on a different theory of negligence. In Schwartz v. Swan, 63 Ill.App.2d 148, 211 N.E.2d 122 (1965) a plaintiff who was injured in one automobile accident on August 13 and another one on August 23 was permitted to join the two defendants in the same suit under her allegation that both contributed to her injuries. In Tanbro Fabrics Corp. v. Beaunit Mills, Inc., 4 A.D.2d 519, 167 N.Y.S.2d 387 (1957) a plaintiff was permitted to join as defendants the seller and the seller's supplier of yarn that proved to be defective. In the opinion the court said: "It should be beyond argument by now, that it is no longer a bar to joinder . . . that there is not an identity of duty or contract upon which to assert alternative

Counterclaims. A counterclaim, as the name suggests, is a claim which the defendant asserts against the plaintiff. It is an invention of the codes. At common law a defendant could file a plea of recoupment under which he could introduce evidence tending to diminish or defeat the claim of the plaintiff, but it had to be something growing out of the transaction sued upon, and in no event could the defendant procure an affirmative judgment against the plaintiff. In equity the courts would, under some circumstances permit a set-off of mutual debts of the parties.[27] The codes provided for a defendant's remedy broader than either. The early codes authorized counterclaims in two situations: (1) where the claim arose out of the same transaction upon which plaintiff sued,[28] and (2) in an action on contract, any other cause of action on contract,[29] and the codes permitted the counterclaim, not merely to diminish or defeat the plaintiff's cause, but to provide the basis for an affirmative judgment against the plaintiff.[30] Later code provisions in some states broadened the scope of counterclaims to include any claim which the defendant had against the plaintiff.[31] Some further provided that defendants could file cross-claims against each other.[32] These more liberal

---

liability. It is still necessary, of course, that there be a finding that the alternative liability arises out of a common transaction or occurrence involving common questions of fact and law." Id. at 524, 167 N.Y.S.2d at 392. In Akely v. Kinnicutt, 238 N.Y. 466, 144 N.E. 682 (1924) 193 plaintiffs were permitted to join, each alleging a separate cause of action for fraud in the sale by the defendant of its corporate stock. A federal court distinguished the Akely case in Sun-X Glass Tinting of Mid-Wisconsin v. Sun-X Int'l., 227 F.Supp. 365 (W.D.Wis.1964) on the ground that in Akely there was a single fraudulent representation made to all plaintiffs in the company's prospectus, whereas in the instant case there was no common misrepresentation made to all plaintiffs, but a series of similar ones to each plaintiff.

27. Clark supra n. 2 at 633–36; Koffler & Reppy, Common Law Pleading (1969) 515–17.

28. The two-car automobile collision is perhaps the most fruitful source of the "same transaction" type of

counterclaim. See Haut v. Gunderson, 54 N.D. 826, 211 N.W. 982 (1926).

29. Clark, supra n. 2 at 642.

30. Clark, supra n. 2 at 651.

31. Such provisions frequently divided counterclaims into two classes: (1) compulsory counterclaims—those growing out of the same transaction—which must be asserted in the action or they were waived, see Keller v. Keklikian, 362 Mo. 919, 244 S.W.2d 1001 (1951), and (2) permissive counterclaims—all others—which defendant could assert or save for another suit, see Jones v. Mortimer, 28 Cal.2d 627, 170 P.2d 893 (1946).

32. In Liebhauser v. Milwaukee Elec. Ry. & Light Co., 180 Wis. 468, 193 N.W. 522 (1923) the plaintiff, a passenger on the street car, was injured when it struck a car belonging to the other defendant. She sued both, and the individual defendant cross-claimed against the street car company for the property damage to his car. The code section authorizing one de-

code amendments were forerunners of the federal rules, and will be discussed more fully in connection with them.

SECTION 3. UNDER THE FEDERAL RULES

The federal rules were drafted after nearly a century of experience under the codes. They brought to the federal courts the great reforms of the codes in a refined and corrected form, and they devised some innovations of their own.

Joinder of causes. The federal rules made two significant changes. The first was a change in nomenclature. They discarded the phrase "cause of action" and substituted for it "claim for relief." It was thought that this might overcome some of the confusion in the cases which employed different definitions of the old term. The second change was more substantial. The difficulties caused by the complex joinder provisions of the codes were overcome by the simple expedient of removing all restrictions on joinder. The rule provided that a party "may join, either as independent, or as alternate claims, as many claims, legal, equitable, or maritime, as he has against an opposing party." [33] There was no requirement that the claims be related in any way, or that they be of the same class. If a plaintiff had a dozen different claims against a defendant, each of a different kind, arising out of a different transaction, and seeking a different kind of relief, he could join them all in the same suit. The philosophy behind such a liberal rule is that when the time comes that parties cannot settle their differences, and one of them brings the matter to court, it is desirable to settle all of their controversies in the same suit. It is of course possible that, if the joined claims are of widely disparate nature a jury may be confused or preju-

---

fendant to cross-claim against another said the relief asked must involve the transaction or property which is the subject matter of the action. A divided court held the cross-claim would not lie since the plaintiff had no interest in his cause of action, nor he in hers. Three justices dissented on the ground the collision was the subject of the action, and not merely plaintiff's legal right. In Wettstein v. Cameto, 61 Cal.2d 838, 841, 40 Cal.Rptr. 705, 395 P.2d 665, 666 (1964), the court says in interpreting the California code, "there is a very shadowy line of distinction between a cross complaint and a counterclaim and a considerable area in which they overlap."

33. Fed.Rules Civ.Proc. 18(a). See Moon v. Brewer, 89 Idaho 59, 402 P.2d 973 (1965), where under a rule identical with Rule 18, the plaintiff was allowed to join a suit for rescission for fraud with a claim for damages due to the fraud. Under the former practice the plaintiff would have been compelled to make an election of remedies, but under the new rule he could plead in the alternative.

diced in trying to handle all of them. If this should seem likely the court is given authority to order separate trials.[34]

Real party in interest. Here the federal rules followed the codes with little or no change, providing that "Every action shall be prosecuted in the name of the real party in interest." [35] The position of the assignee, discussed supra, has been clarified by the Supreme Court in United States v. Aetna Casualty & Surety Co.[36] That was a suit under the federal tort claims act on a claim which had been paid by the insurance company. The court held that, under the rule, if the claim had been paid in full the insurance company was the real party in interest, but that if the subrogation had been only partial then both the insurance company and the original claimant were necessary parties and should be joined.[37] The rule also clears up a conflict of laws point by providing that the capacity of a party to sue or be sued is determined by the law of the domicile of the party.[38]

Standing to sue. May a taxpayer sue to enjoin a program authorized by Congress on the ground that it is unconstitutional? In Massachusetts v. Mellon [39] the Supreme Court held that he could not—that his interest was too remote—that he had no stand-

34. Fed.Rules Civ.Proc. 42(b) which says the court, "in furtherance of convenience or to avoid prejudice, or where separate trials will be conducive to expedition and economy, may order a separate trial." In Carlstrom v. United States, 275 F.2d 802 (9th Cir. 1960), the court says that whether to order separate trials or not rests within the sound discretion of the trial court, which will not be reversed in the absence of abuse. For a case reversing the trial court see Sporia v. Pennsylvania Greyhound Lines, 143 F.2d 105 (3d Cir. 1944), in which P was riding with Q in his car when it collided with D's bus, and both were injured. They joined in suing D who moved to sever the cases of P and Q and to join Q as a defendant with D in P's action so that D would not lose a possible right to contribution between tortfeasors. The lower court denied the motion on the ground there was nothing in the rule covering it, but the appellate court reversed on the ground that essential justice required it. Many codes now contain provisions giving the trial court discretion in ordering separate trials: see Sporn v. Hudson Transit Lines, 265 App. Div. 360, 38 N.Y.S.2d 512 (1942).

35. Fed.Rules Civ.Proc. 17(a).

36. 338 U.S. 366, 70 S.Ct. 207, 94 L.Ed. 171 (1949); accord, Link Aviation, Inc. v. Downs, 117 U.S.App. D.C. 40, 325 F.2d 613 (1963).

37. Where the insurer has paid only part of the loss and sues alone the defendant can compel joinder of the original claimant under Rule 19 to avoid being subjected to a multiplicity of suits. Royal Indem. Co. v. City of Erie, 326 F.Supp. 571 (W.D.Pa.1971).

38. Fed.Rules Civ.Proc. 17(b). Basically, the rule says that capacity to sue shall be determined by state, rather than federal law, but there are exceptions. For an interpretation of the rule see Oskoian v. Canuel, 269 F.2d 311 (1st Cir. 1959).

39. 262 U.S. 447, 43 S.Ct. 597, 67 L.Ed. 1078 (1923).

ing to sue. Forty-five years later, in the case of Flast v. Cohen,[40] the Supreme Court held that he could. The distinction between the two seems to be that in Flast the plaintiff could point to a specific clause in the constitution which limited the spending power of Congress. In the Flast case the Court admitted that standing was one of "the most amorphous [concepts] in the entire domain of public law." [41] Judge Trask, of the Ninth Circuit, put it this way: " the question [of standing] is whether or not that party has a sufficient personal stake in the outcome as to justify the court in entertaining his petition." [42] The necessary interest is usually financial, but it need not be.[43] These cases have raised the current question as to whether non-profit organizations, such as the Sierra Club, have standing to sue private polluters, or even the government, to protect the environment. The majority of federal courts in which the question has arisen have held that such plaintiffs do have standing to sue.[44]

Compulsory joinder of parties. The original federal rule on the subject was entitled "Necessary Joinder of Parties." [45] It spoke in terms of persons "having a joint interest" who "shall be made parties," it spoke of others who, although not indispensable, "ought to be parties," and it prescribed the conditions under which the court could proceed without them if they were not subject to the court's jurisdiction. In short, it very much resembled the procedure under the codes, and, as in the case of the codes, the rule produced some confusion in the cases interpreting it. Courts frequently disagreed in drawing the thin line between "indispensable" and merely "necessary" parties.[46] These diffi-

40. 392 U.S. 83, 88 S.Ct. 1942, 20 L.Ed.2d 947 (1968).

41. Id. at 99, 88 S.Ct. at 1952, 20 L.Ed.2d at 961.

42. Alameda Conservation Ass'n v. State of California, 437 F.2d 1087, 1091 (9th Cir. 1971). Occasionally a statute will specifically authorize taxpayers to sue to restrain illegal expenditure of public funds. See Blair v. Pitchess, 5 Cal.3d 258, 96 Cal.Rptr. 42, 486 P.2d 1242 (1971).

43. Association of Data Processing Organizations, Inc. v. Camp, 397 U.S. 150, 90 S.Ct. 827, 25 L.Ed.2d 184 (1970).

44. Cases holding such plaintiffs have standing to sue: Citizens Committee for the Hudson Valley

v. Volpe, 425 F.2d 97 (2d Cir. 1970); Environmental Defense Fund v. Hardin, 428 F.2d 1093 (D.C.Cir. 1970); Izaak Walton League of America v. St. Clair, 313 F.Supp. 1312 (D.Minn.1970); Parker et al. v. United States, 307 F.Supp. 685 (D.Colo.1969); Pennsylvania Environmental Council, Inc. v. Bartlett, 315 F.Supp. 238 (M.D.Pa.1970). Cases holding contra: Alameda Conservation Ass'n v. State of California, supra n. 42; Sierra Club v. Hickel, 433 F.2d 24 (9th Cir. 1970). See L. Jaffee, Standing Again, 84 Harv.L.Rev. 633 (1971).

45. Fed.Rules Civ.Proc. 19. It remained unchanged until 1966.

46. In Kroese v. General Steel Castings Corp., 179 F.2d 760 (3d Cir. 1950) a preferred shareholder sued

culties led to an extensive revision of the rule in 1966. It would probably be more accurate to say a repeal of the old rule and the substitution of a completely new one in its place.[47]

The new rule does not draw a clear distinction between "necessary" and "indispensable" parties.[48] It does not use the word "necessary" at all but instead speaks of "persons to be joined if feasible." These are defined as persons whose absence will prevent the court from doing complete justice to those already parties, or whose interests may be injuriously affected if the court proceeds without them. The rule then lays down four pragmatic guide-lines to aid the court in determining whether to proceed or to dismiss because the absentee is "indispensable." They are: "first, to what extent a judgment rendered in the person's absence might be prejudicial to him or those already parties; second, the extent to which, by protective provisions in the judgment, by the shaping of relief, or other measures, the prejudice can be lessened or avoided; third, whether a judgment rendered in the person's absence will be adequate; fourth, whether the plaintiff will have an adequate remedy if the action is dismissed for nonjoinder." The new rule is undoubtedly an improvement over the old one since it emphasizes the fact that the line between "necessary" and "indispensable" parties is a shadowy one, dependent upon the facts of the particular case, since it emphasizes

4. guides

the corporation for arrears in dividends, alleging the company had fraudulently favored common stockholders; only 3 of the 12 directors could be served in Pennsylvania (where the suit was brought); the trial court dismissed on the theory that a majority of the board, at least, were indispensable parties, but the appellate court reversed, saying an effective decree could be devised. "Equity courts have known for a long time how to impose onerous alternatives at home to the performance of affirmative acts abroad as a means of getting affirmative acts accomplished." Id. at 765. In Calcote v. Texas Pac. Oil & Gas Co., 157 F.2d 216 (5th Cir. 1946), a suit to cancel an oil and gas lease, it was held that persons holding mineral rights in the land subject to the lease were indispensable parties. In American Ins. Co. v. Bradley Mining Co., 57 F.Supp. 545 (N.D. Cal.1944) a mining property was insured by several insurance companies, some of whom brought an action for a declaratory judgment of non-liability; the court held that the other insurance companies were indispensable parties. Holding contra on comparable facts: Fireman's Fund Ins. Co. v. Crandall Horse Co., 47 F.Supp. 78 (W. D.N.Y.1942). In Greenleaf v. Safeway Trails, 140 F.2d 889 (2d Cir. 1944) the court held that a joint obligor on a contract was not an indispensable party.

47. Rule 19, as amended, is entitled "Joinder of Persons Needed for Just Adjudication." The focus of the rule is shifted from the old concepts of indispensable, necessary and proper parties to the practical feasibility of joinder. Crews v. Blake, 52 F.R.D. 106 (S.D.Ga.1971).

48. Failure to join an "indispensable" party is one of the defenses which is not waived under Rule 12 (h) (2). It can be raised at any time by the court on its own motion: McShan v. Sherrill, 283 F.2d 462 (9th Cir. 1960).

the pragmatic nature of the decision in drawing that line, and since it furnishes some guide-lines. It does not, however blaze a new trail. What it does is make more specific the general definitions announced by the Supreme Court in Shields v. Barrow in 1854.[49]

Permissive joinder of parties. Here the federal rule did no more than adopt the most modern amendments of the codes. Permissive joinder of plaintiffs was permitted if they asserted any right to relief, jointly, severally, or in the alternative; and permissive joinder of defendants was allowed if there was asserted against them jointly, severally, or in the alternative, any right to relief.[50] There are two conditions which must be fulfilled. The rights or duties of the parties so joined must arise out of the same transaction, occurrence, or series of transactions or occurrences.[51] Second, there must be common questions of law or fact.[52] The rule gives the court wide discretion in making "such orders as will prevent a party from being embarrassed, delayed, or put to expense" where these conditions are not met.[53]

49. Shields v. Barrow is discussed in the text at n. 15, supra. The new version of Rule 19 came before the Supreme Court in Provident Tradesmens Bank & Trust Co. v. Patterson, 390 U.S. 102, 88 S.Ct. 733, 19 L.Ed.2d 936 (1968). In reversing the Court of Appeals it said: "The majority of the Court of Appeals read Shields v. Barrow to say that a person whose interests 'may be affected' by the decree of the court is an indispensable party, and that all indispensable parties have a 'substantive right' to have suits dismissed in their absence. We are unable to read Shields as saying either. It dealt only with persons whose interests must, unavoidably, be affected by a decree and it said nothing about substantive rights. Rule 19(b), which the Court of Appeals dismissed as an ineffective attempt to change the substantive rights stated in Shields, is, on the contrary, a valid statement of the criteria for determining whether to proceed or dismiss in the forced absence of an interested person." Id. at 125, 88 S.Ct. at 746, 19 L.Ed. 2d at 953.

In Banks v. Seaboard Coast Line R. R., 51 F.R.D. 304 (N.D.Ga.1970) a black railroad employee sued the railroad and the Union alleging racial discrimination; the court held that the relief asked for by the plaintiff, if granted, would affect the seniority of white employees, and that they were therefore indispensable parties. The court cited Shields and commented: "Contrary to plaintiff's assertion, the revision of the Federal Rules did not make pre-revision principles obsolete." Id. at 305. In Crews v. Blake, supra n. 47, the court said the 1966 amendment shifts the focus from concepts of indispensable, necessary and proper parties to the practical feasability of joinder.

50. Fed.Rules Civ.Proc. 20(a).

51. Kenvin v. Newburger, Loeb & Co., 37 F.R.D. 473 (S.D.N.Y.1965).

52. Federal Housing Adm'r v. Christianson, 26 F.Supp. 419 (D. Conn.1939).

53. Fed.Rules Civ.Proc. 20(b).

Counterclaims. Basically, the federal rule on counterclaims followed the more modern codes,[54] providing for compulsory counterclaims (those arising out of the transaction or occurrence that is the subject matter of the opposing party's claim)[55] and permissive counterclaims (any others). The original rule, in defining compulsory counterclaims, made an exception of a claim which was already the subject of another pending action. The purpose of the exception was to prevent one party from compelling the other to try his case in a court not of his own choosing.[56] A second exception was added by an amendment to the rule in 1963. It provided that a counterclaim was not compulsory where "the opposing party brought suit upon his claim by attachment or other process by which the court did not acquire jurisdiction to render a personal judgment on that claim."[57] The rules had just been amended to permit a plaintiff to start a quasi in rem suit in the federal courts by attachment or garnishment.[58] It was thought that one whose property was attached under the new procedure and who wished to come in and defend it should not be obliged also to assert a counterclaim but should be permitted to do so at his election. The rule provides that a claim which matured, or was acquired by the pleader after the service of his pleading may, with the permission of the court be presented by supplemental pleading.[59] It also provides that the court may, in its discretion, permit a pleader to set up a counterclaim which, through inadvertence or excusable neglect, he failed to plead within the time prescribed by the rules.[60] Under the rule a party may file a cross-claim against the co-party if it relates to the original action, a counterclaim therein, or any property which is the subject matter of the original action.[61] The rule was amend-

---

54. Fed.Rules Civ.Proc. 13.

55. "[A] counterclaim is compulsory if it bears a 'logical relationship' to an opposing party's claim . . .. The phrase 'logical relationship' is given meaning by the purpose of the rule which it was designed to implement. Thus, a counterclaim is logically related to the opposing party's claim where separate trials on each of their respective claims would involve a substantial duplication of effort and time by the parties and the courts." Great Lakes Rubber Corp. v. Herbert Cooper Co., 286 F.2d 631, 634 (3d Cir. 1961).

56. Union Paving Co. v. Downer Corp., 276 F.2d 468 (9th Cir. 1960).

57. Fed.Rules Civ.Proc. 13(a) (2).

58. Fed.Rules Civ.Proc. 4(e).

59. Fed.Rules Civ.Proc. 13(e).

60. Fed.Rules Civ.Proc. 13(f).

61. Fed.Rules Civ.Proc. 13(g). In Danner v. Anskis, 256 F.2d 123 (3d Cir. 1958) the court held a plaintiff could not file a cross-claim against a co-plaintiff and states: "The purpose of Rule 13(g) is to permit a defendant to state as a cross-claim a claim against a co-defendant growing out of the transaction or occurrence that is the subject matter of the original action, and to permit a plaintiff against whom a defendant has filed

ed again in 1966 to provide that "persons other than those made parties to the original action may be made parties to a counterclaim or cross-claim in accordance with the provisions of Rules 19 and 20." [62] The overall purpose of the rule is to dispose of as many cognate claims as possible in the same law suit,[63] but the possible combinations of parties and claims is somewhat staggering. With this in mind, no doubt, the framers of the rule added a final subsection as a reminder that the court has power to order separate trials and to render separate judgments.[64]

SECTION 4. SPECIAL SITUATIONS

Third-party practice. Third-party practice, or impleader, which existed under a few of the more modern codes,[65] was included in the federal rules.[66] It is a device by which the defendant can bring in third parties and make them a part of the law suit. A few examples will illustrate the circumstances under which it is available. In Jeub v. B/G Foods, Inc.,[67] the plaintiff sued the defendant for damages for personal injuries allegedly resulting from eating contaminated ham which was served in the defendant's restaurant. The defendant claimed the canned ham was bought from Swift & Co., and that if it was unwholesome it was entirely the fault of Swift. The court permitted the defendant to "implead" Swift as a third-party defendant. Thus, in the same law suit, if it was held that the plaintiff could recover against the defendant, the court could try the issue of whether the fault was primarily that of Swift, and if so, it could give the defendant a judgment against Swift.[68] Another case illustrating the operation of the rule is Baker v. Moors,[69] an automobile acci-

---

a counterclaim to state as a cross-claim against a co-plaintiff a claim growing out of the transaction or occurrence that is the subject matter of the counterclaim or relating to any property that is the subject matter of the counterclaim. This, we think, is the clear intent of the language of the rule. In other words, a cross-claim is intended to state a claim which is ancillary to a claim stated in a complaint or counterclaim which has previously been filed against the party stating the cross-claim." Id. at 124.

62. Fed.Rules Civ.Proc. 13(h).

63. If a federal court has jurisdiction to entertain the original claim it has ancillary jurisdiction to en-

tertain a compulsory counterclaim or a cross-claim. Glen Falls Indem. Co. v. United States, 229 F.2d 370 (9th Cir. 1955).

64. Fed.Rules Civ.Proc. 13(i).

65. Hejza v. New York Cent. R. R., 230 App.Div. 624, 246 N.Y.S. 34 (1930).

66. Fed.Rules Civ.Proc. 14.

67. 2 F.R.D. 238 (D.Minn.1942).

68. Accord: Roth v. Great A. & P. Tea Co., 12 F.R.D. 383 (E.D.N.Y. 1952).

69. 51 F.R.D. 507 (W.D.Ky.1971).

dent case in which the plaintiff sued for personal injuries. One of the defendants was the driver of the car, and there was some question as to whether he was driving it with the owner's permission, and thus whether he was covered by the owner's liability policy. The driver defendant moved to bring in the insurance company as a third-party defendant. The court granted the motion. It said that the mere fact that the ancillary controversy between the driver and the insurance company "involves a matter of contract, while the primary controversy between plaintiffs and the original defendants involves a matter of tort is not an adequate reason to disallow impleader." [70] Thus the issue of the tort liability of the defendant to the plaintiff, and the contract liability of the insurance company under its policy will be disposed of in the same suit.[71]

The rule does not give the defendant the right to implead anyone against whom he has a claim. The language of the rule is that he may implead "a person not a party to the action who is or may be liable to him for all or part of the plaintiff's claim against him." [72] In United States v. Joe Grasso & Son, Inc.,[73] the court said: "an entirely separate and independent claim cannot be maintained against a third party under Rule 14, even though it does arise out of the same general set of facts as the main claim." [74] That impleader is permitted "only in cases where the third party's liability was in some way derivative of the outcome of the main claim." [75] That was a case in which the plaintiff, the owner of a fleet of fishing boats, sued for a refund of federal employment taxes. The government sought to implead the captains of the boats on the theory that if the owner were not liable for the taxes the captains were, but the motion was denied.[76]

Nor does the rule give the defendant the absolute right to implead a third person even if he comes within the letter of the

70. Id. at 509.

71. Accord: Pioneer Mut. Compensation Co. v. Cosby, 125 Colo. 468, 244 P.2d 1089 (1952) (under a Colo. rule identical with Fed.Rule 14); Contra: American Zinc Co. v. H. H. Hall Constr. Co., 21 F.R.D. 190 (E.D.Ill.1957).

72. Fed.Rules Civ.Proc. 14(a).

73. 380 F.2d 749 (5th Cir. 1967).

74. Id. at 751.

75. Id. at 751.

76. Accord: United States v. De-Haven, 13 F.R.D. 435 (W.D.Mich. 1953). See Brown v. Cranston, 132 F.2d 631 (2d Cir. 1942), where the court would not allow the defendant to implead a joint tort feasor because under the applicable law one tort feasor did not have a claim for contribution from another until a joint money judgment had been recovered against two or more defendants and until more than the claimant's share had been paid.

discretion

rule. The cases have interpreted the rule as giving the <u>trial court</u> <u>discretion in the matter</u>. Thus, in Goodhart v. United States Lines Co.,[77] a personal injury suit against a company based upon the alleged negligence of its employee, the court refused the defendant permission to implead the employee. It took judicial notice of the fact the employee would not be financially able to indemnify the defendant to any substantial extent, it surmised the defendant's purpose was to enlist the sympathy of the jury if it believed the employee would be responsible, or to bring pressure on the employee to cooperate. "Neither of these pleas recommends itself to the court," it said, "as a subject for exercise of the court's discretion. Such legitimate claim as defendant may have against the hi-lo operator is amply protected by defendant's right to bring a separate suit." [78] As Professor Wright points out, "There should be little occasion, however, to deny impleader. The power to order separate trial of separate issues, under Rule 42(b), is sufficient to prevent any harm from impleader." [79]

It is generally held that only one who was not a party to the original action may be impleaded as a third-party defendant, since the normal procedures of counterclaim and cross-claim are adequate to take care of the situation.[80] The rule does, however, provide for two extensions of the impleader process: (a) a third-party defendant, who has been impleaded, may himself implead "any person not a party   .   .   .   who is or may be liable to him   .   .   ." [81]   (b) a plaintiff against whom a counterclaim has been asserted "may cause a third party to be brought in under circumstances which under this rule would entitle a defendant to do so." [82] Thus it is possible for the situation to become somewhat complicated. However, it is encouraging to note that if the federal court had jurisdiction of the original action, the jurisdiction extends to all such third party claims, and no independent federal grounds are necessary.[83]

Interpleader. Interpleader was an ancient remedy by which one could protect himself against the risk of double or multiple

---

77. 26 F.R.D. 163 (S.D.N.Y.1960).

78. Id. at 164. But see Noland Co. v. Graver Tank & Mfg. Co., 301 F. 2d 43 (4th Cir. 1962) in which, after a proper impleader, the court allowed the third-party plaintiff to include non-related claims against the third-party defendant.

79. Wright, Law of Federal Courts (2d ed. 1970) [Hereinafter referred to as Wright], 333.

80. Horton v. Continental Can Co., 19 F.R.D. 429 (D.Neb.1956). Cf. United States v. Nicholas, 28 F.R. D. 8 (D.Minn.1961).

81 Fed.Rules Civ.Proc. 14(a).

82. Fed.Rules Civ.Proc. 14(b).

83. James Talcott, Inc. v. Allahabad Bank Ltd., 444 F.2d 451 (5th Cir. 1971); Dery v. Wyer, 265 F.2d 804 (2d Cir. 1959).

liability when he was being pressed by rival claimants to property in his possession or to a debt which he owed.[84]　He could bring the property or money into court, or acknowledge the debt, and then file a petition asking the court to summon the claimants and adjudicate the rival claims.　Since the plaintiff was disinterested, the court could enter a decree discharging him from liability and proceed to adjudicate the rights of the claimants.[85] If the subject matter of the dispute was tangible property the court could treat the proceeding as one in rem and finally dispose of the case even if one or more of the claimants were non-residents.[86]　However, if a mere debt was involved, interpleader was treated as an in personam action, and the court could not adjudicate the rights of a claimant who was not subject to its in personam jurisdiction.　Such was the holding in the famous case of New York Life Insurance Co. v. Dunlevy.[87]　In that case there were rival claimants to the proceeds of a life insurance policy, one of whom lived in Pennsylvania and the other in California.　The company brought an interpleader action in a Pennsylvania court; both claimants were duly notified, but only the

84. Under the old equity practice the remedy of interpleader was subject to four restrictions: (1) The same thing, debt or duty must have been claimed by both or all of the parties against whom relief was asked, (2) All their titles or claims must have derived from a common source, (3) The plaintiff must not have or claim, any interest in the matter, and (4) The plaintiff must have incurred no independent liability to either of the claimants. A bill in the nature of interpleader was available where the plaintiff was not disinterested. 4 Pomeroy, Equity Jurisprudence (5th ed. 1941) § 1322. Under the modern version of interpleader most of the old restrictions have been swept away. In John A. Moore & Co. v. McConkey, 203 S.W.2d 512, 514 (Mo.App. 1947), the court said today the sole test of the right to maintain the bill is "that plaintiff should be possessed of money or property which he owes, if money to someone else, or, if property, belongs to someone else, and which is claimed by defendants or some of them, and by reason of diverse claims of defendants or some of them, the plaintiff has a reasonable bona fide doubt, either growing out of a question of law or fact, as to which one of the rival claimants is legally entitled thereto." See also Hancock Oil Co. v. Independent Distrib. Co., 24 Cal.2d 497, 150 P.2d 463 (1944).

85. In Pan Am. Fire & Cas. Co. v. Revere, 188 F.Supp. 474 (E.D.La. 1960) plaintiff insured a bus which was involved in an accident resulting in multiple claims, the aggregate of which was far above the policy limits; it was held that it could interplead the claimants, even though it was denying liability and thus was not disinterested. Under the old rule this would have been a bill in the nature of interpleader, requiring some additional equitable ground, but the court said exposure to multiple liability in excess of policy limits was sufficient. Where the plaintiff is entirely disinterested and pays the money into court, he is not liable for interest: Powers v. Metropolitan Life Ins. Co., 439 F.2d 605 (D.C. Cir. 1971).

86. United States v. Estate of Swan, 441 F.2d 1082 (5th Cir. 1971); Georgia Sav. Bank & Trust Co. v. Sims, 321 F.Supp. 307 (D.Ga.1971).

87. 241 U.S. 518, 36 S.Ct. 613, 60 L.Ed. 1140 (1916).

one from Pennsylvania appeared. The court held a hearing and found for him. Thereafter the other claimant sued the company in a federal court in California which held that the Pennsylvania judgment was not a bar, and it found for her. Thus the company had to pay twice. The case dramatically illustrated the weakness of the remedy: unless all claimants were subject to the in personam jurisdiction of the court, its decree could not afford full protection. The federal courts were, moreover, in no better position than the state courts, because their process generally did not reach beyond the borders of the state in which they sat.[88] This situation led to the passage of the federal interpleader act.

The federal act undertook to furnish an adequate forum for interpleader cases. Under it the minimum amount in controversy was set at the low figure of $500,[89] the usual requirement for complete diversity of citizenship between the parties was modified by providing the court would have jurisdiction if there was diversity among the claimants,[90] the venue could be laid in the district where any claimant resided,[91] and service of process could be made anywhere in the United States.[92] The requirement which gave the courts the most trouble was the one about diversity. In the usual diversity case there must be complete diversity of citizenship as between the parties plaintiff and defendant.[93] Under the interpleader act the citizenship of the plaintiff is made immaterial. Is this permissible under the constitution, and if it is, must there be complete diversity among the claimants? The question was answered in the leading case of Haynes v. Felder [94] which involved a dispute over the ownership of $43,000 in a thermos jug which a plumber's helper had uncovered when digging a ditch in the basement of the Felder home. The jug was given to a bank which brought an interpleader action against the seven persons who claimed it, or an interest in it. All were citizens of Texas except one of the Felder heirs, who was a citizen of Tennessee. Although the court admitted that the case presented the absolute minimum of diversity which can arise it was held sufficient to give the court jurisdiction, bearing in mind the beneficent purpose of the congressional act. The minimum diversity doctrine was reaffirmed by the

88. Fed.Rules Civ.Proc. 4(f).

89. 28 U.S.C.A. § 1335 (as opposed to the usual $10,000 limit, 28 U.S. C.A. § 1332(a).

90. Id.

91. 28 U.S.C.A. § 1397.

92. 28 U.S.C.A. § 2361.

93. Strawbridge v. Curtiss, 7 U.S. (3 Cranch) 267, 2 L.Ed. 435 (1806).

94. 239 F.2d 868 (5th Cir. 1957).

Supreme Court in the case of State Farm Fire & Casualty Co. v. Tashire.[95]

Since the whole theory of interpleader is to prevent double or multiple liability where there are rival claimants *to the same claim or property*, it is not available where the persons sought to be interpleaded have separate claims against the plaintiff.[96]

There are two types of interpleader in the federal courts. The one we have been discussing is statutory interpleader, the remedy provided by the federal act. This new remedy did not, however, do away with the traditional remedy which was in existence before the statute was passed.[97] The traditional remedy still lives, but it is governed by Federal Rule 22. The difference between the two remedies is that if one proceeds under the Rule he must meet the normal jurisdictional requirements of federal courts, i. e., the amount involved must exceed $10,000, complete diversity must exist as between plaintiff and defendants, the normal venue statute applies, and service of process is only statewide. One might then ask why anyone would desire to proceed under the more stringent requirements of the rule when the statutory route was open to him. One answer is that if all of the claimants are citizens of the same state, the statutory remedy is not open to him, but the remedy under the rule may be.[98]

Intervention. Intervention is the process by which one who is not a party to a lawsuit seeks to become a party. The procedure under the codes was far from uniform, but generally, in order for an outsider to be accorded the privilege of becoming a party to a lawsuit it was incumbent upon him to show that he was interested in the subject matter of the suit, or the property involved

---

95. 386 U.S. 523, 87 S.Ct. 1199, 18 L.Ed.2d 270 (1967).

96. Knoll v. Socony Mobil Oil Co., 369 F.2d 425 (10th Cir. 1966); Klaber v. Maryland Cas. Co., 69 F.2d 934 (8th Cir. 1934); Trowbridge v. Prudential Ins. Co., 322 F.Supp. 190 (S.D.N.Y.1971).

97. This is made explicit by Fed. Rules Civ.Proc. 22(2).

98. In John Hancock Mut. Life Ins. Co. v. Kraft, 200 F.2d 952, 953 (2d Cir. 1953) the court said: "If jurisdiction of the District Court depended upon 28 U.S.C.A. § 1335, lack of diversity of citizenship be-

tween the adverse claimants would be a fatal objection. But that section did not abolish the equitable remedy of interpleader which has long existed under 28 U.S.C.A. § 1332, where there is diversity of citizenship between the stakeholder and the claimants."

There may be cases in which neither type of interpleader is available in a federal court. Such a case was United Benefit Life Ins. Co. v. Leech, 326 F.Supp. 598 (E.D.Pa. 1971); since the rival claimants were citizens of the same state, statutory interpleader would not lie, and since the amount in controversy was less than $10,000 there was no jurisdiction under Rule 22.

in the suit,[99] and that his interests were not adequately represented by the existing parties.[100] Moreover, his application to intervene must have been made made within a reasonably prompt time after he became aware of the litigation.[101]

The original federal rule [102] sought to liberalize intervention, and in so doing it caused problems requiring several subsequent amendments to the rule. It distinguished between intervention of right and permissive intervention. In the former category it included the following: (1) when a United States statute confers an unconditional right to intervene; [103] (2) when the applicant's interest is or may be inadequately represented by existing parties and he is or may be bound by the judgment; [104] and (3) when he may be adversely affected by the disposition of property in the custody of the court.[105] Permissive intervention was authorized (1) when a United States statute confers such a right, or (2) when the applicant's claim or defense and the main action have a common question of law or fact. In Sam Fox Publishing Co. v. United States,[106] the Supreme Court placed a narrow construction on the provision relating to intervention as a matter of right. It held that an applicant could not intervene unless he would be bound by the decree, and he would not be bound by the decree unless he were adequately represented. As so construed the rule posed an impossible dilemma. As one commentator put it:

> The practical effect of the *Sam Fox* case is to run a blue line through 23(a) (2), and to restrict intervention as of right to situations where a statute of the United

---

99. In Brune v. McDonald, 158 Or. 364, 370, 75 P.2d 10, 13 (1938) the court said: "The generally accepted rule is that the right or interest which will authorize a third person to intervene must be of such a direct and immediate character that the intervener will either gain or lose by the direct legal operation of the judgment." See also Edgington v. Nichols, 242 Iowa 1091, 49 N.W.2d 555 (1951).

100. Potlatch Lumber Co. v. Runkel, 16 Idaho 92, 101 P. 396 (1909); Wharff v. Wharff, 244 Iowa 496, 56 N.W.2d 1 (1953).

101. Allen v. California Water & Tel. Co., 31 Cal.2d 104, 187 P.2d 393 (1947).

102. Fed.Rules Civ.Proc. 24.

103. See 28 U.S.C.A. § 2403 which provides that in any action in which the United States or a government agency is not a party, in which the constitutionality of any Act of Congress is drawn in question "the court shall certify such fact to the Attorney General, and shall permit the United States to intervene."

104. Clark v. Sandusky, 205 F.2d 915 (7th Cir. 1953); Knapp v. Hankins, 106 F.Supp. 43 (E.D.Ill.1952).

105. Formulabs, Inc. v. Hartley Pen Co., 275 F.2d 52 (9th Cir. 1960); Wolpe v. Poretsky, 144 F.2d 505 (D.C.Cir. 1944).

106. 366 U.S. 683, 81 S.Ct. 1309, 6 L.Ed.2d 604 (1961).

States confers an unconditional right to intervene, and to cases involving property which is *in custodia legis*. Whether this was the intention of the draftsmen of this rule, or of the court in deciding the *Sam Fox* case is open to question. At any rate the case may cause the Advisory Committee on Civil Rules to take another hard look at the problem.[107]

The committee apparently did take another look for the rule was amended in 1966 to permit intervention as of right by eliminating the requirement that he must be *bound* by the judgment and substituting "that the disposition of the action may as a practical matter impair or impede his ability to protect" his interest.[108] The Supreme Court, in a later case, acknowledged that the amendment liberally extended the right to intervene.[109] One Court of Appeals has suggested that the amendment was not merely for the purpose of "overruling" Sam Fox, but was to coordinate it with the rules on joinder. It said:

> As the Advisory Committee's notes reflect, there are competing interests at work in this area. On the one hand, there is the private suitor's interests in having his own lawsuit subject to no one else's direction or meddling. On the other hand, however, is the great public interest, especially in these explosive days of ever-increasing dockets, of having a disposition at a single time of as much of the controversy to as many of the parties as is fairly possible consistent with due process. [110]

Notwithstanding the amendment and the cases which liberally interpret it, there are still courts which hold the right to intervene within narrow limits and still cleave to the philosophy expressed by Sam Fox.[111]

---

107. Green, Federal Jurisdiction & Practice (1961 Ann.Survey of Am. Law) 481, 492.

108. Fed.Rules Civ.Proc. 24(a) (2).

109. Cascade Natural Gas Corp. v. El Paso Natural Gas Co., 386 U.S. 129, 87 S.Ct. 932, 17 L.Ed.2d 814 (1967).

110. Atlantis Dev. Corp. v. United States, 379 F.2d 818, 824 (5th Cir. 1967).

111. In Hodgson v. United Mine Workers, 51 F.R.D. 270, 273 (D.D. C.1970) the court said, "One may not intervene as a matter of right

in the litigation of others unless he shows the equivalent of being legally bound by the decree in their case . . .", citing Sam Fox. In Spangler v. Pasadena City Bd. of Educ., 427 F.2d 1352, 1354 (9th Cir. 1970) the Board of Education approved a plan of integration, which was approved by the District Court, and the Board decided not to appeal; dissatisfied parents of children who would be affected had been denied permission to intervene; in affirming the ruling the appellate court said the decision not to appeal "was made following public hearings at which appellants had full opportunity to influence the Board's decision. That deci-

Class actions. "It is a principle of general application in Anglo-American jurisprudence that one is not bound by a judgment in personam in a litigation in which he is not designated as a party or to which he has not been made a party by service of process . . . . To these general rules there is a recognized exception, to an extent not precisely defined by judicial opinion, the judgment in a 'class' or 'representative' suit, to which some members of the class are parties, may bind members of the class or those represented who were not made parties to it." [112]

The class action, of which the Supreme Court was speaking, in the above quotation, was an invention of the courts of equity where the persons who would be affected by a decree were so numerous that it would be impossible, or at least impracticable, to bring them all in as parties.[113] In such circumstances, if the persons so affected all belonged to a well defined class, if they were jointly interested in the relief which was asked, or if their individual interests were identical, and if the parties before the court adequately represented those interests, the court could proceed without them and they would be bound by the final decree in the case. The codes, which eliminated the distinction between legal and equitable actions, tucked in a succinct clause preserving the class action. The typical code provision, often merely part of the section on joinder, says "and when the question is one of a common or general interest, of many persons, or when the parties are numerous, and it is impracticable to bring them all before the court, one or more may sue or defend for the benefit of all." [114] The courts, in interpreting this section, held that it applied to "legal" as well as "equitable" cases, thus very greatly enlarging the scope of the device.[115]

sion was within the competence of the Board in balancing many competing factors against the relatively modest restraint imposed by the decree."

112. Hansberry v. Lee, 311 U.S. 32, 40–41, 61 S.Ct. 115, 117, 85 L.Ed. 22, 26 (1940).

113. One of the leading cases on the essentials of a class suit in equity is Smith v. Swormstedt, 57 U.S. (16 How.) 288 (1853). See also Supreme Tribe of Ben-Hur v. Cauble, 255 U.S. 356, 41 S.Ct. 338, 65 L.Ed. 673 (1921).

114. West's Ann.Cal.Code Civ.Proc. § 382; Clark, supra n. 2 at 396.

115. A typical case involving equitable relief was Jellen v. O'Brien, 89 Cal.App. 505, 264 P. 1115 (1928) in which the plaintiff, the secretary of the San Francisco Furniture Dealers Ass'n, sued to enjoin the Chief of Police from enforcing an allegedly void ordinance which required all dealers to pay a $25 quarterly license fee, in which the court held a class action was proper. For an action involving "legal" relief see Daar v. Yellow Cab Co., 67 Cal.2d 695, 63 Cal.Rptr. 724, 433 P.2d 732 (1967), in which the court permitted a class action by a taxicab customer on behalf of himself and of all others similarly situated to recover excessive charges by the company for the use of its cabs

Notwithstanding the expanded scope of the device under the codes the courts have traditionally been very cautious in permitting its use lest a judgment will deprive one who is not a party, to his day in court.[116] If the non-party has a vital interest in the litigation, and if it is a true class action, he will be concluded by the judgment, whichever way it goes. Consequently the courts took pains to see that he was a member of a definitely ascertainable class, that his interest was identical with other members of the class, and that those interests were adequately represented. When the federal rules were drafted, the framers undertook to be more precise than the makers of the codes in defining class actions. The original federal rule limited the class action to cases in which the persons constituting the class were "so numerous as to make it impracticable to bring them all before the court" and provided that those made parties must "fairly insure" adequate representation of all,[117] and it then spelled out three types of class actions, which have come to be known as "true," "hybrid," and "spurious." [118] The difference was in the character of the right sought to be enforced for or against the class. The first two closely resembled the old equity class action. The third—the "spurious"—more closely resembled the liberal code provisions for permissive joinder of parties.[119] In practice the rule proved difficult to apply because it was couched in terms of abstract legal rights, the differences between the three types of actions proved obscure and uncertain,[120] the conclusive effect of

over a four-year period. In Fanucchi v. Coberly-West Co., 151 Cal. App.2d 72, 311 P.2d 33 (1957), 18 plaintiffs, representing a class of 350 cotton growers, were permitted to bring a class action against the ginning company for the recovery by each, of the amount it had been short-changed because of an arbitrary and illegal formula used by the company in computing amounts due for cotton seed. Compare Weaver v. Pasadena Tournament of Roses, 32 Cal.2d 833, 198 P.2d 514 (1948), a suit by four plaintiffs on behalf of themselves and all others similarly situated, to collect statutory penalties ($100 & expenses) for the defendant's refusal to sell them Rose Bowl tickets after they had stood in line and had priority stubs. The court held a class action was not proper since the cause of action of each was separate, and that as to each there would be separate questions such

as whether the person was over 18, whether he had tendered the price, whether he was boisterous, under the influence, or of immoral character. Said the court: "In the present case there is no ascertainable class . . .. Rather, there is only a large number of individuals, each of whom may or may not have, or care to assert, a claim." Id. at 839, 198 P.2d at 518.

116. Brenner v. Title Guar. & Trust Co., 276 N.Y. 230, 11 N.E.2d 890 (1937).

117. Fed.Rules Civ.Proc. 23(a).

118. See discussion in Wright, supra n. 79 at 310; Clark, supra n. 2 at 404.

119. See Brenner, supra n. 116.

120. See System Fed'n. No. 91 v. Reed, 180 F.2d 991 (6th Cir. 1950),

the judgments in the class action was not defined,[121] and the rule did not "squarely address itself to the question of the measures that might be taken during the course of the action to assure procedural fairness, particularly giving notice to members of the class." [122] In this connection the rule was not clear as to whether a nonparty member of the class could intervene to share in the fruits of a judgment,[123] nor the type of notice, if any, to which he was entitled.[124]

In an effort to overcome these difficulties the rule was completely rewritten in 1966. The new rule employed a pragmatic approach, going into great detail to overcome the deficiencies and ambiguities of the old rule.[125] In so doing it succumbed to the vice of becoming prolix and complex. Whether it will accomplish the task for which it was designed remains to be seen.[126] Our present discussion will be limited to a summary of the provisions of the rule and some of the cases interpreting it.

in which the court laments the confusion created by the tripartite division of class actions.

121. In Pentland v. Dravo Corp., 152 F.2d 851 (3d Cir. 1945) the plaintiffs sued for overtime, damages and counsel fees under the Fair Labor Standards Act, claiming to represent about 500 other employees; the court held this was a "spurious" class action which would not bind non-parties, but that others in the class should be given an opportunity to intervene.

122. Advisory Committee notes to the 1966 amendment to the rule, 3B Moore's Fed. Practice 23–24.

123. Union Carbide & Carbon Corp. v. Nisley, 300 F.2d 561 (10th Cir. 1961). This was an antitrust class action by miners who charged a conspiracy regarding the mining and marketing of uranium ore. One question was whether non-party members of the class could intervene, after defendant's liability was determined, to share in the fruits of the judgment. The court acknowledged there was a split of authority on the point but permitted the intervention; it also held the non-party members were not barred by the statute of limitations since they were represented by the plaintiffs, and thus the running of

the statute was tolled. There was a dissent on the ground that a "spurious" class action is merely a permissive joinder device.

124. York v. Guaranty Trust Co., 143 F.2d 503 (2d Cir. 1944).

125. "The principal reason for rewriting Rule 23 in 1966 was to get away from the conceptually-defined categories of the old rule. The new rule does describe categories of cases that may be appropriate for class treatment, and procedural consequences may depend upon which category is involved, but the new categories are described functionally rather than conceptually." Wright, supra n. 79 at 311. See the notes of the Advisory Committee explaining the new rule: 3B Moore's Fed. Practice 23–22 et seq.

126. For critical comments on the new rule see Frankel, Some Preliminary Observations Concerning Civil Rule 23, 43 F.R.D. 39 (1967); Wright, Recent Changes in the Federal Rules of Procedure, 42 F. R.D. 557, 563 (1966); Note, Revised Federal Rule 23, Class Actions: Surviving Difficulties and New Problems Require Further Amendment, 52 Minn.L.Rev. 509 (1967).

5 parts

Unlike Gaul, the rule is divided into five parts. (1) It spells out the four traditional prerequisites for any class action.[127] (2) It defines three types of class action which, although couched in different language, resemble the three types in the original rule. As to type three (common questions of law or fact), which was most troublesome under the old practice, it gives detailed instructions for the guidance of the court.[128] (3) It addresses itself to the duties of the judge in the conduct of class actions, covering four matters: (a) the timing of the decision whether the action may be maintained as a class action, and the possibility of altering or amending it,[129] (b) the type of notice to be given to members of the class,[130] (c) the various types of judgments which may be entered, and (d) the possibility of partial class actions on particular issues, and the division of a class into subclasses. (4) The fourth subdivision of the rule describes the protective orders which the court may make during the course of the litigation (five of them). (5) The final subdivision provides that a class action may not be dismissed or compromised without the approval of the court, and with prior notice given to all members of the class.

Judging by the increasing number of class actions appearing in the advance sheets, and by the new filings as reported in the press, the class action is destined to become one of the most widely used instruments of social control. It is not, of course, adaptable to every situation, and the minimum prerequisites must be

---

127. Fed.Rules Civ.Proc. 23(a) which authorizes a class action "only if (1) the class is so numerous that joinder of all members is impracticable, (2) there are questions of law or fact common to the class, (3) the claims or defenses of the representative parties are typical of the claims or defenses of the class, and (4) the representative parties will fairly and adequately protect the interests of the class."

128. Fed.Rules Civ.Proc. 23(b) (3). Under this subsection the court must make two "findings": (1) "that the questions of law or fact common to the members of the class predominate over any questions affecting only individual members," and (2) "that a class action is superior to other available methods for the fair and efficient adjudication of the controversy." In making these findings,

says the rule, the court should consider: "(A) the interest of members of the class in individually controlling the prosecution or defense of separate actions; (B) the extent and nature of any litigation concerning the controversy already commenced by or against members of the class; (C) the desirability or undesirability of concentrating the litigation of the claims in the particular forum; (D) the difficulties likely to be encountered in the management of a class action."

129. Fed.Rules Civ.Proc. 23(c) (1).

130. Fed.Rules Civ.Proc. 23(c) (2). The essence of the provision is that all members of the class must be notified, and anyone who does not wish to be bound by the judgment must advise the court to that effect, otherwise he will be bound.

minimum prerequisites

met.[131]　There must be a definitely ascertainable class,[132] with common interests in a cause, be they joint or several,[133] the members comprising the class must be so numerous that it would be impracticable to bring them all in as parties,[134] and those who undertake the suit must afford adequate representation for the non-parties.[135]　Even though these prerequisites have been met in an individual case, and even though the courts are inclined to be liberal in their interpretation of the rule,[136] the road to victory

131. Alameda Oil Co. v. Ideal Basic Indus. Inc., 326 F.Supp. 98 (D.Colo. 1971).

132. In DeBremaecker v. Short, 433 F.2d 733, 734 (5th Cir. 1970) the court said: "It is elementary that in order to maintain a class action, the class sought to be represented must be adequately defined and clearly ascertainable . . . . These requirements were not, in our opinion, satisfied. A class made up of 'residents of this State active in the "peace movement" . . . .' does not constitute an adequately defined or clearly ascertainable class contemplated by Rule 23 . . . ." Compare Sultan v. Bessemer-Birmingham Motel Associates, 322 F.Supp. 86 (S.D.N.Y.1970) where the class "consists of at least 180 persons, all of whom would be affected by a common fraud . . . ." Id. at 91. See also Wilson v. Kelley, 294 F.Supp. 1005 (N.D.Ga.1968).

133. Dolgow v. Anderson, 43 F.R.D. 472 (E.D.N.Y.1968); Sultan v. Bessemer-Birmingham Motel Associates, supra n. 132.

134. The answer to the question of how many persons are required to make the class "too numerous", depends upon the circumstances of the particular case. Smith v. Board of Education, 365 F.2d 770 (8th Cir. 1966). In Philadelphia Elec. Co. v. Anaconda American Brass Co., 43 F.R.D. 452 (E.D.Pa. 1968) the court held that a class of only 25 members met the requirement. In Sultan v. Bessemer-Birmingham Motel Associates, supra n. 132, the class was 180. The number may be too large instead of too small. In Eisen v. Carlisle & Jacquelin, 391 F.2d 555 (2d Cir. 1968) the court held that a class comprised of 3,750,000 persons was not too large. But see the dissenting opinion of Chief Judge Lumbard in which he held the suit was unmanageable: "What could be less of a class action than a suit where there are more than 3,750,000 potential plaintiffs living in every state of the union and in almost every foreign country?" Id. at 570.

135. "Because members of the class are bound—even though they may not be actually aware of the proceedings—by the judgment in a Rule 23 action unless they affirmatively exercise their option to be excluded, the requirement of adequate representation must be stringently applied": Alameda Oil Co. v. Ideal Basic Indus., Inc., supra n. 131 at 103. See also Eisen v. Carlisle & Jacquelin, supra n. 134.

136. Green v. Wolf Corp., 406 F.2d 291 (2d Cir. 1968); Eisen v. Carlisle & Jacquelin, supra n. 134; Sultan v. Bessemer-Birmingham Motel Associates, supra n. 132; Dolgow v. Anderson, supra n. 133. But see Milberg v. Western Pac. R. R., 51 F.R.D. 280, 282 (S.D.N.Y.1970), wherein the court says: "It is not disputed by any of the parties involved in this litigation that class actions have been liberally allowed with respect to the securities field . . . . However, before litigation can proceed as a class action, the parties seeking to have it so designated must make a preliminary showing that there is a substantial possibility of success . . . . No such showing has been made in the case now before us."

in a class action may be hedged about with many difficulties. This is best illustrated by examining representative cases in those type-situations in which class actions are most commonly used.

Treble damage suits for violations of the antitrust laws would seem to be ideal subjects for class actions. They frequently involve conspiracies between large corporations to fix prices which injure great segments of the public. Such actions are becoming increasingly popular, but they pose many problems. Eisen v. Carlisle & Jacquelin,[137] one of the most cited cases, illustrates the point. The plaintiff, suing for himself and all others similarly situated, brought suit against a number of brokerage firms charging a conspiracy by them to charge excessive commissions in the handling of "odd-lot" securities.[138] The District Court dismissed the case, holding that a class action would not lie because the plaintiff could not adequately protect the interests of the members of the class,[139] and because the notice required by the rule [140] and by due process [141] could not be given. The class whom plaintiff purported to represent consisted of approximately 3,750,000 customers of brokers whom it was alleged had been charged excessive commissions. Under the rule each was entitled to notice, and the evidence showed that even notice by mailing would cost $400,000. A divided Court of Appeals reversed and remanded "for a prompt and expeditious evidentiary hearing, with or without discovery proceedings, on the questions of notice, adequate representation, effective administration of the action and any other matters which the District Court may consider pertinent and proper." [142] In Philadelphia Electric Co. v. Anaconda American Brass Co.,[143] the plaintiffs brought a treble damage antitrust suit against thirteen defendants, alleging a conspiracy to charge excessive prices for their products. The "classes" whom the plaintiffs sought to represent in the suit were (1) "All state and

---

137. Supra n. 134.

138. An "odd lot" is a sale of less than 100 shares, which is not covered by the normal rule on commissions.

139. Fed.Rules Civ.Proc. 23(a) (4).

140. Fed.Rules Civ.Proc. 23(c) (2).

141. The "due process" requirements of notice were explained in Mullane v. Central Hanover Bank & Trust Co., 339 U.S. 306, 70 S.Ct. 652, 94 L.Ed. 865 (1950), which, although adopting a pragmatic point of view, said the notice must be

such as one desiring to actually inform the party might reasonably adopt to accomplish it.

142. Eisen v. Carlisle & Jacquelin, supra n. 134, at 570. On remand to the District Court it held hearings and, in an extensive opinion held the suit was maintainable as a class action and should go forward, subject to another hearing regarding the assessment of the costs of the notice required by Rule 23. Eisen v. Carlisle & Jacquelin, 52 F.R.D. 253 (S.D.N.Y. 1971).

143. 43 F.R.D. 452 (E.D.Pa.1968).

municipal governments, governmental authorities, and sub-divisions in the United States . . ." (2) "Non-profit cooperative membership corporations engaged in supplying electricity to their members in rural areas . . ." and (3) "Approximately 16,000 (later revised to 18,000) builders of home and apartment dwellings throughout the United States . . .".[144] In a long opinion the District Court struggled with the classes and sub-classes, finally concluding that a class action would lie as to some categories but that as to the "builders class" it should be limited to "builders whose building operations occurred within the Eastern District of Pennsylvania." [145] West Virginia v. Chas. Pfizer & Co.[146] was a treble damage suit against a number of drug companies, alleging a conspiracy to charge exorbitant prices for antibiotic drugs. The classes represented were (1) states, counties, cities and their political subdivisions and agencies, and (2) wholesalers, retailers, and individual consumers. While the case was in the pretrial stage the defendants offered to settle it for $100,000,000. One of the knotty problems for the District Court, in determining whether to approve the settlement, was to decide how it should be apportioned among the claimants, especially in view of the argument that the wholesalers and retailers should get none of it since they merely passed the overcharge on to their customers.[147]

Fraud in the sale of securities represents another area in which the class action has been frequently employed to provide a remedy. In Alameda Oil Co. v. Ideal Basic Industries, Inc.,[148] 132 stockholders were permitted to maintain a class action, representing all the stockholders of the company, to upset a merger which they allege was effected by false and fraudulent misrepresentations in violation of the Securities Exchange Act. Even though the purchasers of stock did not all receive the identical false prospectus and there were questions of individual reliance on the part of each purchaser, the court held a class action would lie.[149]

144. Id. at 456.

145. Id. at 464.

146. 440 F.2d 1079 (2d Cir. 1971).

147. The Court of Appeals affirmed, stating: "It appears to be well settled that in reviewing the appropriateness of the settlement approval, the appellate court should only intervene upon a clear showing that the trial court was guilty of an abuse of discretion." Id. at 1085. For other representative antitrust cases see Gold Strike Stamp Co. v. Christensen, 436 F.2d 791 (10th Cir. 1970); Illinois v. Harper & Row Publishers, Inc., 301 F. Supp. 484 (D.Ill.1969), annotated in 6 A.L.R. Fed. 19 (1971).

See Dole, The Settlement of Class Actions for Damages, 71 Colum.L. Rev. 971 (1971).

148. Supra n. 131.

149. Supra n. 136.

In Sultan v. Bessemer-Birmingham Motel Associates [150] the court points out that in the stock fraud cases there is usually a large number of persons asserting small claims, too small and too many to warrant individual actions. After citing previous cases the court says, "The utility of the class action procedure in litigation involving fraud in the sale of securities has been constantly and regularly recognized." [151] Closely allied to the type of action we have been discussing is the stockholders' derivative action. It typically involves a situation in which the officers and directors of a corporation are manipulating the affairs of the company to make secret personal profits at the expense of the stockholders.[152] When minority stockholders, becoming aware of this, cannot obtain any relief by utilizing the normal channels within the corporation they may sue the officers and directors. This, in a true sense, is a representative suit, because the plaintiffs are suing on behalf of the corporation and a recovery will benefit all of the stockholders. In 1966, when the rule was amended, a special rule was added, prescribing the procedure in such cases.[153]

The law has never been completely indifferent to the plight of the person who has suffered only a small legal wrong. He, as in the case of anyone else, may sue, but the expense involved may make litigation prohibitive. In recent years we have become much more conscious of the rights of consumers, as a class, and they have been accorded increasing legal protection, from governmental regulatory agencies, and from the courts. The fraud cases and antitrust cases we have been discussing often redound to the benefit of the ultimate consumer. However, they leave untouched a large area in which consumers are illegally exploited. May

---

150. 322 F.Supp. 86 (S.D.N.Y.1970).

151. Id. at 90.

152. For a description of this type of action see Surowitz v. Hilton Hotels Corp., 383 U.S. 363, 86 S.Ct. 845, 15 L.Ed.2d 807 (1966).

The stockholders derivative suit was a device which lent itself to abuse by unscrupulous clients represented by unscrupulous attorneys. A person could acquire a few shares of stock in a company and then bring a stockholders derivative action against it, although completely unfounded, hoping that the company would pay a few thousand dollars in settlement rather than fight it, since such litigation is expensive. To combat this evil, some states have passed statutes providing that, in order to bring such an action, the plaintiff must post a bond guaranteeing the payment of costs and attorney fees if the suit fails. In Cohen v. Beneficial Indus. Loan Corp., 337 U.S. 541, 69 S.Ct. 1221, 93 L.Ed. 1528 (1949) the Supreme Court held that, in a diversity case, a federal court must respect and enforce such a statute. The provisions of old Rule 23(b), and the new Rule 23.1, which supplants it, contain further provisions designed to prevent the bringing of such "strike" suits.

153. Fed.Rules Civ.Proc. 23.1. For a case under the new rule see Kauffman v. Dreyfus Fund, Inc., 434 F.2d 727 (3d Cir. 1970).

such consumers, or some of them, band together and bring a class action? Prior to the amendment of the rule in 1966 there was considerable doubt on the subject, at least as far as the federal courts were concerned because, in the federal courts there is a jurisdictional minimum of $10,000,[154] and it was doubtful whether multiple claimants could aggregate their claims to make up the jurisdictional amount.[155] The situation looked more promising after the amendment. In Gas Service Co. v. Coburn [156] aggregation was permitted. That was a class action on behalf of 18,000 customers, who lived outside of the limits of Kansas municipalities, who had been illegally charged a city tax on natural gas. Aggregation was permitted in Berman v. Narragansett Racing Association,[157] a class action on behalf of race horse owners, who had been wrongfully denied their share of the winnings because of the use of an erroneous formula by the defendant. In that case the court held the jurisdictional amount should be determined by the total sum owed by the defendant, that it had no interest in how the fund would be apportioned among the plaintiffs, and that "The interests of the plaintiffs, *vis a vis* the matter in controversy, are 'common and undivided' and the fact that their interests are separable among themselves is immaterial." [158] Notwithstanding the appealing logic and fairness of these cases, their precedent value was short-lived. They were reversed by the Supreme Court in the case of Snyder v. Harris,[159] holding that the matter involved the jurisdiction of the District Court, which was fixed by Congress, and which could not be expanded by the procedural rule.[160] A strong dissenting opinion said the effect of the decision "is substantially to undermine a generally welcomed and long-needed reform in federal procedure . . . . The artificial, awkward and unworkable distinctions between 'joint,' 'common,' and 'several' claims and between 'true,' 'hybrid,' and 'spurious' class actions which the amendment of Rule 23 sought to terminate is now re-established in federal procedural law." [161]

154. 28 U.S.C.A. §§ 1331, 1332.

155. Booth v. General Dynamics Corp., 264 F.Supp. 465 (N.D.Ill. 1967).

156. 389 F.2d 831 (10th Cir. 1968).

157. 414 F.2d 311 (1st Cir. 1969).

158. Id. at 316.

159. 394 U.S. 332, 89 S.Ct. 1053, 22 L.Ed.2d 319 (1969).

160. The majority opinion, written by Mr. Justice Black, states: "We have consistently interpreted the jurisdictional statute passed by Congress as not conferring jurisdiction where the required amount in controversy can be reached only by aggregating separate and distinct claims. The interpretation of that statute cannot be changed by a change in the Rules." Id. at 338, 89 S.Ct. at 1057, 22 L.Ed.2d at 324–25.

161. Id. at 342–43, 89 S.Ct. at 327–28, 22 L.Ed.2d at 1060.

Despite the dampening effect of Snyder v. Harris the consumer class action is not a dead letter, even in the federal courts. No jurisdictional minimum is required in antitrust cases,[162] which can be an effective means of protecting consumers' rights, nor in civil rights cases.[163] Moreover, as pointed out by Professor Wright, it is within the competence of Congress to overrule Snyder by providing that "in any case permitted to be maintained as an action under the Federal Rules of Civil Procedure, the aggregate claims for or against all members of the class shall be regarded as the matter in controversy." [164] Moreover, it should not be forgotten that class actions are also available in the state courts.[165]

---

162. 15 U.S.C.A. § 15; 28 U.S.C.A. § 1337.

163. 28 U.S.C.A. § 1343. For representative civil rights class actions see: Cash v. Swifton Land Corp., 434 F.2d 569 (6th Cir. 1970); Jenkins v. United Gas Corp., 400 F.2d 28 (5th Cir. 1968); Potts v. Flax, 313 F.2d 284 (5th Cir. 1963); Laffey v. Northwest Airlines, Inc., 321 F.Supp. 1041 (D.D.C.1971).

164. Wright, supra n. 79 at 316. For a discussion of bills which have been introduced in Congress to expand federal class actions for the protection of consumers, see: Note, Federal Jurisdiction—Protective Jurisdiction and Adoption as Alternative Techniques for Conferring Jurisdiction on Federal Courts in Consumer Class Actions, 69 Mich.L.Rev. 710 (1971).

165. Vasquez v. Superior Court, 4 Cal.3d 800, 805, 94 Cal.Rptr. 796, 798, 484 P.2d 964, 966 (1971): "We consider whether a group of consumers who have bought merchandise under installment contracts may maintain a class action seeking rescission of the contracts for fraudulent misrepresentation on behalf of themselves and others similarly situated, against both the seller of a product and the finance company to which the installment contracts were assigned. We conclude that such an action will lie against the seller under the principles set forth in Daar v. Yellow Cab Co. (1967) 67 Cal.2d 695, 63 Cal.Rptr. 724, 433 P.2d 732, and that the assignee of the contract is a proper party to such an action under the circumstances presented here."

CHAPTER V. PLEADING

SECTION 1. INTRODUCTION

Definition. Pleading is the process by which the parties present their controversy to the court for determination. In early England the parties appeared before the court and orally stated their respective contentions, probably shouting simultaneously and creating confusion rather than understanding. It has been said that the greatest invention in procedure was the requirement that the parties speak one at a time.[1] A development of almost equal importance was that the pleadings be reduced to writing. The document containing the plaintiff's grievance against the defendant was called the declaration; today we call it a complaint. The defendant's contentions were contained in a document called a plea; today we call it an answer. The plaintiff was permitted to respond to the plea in a document called a replication, to which the defendant could respond by a rejoinder. This process, of filing alternate pleadings, was carried on until the parties were "at issue," which meant that one would affirm and the other deny an essential matter of fact or law. The collective documents were called the pleadings, which may be defined as the formal written contentions of the parties. They served as the blueprints of the trial.

Purposes of pleading.[2] The pleadings serve the following functions: (1) to narrow the issues to be tried,[3] (2) to give notice to the parties in order to avoid surprise at the trial,[4] (3) to give notice to the court of the nature of the case,[5] (4) to serve as a permanent record and as a basis for res judicata,[6] and (5) to

---

1. "In the whole history of law and order, the longest step forward was taken by primitive man, when, as if by common consent, the tribe sat down in a circle and allowed one man to speak at a time. An accused who is shouted down has no rights whatever. Unless people have an instinct for procedure, this conception of basic human rights is a waste of effort, and whenever we see a negation of those rights it can be traced to a lack, an inadequacy, or a violation of procedure." Judge Curtis Bok, quoted in 55 A.B.A.J. 389 (May 1969).

2. See generally: Cleary, The Uses of Pleading, 40 Ky.L.J. 46 (1951); Clark, Simplified Pleading, 2 F.R.D. 456 (1943).

3. Keller-Dorian Colorfilm Corp. v. Eastman Kodak Co., 10 F.R.D. 39 (S.D.N.Y.1950).

4. Porter v. Shoemaker, 6 F.R.D. 438 (M.D.Pa.1947).

5. McKyring v. Bull, 16 N.Y. 297 (1857).

6. Brown v. Seaboard Air Line R. R., 91 Ga.App. 35, 84 S.E.2d 707 (1954).

dispose of cases without trial where the pleadings revealed there were no real issues of fact to be tried.[7]

Issue formulation—how the pleadings work. The pleadings are supposed to define the issues. How is this done? It is done by a process of logical reasoning. We start with Aristotle's famous syllogism:

All men are mortal (major premise)

I am a man (minor premise)

Therefore I am mortal (conclusion).

Every pleading, except a denial and a demurrer, can be analogized to a syllogism. The major premise is the rule of law involved which is never explicitly stated in the pleading because the court is presumed to know the law.[8] The minor premise consists of the facts which the pleader claims bring his case within the operation of the rule of law embodied in the major premise. These facts are pleaded as his cause of action, in the case of a plaintiff. The conclusion is the demand for judgment according to the law. Let us suppose that plaintiff's complaint (oversimplified) alleged that the defendant, while driving his car, ran over the plaintiff, inflicting severe bodily injury for which he demands judgment in the amount of $100,000. The major premise upon which plaintiff relies, is the assumed rule of law to the effect that one who injures another is liable for the damages caused. The minor premise, of course, is that the defendant did just that. The conclusion inevitably follows: judgment for the plaintiff. How may the defendant attack this complaint? He may challenge the major premise. He may claim there is no such rule of law. It is too broad. The true rule is that one who *negligently* or *wilfully* injures another is liable in damages. If he wishes to challenge the major premise, he does it by filing a demurrer, the effect of which is to admit, for the purposes of argument that plaintiff's facts are true, but to assert that there is no rule of law which affords legal relief under them.[9] If he does this, he has raised an issue of law which must be decided by the judge. If the judge rules in his favor, the demurrer will be sustained, which means that plaintiff will be out of court unless he amends his complaint

demurrer

---

7. Manwill v. Oyler, 11 Utah 2d 433, 361 P.2d 177 (1961).

8. Tag v. Linder, 87 Ohio App. 302, 94 N.E.2d 383 (1949).

9. The major premise is the rule of substantive law which establishes plaintiff's right to redress against the defendant. If no such rule exists the case should be dismissed. Hoshman v. Esso Standard Oil Co., 263 F.2d 499 (5th Cir. 1959); Keister's Adm'r v. Keister's Ex'rs, 123 Va. 157, 96 S.E. 315 (1918); Vogel v. Hearst Corp., 116 N.Y.S.2d 905 (Sup., 1952).

to allege facts which will bring it within a rule of law which the court will recognize. Let us suppose he amends and alleges that the defendant so negligently drove his car that he ran over the plaintiff inflicting severe bodily injury, etc. How may the defendant attack the complaint, as amended? He may do so in either of two ways.[10] (1) He may file a plea denying the plaintiff's facts, in which case the parties are at issue and ready for trial. (2) He may confess the plaintiff's facts and allege new facts to invoke another rule of law. This is known as a plea in confession and avoidance. In this case the syllogism would be: major premise, a plaintiff who is guilty of contributory negligence is debarred from recovery; minor premise, plaintiff was guilty of contributory negligence; conclusion, plaintiff is debarred from recovery. The plaintiff could attack this plea in any of the three ways which were open to the defendant when he was attacking the complaint. He could attack the major premise by demurring, but that would be fruitless in this case since the rule of law is well settled. Secondly he could file a replication denying the new facts which the defendant had alleged. If he did this, the parties would be at issue and ready for trial. Or, thirdly, he could file a replication alleging new facts to invoke another rule of law. Again, this would be confession and avoidance. The new syllogism would be: major premise, contributory negligence is not available as a defense to a defendant who had the last clear chance to avoid the accident; minor premise, defendant had the last clear chance to avoid the accident; conclusion, contributory negligence is not available as a defense to this defendant. Theoretically the defendant would have three ways of attacking this pleading, and so on ad infinitum. Ultimately an issue would be reached and the case would be ready for trial. In practice it usually took no more than three or four rounds to produce an issue.[11]

Allocating the burden. In order to render a just decision in any case the court should be in possession of all relevant facts. The responsibility of placing the facts before the court rests with the parties, and the allocation of the burden as between the parties is determined by the procedural rules which have been developed during the centuries.[12] The plaintiff's burden is to allege in his complaint (and be ready to prove) all of the facts con-

---

10. Adams v. Way, 32 Conn. 160 (1864).

11. Koffler & Reppy, Common Law Pleading (1969) 380 [Hereinafter in this chapter cited as Koffler & Reppy].

12. Cleary, Presuming and Pleading: An Essay on Juristic Immaturity, 12 Stan.L.Rev. 5 (1959).

stituting his cause of action. What those facts are, in any given case, must be determined by the substantive law under which plaintiff seeks to recover (the major premise). The defendant's burden is to plead (and be ready to prove) the facts constituting his defense, if he is making a plea in confession and avoidance. What these facts are will likewise be determined by the substantive law of his defensive major premise. In modern parlance we refer to them as affirmative defenses, meaning the defendant has the burden to plead and prove them. There are some pragmatic exceptions to these logical rules. For example, if a plaintiff is suing to recover the amount of a promissory note, one of the elements of his cause of action, which he must allege, is non-payment of the note by the defendant. It would seem that if the defendant denied this allegation the parties would be at issue on the question of payment. However, payment is regarded as an affirmative defense which must be pleaded by the defendant.[13] Illogical as this may seem, it may be justified on the pragmatic ground that it is easier to prove a positive fact than a negative one. Another example may be found in the libel and slander cases in which it is held that the plaintiff must allege the falsity of the defamatory words in order to state a cause of action. Again, it would seem that if the defendant merely denied such an allegation the parties would be at issue, but the law is otherwise. Truth is an affirmative defense which must be pleaded by the defendant.[14] The task of determining who has the pleading burden on various matters is made much easier under the federal rules which list nineteen issues in which the burden is on the defendant and then, in an abundance of caution, add ". . . and any other matter constituting an avoidance or affirmative defense."[15]

Modern pleading. In the United States pleading has gone through three stages. The first we inherited from England, a complex system with two sets of courts, law and equity, each with its technical and formalized rules of pleading.[16] The second stage began with the Field Code in 1849, which was the result of a

13. Clark, Code Pleading (2d ed. 1947) 610, 615 [Hereinafter in this chapter cited as Clark].

14. Holliday v. Great A. & P. Tea Co., 256 F.2d 297 (8th Cir. 1958); Garcia v. Hilton Hotels Int'l, 97 F. Supp. 5 (D.Puerto Rico 1951); Fowler v. Donnelly, 225 Or. 287, 358 P.2d 485 (1960).

15. Fed.Rules Civ.Proc. 8(c).

16. The common law courts of England operated under a system which required a different type of pleading for each of the many forms of action. To bring a suit, plaintiff would select one of the forms of action and procure a writ, which was practically his ticket of admittance to the court. Tort actions were divided into trespass, trespass on the case, trover, detinue, and replevin. Contract ac-

great procedural reform in the State of New York.[17] The code merged law and equity, abolished the old common law forms of action, provided for but one form known as a Civil Action, and simplified pleading by requiring the facts to be stated in ordinary and concise language.[18] The Field Code inspired similar changes in many states. The third stage began with the promulgation of the Federal Rules of Civil Procedure in 1938. They were the result of a long campaign to simplify and standardize procedure in the federal courts.[19] Prior to that time the federal courts had continued the dichotomy between law and equity, although administered by the same court, but used different procedural rules for each. An equity case was governed by equity rules promulgated by the Supreme Court. Procedure in a law case was governed by the Conformity Act which said that the procedure in a federal court should conform, as near as may be, to the procedure of the state in which it sat.[20] The new rules did for the fed-

---

tions were divided into debt, covenant, special assumpsit, and general assumpsit. The distinctions between them were very fine. For instance, trespass would lie for direct injury but not for consequential injury. In Reynolds v. Clarke, 1 Stra. 634, 636, 93 Eng.Rep. 747, 748 (K.B.1726), a leading case, the court explained, "if a man throws a log into the highway, and in that act hits me, I may maintain trespass, because it is an immediate wrong; but if as it lies there I tumble over it, and receive an injury, I must bring an action upon the case; because it is only prejudicial in consequence." See also Scott v. Shepherd, 3 Wilson 403 (K.B.1773). If a plaintiff chose the wrong form of action he was thrown out of court. Moreover, if a plaintiff could not find an appropriate writ to fit his case he had no remedy. The inflexibility and harshness of the common law led to the development of the courts of Chancery (Equity) which would sometimes give relief where the common law remedy was inadequate or nonexistent. The Chancery courts exercised broad discretion in granting or refusing remedies, and their procedure differed entirely from the common law courts. See Maitland, The Forms of Action at Common Law (1936); Adams, The Origin of English Equi-

ty, 16 Colum.L.Rev. 87 (1916); Koffler & Reppy, supra n. 11 at 19–21.

17. Millar, Civil Procedure of the Trial Court in Historical Perspective 52 (1952); Hepburn, The Development of Code Pleading 18–19 (1897); Weinstein & Distler, Drafting Pleading Rules, 57 Colum.L. Rev. 518 (1957).

18. Old habits die hard. Under the common law actions of assumpsit one could plead the bare legal conclusion that the defendant owed the plaintiff for goods or wares or for services. These were known as the common counts. Although they did not comply with the "facts" required by the codes, the courts continued to permit counsel to use them. Abadie v. Carrillo, 32 Cal. 172 (1867). Even today they are permitted: Moya v. Northrup, 10 Cal.App.3d 276, 88 Cal.Rptr. 783 (1970). They can also be used under the federal rules. See Official Forms 5, 6, 7.

19. Clark & Moore, A New Federal Civil Procedure: I. The Background 44 Yale L.J. 387 (1935).

20. Wright, Law of Federal Courts (2d ed. 1970) [Hereinafter referred to as Wright] 255–57.

one form of action

eral courts what the Field Code had done for the states: merged law and equity into one system, created one form of action known as a "civil action," and greatly simplified pleading, going much further than the codes. They did two other things: they standardized procedure in the federal courts, making it uniform throughout the country, and they provided an effective means of discovery before trial which took over a great share of the burden formerly carried by pleading.

It would be a mistake to think that the boundaries between the three stages of development in pleading are sharply defined. The Field Code, adopted in New York in 1849, was recognized as a great step forward. Some states practically copied it, some adopted it with major or minor modifications, and some ignored it, remaining faithful to the common law tradition.[21] In the ninety year interval between the Field Code and the federal rules, procedural reform in the states was on a sporadic and piecemeal basis. The adoption of the federal rules in 1938 gave a new impetus to movements for the improvement of procedure. The rules had a greater effect, in a shorter time, than did the code. Today about half the states have revised their procedure to virtual conformity with the federal rules and practically all states have borrowed something from them.[22] Consequently, today the federal rules dominate the scene, a diminishing number of states cleave to the codes, and only traces of the common law-equity complex are to be found.

SECTION 2. THE COMPLAINT

In general. The principal pleading on the part of the plaintiff is the complaint which consists of (1) a caption specifying the court in which the action is brought and the names of the parties, (2) the body of the complaint which sets out the cause of action or claim for relief, and (3) the prayer or demand for judgment. Under the codes the body of the complaint must set forth "a plain and concise statement of the facts constituting the cause of action without unnecessary repetition."[23] Under the federal rules the body of the complaint must contain "a short and plain statement of the claim showing that the pleader is entitled to relief."[24] The reason for the difference is that the phrase "cause of action"

---

21. Clark, supra n. 13 at 21–31.

22. Wright, supra n. 20 at 260; 1 Barron & Holtzoff (Wright ed.) §§ 9–9.53.

23. Clark, supra n. 13 at 210.

24. Fed.Rules Civ.Proc. 8(a).

caused so much trouble under the codes.[25]   Courts disagreed on definitions of the phrase, some defining it narrowly in terms of technical legal rights and duties and others defining it broadly, from a layman's point of view, as a group of operative facts.[26] These theoretical differences resulted in practical difficulties. For instance, if a brakeman sustained injuries while on the job in interstate commerce and he sued for damages under the common law, under the New Jersey Employer's Liability Act, and under the Federal Employer's Liability Act, has he stated more than one cause of action, and must he state them in different counts?[27]   Or, if a plaintiff is injured in an automobile accident and his car is damaged, does he have one or two causes of action? If he sued for the damage to his car and recovered, could he later bring an action for his personal injuries, or would he be met with a plea of res judicata because he had "split" his cause of action?[28]

Form of allegations. The mandate of the codes was to state the *facts* constituting the cause of action in ordinary and concise language. Simple as this seems the section has caused almost unbelievable trouble. The difficulty arises from the meaning of the word "facts." What is an allegation of fact? If the plaintiff alleges that she is a widow, is that an allegation of fact? Or is it a conclusion? Is it a conclusion from a group of unstated facts: that while single and of marriageable age she went through a valid marriage ceremony before someone authorized to perform marriages and that thereafter her husband disappeared and has not been heard of for more than seven years and is therefore pre-

25. It had also caused trouble at common law, from which the codes borrowed it. Koffler & Reppy, supra n. 11 at 86.

26. For a very thorough discussion of the various theories as to what constitutes a cause of action see Clark, supra n. 13 at 127–48. The Supreme Court has remarked how "futile is the attempt to define a 'cause of action' without reference to the context." Gully v. First Nat'l Bank in Meridian, 299 U.S. 109, 117, 57 S.Ct. 96, 100, 81 L.Ed. 70, 74 (1936).

27. Held that he had stated but one cause of action: Payne v. New York, Susquehanna & West. R. R., 201 N.Y. 436, 95 N.E. 19 (1911).

28. In Clancey v. McBride, 338 Ill. 35, 40, 169 N.E. 729, 731 (1929) the court held there were two causes of action and therefore the plaintiff was not barred from bringing the second suit: "The differences in the rules governing assignability and subrogation, in the methods of enforcement, in the evidence required to sustain, in the distribution of the proceeds, and in the periods of limitation, above stated, militate against the doctrine that out of a single wrongful act only one cause of action to redress injury to the person and damage to property can arise." In Rush v. City of Maple Heights, 167 Ohio St. 221, 147 N.E.2d 599 (1958) the court held there was but one cause of action and hence the second suit was barred. One reason for preferring this rule, said the court, was to prevent a multiplicity of actions.

But....

sumed dead? And if it is a conclusion, and not a fact, is it a conclusion of fact or a conclusion of law? If it is an impermissible conclusion, then must the plaintiff allege all of the above unstated facts? Are they facts, or merely evidence of her widowhood which is the real fact? This little exercise in semantics may seem inane, but it is the type of thing the courts have been struggling with ever since the first code was adopted in New York in 1849. Out of this morass has come the "rule" that when the code says to plead "facts", it means ultimate or operative facts and not conclusions or evidence.[29] The distinction between facts, evidence and conclusions is virtually impossible to draw because it is merely a difference in degree of specificity.[30] However, under the codes the courts require the pleader to distinguish between them and to search the cases for authorities which have approved or disapproved particular allegations.[31]

Not only must the pleader under the codes steer the narrow course between conclusions and evidence and plead only facts, he must allege them positively, and not alternatively[32] or hypothet-

29. The Evergreens v. Nunan, 141 F. 2d 927 (2d Cir. 1944); Dino, Inc. v. Boreta Enterprises, Inc., 226 Cal. App.2d 336, 38 Cal.Rptr. 167 (1964); Oliver v. Coffman, 112 Ind. App. 507, 45 N.E.2d 351 (1942).

30. Clark, supra n. 13 at 225–39; Cook, Statements of Fact in Pleading Under the Codes, 21 Colum.L. Rev. 416 (1921); Cook, 'Facts' and 'Statements of Fact,' 4 U.Chi.L.Rev. 233 (1937); Morris, Law and Fact, 55 Harv.L.Rev. 1303 (1942); Gavit, Legal Conclusions, 9 Ind.L.J. 109 (1933).

31. The following are illustrative: McCaughey v. Schuette, 117 Cal. 223, 48 P. 1088 (1897) ("Defendants delivered to Plaintiff their grant deed of premises" held bad as a statement of evidentiary facts); Southern Ry. v. King, 217 U.S. 524, 538, 30 S.Ct. 594, 598 (1910) (holding an allegation that D was negligent for violating safety regulation was bad as conclusion, with Holmes, J. dissenting: "The statement may be called a conclusion, but it is a conclusion of fact, just as the statement that a certain liquid was beer is a conclusion of fact from certain impressions of taste, smell and sight."); Jones v. Green,

66 Idaho 731, 168 P.2d 834 (1946) ("lodged in jail without any right or authority" held bad as legal conclusion); Kramer v. Kansas City Power & Light Co., 311 Mo. 369, 279 S.W. 43 (1925) (where court holds general allegations of negligence bad as conclusions, but a dissenting opinion says they are sufficient unless attacked by a motion to make more definite); Gillispie v. Goodyear Serv. Stores, 258 N.C. 487, 128 S.E.2d 762 (1963) (case gives various examples of legal conclusions); Gabel v. Frantz, 65 York 28 (Pa.C.P.1950) ("that she is the common law wife of the decedent" held a permissible conclusion of fact); Thomas v. Hempt Bros., 74 D. & C. 213 (Pa.C.P.1950) (holding that an allegation that plaintiff's work was solely in interstate commerce was a legal conclusion); In re Goldsberry's Estate, 95 Utah 379, 81 P.2d 1106 (1938) (holding that allegations of fraud and undue influence were legal conclusions).

32. Pavalon v. Thomas Holmes Corp., 25 Wis.2d 540, 131 N.W.2d 331 (1964); Robertson v. Nat Kaiser Inv. Co., 82 Ga.App. 416, 61 S.E.2d 298 (1950); Macurda v. Lewiston Journal Co., 104 Me. 554,

ically.[33] Perhaps the principal reason for this was that alternative or hypothetical allegations were at best uncertain and possibly evasive. Some courts would permit alternative allegations if both alternatives were good, but would condemn them if one alternative was bad, on the theory that a chain is no stronger than its weakest link.[34] Faced with this dilemma, what could a plaintiff do if he were genuinely uncertain as to what the facts were? Could he draft his complaint in such a way as to set up two causes of action, in separate counts, alleging a different version of the facts in each, with the idea that it would be for the jury to decide what the facts actually were after hearing the evidence? The early code cases held that this also was bad, that a plaintiff could not allege inconsistent counts.[35] The harshness of this position led to reform, even under the codes, permitting alternative allegations [36] and inconsistent counts.[37]

The code-makers had sought to eliminate the technicality of the common law by abolishing the forms of action and providing that the plaintiff should state the facts constituting his cause of action in concise language. In interpreting the codes the courts brought technicality back into the picture, perhaps unavoidably, by their diverse definitions of cause of action and facts. The drafters of the new federal rules sought to avoid these pitfalls which had been plaguing the profession for nearly a century. They discarded the "cause of action" and they discarded "facts." The new rules provided that the complaint should contain "a short and plain statement of the claim showing that the pleader is entitled to relief." [38] They provided that "each averment of a pleading shall be simple, concise, and direct," and that "no tech-

72 A. 490 (1908). Concerning the use of the phrase "and/or" one court has said: "It is one of those inexcusable barbarisms which was sired by indolence and damned by indifference, and has no more place in legal terminology than the vernacular of Uncle Remus has in Holy Writ." Cochrane v. Florida E. Coast Ry., 107 Fla. 431, 435, 145 So. 217, 218 (1932).

33. Mountford v. Cunard S.S. Co., 202 Mass. 345, 88 N.E. 782 (1909).

34. Jamison v. King, 50 Cal. 132 (1875); see cases supra n. 32; Clark, supra n. 13 at 254–58; McDonald, Alternative Pleading: I, 48 Mich.L.Rev. 311 (1950); McDonald, Alternative Pleading in the United States: I, 52 Colum.L.Rev. 443 (1952).

35. Oklahoma Wheat Pool Term. Corp. v. Rodgers, 180 Okl. 623, 70 P.2d 1080 (1937).

36. Foreman & Clark Corp. v. Fallon, 3 Cal.3d 875, 479 P.2d 362, 92 Cal.Rptr. 162 (1971).

37. McCormick v. Kopmann, 23 Ill. App.2d 189, 161 N.E.2d 720 (1959); Downs v. Exchange Nat'l Bank, 24 Ill.App.2d 24, 163 N.E.2d 858 (1959); Young v. George C. Fuller Contracting Co., 12 N.J.Super. 554, 80 A.2d 135 (1951); Taiyo Trading Co. v. Northam Trading Corp., 1 F.R.D. 382 (S.D.N.Y.1940).

38. Fed.Rules Civ.Proc. 8(a).

nical forms of pleading or motions are required." [39] They expressly permitted alternative and hypothetical pleading, "either in one count or defense or in separate counts or defenses" and provided that "when two or more statements are made in the alternative and one of them if made independently would be sufficient, the pleading is not made insufficient by the insufficiency of one or more of the alternative statements." [40] Finally, they provided that "A party may also state as many separate claims or defenses as he has regardless of consistency . . . ." [41] An Appendix to the rules sets forth 32 pleading forms. As originally promulgated the forms were intended for illustration only. They met with general acceptance by most of the federal courts,[42] but there were some which insisted on the stricter fact pleading of the codes.[43] This led to an amendment of the rules in 1946, effective in 1948, which stated "The forms contained in the Appendix of Forms are sufficient under the rules . . . ." [44] The result is that if one of the forms in the Appendix fits the pleader's case it may be used with confidence that it will withstand a motion to dismiss. It may not withstand a motion to make more definite.[45] When the pleader does not follow one of the forms, either because he cannot find one which fits his case or because he wishes to plead in more detail, he can proceed with some confidence that the court will give a liberal construction to his pleading.[46] That has been true at least since the case of Conley v. Gibson,[47] decided by the Supreme Court in 1957, in which the court said that "a complaint should not be dismissed for failure to state a claim unless it appears beyond doubt that the plaintiff can prove no set of facts in support of his claim which would entitle him to relief." [48]

39. Id. 8(e) (1).

40. Id. 8(e) (2).

41. Id.

42. Sierocinski v. E. I. DuPont De-Nemours & Co., 103 F.2d 843 (3d Cir. 1939); Swift & Co. v. Young, 107 F.2d 170 (4th Cir. 1939); Sparks v. England, 113 F.2d 579 (8th Cir. 1940).

43. Foley-Carter Ins. Co. v. Commonwealth Life Ins. Co., 128 F.2d 718 (5th Cir. 1942).

44. Fed.Rules Civ.Proc. 84.

45. Fennell v. Svenska Amerika Linien, 23 F.R.D. 116 (D.Mass.1958).

46. Dioguardi v. Durning, 139 F.2d 774 (2d Cir. 1944); Willis v. Reddin, 418 F.2d 702 (9th Cir. 1969).

47. 355 U.S. 41, 78 S.Ct. 99, 2 L.Ed. 2d 80 (1957).

48. Id. at 45–46, 78 S.Ct. at 102, 2 L.Ed.2d at 84. See also Brown v. Western R.R. of Ala., 338 U.S. 294, 70 S.Ct. 105, 94 L.Ed. 100 (1949). The Brown case was not construing the federal rules; it was a FELA case brought in a state court which construed the complaint most strongly against the plaintiff and dismissed. The Supreme Court reversed holding the complaint should be liberally construed since plaintiff was claiming a right based on an act of Congress. See gener-

Pleading special matters. Notwithstanding the liberality of the federal rules, they require certain matters to be set forth with particularity. *Fraud* is one of them.[49] This is a carry-over from the code rule requiring explicit details of the fraud to be set forth, probably because fraud was a disfavored action, the defendant's morality was put in issue, and he was entitled to full notice of the claim.[50] *Special damage* is another matter which, under the rules, must be pleaded with particularity.[51] This is again a carry-over from the code rule, based upon the idea of giving notice to the defendant if the plaintiff is claiming damages which are not the natural and expected consequence of his alleged wrongful act.[52] *Conditions precedent* likewise has a special federal rule

---

ally Clark, Pleading Under the Federal Rules, 12 Wyo.L.J. 177 (1958); McCaskill, The Modern Philosophy of Pleading: A Dialogue Outside the Shades, 38 A.B.A.J. 123 (1952).

49. Fed.Rules Civ.Proc. 9(b) ("the circumstances constituting fraud or mistake shall be stated with particularity"). In Consumers Time Credit, Inc. v. Remark Corp., 227 F.Supp. 263 (E.D.Pa.1964) an allegation that transfers were made "with the intent to defraud the plaintiff" was held sufficient. Some courts would require greater particularization, Barron & Holtzoff, Federal Practice and Procedure, Rules ed., Vol. 1A, § 302. It can, however, be overdone. In Carrigan v. California State Legislature, 263 F.2d 560 (9th Cir. 1959) the plaintiff's complaint was 188 pages which the court held was a violation of Rule 8(a) ("a short and plain statement of the claim"). In Buckley v. Altheimer, 2 F.R.D. 285 (N.D.Ill.1942) the plaintiff's complaint was 260 pages plus 43 pages of exhibits which the court held should be stricken as a gross violation of the rules. In Jannes v. Microwave Communications, Inc., 325 F.Supp. 896, 897 (N.D.Ill.1971), the court dismissed the complaint "because of the plaintiff's repeated and flagrant disregard of the directives set forth in Rule 8(a)." The complaint (the plaintiff's third try) consisted of 31 pages containing 33 paragraphs with 54 subparagraphs.

50. Clark, supra n. 13 at 311–16.

51. Fed.Rules Civ.Proc. 9(g). The following cases held evidence of special damages inadmissible because not pleaded: Niedland v. United States, 338 F.2d 254 (3d Cir. 1964) (expenditures for hiring a substitute); Howard v. Barr, 114 F. Supp. 48 (D.Ky.1953) (medical expenses); Burlington Transp. Co. v. Josephson, 153 F.2d 372 (8th Cir. 1946) (loss for remodeling an apartment). In Great Am. Indem. Co. v. Brown, 307 F.2d 306 (5th Cir. 1962) the court held that itemization was not necessary if they were pleaded, since the defendant could get the details through the discovery procedure.

52. The following cases held evidence inadmissible because special damages had not been alleged: Ziervogel v. Royal Packing Co., 225 S.W.2d 798 (Mo.1949) (increased blood pressure and injury to shoulder); Hobbs v. Carolina Coca-Cola Bottling Co., 194 S.C. 543, 10 S.E. 2d 25 (1940) (expenses for hiring a substitute); Keefe v. Lee, 197 N.Y. 68, 90 N.E. 344 (1909) (loss of hearing and deafness not admissible under an allegation that he is seriously and permanently injured in his head). Compare Varley v. Motyl, 139 Conn. 128, 90 A.2d 869 (1952) under which evidence of a pre-existing heart condition was held admissible under an allegation that the accident affected and injured his heart. See generally Clark, supra n. 13 at 327–30.

which adopts the reformed code procedure.[53]   The common law rule was that a plaintiff suing on a contract must plead specifically performance of all conditions precedent.[54]   This rule was modified by many of the codes to provide that it was sufficient for the plaintiff to allege that all conditions precedent have been performed and putting the burden on the defendant of pleading non-performance of any particular conditions which he claimed had not been performed.[55]   This shifting of the burden was thought to be fair, due to the vast increase in conditions found in small type in many modern contracts.   Other pleading problems in relation to contracts present few difficulties today.   In the federal courts the manner of alleging the promise, or contract, is taken care of in the forms supplied in the Appendix.   Under the codes the contract may be pleaded by setting it forth in the complaint or by attaching it as an exhibit or, if it is an oral contract, by alleging the elements of the contract.[56]   *Consideration*, which, under the common law had to be pleaded with great particularity,[57] may now be alleged in general terms in many of the code states.[58] *Negligence* has ceased to be a serious pleading problem under the federal rules due to the fact that the approved forms in the Appendix permit the plaintiff to allege the particular act which the defendant did, characterize it as having been negligently done, and state that it resulted in the injuries which he received.[59]   In the states in which codes are still in effect the task of properly alleging negligence may present difficulties.[60]

---

53.   Fed.Rules Civ.Proc. 9(c).

54.   Koffler & Reppy, supra n. 11 at 133, 328.

55.   The first problem is to determine whether the condition is a condition precedent (performance of which must be alleged by the plaintiff) or a condition subsequent (breach of which must be alleged by the defendant). See Title Guar. & Sur. Co. v. Nichols, 224 U.S. 346, 32 S.Ct. 475, 56 L.Ed. 795 (1912). Cases holding general allegation of performance sufficient: Blasingame v. Home Ins. Co., 75 Cal. 633, 17 P. 925 (1888); Parkinson v. Roberts, 78 Wyo. 478, 329 P.2d 823 (1958); Reichhold Chems., Inc. v. Wells, 189 Misc. 188, 70 N. Y.S.2d 805 (N.Y.1947) (but holding if the condition is one to be performed by a third party and not the plaintiff, the plaintiff must allege facts constituting perform-

ance); Harty v. Eagle Indem. Co., 108 Conn. 563, 143 A. 847 (1928).

56.   Riley v. White, 231 S.W.2d 291 (Mo.1950); Holly Sugar Corp. v. McColgan, 18 Cal.2d 218, 115 P.2d 8 (1941); Clark, supra n. 13 at 276.

57.   Koffler & Reppy, supra n. 11 at 325–28.

58.   Considine v. Gallagher, 31 Wash. 669, 72 P. 469 (1903); Clark, supra n. 13 at 279–80.

59.   There are a few federal cases holding a general allegation of negligence is insufficient, despite the rules and the approved forms: Bush v. Skidis, 8 F.R.D. 561 (E.D. Mo.1948); Dunahoo v. New York Cent. R. R., 15 F.R.S. 8a432, Case 1 (1951).

60.   Holding general allegations of negligence are sufficient: Rannard

SECTION 3. THE ANSWER

In general. The principal pleading on the part of the defendant is the answer. It must contain a denial of all of the allegations of the complaint which the defendant wishes to controvert. It is possible for him to make a general denial of all allegations of the complaint, or he may deny specific ones and admit others.[61] Failure to admit or deny an allegation is equivalent to an admission.[62] The answer may also contain any affirmative defenses which the defendant may have, which should be stated separately.[63] In addition the answer may contain a statement of any counterclaim which the defendant has against the plaintiff and which is legally available to him in the action.[64] The formal structure of the answer is the same under the codes and under the federal rules. The chief differences are in (1) the manner of alleging facts, which follows the same pattern as in the complaint, (2) the affirmative defenses available to the defendant, and (3) the counterclaims available to the defendant.

Denials. At common law one of the favorite pleas was the "general issue" which put the plaintiff to proof of his cause of action. In trespass the plea was "not guilty," in an action of debt the plea was "nil debit," in an action of assumpsit the plea was "non assumpsit." Since some affirmative defenses were admissible under the general issue the plaintiff was kept in the

---

v. Lockheed Aircraft Corp., 26 Cal. 2d 149, 157 P.2d 1 (1945); Kauffroath v. Wilbur, 66 Ariz. 152, 185 P.2d 522 (1947); Wylie v. Stevens, 261 App.Div. 1031, 26 N.Y.S.2d 484 (1941). Holding general allegations of negligence were insufficient: Davis v. Aiken, 111 Ga.App. 505, 142 S.E.2d 112 (1965); Poldon Eng'r. & Mfg. Co. v. Zell Elec. Mfg. Co., 1 Misc.2d 1016, 156 N.Y.S.2d 169 (1955); Turner v. Craney, 254 App.Div. 919, 5 N.Y.S.2d 641 (1938). In the jurisdictions in which freedom from fault is an element of plaintiff's cause of action a complaint will be dismissed if it does not contain such an allegation: Prater v. Buell, 336 Ill.App. 533, 84 N.E.2d 676 (1949); Hatch v. Merigold, 119 Conn. 339, 176 A. 266 (1935). Where a plaintiff intends to rely upon the doctrine of res ipsa loquitur, there are three different rules: (1) Where specific acts of negligence are pleaded the

right to rely on the presumption is lost, (2) The plaintiff is not deprived of the doctrine by pleading specific acts of negligence, (3) Where the plaintiff pleads specific acts of negligence he is limited on his proof to such acts, but as to them he may invoke the doctrine. These rules are discussed in Armstrong v. Wallace, 8 Cal.App.2d 429, 47 P.2d 740 (1935).

61. Clark, supra n. 13 at 577; Fed. Rules Civ.Proc. 8(b).

62. Canfield v. Tobias, 21 Cal. 349 (1863); Clark, supra n. 13 at 580; Sinclair Ref. Co. v. Howell, 222 F. 2d 637 (5th Cir. 1955); Fed.Rules Civ.Proc. 8(d).

63. Clark, supra n. 13 at 577; Fed. Rules Civ.Proc. 8(c).

64. Clark, supra n. 13 at 638; Fed. Rules Civ.Proc. 13.

dark as to what the defense really was.[65] The fact-pleading of the codes sought to diminish the element of ambush and surprise in pleading. Hence, although a general denial was still available it was seldom used since it was a rare case in which the defendant could honestly deny all of the allegations of the complaint.[66] Under many of the codes the pleadings must be verified (sworn to) by the parties,[67] and under the federal rules each pleading must be signed by the attorney, which constitutes a certificate of his good faith in filing it.[68]

The alternative to the general denial is the specific denial. The defendant may select the allegations in the complaint which he wishes to deny and then specifically deny them, or, he may select the allegations in the complaint which he wishes to admit, specifically admit them and then deny each and every allegation not expressly admitted. There is some danger in employing the former method due to a doctrine known as the "negative pregnant," which is a denial in form, but which is pregnant with an admission. Negatives pregnant come in two varieties. One is the literal denial.[69] If the complaint alleges that the defendant was driving his car at 75 miles an hour and the defendant denies that he was driving his car at 75 miles an hour, this would be an admission that he may have been driving it at any other speed, i. e., 74 or 76 miles per hour. The other type of negative pregnant is the conjunctive denial.[70] If the complaint alleges that the defendant was careless and negligent and reckless and the defendant denies that he was careless and negligent and reckless this would constitute an admission that he was guilty of any combination less than all three. To avoid this the defendant should have denied the facts in the disjunctive, i. e., denied that he was careless *or* negligent *or* reckless. Another type of denial which has been held bad is the argumentative denial which consists of making a contradictory statement rather than a categorical denial.[71] For example, if the complaint alleges that the defendant

[Margin note: Negative pregnant]

65. Koffler & Reppy, supra n. 11 at 457 et seq.

66. United States v. Long, 10 F.R.D. 443 (D.Neb.1950).

67. Clark, supra n. 13 at 215.

68. Fed.Rules Civ.Proc. 11.

69. Wingfoot Cal. Homes Co. v. Valley Nat'l Bank, 80 Ariz. 133, 294 P.2d 370 (1956) (holding that where defendant merely denies a debt in the precise sum alleged, it is an admission of any lesser sum); Harden v. Atchison & Neb. R. R., 4 Neb. 521 (1876); Chastain v. Consolidated Credit Co., 113 Ga.App. 225, 147 S.E.2d 807 (1966) (denying designated paragraphs of complaint "as pleaded" held evasive—a variety of literal denial).

70. Spencer v. Turney & Co., 5 Okla. 683, 49 P. 1012 (1897).

71. Dons Club v. Anderson, 83 Ariz. 94, 317 P.2d 534 (1957).

was in Chicago on a certain date and the answer alleges that on said date he was in New York, this might be held bad as an argumentative denial. In each of these situations, if the court holds the denial is insufficient, then the allegation is deemed admitted. The only sound reason for these highly technical rules is that such denials are evasive. In view of the modern trend towards liberality in pleading and the availability of pretrial discovery to avoid surprise, it is believed that technical rules such as these will fall into disuse.[72] The best way to avoid all such pitfalls is to carefully select those allegations in the complaint which are true, admit them, and then deny each and every other allegation in said complaint.[73]

It often happens that a defendant honestly does not know whether or not certain allegations in the complaint are true, and yet, under the code or the rules, he must admit or deny them. The federal rules take care of this situation by providing: "If he is without knowledge or information sufficient to form a belief as to the truth of an averment, he shall so state and this has the effect of a denial."[74] The codes have similar provisions with slight variations in wording.[75] Such provisions are subject to abuse by a defendant who wishes to be evasive. To counteract this tendency the courts have been quite strict in holding that a defendant may not use this form of denial when responding to allegations of fact which are presumably within his own knowledge.[76] They have also insisted that if a defendant wishes to employ this form he must comply strictly with the prescribed language.[77]

Where the plaintiff has pleaded performance of all conditions precedent in a contract, a simple denial will not put the matter in issue. Both under the codes [78] and under the rules [79] the burden

---

72. State v. Means, 71 Nev. 340, 291 P.2d 909 (1955); Clark, supra n. 13 at 590.

73. Zielinski v. Philadelphia Piers, Inc., 139 F.Supp. 408 (E.D.Pa.1956).

74. Fed.Rules Civ.Proc. 8(b).

75. One type of code provision permits a defendant "to deny any knowledge or information sufficient to form a belief." Another type permits the defendant to deny "upon information and belief." Clark, supra n. 13 at 593.

76. Clanton's Auto Auction Sales, Inc. v. Campbell, 230 S.C. 65, 94

S.E.2d 172 (1956); Oliver v. Swiss Club Tell, 222 Cal.App.2d 528, 35 Cal.Rptr. 324 (1963) (also holding a defendant is not permitted to use this form of denial regarding allegations of facts which are a matter of public record).

77. Oliver v. Swiss Club Tell, supra n. 76; Mahanor v. United States, 192 F.2d 873 (1st Cir. 1951).

78. Moore v. Schoen, 313 Ill.App. 367, 40 N.E.2d 562 (1942).

79. Reynolds-Fitzgerald, Inc. v. Journal Publishing Co., 15 F.R.D. 403 (S.D.N.Y.1954).

is placed upon the defendant to specify wherein plaintiff has failed to perform. If he merely denies the general allegation of performance the cases hold he has admitted it.

Affirmative defenses. Affirmative defenses, in modern pleading, roughly correspond to the common law pleas of confession and avoidance.[80] Under the codes they were not called affirmative defenses. The typical code provision was "a statement of any new matter constituting a defense," [81] and the codes did not elaborate.[82] The federal rules, on the other hand, list 19 specific affirmative defenses.[83] The purpose of requiring new matter or affirmative defenses to be pleaded is to give the plaintiff notice. As a rule of thumb, any evidence which will not be admissible under a denial must be pleaded as an affirmative defense.[84] If it is not pleaded and the plaintiff objects to the evidence at the trial, the evidence will be excluded.[85]

fed.

Inconsistent defenses. Where the evidence is conflicting neither party can be sure what a jury will find the facts to be. In this situation a defendant may wish to plead inconsistent defenses. Under most codes he was permitted to do so,[86] and the federal rules explicitly state that "A party may . . . state as many separate claims or defenses as he has regardless of consistency." [87] If the defendant has pleaded inconsistent defenses may the plaintiff require him to elect between them after the evidence has been presented at the trial? There are cases holding both ways,[88] but probably the better view is not to require the

---

80. Clark, supra n. 13 at 597.

81. Id. at 577.

82. Id. at 611.

83. Fed.Rules Civ.Proc. 8(c).

84. Chesapeake & O. Ry. v. Carmichael, 298 Ky. 769, 184 S.W.2d 91 (1944); Denham v. Cuddeback, 210 Or. 485, 311 P.2d 1014 (1957); 91065 Corp. v. Industrial Nat'l Bank, 94 R.I. 424, 181 A.2d 239 (1962). See Clark, supra n. 13 at 606.

85. Orient Ins. Co. v. Northern Pac. Ry., 31 Mont. 502, 78 P. 1036 (1905) (contributory negligence); Fort Dodge Hotel Co. v. Bartelt, 119 F.2d 253 (8th Cir. 1941); Snow v. Chatfield, 11 Mass. (Gray) 12 (1858) (justification); Girardi v. Gates Rubber Co., 253 F.Supp. 690

(N.D.Cal.1965) (statute of limitations); Ellis v. Black Diamond Coal Mining Co., 265 Ala. 264, 90 So.2d 770 (1956) (statute of limitations); McKyring v. Bull, supra n. 5 (payment); Brearton v. DeWitt, 252 N. Y. 495, 170 N.E. 119 (1930) (illegality).

86. Byk v. Weber, 186 Misc. 456, 60 N.Y.S.2d 426 (1946); Shallcross v. West Jersey & Seashore R. R., 75 N.J.L. 395, 67 A. 931 (1907); Clark, supra n. 13 at 629.

87. Fed.Rules Civ.Proc. 8(e) (2).

88. Cases requiring election: Wigton v. McKinley, 122 Colo. 14, 221 P.2d 383 (1950); Schochet v. General Ins. Co., 204 Minn. 610, 284 N. W. 886 (1939). Cases not requiring election: Fidelity & Deposit Co. of Md. v. Krout, 146 F.2d 531 (2d Cir. 1945); Shuffelberger v. Hop-

election.[89] The case should be submitted to the jury under proper instructions and permit the jury to find the facts. As one court remarked, any other rule would nullify the salutory purposes of alternative pleading.[90]

Counterclaims. In addition to denials and affirmative defenses, the answer may contain counterclaims which the defendant may have against the plaintiff. Counterclaims were unknown to the common law; it provided only a plea of set-off or recoupment, the maximum effect of which was to reduce the amount of the plaintiff's claim.[91] A counterclaim, on the other hand, may result in an affirmative judgment against the plaintiff greatly in excess of his original demand. The early code provisions restricted counterclaims to those arising out of the same transaction or, in an action on contract, any other cause of action also on contract.[92] Some modern codes, and the federal rules, broaden the counterclaim to include any cause of action which the defendant has against the plaintiff.[93] This is in accord with modern trends toward judicial economy: to settle as many claims as possible in one litigation.

Where two automobiles collide at an intersection injuring both drivers, each may have a cause of action or claim for relief against the other. Which will be the counterclaim depends upon who first brings suit. Consequently, the same rules of pleading regarding the statement of the facts constituting the cause of action or claim for relief will apply to the statement of the counterclaim. There are, however, some problems peculiar to counterclaims. One of them is whether a defendant has a choice of asserting his claim as a counterclaim or as a separate suit. The federal rules, and some codes, provide that a defendant must plead a counterclaim if it arises out of the transaction or occurrence that is the subject matter of the plaintiff's suit.[94] Other-

kins, 177 Kan. 513, 280 P.2d 933 (1955).

89. "I see no basis for requiring an election .   . .. Where the judicial treatment of the facts is in doubt, justice demands that the litigant be permitted to assert alternative positions which depend upon the successful determinations of the issues raised by the facts." Chirelstein v. Chirelstein, 8 N.J. Super, 504, 511, 73 A.2d 628, 632 (1950).

90. McCormick v. Kopmann, supra n. 37.

91. Koffler & Reppy, supra n. 11 at 515–17.

92. Clark, supra n. 13 at 642.

93. Id. 644; Fed.Rules Civ.Proc. 13 (b).

94. Fed.Rules Civ.Proc. 13(a); West's Ann.Cal.Code Civ.Proc. § 439. What constitutes a "transaction" within the meaning of the rule can be troublesome. In Mulcahy v. Duggan, 67 Mont. 9, 16, 214 P. 1106, 1109 (1923) the suit was for an assault and battery which occurred on May 17; the defendant

wise, it is what is known as a permissive counterclaim which may or may not be asserted as such at the pleasure of the defendant.[95] A defendant may not, however, split his cause of action against the plaintiff, using part of it as a defense to the suit and saving the rest for a separate action.[96]

An occasional case presents a curious problem involving counterclaims and the statute of limitations. Again, let us suppose the intersection accident. The plaintiff files suit the day before the statute of limitations has run and the defendant is served with process a few days later. Is the counterclaim barred by the statute? There is authority both ways, but the better view seems to be that the counterclaim is not barred.[97] One court has said that, apart from the demands of simple justice, such a rule will "have the beneficial effect of tending to discourage the filing of frivolous claims just before the running of the statute of limitations." [98]

SECTION 4. THE DEMURRER

The demurrer is the device which the common law and the codes provided for the purpose of challenging the legal sufficiency of an opponent's pleading.[99] The Federal Rules of Civil Pro-

sought to plead a counterclaim for a libel which occurred on May 8; it appeared that it was the libel which caused the assault and battery; the court applied a nontechnical definition to the word "transaction" which it said embraced both events because of the causal relationship, stating, "The purpose of this statute is to enable and require parties to adjust in one action the various differences which grow out of any given transaction." In Williams v. Robinson, 1 F.R.D. 211, 213 (D.D.C. 1940), the court said, in defining "transaction" as used in Rule 13(a), "A familiar test may be applied by inquiring whether the same evidence will support or refute the opposing claims." (Here the plaintiff was named as a corespondent in a divorce action, and the court held that his action for libel based on the allegations of the husband did not grow out of the same transaction.)

Where a plaintiff's case is dismissed, on motion, before the time the defendant is required to an-

swer, he is not required to file a compulsory counterclaim, but may bring a separate action. Lawhorn v. Atlantic Ref. Co., 299 F.2d 353 (5th Cir. 1962).

95. There is no restriction on the type of permissive counterclaim which may be asserted under Rule 13(b). Kuenzel v. Universal Car-Loading & Distrib. Co., 29 F.Supp. 407 (E.D.Pa.1939).

96. Derderian v. Union Market Nat'l Bank, 326 Mass. 538, 95 N.E.2d 552 (1950); Mitchell v. Federal Intermediate Credit Bank, 165 S.C. 457, 164 S.E. 136 (1932).

97. Sullivan v. Hoover, 6 F.R.D. 513 (D.D.C.1947) (holding the counterclaim is barred); Azada v. Carson, 252 F.Supp. 988 (D.Hawaii 1966) (holding the counterclaim is not barred).

98. Azada v. Carson, op. cit. at 989.

99. The defect in the pleading challenged could be either one of form

fed.: motion to dismiss replaces demurrer

cedure abolished the demurrer but substituted for it the motion to dismiss which serves the same purpose.[100] Unlike the complaint and the answer, a demurrer does not allege facts. What it does is to challenge the legal sufficiency of the facts which the opponent has alleged.[101] In other words, the demurrer admits, for the purposes of argument, that the facts alleged are true, but it avoids the conclusion the pleader wishes drawn from those facts by pointing out that the facts are insufficient under the law to constitute a cause of action or a defense.[102] Viewed in a different light, a demurrer is a screening device to eliminate cases at the pleading stage which do not have enough substance to warrant a trial. The party who files the demurrer is in effect saying to the court: even if my opponent is able to prove all the

or substance. The discussion in the text is limited to defects of substance. The original New York Code specified six grounds of demurrer to the complaint: (1) no jurisdiction over the person or subject matter, (2) plaintiff lacks legal capacity to sue, (3) another action pending between the same parties, (4) defect of parties, (5) improper joinder of causes of action, and (6) the complaint does not state facts sufficient to constitute a cause of action. First Rep. Com'rs on Prac. and Pl., N.Y.1848, § 122. Some codes include ambiguity or uncertainty as a ground of demurrer: West's Ann.Cal.Code Civ.Proc. § 430.

100. Investors Syndicate of America Inc. v. City of Indian Rocks Beach, 434 F.2d 871 (5th Cir. 1970); Fed. Rules Civ.Proc. 12(b), which states seven grounds. Rule 12(f), Motion to Strike, serves the same purpose as a demurrer to the answer.

101. Usually if a defense is not interposed at the proper time, it is waived. Under the codes this was not true regarding lack of jurisdiction over the subject matter or failure to state facts sufficient to constitute a cause of action. They could be raised at any time. Jacobus v. Colgate, 217 N.Y. 235, 111 N.E. 837 (1916); Redondo Improvement Co. v. City of Redondo Beach, 3 Cal.App.2d 299, 39 P.2d 438 (1934); Watson v. Lee County, 244 N.C. 508, 31 S.E.2d 535 (1944).

This is one situation in which the federal rules are less liberal than the codes. Rule 12(h) provides that "A defense of failure to state a claim upon which relief can be granted . . . and an objection of failure to state a legal defense to a claim may be made in any pleading permitted or ordered under Rule 7(a), or by motion for judgment on the pleadings, or at the trial on the merits." If not so raised in one of these three ways, the objection will be deemed waived: Black, Sivalls & Bryson v. Shondell, 174 F.2d 587 (8th Cir. 1949); Elbinger v. Precision Metal Workers Corp., 18 F.R.D. 467 (E.D. Wis.1956).

A motion for judgment on the pleadings, mentioned in the federal rule, and also available under the codes, was another method of raising the sufficiency of a pleading. The motion could be made by either party after the pleadings had been completed, and it served the same purpose as a demurrer by challenging the sufficiency of the opponent's pleading: Falick v. Sun N Sea, Inc., 81 So.2d 749 (Fla.1955); Norman v. Leach, 208 Okl. 25, 252 P.2d 1020 (1953); Page v. North Carolina Mut. Life Ins. Co., 207 S. C. 277, 35 S.E.2d 716 (1945).

102. A motion to dismiss under the federal rules has the same effect: Stanton v. United States, 434 F.2d 1273 (5th Cir. 1970).

facts which he has alleged, his case would have to be dismissed because there is no applicable law to support it.

One of the cardinal rules which courts apply when ruling on a demurrer to a complaint is that the decision must be made on the basis of the facts alleged on the face of the complaint.[103]   A demurrer may not contradict facts properly alleged, nor may it allege facts in avoidance of or supplementary to the facts alleged in the complaint.[104]   For example, the defense of the statute of limitations may not be raised by demurrer where the statutory bar does not appear from the facts alleged in the complaint.[105] However, if a complaint contains allegations of facts which constitute a prima facie defense to the cause of action without alleging other facts to negate or avoid them the complaint will be demurrable because on its face it shows a defense.[106]   As stated in a previous section, under the codes the plaintiff must allege ultimate facts and not mere conclusions or evidence.[107]   Consequently a complaint which is deficient in alleging sufficient ultimate facts will not be saved by allegations of conclusions or evidence.   Nor can a plaintiff save his complaint by alleging facts which are contrary to facts of which the court is required to take judicial notice.[108]   Bearing these qualifications in mind, if a com-

103. Ghiradelli v. Greene, 56 Cal. 629 (1880); Augusta & S. R. R. v. Lark, 97 Ga. 800, 25 S.E. 175 (1896); Metzger v. Canadian & European Credit Sys. Co., 59 N.J.L. 340, 36 A. 661 (1896); McDowell v. Blythe Bros., 236 N.C. 396, 72 S.E.2d 860 (1952).

104. Such a demurrer was known as a "speaking demurrer" and was not permitted. See the cases cited in n. 105, infra. Under the federal rules some courts tolerate "speaking motions" on the theory that the liberal discovery rules make the pleadings less important. Benson v. Export Equip. Corp., 49 N.M. 356, 164 P.2d 380 (1945).

105. Wall v. Chesapeake & O. R. R., 200 Ill. 66, 65 N.E. 632 (1902). Compare Taylor v. Houston, 93 U. S.App.D.C. 391, 211 F.2d 427 (1954), which permitted the statute of limitations to be raised by a motion to dismiss under Rule 12(b) (6).

106. Casualty Ins. Co. v. Rees Inv. Co., 14 Cal.App.3d 16, 92 Cal.Rptr.

857 (1971) (facts alleged showed claim was barred by the statute of limitations, and no facts were alleged which would negative this defense); Scott v. Statesville Plywood & Veneer Co., 240 N.C. 73, 81 S.E.2d 146 (1954) (libel suit in which the allegations in the complaint showed that the defamatory statements were privileged); Penton v. Canning, 57 Wyo. 390, 118 P.2d 1002 (1941) (malicious prosecution suit in which the complaint showed a magistrate had found probable cause to hold the plaintiff); Leggett v. Montgomery Ward & Co., 178 F.2d 436 (10th Cir.1949) (malicious prosecution suit in which the complaint showed the plaintiff had waived a preliminary hearing).

107. Supra, Sec. 2.

108. Nicketta v. National Tea Co., 338 Ill.App. 159, 87 N.E.2d 30 (1949) (in which the court took judicial notice that it was impossible to get trichinosis from eating pork which was properly cooked); Hancock Nat'l Bank v. Ellis, 166 Mass.

plaint states facts sufficient to constitute *any* cause of action, a demurrer to it should not be sustained even though the facts stated do not warrant the specific relief demanded in the prayer.[109]

The present situation in the federal courts presents a slightly different picture. The rules abolish "cause of action" and substitute "claim for relief." They abolish "demurrer" and substitute "motion to dismiss." Is this more than a mere change in nomenclature? It is submitted that it is. The federal courts no longer struggle with the distinctions between facts and conclusions, and under the liberal pleading edict of the Supreme Court [110] they will not sustain a motion to dismiss unless it appears almost inconceivable that, under his pleading, the plaintiff could produce evidence justifying some form of relief.[111] This judicial attitude is due, in part, to the general liberal philosophy of the new rules, in part to the conviction that pleadings are a poor device for screening cases, and in part to the existence of a better screening device, the motion for summary judgment.[112]

Mention should be made of two of the common law rules relating to demurrers which, although modified, are still reflected in modern practice. (1) The common law rule was that a demurrer would search the record and be sustained against the first bad pleading.[113] To illustrate: the pleadings in a case might consist of a complaint, an answer, a replication, and a rejoinder; if the plaintiff filed a demurrer to the rejoinder it would search

414, 44 N.E. 349 (1896) (in which a Mass. court refused to take judicial notice of the statutes of Kansas); Southern Ry. v. Covenia, 100 Ga. 46, 29 S.E. 219 (1896) (in a death case for loss of services of child the court took judicial notice that a child under two years of age was incapable of rendering services); Clough v. Goggins, 40 Iowa 325 (1875) (in which the court took judicial notice that the day upon which notes were executed was Sunday); Colvig v. R.K.O. Gen., Inc. 232 Cal.App.2d 56, 42 Cal.Rptr. 473 (1965) (in which the court took judicial notice of the official acts of the judicial department of the state); Hancock v. Burns, 158 Cal.App.2d 785, 323 P. 2d 456 (1958).

109. Berryman v. Berryman, 115 Colo. 281, 172 P.2d 446 (1946); Clark, The Complaint in Code

Pleading, 35 Yale L.J. 259, 285, 290 (1926). Likewise, if two defendants file a joint demurrer it should be overruled if the complaint states a cause of action against either defendant: Myers v. County of Orange, 6 Cal.App.3d 626, 86 Cal. Rptr. 198 (1970).

110. Conley v. Gibson, supra n. 47.

111. Delaware Floor Prods. v. Franklin Distribs., 12 F.R.D. 114 (E.D.Pa.1951). Cf. Sparks v. Chicago & E. I. R.R., 42 F.Supp. 1019 (E.D.Ill.1942), where the court sustained a motion to dismiss, with leave to file an amended complaint.

112. See infra Sec. 8.

113. Humphreys v. Bethily, 2 Vent. 198, 86 Eng.Rep. 391 (1690); Koffler & Reppy, supra n. 11 at 400.

the record and be sustained against the first bad pleading, which might be the complaint. This was one of the few instances of judicial economy in the common law days. Today the doctrine has little application due to the fact we have shortened the pleadings to a complaint, an answer, and sometimes a reply.[114] (2) In the early common law, cases were actually disposed of on demurrer. If a court sustained a defendant's demurrer to a complaint he was awarded a judgment on the merits; if the demurrer was overruled the plaintiff recovered judgment on the merits.[115] This was a very harsh rule and was ultimately relaxed, even at common law. Today, after a ruling on a demurrer the party against whom the ruling was made may generally replead. In other words, if a demurrer is sustained against a complaint the plaintiff will be given leave to file an amended complaint; if the demurrer is overruled, the defendant may answer.[116]

SECTION 5.   OTHER PLEADINGS

The reply. One of the principal aims of the common law system of pleading was to narrow the issues to be tried. In the quest for this goal the pleadings were carried on and on in an effort to reach a single issue, if possible. The codes drastically curtailed the pleadings. Under some codes there was merely a complaint, an answer and a demurrer, with a provision that new matter (affirmative defenses) in the answer would be deemed denied or avoided.[117] In others a reply was necessary to respond to new matter in the answer, and in still others a reply was necessary only to respond to a counterclaim or cross complaint.[118] Under the federal rules a reply is necessary to a counterclaim, and the court may order a reply to an answer.[119] The rules further provide that averments in a pleading to which a responsive pleading is required are admitted when not denied in the responsive pleading, but that averments in a pleading to which no responsive pleading is required shall be taken as denied or avoided.[120] Under these rules no reply is necessary to affirmative

---

114. The doctrine is shrunken in size but not dead. Watertown Milk Producers Coop. v. Van Camp Packing Co., 199 Wis. 379, 226 N.W. 378 (1929); Gunder v. New York Times, 37 F.Supp. 911 (S.D.N.Y.1941).

115. Koffler & Reppy, supra n. 11 at 405.

116. Hutchins v. Libby, 149 Me. 371, 103 A.2d 117 (1953); Gignac v. King, 118 Vt. 413, 111 A.2d 42 (1955).

117. West's Ann.Cal.Code Civ.Proc., §§ 422, 462.

118. Clark, supra n. 13 at 688–89.

119. Fed.Rules Civ.Proc. 7(a).

120. Fed.Rules Civ.Proc. 8(d).

defenses in an answer.[121]   However if a reply is not filed to a counterclaim, it will be deemed admitted.[122]   Upon request a court may order a reply to an answer, but this is a matter resting within the discretion of the court.[123]

Supplemental pleadings.   Usually the positions of the parties have become crystallized before the suit is brought.   There are situations, however, in which events occurring subsequent to the time the suit is brought may have an effect upon its outcome. When this happens the parties may wish to supplement the pleadings which have already been filed.   A supplemental pleading is one which is limited to alleging facts occurring subsequent to the filing of the original pleading.   Whether or not such a pleading may be filed rests within the discretion of the court.   If permitted, it does not replace the original pleading, as an amended pleading does, but is a supplement to it.   Such pleadings are permitted under the codes [124] and under the federal rules.[125]

discretion

Motions.   Any application for a court order is a motion.   The most common motions during the pleading stage of a lawsuit are (1) a motion to make a pleading more definite and certain, (2) a motion for a bill of particulars, and (3) a motion to strike a pleading or portions thereof.[126]   All three were provided for in the original Federal Rules of Civil Procedure, but in 1948 an amendment deleted the provision for a bill of particulars on the theory that the discovery procedure afforded a sufficient remedy.[127]   The motion to make a pleading more definite is restricted to situations in which the pleading "is so vague or ambiguous that a party cannot reasonably be required to frame a responsive pleading." [128]   The motion to strike may be used only to eliminate

---

121.   Falick v. Sun N Sea, Inc., supra n. 101; Neeff v. Emery Transp. Co., 284 F.2d 432 (2d Cir. 1960).

122.   Peters & Russell v. Dorfman, 188 F.2d 711 (7th Cir. 1951).

123.   Keller-Dorian Colorfilm Corp. v. Eastman Kodak Co., supra n. 3; Beckstrom v. Coastwise Line, 13 F. R.D. 480 (D.Alaska 1953).

124.   Manning v. Hyland, 19 A.D.2d 652, 241 N.Y.S.2d 908 (1963), in which the court permitted the defendant to file a supplemental answer that the parties had intermarried since the personal injury suit was started, thus destroying liability.

125.   Slavenburg Corp. v. Boston Ins. Co., 30 F.R.D. 123 (S.D.N.Y.1962) (supplemental answer permitted which alleged additional breaches of condition in insurance policy, occurring since the suit was filed); Garrison v. Baltimore & O. R. R., 20 F.R.D. 190 (W.D.Pa.1957) (supplemental answer setting up a release not permitted because of inexcusable delay in filing same).

126.   Clark, supra n. 13 at 545.

127.   United States v. Hartmann, 2 F.R.D. 477 (E.D.Pa.1942); Wright, supra n. 20 at 277.

128.   Fed.Rules Civ.Proc. 12(e).   In Mitchell v. E–Z Way Towers, Inc.,

from a pleading "any insufficient defense or any redundant, immaterial, impertinent, or scandalous matter." [129]

SECTION 6. VARIANCE

A variance is the legal term which describes the situation in which evidence offered at the trial went beyond the issues made by the pleadings. Upon proper objection, such evidence was excluded. The rationale for the rule is quite simple: the pleadings are supposed to serve notice to the parties of their respective contentions, and to permit a variance between pleading and proof would sanction surprise and sharp tactics. Under the codes, before pretrial discovery was developed, the courts were quite strict in enforcing the rule against variance. It was frequently said that a plaintiff must recover, if at all, upon the cause of action alleged in his complaint, and not upon some other which might be developed by the proofs at the trial.[130] For instance, in Messick v. Turnage,[131] the plaintiff sued for injuries sustained when a portion of the ceiling in a theater fell and struck her; in her complaint she alleged that the roof leaked, letting in the rain which softened the plaster, causing it to fall; whereas at the trial the proof showed that the water which softened the plaster came from a lavatory on the balcony floor where a drain was clogged with cigarette butts; this was held to be a fatal variance. In Buckley v. Mandel Bros.,[132] another personal injury case, the

269 F.2d 126 (5th Cir. 1959) the court held the motion was not appropriate for securing facts in preparation for trial but should only be used when necessary to draft a responsive pleading. Whether the motion should be granted is largely discretionary with the trial court: Webb v. Webb, 32 F.R.D. 615 (W.D.Mo. 1963); Fennell v. Svenska Amerika Linien, supra n. 45. State court practice is similar: Dansby v. Dansby, 165 Ohio St. 112, 133 N.E. 2d 358 (1956); Driefer v. Hersey Estates Inc., 61 Dauph. 468 (Pa. C.P.1951).

129. Fed.Rules Civ.Proc. 12(f). In United States v. Bize, 86 F.Supp. 939 (D.Neb.1949) the court held matter should not be stricken unless it could have no possible relation to the controversy. In Garcia v. Hilton Hotels Int'l., Inc., 97 F.Supp. 5 (D.Puerto Rico 1951) the

court granted a motion to strike portions of a complaint as redundant, and to require other parts to be made more definite. State court practice is similar: Brown v. Lamb, 112 Ohio App. 116, 171 N.E. 2d 191 (1960); Daniel v. Gardner, 240 N.C. 249, 81 S.E.2d 660 (1954); Krausnick v. Haegg Roofing Co., 236 Iowa 985, 20 N.W.2d 432 (1945); Symington v. Haxton, 195 App.Div. 85, 186 N.Y.S. 397 (1921).

130. Mondran v. Goux, 51 Cal. 151 (1875).

131. 240 N.C. 625, 83 S.E.2d 654 (1954). Accord: Wilkins v. Commercial Fin. Co., 237 N.C. 396, 75 S.E.2d 118 (1953); Bowen v. Darden, 233 N.C. 443, 64 S.E.2d 285 (1951).

132. 333 Ill. 368, 164 N.E. 657 (1929). Accord: Ferla v. Rotella, 92 R.I. 460, 169 A.2d 906 (1961); Fuentes

court held there was a fatal variance where the proof showed that the plaintiff's motorcycle ran into the defendant's truck rather than vice versa as the plaintiff had alleged. There has been a tendency in the modern cases to relax the rule regarding variance where the court feels that the party against whom the evidence was offered was not taken by surprise.[133] Even under the more liberal rule, however, there is the danger that a court will hold that there has been a failure of proof and not a mere variance.[134]

SECTION 7.   AMENDMENTS

In general. Pleadings are not an end in themselves, and hence they are subject to amendment. This was true at common law,[135] under the codes,[136] and under the federal rules.[137] Differences have been largely a matter of the degree of liberality with which amendments are permitted. The federal rules provide that a party may amend his pleading once as a matter of right at any time before a responsive pleading is served,[138] or, if no responsive pleading is permitted, within twenty days after it is served; otherwise he may amend only with the consent of the adverse party or by leave of court.[139] The rules further provide that "leave shall be freely given when justice so requires." [140] Notwithstanding the liberality of this language the matter is one resting in the

v. Tucker, 31 Cal.2d 1, 187 P.2d 752 (1947); Manning v. Loew, 313 Mass. 252, 46 N.E.2d 1022 (1943); Hilderbrand v. Anderson, 270 S.W. 2d 406 (Mo.App.1954).

133. Diemer v. Diemer, 8 N.Y.2d 206, 203 N.Y.S.2d 829 (1960); Bridges v. Ingram, 122 Colo. 501, 223 P.2d 1051 (1950).

134. Lewis v. South San Francisco Yellow Cab Co., 93 Cal.App.2d 849, 210 P.2d 62 (1949).

135. Koffler & Reppy, supra n. 11 at 558 et seq.

136. Clark, supra n. 13 at 708 et seq.

137. Fed.Rules Civ.Proc. 15.

138. See Breier v. Northern Cal. Bowling Ass'n, 316 F.2d 787 (9th Cir. 1963), holding that a motion to

dismiss is not a "responsive pleading" and therefore a plaintiff could amend his complaint as a matter of right even after the defendant had filed a motion to dismiss.

139. Fed.Rules Civ.Proc. 15(a).

140. Id. For an extreme example of the liberality with which amendments are allowed see Emich Motors Corp. v. General Motors Corp., 229 F.2d 714 (7th Cir. 1956). Plaintiff brought an antitrust suit in 1941 and won a verdict for more than a million dollars, which was reversed for a new trial. Later, in an unrelated case, the Supreme Court held that the Illinois statute of limitations applied to antitrust cases, and thereafter (ten years after the Emich case had been started) the defendant was permitted to file an amended answer pleading the statute of limitations.

sound discretion of the trial court which will not be reversed except for abuse.[141]

Amendments to conform to the evidence. The rule against variance between the pleadings and the proof has been softened by modern code provisions which make a variance immaterial unless it has misled a party to his prejudice.[142] Even a material variance may be cured by an amendment upon such terms as may be just. The federal rules have substantially similar provisions.[143] They go somewhat further in providing, "When issues not raised by the pleadings are tried by express or implied consent of the parties, they shall be treated in all respects as if they had been raised by the pleadings. Such amendment of the pleadings as may be necessary to cause them to conform to the evidence . . . may be made . . . at any time, even after judgment." [144] Most courts have been liberal in interpreting this rule,[145] but there is some authority to the effect that amendments to conform to the evidence will not be allowed where the proffered amendment sets forth a completely new cause of ac-

141. Zenith Radio Corp. v. Hazeltine Research, Inc., 401 U.S. 321, 91 S.Ct. 795, 28 L.Ed.2d 77 (1971). In Friedman v. Transamerica Corp., 5 F.R.D. 115 (D.Del.1946) the plaintiff asked leave to amend his complaint for a fourth time, which the court refused. See also Tingley v. Times Mirror, 151 Cal. 1, 89 P. 1097 (1907) in which the court refused leave to amend an answer setting up a new defense because the request came too late and no excuse for the tardiness was shown.

142. West's Ann.Cal. Code Civ.Proc., §§ 469, 470.

143. Fed.Rules Civ.Proc. 15(b).

144. Id. Such a rule does not prevent a party from objecting to a material variance where he is really taken by surprise: Texas Employers' Ins. Ass'n v. Dillingham, 262 S.W.2d 748 (Tex.Civ.App.1953). The court may permit a trial amendment but only on terms which are just, which, in most cases would be to require a postponement to enable the objecting party to prepare to meet the new evidence.

145. Slavitt v. Kauhi, 384 F.2d 530 (9th Cir. 1967) (holding the trial court abused its discretion in denying an amendment to the complaint, at the close of the evidence, to add a ground of negligence to the case which initially was one of wilful assault); Niedland v. United States, 338 F.2d 254 (3d Cir. 1964) (evidence of special damages, not pleaded, but which went in without objection. The court said had the defendant objected the court could have allowed an amendment, and if the defendant was taken by surprise, the court could have granted a continuance); Robbins v. Jordan, 86 U.S.App.D.C. 304, 181 F. 2d 793 (1950) (holding the trial court abused its discretion in refusing an amendment, but could have granted a continuance); Knudson v. Boren, 261 F.2d 15 (10th Cir. 1958) (permitting evidence of unpleaded special defense which came in without objection); Dacus v. Burns, 206 Ark. 810, 177 S.W.2d 748 (1944) (permitting amendment to conform to the proof); Coburn v. Moore, 322 Mass. 204, 76 N.E.2d 640 (1948) (permitting amendment to conform to proof); Thomas v. Newport Oil Corp., 85 R.I. 455, 133 A.2d 631 (1957) (permitting amendment to conform to proof).

tion [146] or changes the theory upon which the case was tried.[147]

Amendments and the statute of limitations. One of the troublesome questions concerning amendments is whether an amendment to a pleading may relate back to the time of the filing of the original pleading in order to avoid the bar of the statute of limitations. The federal rule provides that it does relate back if the matter alleged in the amended pleading "arose out of the conduct, transaction or occurrence set forth or attempted to be set forth in the original pleading." [148] This language is an attempt to avoid the ambiguities in the phrase "cause of action" as used in the codes. The rule was construed by the United States Supreme Court in Tiller v. Atlantic Coast Line Railroad Co.[149] In that case a widow was suing the railroad under the Federal Employers Liability Act, alleging negligence in the operation of the train which killed her husband. After a trial, an appeal, and a reversal for a new trial, the plaintiff was permitted, over objection, to amend her complaint to allege a violation of the Federal Boiler Inspection Act. The amendment was filed after the three year statute of limitations had run, and the question was whether the amendment would relate back to the time of filing the original suit. The Supreme Court held that it would, stating that the amendment and the original complaint related to the "same general conduct, transaction and occurrence which involved the death of the deceased . . .. There is no reason to apply a statute of limitations when, as here, the respondent has had notice from the beginning that petitioner was trying to enforce a claim against it because of the events leading up to the death of the deceased in the respondent's yard." [150] Most courts have likewise given a liberal interpretation to the rule.[151]

Counterclaims pose an interesting problem: may an amendment to an answer which includes an omitted counterclaim relate back to save it from the statutory bar? It could if it arose out of the same "conduct, transaction or occurrence" and if Rule 15 (c) applied. However, there is a special rule on counterclaims, Rule 13(f) which provides, "When a pleader fails to set up a

146. Standard Title Ins. Co. v. Roberts, 349 F.2d 613 (8th Cir. 1965).

147. Hagans v. Hagans, 215 A.2d 842 (D.C.Ct.App.1966).

148. Fed.Rules Civ.Proc. 15(c).

149. 323 U.S. 574, 65 S.Ct. 421, 89 L.Ed. 465 (1945).

150. Id. at 581, 65 S.Ct. at 424, 89 L.Ed. at 471–72.

151. Green v. Walsh, 21 F.R.D. 15 (E.D.Wis.1957); Blair v. Durham, 134 F.2d 729 (6th Cir. 1943); Wennerholm v. Stanford Univ., 20 Cal. 2d 713, 128 P.2d 522 (1942) (interpreting Cal.Code); Harriss v. Tams, 258 N.Y. 229, 179 N.E. 476 (1932) (under N.Y. Code); Levey v. Newark Beth Israel Hosp., 17 N.J.Super. 290, 85 A.2d 827 (1952) (saying the question is whether the "gist" of the cause of action remains the same).

counterclaim through oversight, inadvertence, or excusable neg-lect, or when justice requires, he may by leave of court set up the counterclaim by amendment." [152]   The rule says nothing about the amendment relating back, and there is authority to the ef-fect that the newly pleaded counterclaim will be barred.[153]

It is one thing to permit an amendment to relate back as ap-plied to parties before the court from the beginning of the suit. It is quite another to permit it to relate back as applied to a new party who is sought to be added by the amendment and against whom the statute of limitations has run.   The federal rule covers this situation by providing that such an amendment may relate back only if the claim against the new party arose out of the "con-duct, transaction or occurrence" set forth in the original plead-ing, and also providing the new party knew or should have known of the institution of the original suit so that he will not be preju-diced in maintaining his defense on the merits.[154]   As might be expected, the cases interpreting these provisions go both ways, depending on the facts of the particular case.[155]

SECTION 8.   SUMMARY JUDGMENT

A device has been developed in recent decades to pre-test the issues made by the pleadings to determine whether or not they are substantial enough to warrant a trial.   It is the motion for sum-mary judgment.[156]   Such a motion assumes the existence of is-sues made by the pleadings but it challenges the genuineness of those issues.[157]   In its simplest form the motion will be accom-panied by affidavits of persons having personal knowledge of the facts to show that the issues made by the pleadings have no foun-

152. Fed.Rules Civ.Proc. 13(f).

153. Stoner v. Terranella, 372 F.2d 89 (6th Cir. 1967).   The case is questioned in Wright, supra n. 20 at 276.

154. Fed.Rules Civ.Proc. 15(c).

155. Cases permitting the amend-ment: Meredith v. United Air Lines, 41 F.R.D. 34 (S.D.Cal.1966); Adams v. Beland Realty Corp., 187 F.Supp. 680 (E.D.N.Y.1960); cases denying the amendment: Aarhus Oliefabrik, A/S v. A. O. Smith Corp., 22 F.R.D. 33 (E.D.Wis.1958); Lomax v. United States, 155 F.

Supp. 354 (E.D.Pa.1957); Martz v. Miller Bros., 244 F.Supp. 246 (D. Del.1965);   compare   Stauffer   v. Isaly Dairy Co., 4 Ohio App.2d 15, 211 N.E.2d 72 (1965).

156. Fed.Rules Civ.Proc. 56.

157. Adickes v. S. H. Kress & Co., 398 U.S. 144, 90 S.Ct. 1598, 26 L. Ed.2d 142 (1970); Lane v. Grey-hound Corp., 13 F.R.D. 178 (E.D. Ky.1952); R. D. Reeder Lathing Co. v. Allen, 66 Cal.2d 373, 425 P. 2d 785 (1967); Incorporated Soc. of St. Maria del Buoncammino New York v. Lorusso, 5 Misc.2d 551, 161 N.Y.S.2d 483 (1957).

dation in truth or in fact.[158] If the opponent files no counter-affidavits, he has in effect admitted that the pleading issue was a spurious one, and the court will then enter a summary judgment against him.[159] If he files counter-affidavits to support the position he took in his pleading the motion will be denied. A motion for summary judgment may be supported by other sworn statements of facts appearing in the record of the case such as the pretrial discovery depositions of the parties,[160] answers to discovery interrogatories,[161] or admissions made at a pretrial conference.[162] In whatever form the supporting material occurs it must establish beyond question that the issues made by the pleadings are not genuine because the motion is not a substitute for trial.[163] Before a court may properly grant such a motion it must clearly appear that the moving party is entitled to judgment as a matter of law,[164] viewing the supporting material in the light most favorable to his opponent.[165] Notwithstanding the heavy burden resting on one making such a motion many cases are dis-

158. Alderman v. Baltimore & O. R. R., 113 F.Supp. 881 (S.D.W.Va. 1953); Dyer v. MacDougall, 201 F. 2d 265 (2d Cir. 1952); Dwan v. Massarene, 199 App.Div. 872, 192 N.Y.S. 577 (1922).

159. Chenoweth v. Epperson, 3 Ariz. App. 316, 414 P.2d 165 (1966); Chartier v. Empire Mut. Ins. Co., 34 F.R.D. 217 (E.D.Pa.1964). The affidavits must be made by one having personal knowledge of the facts, and the facts alleged in the affidavits must show there is no genuine issue: Adickes v. S. H. Kress & Co., supra n. 157; Lundeen v. Cordner, 354 F.2d 401 (8th Cir. 1966); Maltby v. Shook, 131 Cal.App.2d 349, 280 P.2d 541 (1955).

160. Dale Hilton, Inc. v. Triangle Publications, Inc., 27 F.R.D. 468 (S.D.N.Y.1961); DiSabato v. Soffes, 9 A.D.2d 297, 193 N.Y.S.2d 184 (1959); Forman v. Silver, 313 S. W.2d 420 (Ky.Ct.App.1958).

161. American Airlines v. Ulen, 87 U.S.App.D.C. 307, 186 F.2d 529 (1949).

162. Burke v. Owens Ill. Glass Co., 86 F.Supp. 663 (S.D.W.Va.1949).

163. Sartor v. Arkansas Natural Gas Corp., 321 U.S. 620, 64 S.Ct. 724, 88 L.Ed. 967 (1944); Thomas v. Martin, 8 F.R.D. 638 (E.D.Tenn. 1949); Whaley v. Fowler, 152 Cal. App.2d 379, 313 P.2d 97 (1957).

164. Sartor v. Arkansas Natural Gas Corp., supra n. 163; Chenoweth v. Epperson, supra n. 159; Burke v. Owens Ill. Glass Co., supra n. 162.

165. Giordano v. Lee, 434 F.2d 1227 (8th Cir. 1971); Dale Hilton, Inc. v. Triangle Publications, Inc., supra n. 160; Whaley v. Fowler, supra n. 163. Occasionally the members of a court will be in sharp disagreement among themselves as to whether a summary judgment is proper in an individual case. One of the most interesting of such cases is Arnstein v. Porter, 154 F. 2d 464 (2d Cir. 1946) in which Judge Clark and Judge Frank sharply disagreed on the propriety of such a judgment in a case in which Cole Porter was being sued for plagiarism. For an account of the friendly feud between these judges on this and other cases see Schick, Judicial Relations on the Second Circuit, 1941–1951, 44 N.Y. U.L.Rev. 939 (1969).

posed of by summary judgment.[166] Even though the moving party may not be entitled to a summary judgment on the whole case, he may be entitled to a partial summary judgment on the issue of liability [167] or on some of the counts in a complaint which contains more than one claim.[168]

166. Cases granting summary judgments: Chenoweth v. Epperson, supra n. 159; Alderman v. Baltimore & O. R. R., supra n. 158; Burke v. Owens Ill. Glass Co., supra n. 162; Dale Hilton, Inc. v. Triangle Publications, Inc., supra n. 160; Forman v. Silver, supra n. 160; Cooper v. R. J. Reynolds Tobacco Co., 256 F. 2d 464 (1st Cir. 1958); DiSabato v. Soffes, supra n. 160; Lundeen v. Cordner, supra n. 159. Cases denying summary judgments: Whaley v. Fowler, supra n. 163; Cross v. United States, 336 F.2d 431 (2d Cir. 1964).

A summary judgment may be entered in favor of one who has the burden of proof and infringes no constitutional rights: Continental Cas. Co. v. American Sec. Co., 443 F.2d 649 (D.C.Cir. 1970); Investment Co. v. I. R. T. Co., 235 N.Y. 133, 139 N.E. 216 (1923).

167. American Airlines v. Ulen, supra n. 161; DiSabato v. Soffes, supra n. 160.

168. Dyer v. MacDougall, supra n. 158.

CHAPTER VI. DISCOVERY AND PRETRIAL

SECTION 1. ORIGIN AND PURPOSE

There was a time when issues of fact in a lawsuit were decided by trial by battle. This primitive method has long since been replaced by trial by jury. Nevertheless, our modern system has within it traces of our barbaric past. We still subscribe to the adversary theory of justice which is bottomed on the implicit assumption that a lawsuit is a fight, that each party must exert his utmost energy to overcome his opponent, and that when the dust of battle settles in the legal arena, justice will emerge triumphant. The theory possesses a certain charm and it frequently works, at least in the cases in which the parties are evenly matched. Where, however, one party is represented by a seasoned veteran of many legal battles and the other is represented by a tyro fresh from law school, justice is often smothered in the dust, and the decision in the case is awarded as a prize for the skill of counsel. For centuries, under our adversary system of justice, surprise has been regarded as a legitimate trial tactic. The biographies of great trial lawyers are full of instances of how they carried the day by taking their opponents unawares. The reason they could do this was that there was no effective way in which opposing counsel could find out, in advance of trial, the nature of the evidence which would be presented. The pleadings were supposed to give notice of what the case was about, but they were couched in general terms, stating only the ultimate facts, but giving no indication of the evidence which would be used to support them. The only common law discovery device was the motion for a bill of particulars which, if granted, would require the plaintiff to itemize the account upon which he was suing.[1] The bill of discovery in equity was limited to situations in which the plaintiff was seeking discovery of facts to support his action at law; it offered no relief to a plaintiff who was seeking to find out about his opponent's case.[2] The nineteenth century reforms of the codes did little to broaden the scope of discovery although, by the merger of law and equity, they eliminated the necessity of a separate suit in equity.[3] It was not until the adoption of the federal

---

1. Sunderland, Cases & Materials on Trial and Appellate Practice (2d ed. 1941) pp. 1–4; James, Civil Procedure (1965) pp. 179–82.

2. Sinclair Ref. Co. v. Jenkins Petroleum Process Co., 289 U.S. 689,

53 S.Ct. 736, 77 L.Ed. 1449 (1933); Kelly v. Nationwide Mut. Ins. Co., 23 Ohio Op.2d 29, 188 N.E.2d 445 (C.Pl., Ashtabula Cty.1963).

3. Downie v. Nettleton, 61 Conn. 593, 24 A. 977 (1892).

rules of civil procedure in 1938 that a new philosophy of pretrial discovery was written into the law.[4]

The new rules did not abolish the adversary theory of justice, but they provided a handicapping device by means of which the battle in the judicial arena became a fairer contest and greatly enhanced the possibility that at the end justice would, in fact, emerge triumphant. In short, they eliminated surprise as a legitimate courtroom tactic.[5] They did this by providing tools, available to both parties, for discovering in advance of the trial all of the relevant facts about the case. The contest between an experienced lawyer on one side and a beginner on the other was still an unequal contest, but the diligent beginner was given the opportunity to arm himself with a full knowledge of the facts of the case before he went into court. The primary purpose of the discovery process was to insure that the facts would be fully disclosed at the trial. There were two incidental benefits: (1) pretrial disclosure of the facts would often shorten the trial by eliminating issues about which there was no genuine dispute, and (2)

---

4. Prior to the adoption of the federal rules a few states had expanded the scope of discovery beyond the traditional lines. Ragland, Discovery Before Trial (1932) 1–5; James, Discovery, 38 Yale L.J. 746 (1929).

5. The leading case on the federal rules relating to discovery is Hickman v. Taylor, 329 U.S. 495, 67 S.Ct. 385, 91 L.Ed. 451 (1947). The court said: "We agree, of course, that the deposition-discovery rules are to be accorded a broad and liberal treatment. No longer can the time-honored cry of 'fishing expedition' serve to preclude a party from inquiring into the facts underlying his opponent's case. Mutual knowledge of all of the relevant facts gathered by both parties is essential to proper litigation. To that end, either party may compel the other to disgorge whatever facts he has in his possession." Id. at 507, 67 S.Ct. at 392, 91 L.Ed. at 460. In United States v. Procter & Gamble Co., 356 U.S. 677, 78 S.Ct. 983, 2 L.Ed.2d 1077 (1958) the court said, in reference to the discovery rules: "They together with pretrial procedures make a trial less a game of blind man's buff and more a fair contest with the basic issues and facts disclosed to the fullest practicable extent." Id. at 682, 78 S.Ct. at 986, 2 L.Ed. 2d at 1082. In Burton v. Weyerhaeuser Timber Co., 1 F.R.D. 571 (D.Or.1941) the court said: "I can sympathize with the desire of counsel, experienced in the older forms of practice, to withhold disclosure of such dramatic issues until the midst of trial, but it must be made clear that surprise, both as a weapon of attack and defense, is not to be tolerated under the new Federal procedure . . . the new rules outlaw the sporting theory of justice from Federal courts." Id. at 573. In Boldt v. Sanders, 261 Minn. 160, 111 N.W.2d 225 (1961), in denying the defendant's contention that evidence which is to be used for impeachment should be immune from discovery, the court says, "For us to revert to this philosophy would be judicial retrogression undermining the whole purpose of the rules of civil procedure. It would inevitably lead us back to the 'poker hand' conception of litigation, rewarding artifice and camouflage." Id. at 164, 111 N.W. 2d at 227–28.

such disclosure often resulted in a settlement of the case, thus eliminating the trial altogether.[6]

The discovery rules have been in force in all United States District Courts since 1938. They have also been adopted, in whole or in part, by a majority of the states. Experience under the rules has proved their worth, and the reaction of the bar has been generally favorable.[7] As in the case of any new statute or set of rules, defects and ambiguities have appeared. Some of these have been corrected by ad hoc amendments. Others have been corrected by a revision of the rules in 1970.[8] The changes have been in regard to detail rather than substance, and they will be noted in the following discussion.

SECTION 2. SCOPE OF DISCOVERY

In general. The heart of the discovery process is Rule 26(b) which defines its scope. The 1970 amendment adds to the rule by making certain matters more specific, but it does not alter the

---

6. Pretrial discovery is discussed in the following articles: James, The Revival of Bills of Particulars under the Federal Rules, 71 Harv.L. Rev. 1473 (1958); Louisell, Discovery Today, 45 Cal.L.Rev. 486 (1957); Louisell, Discovery and Pre-Trial Under the Minnesota Rules, 36 Minn.L.Rev. 633 (1952); Speck, The Use of Discovery in United States District Court, 60 Yale L.J. 1132 (1951); Rosenberg, Sanctions to Effectuate Pretrial Discovery, 58 Colum.L.Rev. 480 (1958); Tolman, Discovery Under the Federal Rules: Production of Documents and the Work Product of the Lawyer, 58 Colum.L.Rev. 498 (1958); Weinstein, Glei & Kay, Procedure for Obtaining Information Before Trial, 35 Tex.L.Rev. 481 (1957).

7. Wright, Law of Federal Courts, 354–55 (1970); Holtzoff, The Elimination of Surprise in Federal Practice, 7 Vand.L.Rev. 576 (1954). For a critical view see Hawkins, Discovery and Rule 34: What's So Wrong About Surprise? 39 A.B.A.J. 1075 (1953).

8. The amendments to the discovery rules in 1970 constituted the first comprehensive revision since 1938. The amendments clarified the scope of discovery, improved its mechanics, and rearranged the rules in a more logical sequence. The original version of Rule 26, which contained the crucial section on scope, dealt only with depositions, and the scope section, 26(b), was incorporated by reference in some of the other rules. In the 1970 revision, Rule 26 becomes a general rule applicable to all of the discovery tools. This resulted in a necessary rearrangement of the rules which is shown in the following table:

Old Rule No.	New Rule No.
26(a)	30(a), 31(a)
26(c)	30(c)
26(d)	32(a)
26(e)	32(b)
26(f)	32(c)
30(a)	30(b)
30(b)	26(c)
32	32(d)

See the explanation of the Advisory Committee in 4 Moore's Federal Practice (2d ed. 1970) [Hereinafter cited as Moore] R 26[4], pp. 26–24–28.

substance of the original rule. It provides that any party may obtain discovery

> .   .   .   regarding any matter, not privileged, which is relevant to the subject matter involved in the pending action, whether it relates to the claim or defense of the party seeking discovery or to the claim or defense of any other party, including the existence, description, nature, custody, condition and location of any books, documents, or other tangible things and the identity and location of persons having knowledge of any discoverable matter. It is not ground for objection that the information sought will be inadmissible at the trial if the information sought appears reasonably calculated to lead to the discovery of admissible evidence.[9]

The scope of pretrial discovery under the rule is extremely broad. It relates to practically any matter relevant to the case and it is not restricted to evidence which will be admissible at the trial. With few exceptions, which will be noted later, this broad grant of inquisitorial power extends to all of the tools of discovery. This may best be illustrated by a hypothetical example. Let us assume the case of a young lawyer representing a defendant who is being sued by a plaintiff seeking damages for injuries received in an automobile accident. He may promptly take the deposition of the plaintiff, herself,[10] which means that he may cross-examine her under oath and make her tell everything she knows about the accident, including the names and addresses of all persons who have any knowledge relating to it.[11] He may then take the depositions of all of them, questioning them, under oath, what they know about the case, and whether they know any other witnesses. In the course of this examination he may inquire about the plaintiff's documentary evidence, her doctor and hospital bills, garage repair bills, police reports, photographs and X-rays, and the names of the expert witnesses she intends to use at the trial. He may then demand the production of these documents for inspection and copying.[12] He may also require the plaintiff to submit to a physical examination by a doctor ap-

---

9. In the 1970 edition this is Rule 26(b) (1).

10. "After commencement of the action, any party may take the testimony of any person, including a party, by deposition upon oral examination." Rule 30(a).

11. Abbatemarco v. Colton, 31 N.J. Super. 181, 106 A.2d 12 (1954);

Hitchcock v. Ginsberg, 240 Iowa 678, 37 N.W.2d 302 (1949).

12. "Any party may serve on any other party a request (1) to produce and permit the party making the request, or someone acting in his behalf, to inspect and copy, any designated documents   .   .   .." Rule 34(a).

pointed by the court.[13] In this way, if he is diligent, the young lawyer should be able to prepare himself and his client for trial and walk into the courtroom with some assurance that he will not be ambushed by his adversary. Likewise, if his adversary has diligently employed the discovery procedure, he too should enjoy the same confidence.

Limitations. The scope of discovery, although very broad, is not without its limitations. The first is that the matter sought, be not privileged. This has been interpreted to mean, that the matter is not covered by one of the traditional privileges of the law of evidence growing out of a confidential relationship, as that of attorney-client, doctor-patient, and priest-penitent.[14] Evidence may be inadmissible at the trial for other reasons, i e., hearsay, but this does not protect it from discovery, because the rule specifically states that "it is not ground for objection that the information sought will be inadmissible at the trial if the information sought appears reasonably calculated to lead to the discovery of admissible evidence."[15] In addition to the traditional privileges which render material nondiscoverable the courts have recognized a privilege against discovery, where to allow it might endanger the national security or disclose military secrets.[16]

In Hickman v. Taylor [17] the Supreme Court created another small area of nondiscoverable facts. The suit was for the wrongful death of four crew members when the tug J. M. Taylor sank. In anticipation of litigation, the attorney for the owners of the tug interviewed the surviving members of the crew, and others, taking written statements from some and making memoranda of the oral statements of others. When the suit was filed the attorneys for the plaintiffs sought, by means of pretrial discovery, to obtain copies of the written statements of the crew members and copies of the memoranda of counsel regarding the oral statements and other matters. The defendants refused to comply, invoking the attorney-client privilege. The Supreme Court held there was no privilege since the requested material was obtained

---

13. "When the mental or physical condition (including the blood group) of a party . . . is in controversy, the court in which the action is pending may order the party to submit to a physical or mental examination by a physician." Rule 35(a).

14. United States v. Reynolds, 345 U.S. 1, 73 S.Ct. 528, 97 L.Ed. 727 (1953).

15. Rule 26(b) (1).

16. Machin v. Zuckert, 114 U.S.App. D.C. 335, 316 F.2d 336 (1963); Snyder v. United States, 20 F.R.D. 7 (E.D.N.Y.1956).

17. Supra n. 5.

by the lawyer from third persons and not from the client. The court held, however, that the requested material was the "work product" of the attorney and enjoyed something akin to a quasi-privilege. In other words, the matter was prima facie exempt from discovery. The court indicated that upon a showing of real necessity such material was subject to pretrial discovery. Hickman is vague in two respects: (1) exactly what is included in the "work product" of the attorney, and (2) what showing of "necessity" must be made to subject such material to the discovery process. As might be expected, courts have differed on the answers to these questions. In Alltmont v. United States [18] the court held that the work product doctrine applied to statements of witnesses secured by agents of the F.B.I. It said, "While the language of the Supreme Court was here necessarily directed to statements obtained personally by Fortenbaugh as counsel for the adverse party, since only such statements were involved in the Hickman case, we think that its rationale has a much broader sweep and applies to all statements of prospective witnesses which a party has obtained for his trial counsel's use." A similar result was reached in Snyder v. United States [19] which held that the record of the Aircraft Accident Board could not be reached, since under the Hickman doctrine the investigation need not be made by the attorney personally. Other courts have taken the position that the work product exemption should be narrowly construed and should not shield from discovery material obtained by insurance claim agents and others. [20]

The 1970 amendment to Rule 26(b) is an attempt to clear up some of the difficulties encountered in the application of the work product doctrine of the Hickman case. A new subsection to the rule, under the heading of "Trial Preparation: Materials" [21] provides that "documents and tangible things" which were prepared in anticipation of litigation or for trial, are discoverable "only upon a showing that the party seeking discovery has substantial need of the materials in the preparation of his case and that he is unable without undue hardship to obtain the substantial equivalent of the materials by other means." Whether or not the quoted language does anything more than rephrase the "good cause" doctrine as spelled out by the cases, time alone will tell. The

18. 177 F.2d 971, 976 (3d Cir. 1949).

19. Supra n. 16.

20. Southern Ry. v. Lanham, 403 F. 2d 119 (5th Cir. 1969); Burke v. United States, 32 F.R.D. 213 (E.D. N.Y.1963); Shepherd v. Castle, 20 F.R.D. 184 (W.D.Mo.1957); Beyer v. Keller, 11 A.D.2d 426, 207 N.Y. S.2d 591 (1960); Monier v. Chamberlain, 35 Ill.2d 351, 221 N.E.2d 410 (1966); Grew v. Brunner, 1 Pa. D. & C.2d 754 (Phila.C.Pl.1955).

21. Rule 26(b) (3).

amendment does, however, explicitly clarify several things which had been troublesome. It includes in the trial preparation materials, for which a showing must be made, materials prepared "by or for another party or by or for that other party's representative (including his attorney, consultant, surety, indemnitor, insurer, or agent)." This should lay to rest the old dispute as to whether material gathered by claim agents, adjustors, and lay agents is discoverable, and in so doing it narrows the scope of discovery unless a special showing of hardship is made. The amendment also undertakes to safeguard the real work product of the lawyer from discovery by the following explicit statement: "In ordering discovery of such materials when the required showing has been made, the court shall protect against disclosure of the mental impressions, conclusions, opinions, or legal theories of an attorney or other representative of a party concerning the litigation."

Prompt investigations of accidents resulting in personal injuries are usually made by claim agents, adjustors for insurance companies, or attorneys. Such investigators customarily take written statements from witnesses, including parties. They seldom furnish copies. Months or years later, when the case is approaching trial, a party or a witness may want to see a copy of the statement which he made. Is it protected from discovery as made in anticipation of litigation? The 1970 amendment to the rule says that it is not; it is a special situation where no showing of hardship or necessity is required.[22]

The 1970 amendment settled another question upon which the courts were in sharp disagreement—whether expert testimony was subject to discovery. In many situations expert testimony is required to prove or disprove a point. A common example is the medical expert to testify to the degree of permanent disability; another, the expert on land values whose testimony will be extremely important in a condemnation case. Under the law

---

22. Id. On this point, prior to the 1970 amendment, the cases were divided. Cf. Safeway Stores, Inc. v. Reynolds, 85 U.S.App.D.C. 194, 176 F.2d 476 (1949); Shupe v. Pennsylvania R. R. 19 F.R.D. 144 (W.D.Pa.1956); with, New York Cent. R. R. v. Carr, 251 F.2d 433 (4th Cir. 1957); Belback v. Wilson Freight Forwarding Co., 40 F.R.D. 16 (W.D.Pa.1966). In explaining the reasons for the exception the Advisory Committee states: "Ordinarily, a party gives a statement without insisting on a copy be- cause he does not yet have a lawyer and does not understand the legal consequences of his actions. Thus, the statement is given at a time when he functions at a disadvantage. Discrepancies between his trial testimony and earlier statement may result from lapse of memory or ordinary inaccuracy; a written statement produced for the first time at trial may give such discrepancies a prominence which they do not deserve." Moore, supra n. 8, R. 26.01[18], pp. 26–49.

of evidence an expert may testify as to his opinion on a hypothetical set of facts; there is no requirement that he have personal knowledge of the facts. Where such opinion evidence is important each side in a lawsuit will employ its own experts. Can one party compel discovery of the opinions of the other side's experts and of the facts upon which the opinions are based?[23] The 1970 amendment of the rule added a subsection which deals separately with experts whom the party expects to call as trial witnesses and those he has retained but does not expect to call.[24] As to the former, the amendment permits discovery of the subject matter on which the expert is expected to testify. As to the latter, discovery is permitted only upon a showing of exceptional circumstances "under which it is impracticable for the party seeking discovery to obtain facts or opinions on the same subject by other means."

Finally, it should be said that the basic limitation on discovery is that the material sought must be "relevant to the subject matter involved in the pending action."[25] Some courts construe relevancy narrowly as encompassing only those matters which would be admissible at the trial,[26] but most courts construe it broadly.[27] Indeed, the rule itself specifies that the material

---

23. In United States v. 364.82 Acres, 38 F.R.D. 411 (N.D.Cal.1965) the court analyzes the cases under three headings: (1) those which refuse to allow any discovery whatever, (2) those which allow discovery of the facts upon which the expert bases his opinion, but not the opinion, and (3) those which allow discovery of both. See the following cases permitting discovery: Franks v. National Dairy Prods. Corp., 41 F.R.D. 234 (W.D.Tex. 1966); United States v. 23.76 Acres, 32 F.R.D. 593 (D.Md.1963); United States v. 50.34 Acres, 13 F.R.D. 19 (E.D.N.Y.1952). In Seven-Up Bottling Co. v. United States, 39 F.R. D. 1, 2 (D.Colo.1966) the court refused to follow the cases denying discovery, saying: "It would, though, appear that the underlying factor which causes the courts to treat expert testimony somewhat differently from testimony of other witnesses is that the party has an investment in the witness. Somehow it is believed that he has bought and paid for the witness and that the other party should not share in his property. We cannot accept this 'oath helper' ap-

proach to discovery." In Knighton v. Villian & Fassio e Compagnia, 39 F.R.D. 11, 13–14 (D.Md.1965) the court allowed discovery of the names of the opponent's experts but said "it is not contemplated that a party will be allowed, by deposition or otherwise, to conduct a preliminary cross-examination of his opponent's experts for the purpose of developing material to be used for impeachment nor to obtain the opinion of his opponent's expert on other facts than those on which he shaped his opinion." On the general question of the discoverability of impeaching evidence see Boldt v. Sanders, supra n. 5; Burton v. Weyerhaeuser Timber Co., supra n. 5.

24. Rule 26(b) (4).

25. Rule 26(b) (1).

26. See e. g., Kelly v. Nationwide Mut. Ins. Co., supra n. 2.

27. See e. g., Pacific Tel. & Tel. Co. v. Superior Court, 2 Cal.3d 161, 84 Cal.Rptr. 718, 465 P.2d 854 (1970).

sought need not be admissible at the trial if it appears reasonably calculated to lead to the discovery of admissible evidence.[28] Most of the litigation involving the meaning of relevancy in this connection dealt with the problem of whether the plaintiff, in a personal injury case, could discover whether or not the defendant was covered by liability insurance and if so the name of the company and the policy limits. Obviously, a plaintiff would desire to have this information in order to determine the settlement value of the case. Defendants frequently refuse to disclose such information voluntarily and resist attempts to obtain it by discovery on the ground it is not relevant because the existence or non-existence of liability insurance is not admissible in evidence, and it is difficult to see how knowledge of the same could lead to the discovery of admissible evidence. The cases on the point are sharply divided.[29] The 1970 amendment added a subsection to the rule resolving the issue in favor of discoverability.[30] In explaining the amendment the Advisory Committee said: "The amendment is limited to insurance coverage, which should be distinguished from any other facts concerning defendant's financial status (1) because insurance is an asset created specifically to satisfy the claim; (2) because the insurance company ordinarily controls the litigation; (3) because information about coverage is available only from defendant or his insurer; and (4) because disclosure does not involve a significant invasion of privacy." [31]

Good cause. Prior to the amendment of the rules in 1970, pretrial discovery was conditioned upon a showing of "good cause" in two situations: (1) where, under Rule 34, a party moved for the production, inspection, or copying of documents, and (2) where, under Rule 35, a party moved for a physical or mental examination of the other party. The courts were not in agreement as to the meaning of "good cause." One line of authority equated it with relevance;[32] another held that more than relevance was

---

28. Rule 26(b) (1).

29. Cases permitting discovery: Cook v. Welty, 253 F.Supp. 875 (D.D.C.1966); Landkammer v. O'Laughlin, 45 F.R.D. 240 (S.D. Iowa 1968); Johanek v. Aberle, 27 F.R.D. 272 (D.Mont.1961). Cases denying discovery: Clauss v. Danker, 264 F.Supp. 246 (S.D.N.Y. 1967); Bisserier v. Manning, 207 F. Supp. 476 (D.N.J.1962); Cooper v. Stender, 30 F.R.D. 389 (E.D.Tenn. 1962).

30. Rule 26(b) (2). The new rule was attacked on constitutional grounds (due process, equal protection, and unlawful search and seizure) but was upheld in Helms v. Richmond-Petersburg Turnpike Authority, 52 F.R.D. 530 (E.D.Va. 1971).

31. Moore, supra n. 8, R. 26.01[18], at 26–44.

32. Houdry Process Corp. v. Commonwealth Oil Ref. Co., 24 F.R.D. 58 (S.D.N.Y.1959); Franks v. National Dairy Prods. Corp., supra n. 23.

required,[33] but perhaps less than the showing needed to overcome the work product exception of the Hickman case.[34] Whether or not good cause existed in any concrete situation depended upon the facts of the particular case.[35] The 1970 amendment eliminated the good cause requirement under Rule 34 but retained it in regard to Rule 35. The effect of the amendment is to widen the scope of discovery in regard to documentary and real evidence. Where the physical or mental condition of a party is in controversy and an examination is requested, a showing of good cause is still required. Our best clue as to what it means in this connection is found in the case of Schlagenhauf v. Holder,[36] in which the Supreme Court said:

> Obviously, what may be good cause for one type of examination may not be so for another. The ability of the movant to obtain the desired information by other means is also relevant.

> Rule 35, therefore, requires discriminating application by the trial judge, who must decide, as an initial matter in every case, whether the party requesting a mental or physical examination or examinations has ade-

33. Guilford Nat'l Bank v. Southern Ry., 297 F.2d 921 (4th Cir. 1962); Martin v. Capital Transit Co., 83 U.S.App.D.C. 239, 170 F.2d 811 (1948).

34. Southern Ry. v. Lanham, supra n. 20.

35. United States v. Procter & Gamble Co., supra n. 5 (civil antitrust suit in which defendants sought the transcript of proceedings before the grand jury, which had failed to indict; held there was no sufficient showing to overcome the policy of secrecy of grand jury proceedings); Hanley v. James McHugh Constr. Co., 419 F.2d 955 (7th Cir. 1969) (denying discovery on the ground the movant should not have the fruits of his opponent's investigations when his own investigations could have produced the statements); United Air Lines, Inc. v. United States, 186 F.Supp. 824 (D.Del.1960) (court grants discovery of record of investigation of airplane crash on ground the circumstances are exceptional, notwithstanding the general rule that production of the statements of

witnesses are not discoverable where the witnesses are themselves available); Currie v. Moore-McCormack Lines, Inc., 23 F.R.D. 660 (D.Mass.1959) (some routine situations carry their own showing of good cause, as where a plaintiff is suing his employer, he is entitled to see the payroll or work records); Blanchet v. Colonial Trust Co., 23 F.R.D. 118 (D.Del.1958) (discovery of secretly made tape recordings of conversations held proper since they were needed for basis of cross-examination or impeachment); United States v. 50.34 Acres, supra n. 23 (appraisal reports of experts in land condemnation case held discoverable under the special circumstances of the case); Naylor v. Isthmian S. S. Co., 10 F.R.D. 128 (S.D.N.Y.1950) (Jones Act case; discovery of statements of crew members of ship permitted even though good cause not shown in view of the "financial straits" of the plaintiff).

36. 379 U.S. 104, 118–19, 85 S.Ct. 234, 243, 13 L.Ed.2d 152, 164 (1964).

quately demonstrated the existence of the Rule's requirements of "in controversy" and "good cause," which requirements, as the Court of Appeals in this case itself recognized, are necessarily related   .   .   . .

Of course, there are situations where the pleadings alone are sufficient to meet these requirements. A plaintiff in a negligence action who asserts mental or physical injury   .   .   .   places that mental or physical injury clearly in controversy and provides the defendant with good cause for an examination to determine the existence and extent of such asserted injury .   .   . .

SECTION 3.   THE TOOLS OF DISCOVERY

The federal rules offer a complete set of tools for the discovery of facts. They are: (1) depositions,[37] (2) interrogatories to the parties,[38] (3) production of documents,[39] (4) physical and mental examination,[40] (5) requests for admissions.[41] A party seeking discovery is not required to elect which tool he will use. Each is designed for a different purpose, and a party may use the tool or tools which fit his particular situation.[42]

Depositions. A deposition is the testimony of a witness who is examined out of court before an official who is empowered to administer an oath,[43] by a party who has given notice to all other parties so that they can be present to cross-examine the deponent. The taking of the testimony of the witness is by questions and answers in much the same way a witness testifies in open court, except that the deposition is being taken outside of a courtroom prior to the trial. Objections to questions may be made but cannot be ruled upon at the time because the person before whom the deposition is being taken is not a judge, but usually a notary public. Such objections will be noted in the stenographic record

37. Rules 30 and 31.

38. Rule 33.

39. Rule 34.

40. Rule 35.

41. Rule 36.

42. Woods, Housing Expediter v. Robb, 171 F.2d 539 (5th Cir. 1948).

43. Rule 28(a) defines such person as "an officer authorized to administer oaths by the laws of the United States or of the place where the examination is held, or before a person appointed by the court in which the action is pending." Rule 28(b) defines the persons before whom depositions may be taken in foreign countries. See e. g., Electric Reduction of Canada v. Crane, 239 Miss. 18, 120 So.2d 765 (1960); Solliday v. District Court, 135 Colo. 489, 313 P.2d 1000 (1957).

which is being made of the deposition and can later be ruled upon by the court.[44] Taking of testimony by depositions was the usual method in the courts of equity, and in this country depositions have long been available as a means of taking testimony of witnesses who will be unable to appear at the trial, for use as evidence at the trial. The innovation of the federal rules is that such depositions may also be taken for discovery purposes.[45] The rules provide that "after commencement of the action, any party may take the testimony of any person, including a party, by deposition upon oral examination." [46] The mechanics for taking the deposition are simple. The party desiring to take the deposition is merely required to give written notice to all other parties, of the time and place for taking the deposition and the names of the witnesses to be examined.[47] A subpoena may be obtained to compel the attendance of a witness if necessary, and it may be a subpoena duces tecum requiring the witness to bring with him designated documents.[48] In case the deponent is a party, no subpoena is necessary,[49] and he may be required to bring designated documents pursuant to another rule.[50] The rules provide that the parties can dispense with the formalities of notice by written stipulation, that the deposition be taken before any person, at any time or place agreed upon.[51] The 1970 amendment to the rules added a new provision that a party may name a corporation, partnership, association, or governmental agency as the deponent and designate the matters upon which he requests examination, and the organization shall then name one or more of its officers,

---

44. Rules 30(c); 32(b).

45. Rule 32 governs the use of depositions at the trial. Before the 1970 amendment it was covered by Rule 26(d). In Hertz v. Graham, 292 F.2d 443 (2d Cir. 1961), the court holds that depositions taken in one case may be used in another against a person who was a party in the first suit and who had an opportunity for cross-examination. In Richmond v. Brooks, 227 F.2d 490 (2d Cir. 1955) depositions taken in California were admitted in evidence in a suit in a federal court in New York.

46. Rule 30(a). In Application of the Royal Bank of Canada, 33 F. R.D. 296 (S.D.N.Y.1963) the court held that depositions could not be taken until after summons had been served in the case since mere filing of the complaint did not constitute the "commencement of the action." Compare Rule 3.

47. Rule 30(b).

48. Rules 30(b); 45(b).

49. Collins v. Wayland, 139 F.2d 677 (9th Cir. 1944).

50. Rule 30(b) (5). This provision was added by the 1970 amendment. The reason for the amendment was that since the requirement of good cause has been removed from Rule 34 (production of documents) a party should be required to bring them at the time of the taking of his deposition rather than requiring a court order under Rule 34. See notes of the Advisory Committee, Moore, supra n. 8, R 30.01[19] at 30–26.

51. Rule 29.

directors, managing agents, or other persons to appear and testify.[52] This greatly relieved the burden upon the seeker of information to find out in advance the persons from whom the information could be obtained.

The foregoing discussion related to depositions taken on oral examinations. Such depositions are easily the most effective because an answer to a question may disclose information or suggest a clue to a new line of inquiry which in turn may open up other areas. There are, however, situations in which the taking of oral depositions will be burdensome and expensive, especially where the witness to be examined lives at a great distance from the forum.[53] This situation is taken care of by another rule which authorizes depositions on written questions.[54] Counsel seeking to take such a deposition prepares a set of questions to be asked the witness, which are served upon opposite parties, who may then prepare cross-questions. A copy of all questions is delivered to the officer designated to take the deposition who then proceeds to take the testimony of the witness by recording his responses to the questions. Taking the deposition in this manner eliminates the necessity of counsel being present.

Interrogatories to parties. There is a much simpler though less thorough device for obtaining information than the deposition. It consists merely of propounding written interrogatories to a party, which must be answered in writing under oath. Rule 33, as amended, permits any party to serve such interrogatories upon any other party.[55] The scope of discovery under this device

---

52. Rule 30(b) (6).

53. Such a case was River Plate Corp. v. Forestal Land, Timber & Ry. Co., 185 F.Supp. 832 (S.D.N.Y. 1960), an antitrust case in which plaintiff sought to take depositions in Argentina and London; because of the complexity of the case, the court ordered the depositions to be taken on oral examination but required the plaintiff to advance travel expenses of counsel to attend the examination, which would be taxed as costs in the event the plaintiff won. In Perry v. Edwards, 16 F.R.D. 131 (W.D.Mo. 1954), where the suit was pending in a Missouri federal court but the defendant lived in Michigan, the court ordered the defendant's deposition taken either in Pontiac, Michigan, or in Kansas City, Missouri, on a shared expense basis.

In Collins v. Wayland, supra n. 49, Oregon plaintiff sued Arizona defendants in an Arizona federal court, and on defendant's motion the court ordered defendant's deposition to be taken in Arizona.

In Carson v. Burlington Northern, Inc., 52 F.R.D. 492 (D.Neb. 1971) the court ordered a deposition taken by video tape, perhaps heralding the use of more scientific methods in court proceedings.

54. Rule 31.

55. Prior to the 1970 amendment the rule permitted service of interrogatories on "adverse" parties. This was construed narrowly as requiring an adverse interest to be shown by the pleadings, e. g., Biddle v. Hutchinson, 24 F.R.D. 256 (M.D.Pa.1959) (codefendants). In Schlagenhauf v. Holder, 379 U.S.

is as broad as it is under the deposition procedure, but the device *-eld.* is restricted to the parties to the action, and cannot be employed in the case of a witness who is not a party.[56] Interrogatories are very useful in obtaining the names and addresses of persons having knowledge of pertinent facts,[57] in obtaining descriptions of documentary evidence in the possession of an adverse party,[58] and in clarifying the pleadings.[59] Answers to interrogatories must be returned within 30 days. Provision is made by the rule for objections to specific interrogatories, plus the reasons for the objections. The party seeking the information may then apply to the court for a ruling on the objections and request an order compelling answers. The 1970 amendments improved the rule by (1) simplifying the mechanics of its operation,[60] (2) resolving a conflict in the cases as to whether interrogatories were confined to matters of "fact" or could also elicit opinions and legal conclu-

104, 85 S.Ct. 234, 13 L.Ed.2d 152 (1964) the Supreme Court gave a more liberal interpretation to "opposing" party under Rule 35. The Advisory Committee states, "Eliminating the requirement of 'adverse' parties from Rule 33 brings it into line with all other discovery rules." Moore, supra n. 8, R 33.01 [6], p. 33–12.

56. Answers to interrogatories may be introduced in evidence at the trial and thus save the expense of subpoenaing witnesses: Drum v. Town of Tonawanda, 13 F.R.D. 317 (W.D.N.Y.1952). In American Airlines v. Ulen, 87 U.S.App.D.C. 307, 186 F.2d 529 (1949) the court held that answers to 55 interrogatories clearly established negligence, therefore the plaintiff was entitled to a partial summary judgment on the question of liability.

57. Hitchcock v. Ginsberg, supra n. 11.

58. In Smith v. Central Linen Serv. Co., 39 F.R.D. 15 (D.Md.1966) the court said that Rule 33 may not be used as the vehicle to obtain copies of documents since that would circumvent the good cause requirement of Rule 34. The requirement of good cause was removed from Rule 34 by the 1970 amendment, but the proper procedure would still be to use Rule 33 to determine the existence of doc-

umentary evidence, and then to move for its production under Rule 34.

59. Bynum v. United States, 36 F.R. D. 14 (E.D.La.1964) holds that a plaintiff may be compelled to answer, under Rule 33, whether he is relying on some specific act of negligence in addition to the res ipsa loquitur doctrine. Hartsfield v. Gulf Oil Corp., 29 F.R.D. 163 (E.D.Pa.1962) held that interrogatories under Rule 33 are appropriate for obtaining a specification of the facts upon which the claim of negligence is founded.

60. The time for responses was increased from 15 to 30 days; answers and objections may be served together, which lessens the opportunity for dilatory tactics; and the burden is on the interrogating party to move the court for an order compelling answers. The Advisory Committee felt the changes would encourage consultation between counsel and minimize the necessity for court intervention in the operation of the rule. Moore, supra n. 8, R 33.01[6] p. 33–10.

Motions to compel answers, or for more complete answers are made under Rule 37(a), which contains no time limits as to when the motion should be made. See Riley v. United Air Lines, 32 F.R.D. 230 (S.D.N.Y.1962).

sions,[61] (3) giving a party the option of producing for inspection his business records which contained the data for answering a particular question,[62] and (4) resolving the conflict in the cases as to the duty of a party to update or supplement his answers.[63]

Production of documents and things. Discovery of documents, tangible things, and other real evidence is covered by Rule 34. Prior to the 1970 amendment discovery of such material was only by court order upon a showing of good cause. The 1970 amendment eliminated the requirement of good cause and it redrafted

61. For a collection of many of the conflicting authorities see Moore, supra n. 8, R 33.17, p. 33–72 et seq.; 2A Barron & Holtzoff, Federal Practice and Procedure (Wright ed. 1961) § 768; see e. g., Leumi Fin. Corp. v. Hartford Accident & Indem. Co., 295 F.Supp. 539 (S.D.N.Y.1969); Zinsky v. New York Cent. R. R., 36 F.R.D. 680 (N.D.Ohio 1964). The 1970 addition to Rule 33(b) reads: "An interrogatory otherwise proper is not necessarily objectionable merely because an answer to the interrogatory involves an opinion or contention that relates to fact or the application of law to fact, but the court may order that such an interrogatory need not be answered until after designated discovery has been completed or until a pretrial conference or other later time."

62. Sometimes answers to interrogatories require a party to engage in burdensome and expensive research into its own business records. The 1970 amendment added a new provision addressed to this situation which provides that "it is a sufficient answer to such interrogatory to specify the records from which the answer may be derived or ascertained and to afford the party serving the interrogatory reasonable opportunity to examine, audit or inspect such records and to make copies, compilations, abstracts or summaries." Rule 33(c). See Triangle Mfg. Co. v. Paramount Bag Mfg. Co., 35 F.R.D. 540 (E.D.N.Y.1964) where, even prior to the amendment, the court entered a Rule 34 order for inspection and copying even though the party had moved under Rule 33. There are other situations in which a court will issue a protective order to prevent abuse of the rule. See, e. g., Frost v. Williams, 46 F.R.D. 484 (D.Md. 1969).

63. It frequently happens that an answer to an interrogatory may be true when made but untrue or inadequate at a later date when the party comes into possession of additional information. The cases were divided upon the duty of a party to up-date his answers. Holding there was such a duty: Abbatemarco v. Colton, supra n. 11; Taggart v. Vermont Transp. Co., 32 F.R.D. 587 (E.D.Pa.1963). Holding there was no such duty: Diversified Prods. Corp. v. Sports Center Co., 42 F.R.D. 3 (D.Md. 1967); Aulgur v. Zylich, 390 S.W. 2d 553 (K.C.Mo.Ct.App.1965). The 1970 amendment adds a subsection to Rule 26 (the general rule relating to all types of discovery) which states that there is no such continuing burden to supplement answers except as follows: (1) regarding the names and addresses of persons having knowledge of the facts, (2) when he obtains information on the basis of which he knows the answer was incorrect when made or "he knows that the response though correct when made is no longer true and the circumstances are such that a failure to amend the response is in substance a knowing concealment," and (3) when the duty to supplement is imposed by order of court, or agreement of the parties. Rule 26(e).

the machinery of the rule so that it operated extrajudicially, with- *w/o order*
out the necessity of obtaining a court order. The present rule
merely requires the party seeking discovery to serve on any other
party a request to produce such materials for inspection and copying. The request must set forth the items to be inspected "either
by individual item or by category, and describe each item with
reasonable particularity." [64] The documents or things to be inspected must be "in the possession, custody or control of the party
upon whom the request is served." [65] The 1970 amendment
greatly broadened the type of material subject to discovery under
the rule,[66] describing it as follows: "any designated documents
(including writings, drawings, graphs, charts, photographs,
phono-records, and other data compilations from which information can be obtained, translated, if necessary, by the respondent
through detection devices into reasonably usable form)." [67] The
new rule thus makes electronically stored data subject to the discovery process. The rule also permits testing and sampling of
any tangible things, and permits "entry upon designated land or
other property . . . for the purpose of inspection and meas-
uring, surveying, photographing, testing, or sampling the property or any designated object or operation thereon." The scope
of the discovery permissible under the rule is governed by Rule
26(b).[68] If the respondent objects to any item, he shall give the

64. Fed.Rules Civ.Proc. 34(b). The quoted language was added in the 1970 amendment to make it clear that reasonable designation by category was sufficient. Cases antedating the amendment had generally so held; see Monier v. Chamberlain, supra n. 20; Houdry Process Corp. v. Commonwealth Oil Ref. Co., supra n. 32.

65. Fed.Rules Civ.Proc. 34(a). The Supreme Court was faced with an interesting case raising the question of what constitutes "control" in Société Internationale v. Rogers, 357 U.S. 197, 78 S.Ct. 1087, 2 L.Ed. 2d 1255 (1958), a suit by a Swiss holding company to recover $100,-000,000 assets seized by the United States government under the Trading with the Enemy Act. The government moved, under Rule 34, for an inspection and copying of a large number of records of a Swiss banking company, an affiliate of the plaintiff. Plaintiff resisted discovery on the ground it did not control the documents because if

it produced them it would be violating the Swiss criminal law. The court held that fear of criminal prosecution would not prevent a finding that the plaintiff had "control" of the documents.

66. Prior to the 1970 amendment, Rule 34 described the material as "any designated documents, papers, books, accounts, letters, photographs, objects, or tangible things."

67. The broader language of the amended rule ("any designated documents") omits specific mention of "papers, books, accounts, letters" which were included in the language of the old rule.

68. Material obtained under Rule 34 or equivalent state procedure, if otherwise admissible, may be introduced into evidence at the trial, but admissibility at the trial is not a prerequisite to discovery. Culligan, Inc. v. Rheaume, 268 Wis. 298, 67 N.W.2d 279 (1954); Beyer v. Keller, supra n. 20, disapproving

reasons for the objection and the matter will be decided by the court.

Physical and mental examinations. When a plaintiff sues for damages for personal injuries allegedly caused by the negligence of the defendant, the latter will, understandably, wish to know: the nature and extent of the injuries, if any; whether or not they will result in permanent disability; and whether they are attributable, in whole or in part, to the alleged accident. He needs this information to determine the settlement value of the case, and also, to prepare to cross-examine the plaintiff's expert witnesses and determine what experts he will call. Rule 35 provides the means by which such information may be obtained. It is, however, not limited to personal injury actions but provides that when the mental or physical condition of a party is in issue, the court, upon motion and for good cause, may order said party to submit to a physical or mental examination by a physician.[69] The person examined is, upon request, entitled to receive a copy of the written report of the examining physician.[70] The rule provides that, by requesting and receiving a copy of the examining physician's report the party examined must, upon request, furnish copies of written reports made by his physicians, and it provides further that he waives any privilege regarding the testimony of every other person who has or thereafter may examine him in respect of the same mental or physical condition. These provisions are calculated to insure the fullest possible pretrial disclosure.[71]

the earlier case of Urbina v. Mc-Lain, 4 A.D.2d 589, 168 N.Y.S.2d 175 (1957).

69. The 1970 amendments to Rule 35 expressly include blood grouping tests within the examination authorized, removing any doubt that the rule may be used in a paternity case. See Beach v. Beach, 72 U.S.App.D.C. 318, 114 F.2d 479 (1940). The amendment also explicitly states that the rule is applicable to "a person in the custody or under the legal control of a party" which takes care of the situation where a parent or guardian is suing to recover for injuries to a minor.

70. The 1970 amendment goes beyond the old rule regarding the right of the party examined to request and receive a copy of the written report of the examining physician, adding "including results of all tests made," which would include such things as X-rays and electrocardiograms.

71. Although the rule provides that the examination may be made upon application and court order, in practice most such examinations are made pursuant to agreement of the parties. In such cases some question has arisen as to whether the provisions of the rule requiring mutual disclosure of reports apply. See Sher v. DeHaven, 91 U.S.App.D.C. 257, 199 F.2d 777 (1952). The 1970 amendment took care of this situation by adding a subsection that the rule "applies to examinations made by agreement of the parties, unless the agreement expressly provides otherwise." Fed.Rules Civ.Proc. 35(b) (3).

The validity of Rule 35 was challenged in the case of Sibbach v. Wilson & Co.,[72] in which the plaintiff claimed the rule invaded the plaintiff's privacy, abridged her substantive rights and thus was beyond the authority granted by Congress to promulgate rules of practice and procedure.[73] In a 5–4 decision the Supreme Court upheld the validity of the rule. In his dissenting opinion, Mr. Justice Frankfurter said, "I deem a requirement as to the invasion of the person to stand on a very different footing from questions pertaining to the discovery of documents, pre-trial procedure and other devices for the expeditious, economic and fair conduct of litigation." [74]

Rule 35 refers to the mental or physical condition of a "party", not merely a plaintiff. In Schlagenhauf v. Holder [75] the Supreme Court held the rule could be applied to a defendant. In that case the plaintiff sued for injuries she had received when the Greyhound bus in which she was riding, ran into the rear end of a tractor-trailer. She sued Greyhound, the bus driver, and the owners of the tractor-trailer. The latter claimed the accident was due solely to the negligence of the bus driver and moved for a physical and mental examination of him on the ground such conditions were "in controversy." In upholding the action of the trial court in ordering the examinations, the court noted the difference between the case of a plaintiff, who puts her physical condition in issue when she sues for damages, and that of a defendant, whose condition is sought to be placed in issue by others. Nevertheless, the court held that, upon a proper showing, the physical or mental examination of a defendant could be ordered.[76] In a dissenting opinion Mr. Justice Douglas said:

> When the defendant's doctors examine plaintiff, they are normally interested only in answering a single question: did plaintiff in fact sustain the specific injuries claimed? But plaintiff's doctors will naturally be inclined to go on a fishing expedition in search of *anything* which will tend to prove that the defendant was unfit to perform the acts which resulted in plaintiff's injury

---

72. 312 U.S. 1, 61 S.Ct. 422, 85 L. Ed. 479 (1941).

73. The Act of Congress which authorized the Supreme Court to promulgate the Rules of Civil Procedure contained the following: "Such rules shall not abridge, enlarge, or modify any substantive right . . .." 28 U.S.C.A. § 2072.

74. 312 U.S. at 18, 61 S.Ct. at 428, 85 L.Ed. at 487.

75. Supra n. 55.

76. The 1970 amendment made no change regarding the necessity of a showing of good cause for an order for examination under the rule. Consequently, the Schlagenhauf case is still good law on what constitutes good cause under the rule.

. . . .. Neither the Court nor Congress up to today has determined that any person whose physical or mental condition is brought into question during some lawsuit must surrender his right to keep his person inviolate.[77]

Requests for admissions. Rule 36 is not really a discovery tool but a device to force admissions in order to narrow the issues and to eliminate the necessity of proof at the trial. Under it a party may serve any other party with a written request to admit specified facts or the genuineness of specified documents. The party served with such a request has thirty days within which to admit or deny the requests or to give his objections and reasons for not complying. If he does nothing, the matters will be deemed admitted for the purposes of the suit. The rule is especially valuable in forcing formal admissions of facts about which there can be no question, frequently laying the foundation for a motion for summary judgment.[78] Under the older versions of the rule, there were differences of judicial opinion as to whether the rule could be used to request admissions of basic issues, or matters of opinion, or of legal conclusions. The 1970 amendments to the rule have resolved most of these questions.[79]

---

77. Supra n. 55 at 125–26, 85 S.Ct. at 246–47, 13 L.Ed.2d at 167–68. In the quotation Mr. Justice Douglas refers to "plaintiff's doctors" and "defendant's doctors." Where an order is made for an examination under the rule, the court appoints the doctors, but as a practical matter the court will usually appoint the doctors suggested by the moving party. In Schlagenhauf the court was requested to appoint a specialist in each of the following fields: (1) internal medicine, (2) opthalmology, (3) neurology, and (4) psychiatry, and for the purpose of offering a choice to the District Court two specialists in three fields and three in the other were suggested. The court appointed all nine. In reversing and remanding for further proceedings the Supreme Court indicated the District Court had been over-generous in ordering examinations. It stated: "This record cannot support even the corrected order which required one examination in each of the four specialties . . . .. Nothing in the pleadings or affidavit would afford a basis for a belief that Schla-

genhauf was suffering from a mental or neurological illness warranting wide-ranging psychiatric or neurological examinations. Nor is there anything stated justifying the broad internal medicine examination." 379 U.S. at 120–21, 85 S.Ct. at 244, 13 L.Ed.2d at 165.

78. Kasar v. Miller Printing Mach. Co., 36 F.R.D. 200 (W.D.Pa.1964); McSparran v. Hanigan, 225 F.Supp. 628 (E.D.Pa.1963); Water Hammer Arrester Corp. v. Tower, 7 F.R.D. 620 (E.D.Wis.1947) (reversed for application of inappropriate sanction: 171 F.2d 877 (7th Cir. 1949); DeRyder v. Metropolitan Life Ins. Co., 206 Va. 602, 145 S.E.2d 177 (1965); Mueller v. Shacklett, 156 Neb. 881, 58 N.W.2d 344 (1953).

79. Prior to the 1970 amendment, the rule provided that the request for admissions could be "of the genuineness of any relevant documents described in and exhibited with the request or of the truth of any relevant matters of fact set forth in the request." The 1970 amendment changed the language

SECTION 4.   SANCTIONS

The discovery rules, in their present form, are based on the assumption that voluntary compliance upon the part of the parties is to be expected. It is only in relation to a physical or mental examination that a court order is required, and this is usually waived by the parties. Nevertheless, if discovery is to be effective, compulsion must be available in case of necessity. It is to be found in Rule 37, which contains a full battery of sanctions.[80] In the event that a party or witness refuses to appear for a deposition, or refuses to answer proper questions, or refuses to answer interrogatories, or to permit inspection of documents, the party seeking discovery may apply to the court for an order compelling compliance. In making the order the court may also make provisions for the protection of the parties to guard against the disclosure of privileged material or to prevent harassment.[81] The court may also order the payment of reasonable expenses, includ-

to read: "of the truth of any matters within the scope of Rule 26(b) set forth in the request that relate to statements or opinions of fact or of the application of law to fact, including the genuineness of any documents described in the request." For the significance of the change see the Advisory Committee's notes in Moore, supra n. 8, R. 36.01 [7], pp. 36–9 et seq. For a general discussion of Rule 36 see Finman, The Request for Admissions in Federal Court Procedure, 71 Yale L.J. 371 (1962).

80. See generally Rosenberg, Sanctions to Effectuate Pretrial Discovery, 58 Colum.L.Rev. 480 (1958).

81. Rule 37(a) (2) provides, in part, "If the court denies the motion in whole or in part, it may make such protective order as it would have been empowered to make on a motion made pursuant to Rule 26(c)." The latter rule provides that any party or person from whom discovery is sought may apply to the court for a protective order; the rule further provides that the court may make "any order which justice requires" and lists eight types of protective orders. In Frost v. Williams, supra n. 62, the court held that the service of 200 interroga-

tories on the defendant in a case arising out of an ordinary rear-end collision was oppressive and warranted the issuance of a protective order. In Triangle Mfg. Co. v. Paramount Bag Mfg. Co., supra n. 62, a patent infringement suit, where inspection of documents and records was ordered, the court appointed a disinterested third person to do the examining, in order to protect the plaintiff against revelation of trade secrets. In River Plate Corp. v. Forestal Land, Timber & Ry. Co., supra n. 53, a private antitrust suit, in ordering depositions to be taken on oral examination in Argentina and London, the court made protective orders regarding the manner of taking, the scope, and the allocation of the expenses involved. In Electric Reduction of Canada v. Crane, supra n. 43, where an application was made to cite a witness for contempt for refusing to answer certain questions in a deposition, the court said a showing would first have to be made that the information called for was pertinent to the issues in the case. In Perry v. Edwards, supra n. 53, the court fixed the place of the taking of an oral deposition in either Kansas City or Pontiac on a shared expense basis.

ing attorney fees, when it finds that the refusal to make discovery was unjustified.[82] Such a provision is a strong deterrent to unreasonable resistance to discovery. The rule also provides an antidote to unreasonable applications to the court for relief where discovery was unjustified, by providing that if the motion is denied, the court may make an order for the payment of expenses unless "the making of the motion was substantially justified or that other circumstances make an award of expenses unjust." [83]

Occasionally a party or a witness will fail to comply or refuse to comply with a court order compelling discovery.[84] In such case the rule gives the court a wide discretion in the selection of sanctions to enforce its order. It may cite the party or witness for contempt of court,[85] enter an order that the facts regarding which discovery was sought will be deemed established for the purpose of the trial,[86] enter an order precluding the disobedient party from supporting or opposing designated claims or defenses, or precluding him from introducing designated matters in evidence,[87] it may strike pleadings or portions thereof,[88] enter a judgment dismissing the action,[89] or a judgment by default,[90] and it may order the payment of costs and expenses.[91]

---

82. Rule 37(a) (4).

83. Id.

84. Under the pre-1970 version of the rule some of the sanctions were for "failure" to comply, and others were for "refusal" to comply, which caused some confusion in the cases. In Société Internationale v. Rogers, supra n. 65, the Supreme Court held that, as used in the rule the two terms were synonomous. The 1970 amendment drops "refusal" and merely uses "failure." There was also some question whether an incomplete answer or an evasive answer was a "refusal" or "failure" within the rule. See Riley v. United Air Lines, supra n. 60. To remedy this the 1970 amendment added: "Evasive or Incomplete Answer. For purposes of this subdivision an evasive or incomplete answer is to be treated as a failure to answer." Rule 37(a) (3).

85. Rule 37(b) (1); 37(b) (2) (D). The sanction of contempt is not available for failure to comply with

an order for a physical or mental examination under Rule 35. Sibbach v. Wilson & Co., supra n. 72.

86. Rule 37(b) (2) (A).

87. Rule 37(b) (2) (B). In Taggart v. Vermont Transp. Co., supra n. 63, the court excluded the testimony of an expert and of an eye witness. In Aulgur v. Zylich, supra n. 63, the court held it was within the discretion of the trial court to admit or reject the evidence of witnesses whose names had not been disclosed. In Abbatemarco v. Colton, supra n. 11, the court held the trial court was clearly within bounds when it refused to admit such evidence.

88. Rule 37(b) (2) (C).

89. Welsh v. Automatic Poultry Feeder Co., 439 F.2d 95 (8th Cir. 1971). This was a case with a long history of the plaintiff's wilful non-

90. See note 90 on page 141.

91. See note 91 on page 141.

SECTION 5. APPELLATE REVIEW

A party who seeks discovery of facts may need them desperately in order to prepare and prove his case. If objections to his attempts to gain the information are erroneously sustained, his cause may be lost. On the other hand a party who resists discovery because the facts sought are privileged or would involve trade secrets, may be ruined if he is erroneously forced to disclose them. May one, in such a situation, get an immediate appeal from what he considers to be an erroneous order? The general rule is that he may not, because discovery orders are interlocutory and hence nonappealable.[92] This is in accord with the rule that, with few exceptions, no appeal lies except from a final judgment.[93] Where a party resists discovery as a result of which

compliance with court orders so the trial court finally imposed the sanction of dismissal with prejudice. The Court of Appeals admitted the sanction was a drastic one but held that, on the record, there was no abuse of discretion, and affirmed.

90. In Scherrer v. Plaza Marina Commercial Corp., 16 Cal.App.3d 520, ——, 94 Cal.Rptr. 85, 87 (1971), the court said: "The ultimate sanction of default against a litigant who wilfully fails to appear for the taking of his deposition is a drastic penalty which should be sparingly used; ordinarily, it should be used only when lesser sanctions have failed." In that case, however, the court upheld the imposition of the sanction where the corporation's president and counsel not only failed to appear at two deposition hearings, and a pretrial conference, but also failed to appear at a hearing on a motion to strike the answer to a cross-complaint. See also Diaz v. Southern Drilling Corp., 427 F.2d 1118 (5th Cir. 1970); Haney v. Woodward & Lothrop, Inc., 330 F.2d 940 (4th Cir. 1964); Unger v. Los Angeles Transit Lines, 180 Cal.App.2d 172, 4 Cal.Rptr. 370 (1960).

In Transworld Airlines, Inc. v. Hughes, 449 F.2d 51 (2d Cir. 1971) the court upheld a default judgment of $145,448,141.07 against Howard Hughes as a sanction for his continued refusal to appear for a deposition. This probably set an all-time record. The only modification of the judgment by the appellate court was to add that it should carry interest of $7\frac{1}{2}\%$ until paid.

91. Gamble v. Pope & Talbot, Inc., 191 F.Supp. 763 (E.D.Pa.1961).

92. Louie v. Carnevale, 443 F.2d 912 (9th Cir. 1971); Republic Gear Co. v. Borg-Warner Corp., 381 F.2d 551 (2d Cir. 1967).

93. 28 U.S.C.A. § 1291: "The courts of appeals shall have jurisdiction of appeals from all final decisions of the district courts of the United States. . . ." 28 U.S.C.A. § 1292 states the few exceptions none of which is here applicable except possibly § 1292(b) which states that when a district court judge is of the opinion that an interlocutory order "involves a controlling question of law as to which there is substantial ground for difference of opinion and that an immediate appeal from the order may materially advance the ultimate termination of the litigation", he may so certify, and the court of appeals may then, in its discretion, permit the appeal. See Hanley v. James McHugh Constr. Co., supra n. 35.

In Cobbledick v. United States, 309 U.S. 323, 325–26, 60 S.Ct. 540, 541,

the trial court dismisses his case,[94] or enters a default judgment against him,[95] an immediate appeal will lie because the sanction imposed was a final judgment. Where a party resists discovery and is cited for contempt of court, an immediate appeal will also lie because of the severity of the sanction.[96] Aside from these situations the law is far from clear as to the possibility of immediate appellate review of interlocutory discovery orders. Where it is held to be available, it is not by way of appeal, but by the use of one of the great writs which appellate courts sometimes issue in their superintending control over inferior courts. Where a showing is made that great hardship may result if an immediate review is not had, appellate courts, in their discretion, frequently review discovery orders by writs of mandamus,[97] or prohibition.[98]

SECTION 6. PRETRIAL PROCEDURE

The discovery procedure was one of the great contributions of the Federal Rules. Another innovation, not of the same magnitude, but closely related to discovery, was the establishment of a pretrial procedure.[99] Rule 16 provides that in any action the

84 L.Ed. 783, 785 (1940) the Supreme Court held an order denying a motion to quash subpoenas duces tecum was not appealable. In explaining the rule of finality Mr. Justice Frankfurter said: "To be effective, judicial administration must not be leaden-footed. Its momentum would be arrested by permitting separate reviews of the component elements in a unified cause. . . . the requirement of finality will be enforced not only against a party to the litigation but against a witness who is a stranger to the main proceeding."

94. United States v. Procter & Gamble Co., supra n. 5; Richmond v. Brooks, supra n. 45; Collins v. Wayland, supra n. 49; Lang v. Morgan's Home Equip. Corp., 6 N. J. 333, 78 A.2d 705 (1951).

95. Diaz v. Southern Drilling Co., supra n. 90.

96. Hickman v. Taylor, supra n. 5; Sibbach v. Wilson & Co., supra n. 72; Southern Ry. v. Lanham, supra n. 20.

97. Schlagenhauf v. Holder, supra n. 55; Padovani v. Bruchhausen, 293 F.2d 546 (2d Cir. 1961); Burke v. Superior Court, 71 Cal.2d 276, 78 Cal.Rptr. 481, 455 P.2d 409 (1969).

98. Pacific Tel. & Tel. Co. v. Superior Court, supra n. 27; Kaiser Foundation Hospital v. Superior Court, 275 Cal.App.2d 801, 80 Cal. Rptr. 263 (1969); Solliday v. District Court, supra n. 43; Boldt v. Sanders, supra n. 5. Some courts use the writ of certiorari: Brooks v. Owens, 97 So.2d 693 (Fla.1957).

99. For a history of the development of the pretrial conference in England and in the United States see Sunderland, The Theory and Practice of Pre-Trial Procedure, 36 Mich.L.Rev. 215 (1937). For a description of pretrial under the federal rules see: Clark, To an Understanding Use of Pre-Trial, 29 F.R.D. 454 (1961); Holtzoff, Federal Pretrial Procedure, 11 Amer.U.L.Rev. 21 (1962); Vestal, The Pretrial Conference and the Recalcitrant Attorney: A Study in Judicial Power, 48 Iowa L.Rev. 761 (1963).

court may direct the attorneys for the parties to appear before it for a conference to consider the simplification of the issues, possible amendments to the pleadings, the possibility of admissions of facts or documents to avoid unnecessary proof, the limitation of the number of expert witnesses, the possibility of reference of some issues to a master, and "such other matters as may aid in the disposition of the action." The purpose of the conference is not to serve as a substitute for the trial but to streamline the trial.[100] The pretrial conference may also serve as a catalyst for the settlement of the case, thus eliminating the trial entirely. By the time of the pretrial conference, if counsel have been diligent in the use of the discovery machinery, each knows fairly well the strength of his opponent's case, and with a little encouragement by the judge, in an impartial capacity, they may be moved to settle instead of litigate.[101] The rule provides that, at the conclusion of the conference the judge shall make an order which recites the action taken, the agreements reached, the limitation of issues, and the amendments to the pleadings.[102] It provides that "such order when entered, controls the subsequent course of the action, unless modified at the trial to prevent manifest injustice." [103] In the absence of such an amendment,[104] a party who is precluded by the judge from going

100. Lynn v. Smith, 281 F.2d 501 (3d Cir. 1960); Burton v. Weyerhaeuser Timber Co., supra n. 5; Padovani v. Bruchhausen, supra n. 97 at 550, in which Judge Clark said it leads to "better justice more shortly and efficiently obtained."

101. Opinions differ as to how active a part the judge should take in attempting to secure a settlement of the case. See Brennan, Introduction to the Problem of the Protracted Case, 23 F.R.D. 376 (1958); Clark, Objectives of Pre-Trial Procedure, 17 Ohio St.L.J. 163 (1956); Wright, The Pre-Trial Conference, 28 F.R.D. 141 (1960).

102. In making the order the judge is not restricted to the formal agreements of counsel. In Life Music, Inc. v. Edelstein, 309 F.2d 242, 243 (2d Cir. 1962), the court said: "It could hardly have been intended that if, as a result of all this, the judge finds that the parties are really in accord, he may not issue an order defining their 'agreement' simply because one of

them refuses a formal manifestation of assent. Although 'agreement' usually connotes a voluntary undertaking of two or more parties, this is not its only meaning. We characterize readings on scientific instruments as in agreement, although the instruments have not said they were . . .. We hold that the judge was not stripped of jurisdiction to limit the issues under Rule 16 by the lack of petitioner's formal assent."

103. United States v. Hougham, 364 U.S. 310, 81 S.Ct. 13, 5 L.Ed.2d 8 (1960), holding that the pretrial order conclusively established the issues and superseded the pleadings. States adopting the federal procedure are in accord: Baird v. Hodson, 161 Cal.App.2d 687, 327 P.2d 215 (1958).

104. In Laguna v. American Export Isbrandtsen Lines, Inc., 439 F.2d 97, 103 (2d Cir. 1971) a divided court held the trial judge had abused his discretion in refusing an amendment of the pretrial order.

beyond the scope of the pretrial order at the trial has little hope of a reversal in the appellate court.[105]

SECTION 7. THE "BIG" CASE

The massive antitrust suit, often involving multiple plaintiffs and multiple defendants, has created serious problems in judicial logistics.[106] In the early part of the last decade it really became critical when, in the electrical appliance antitrust litigation, over 1900 suits were filed in 36 federal judicial districts. All of the cases involved common questions of law and fact. The pretrial proceedings in these cases, even though informally coordinated, produced over 1.5 million documents.[107] A committee of the Judicial Conference of the United States was established to aid in the administration of these cases. The committee worked out a national discovery program to minimize the duplication of deposi-

Judge Lumbard, dissenting, said: "In these days when delays in the trial of most civil jury cases in the Southern District now exceed two years from the time the case is at issue, I see no reason whatever for holding that the trial judge abused his discretion in refusing to permit plaintiff to amend his complaint on five days' notice before the case was reached for trial on June 17, 1970, a maneuver which undoubtedly would have required an adjournment of the trial had the trial judge permitted it."

105. McKey v. Fairbairn, 120 U.S. App.D.C. 250, 345 F.2d 739 (1965) (holding trial judge did not abuse discretion in refusing to permit appellant to change the theory adopted in the pretrial conference); Fernandez v. United Fruit Co., 200 F. 2d 414 (2d Cir. 1952) (affirming lower court in preventing plaintiff from going to jury on a theory which was pleaded but which was not included in the pretrial order); Globe Cereal Mills v. Scrivener, 240 F.2d 330 (10th Cir. 1956) (upholding lower court in excluding exhibits not covered by pretrial order); DeCastro & Co. v. Liberty S. S. of Panama, S. A., 186 Cal.App. 2d 628, 9 Cal.Rptr. 107 (1960) (upholding lower court in refusing to permit defendant to go beyond the pretrial order).

There are cases, however, in which an appellate court will reverse for abuse of discretion. In Padovani v. Bruchhausen, supra n. 97, the court reversed because the preclusion order of the trial court was so severe that it practically prevented the plaintiff from introducing any evidence to support his case.

106. McAllister, The Big Case: Procedural Problems in Anti-trust Litigation, 64 Harv.L.Rev. 27 (1950); McAllister, The Judicial Conference Report on the "Big Case": Procedural Problems of Protracted Litigation, 38 A.B.A.J. 289 (1952); Prettyman, Needed: New Trial Technique: Suggestions for the Trial of Complicated Cases, 34 A.B.A.J. 766 (1948); Comment, Pretrial Procedure, A Modern Method of Improving Trials of Law Suits, 25 N.Y.U.L.Rev. 16 (1950).

107. Peterson & McDermott, Multidistrict Litigation: New Forms of Judicial Administration, 56 A.B. A.J. 737 (1970); Neal & Goldberg, The Electrical Equipment Antitrust Cases: Novel Judicial Administration, 50 A.B.A.J. 621 (1964); Neal, Multidistrict Coordination—The Antecedents of § 1407, 14 Antitrust Bull. 99 (1969).

tions and documents. It was out of this experience that a proposal was made to amend the judicial code to make more adequate provisions for multi-district litigation. Congress responded by passing Section 1407 of the Judicial Code,[108] which became
law in 1968. It provides that: "When civil actions involving one
or more common questions of fact are pending in different districts, such actions may be transferred to any district for coordinated or consolidated pretrial proceedings." [109] The transfers are to be made by a panel on multi-district litigation consisting of seven circuit and district judges appointed by the Chief
Justice of the United States. The panel was given authority to,
and has prescribed rules for the conduct of its business.[110] A co-
ordinating committee also prepared a manual for the conduct of
such litigation.[111]

Proceedings for the transfer of a case under this section may
be initiated by a party to any action or by the panel itself. Hearings are held by the panel, after notice to all parties in all actions
in which transfers are contemplated, and the panel then determines whether the transfer shall be made. There is no provision
made for review of its orders except by extraordinary writ. When
a transfer is made, it is for the purpose of centralizing and co-
ordinating the pretrial and discovery procedure and, presumably,
once this is completed, the individual cases will be returned to
their home districts. In other words, a transfer under this section is for one purpose only, and does not amount to a consolidation of the cases for trial. However, in the short time the system
has been in existence, the experience indicates that most of the
cases may be settled, thus eliminating the trials entirely.

Most of the cases handled by the panel are antitrust cases, although a substantial number are disaster cases, and patent and
trademark cases. The Antibiotic Drug Litigation may already
have become more complex than the electrical appliance cases.[112]
The decisions of the panel are now appearing in the Federal Supplement,[113] and the periodical literature of the subject is growing.[114]

---

108. 28 U.S.C.A. § 1407 (Supp. V, 1969).

109. Id.

110. A copy of the rules is contained in the supplement to 28 U.S.
C.A. following § 1407. The rules
are also reprinted in 53 F.R.D. 119
(1971).

111. Manual for Complex and Multidistrict Litigation, with amendments to May 18, 1970 (West Pub.
Co.).

112. In re Antibiotic Drug Antitrust
Litigation, 320 F.Supp. 586 (JPML
1970).

113. In re Oral Contraceptives
Prods. Liab. Litigation, 322 F.Supp.
1011 (JPML 1971); In re Air Fare

114. See note 114 on page 146.

Litigation, 322 F.Supp. 1013 (JPML 1971); In re Carrom Trademark Litigation, 322 F.Supp. 1016 (JPML 1971); In re Willingham Patent, 322 F.Supp. 1019 (JPML 1971); In re Penn. Cent. Sec. Litigation, 322 F.Supp. 1021 (JPML 1971); In re Koratron Patent Litigation, 327 F. Supp. 559 (JPML 1971).

114. Supra n. 107. See also excellent Note: Consolidation and Transfer in the Federal Courts: 28 U.S.C. Section 1407 Viewed in Light of Rule 42(a) and 28 U.S.C. Section 1404(a), 22 Hastings L.J. 1289 (1971).

CHAPTER VII.   THE TRIAL

The sweeping changes which recent decades have brought to jurisdiction, pleading, and pretrial procedure have left the format of the trial relatively unaffected.   The basic steps remain the same: the opening statements of counsel, the presentation of evidence, the motions for nonsuit or directed verdict, the closing arguments of counsel, the judge's charge to the jury, and finally the verdict, often followed by post-trial motions.   The reforms in other areas of procedure have, however, had their effect on the details of trial practice and, most importantly, in the operation of the jury system.

SECTION 1.   OPENING AND CLOSING

In the trial of a law suit the party who has the burden of proof has the right to open and close.   This is usually the plaintiff since it is he who is asking the court for relief.   In rare situations, where the defendant has formally admitted all of the plaintiff's allegations and is relying on an affirmative defense or counterclaim, he will be accorded the right.[1]   The right must be determined from the pleadings since it is important at all stages of the trial.   It is a valuable right, especially in trials to a jury, since the one who opens and closes has the double advantage of creating the first impression, and of having the last word.

The purpose of an opening statement is to give an outline of the case so that the trier of the facts may more easily follow the evidence as it is presented.   It is of less importance where the case is being tried by the judge without a jury since he has probably gained some familiarity with it from the pleadings and pretrial proceedings.   However, when the case is being tried to a jury the importance of the opening statement can hardly be exaggerated because the jury usually comes to the case fresh, with no previous knowledge of the facts.   A clear and cogent statement by counsel, at this time, of the evidence he intends to present not only creates a first impression in the minds of the jurors but will be a great aid to them in putting the picture puzzle together, especially in view of the fact that it is often impossible to present the evidence in a logical and chronological order.   Sometimes a witness is late, or fails to appear, and another must be called out of turn.   The testimony of a witness may have to be interrupted so that a busy medical expert may be accommodated.   If a proper

1.   Carmody v. Kolocheski, 181 Wis. 394, 194 N.W. 584 (1923).

opening statement has been made a jury will understand these things and make necessary adjustments in its thinking. The opening statement is not evidence, as the court will instruct the jury. It is an outline of the evidence counsel hopes to produce. If he has been too optimistic and later fails to produce the evidence he has promised the result may be devastating when opposing counsel reminds the jury of this in his closing argument.[2] If, however, counsel gives the jury a clear picture of the evidence which he can, and later does produce, the opening statement can be a crucial factor in the case. In his opening statement it is improper for counsel to introduce arguments,[3] or to refer to evidence which is inadmissible and prejudicial.[4] Such conduct may call for a reprimand by the judge [5] and may even warrant the granting of a mistrial [6] or be ground for a reversal of the case on appeal.[7] The opening statement of defendant's counsel follows that of the plaintiff unless the court grants him permission to reserve it until he begins the presentation of his evidence.[8] What has been said as to the proper limits of the plaintiff's opening statement also applies to that of the defendant.

After the opening statements of counsel have been made, the plaintiff will then be permitted to present his evidence, and after the defendant has presented his evidence the plaintiff will be permitted to present rebuttal evidence. It is at this stage that his right to close—to have the last word—comes into play.[9]

When the evidence has been completed, and both parties have "rested" their case, counsel will then be permitted to make their closing arguments, or summations, to the jury. Here, again, plaintiff's counsel has the right to go first, and, after the defendant's argument, plaintiff's counsel will be permitted to reply in rebuttal. The purpose of the closing arguments is to aid the jury in analyzing the evidence in the case. At this time counsel may properly argue the case, he may attack his opponent's evi-

---

2. Hutson v. Imperial Royalties Co., 134 Kan. 378, 5 P.2d 825 (1931).

3. Security State Bank v. Baty, 439 F.2d 910 (10th Cir. 1971).

4. Maggio v. City of Cleveland, 151 Ohio St. 136, 84 N.E.2d 912 (1949).

5. If a lawyer repeatedly disregards admonitions from the judge to keep his opening statement within proper bounds, he may be committed for contempt of court. Hallinan v. United States, 182 F.2d 880 (9th Cir. 1950).

6. In re: Appropriation of Easement for Highway Purposes, 118 Ohio App. 207, 193 N.E.2d 702 (1962).

7. Maggio v. City of Cleveland, supra n. 4.

8. Sinclair Co. v. Waddill, 200 Ill. 17, 65 N.E. 437 (1902).

9. Evidence is treated as a special subject in the law school curriculum.

dence as unreasonable, unfounded, or unreliable, and he may attempt to discredit his opponent's witnesses and reinforce the credibility of his own. He may use whatever histrionic ability he possesses and be as eloquent as he pleases as long as he stays "within the record." In other words, he is not permitted to base arguments upon facts which have no support in the evidence which was introduced at the trial,[10] and, in the guise of argument, he is not permitted to testify or introduce new evidence.[11] Such conduct on his part may result in appropriate sanctions against him and his client.

SECTION 2. THE RIGHT TO A JURY TRIAL

The constitutional guarantee. The origin of the jury system in ancient England is obscure, but probably it began as an adjunct to a royal inquest or investigation. Juries of local citizens were empaneled to give information to the king on matters in which he was interested. They were, in a sense, witnesses. Just how they changed into the jury as we know it—a body of disinterested men who were chosen because they had no knowledge of the facts of the case—is shrouded by the mists of time. We do know that it was introduced into the courts of England, in civil and criminal cases, to replace the more ancient methods of trial by battle, and the ordeals of fire, water, and trial by compurgation.[12]

Trial by jury was part of our heritage from England. It was regarded so highly that it was guaranteed by the bill of rights in the federal constitution, and similar guarantees are found in the constitutions of practically all of the states.[13] These provisions do not undertake to define trial by jury nor to specify the types of cases to which the guarantee applies. These were matters of common knowledge, and it was assumed by the men who wrote the constitutions that such definitions were unnecessary—a natural assumption at the time. Jury trials were had as a matter of course in common law actions, but not in suits in equity except in the rare cases in which the chancellor would empanel

---

10. New York Cent. R. R. v. Johnson, 279 U.S. 310, 49 S.Ct. 300, 73 L.Ed. 706 (1929); Hoffman v. Brandt, 65 Cal.2d 549, 421 P.2d 425, 55 Cal.Rptr. 417 (1966); Buehler v. Festus Mercantile Co., 343 Mo. 139, 119 S.W.2d 961 (1938).

11. Gutzman v. Clancy, 114 Wis. 589, 90 N.W. 1081 (1902).

12. Green, Juries and Justice—The Jury's Role in Personal Injury Cases, 1962 U.Ill.L.F. 152, 157.

13. James, Civil Procedure (1965) pp. 337 et seq.

an advisory jury whose verdict he was free to disregard.[14] There was some variation in the language employed in different constitutions by which jury trial was guaranteed; some said it shall be "preserved," [15] others that it shall remain "inviolate," [16] and others that it "shall be held sacred." [17] But whatever language was used, the uniform interpretation of such provisions has been that the right to trial by jury should remain and be preserved as it existed at the time of the adoption of the constitution. There have been many changes in the law since 1791, when the Seventh Amendment was adopted. The common law forms of action have been abolished; law and equity have been merged; many of the old substantive rights have been modified by statute; and old common law remedies have been abolished and replaced by new statutory causes of action. In other words, the general legal climate is not the same today as it was a century and three-quarters ago, and yet, when the question arises in an individual case as to whether one has a constitutional right to a jury trial the answer must be found in history.[18]

In determining the constitutional right to a jury trial one must be careful to distinguish between the federal constitution and state constitutions and between civil cases and criminal cases. In recent decades the Supreme Court has held that some of the guaranteed rights in the first nine amendments are so fundamental that a violation of them would constitute a violation of the due process clause of the Fourteenth Amendment.[19] The Sixth Amendment guaranteeing jury trial in criminal cases is one of them, which is now held to be applicable in both federal and state cases.[20] The Seventh Amendment, however, which guar-

---

14. Klein v. Shell Oil Co., 386 F.2d 659 (8th Cir. 1967).

15. U.S.Const. amend. VII; Alaska Const. art. I, § 16.

16. Cal.Const. art. I, § 7; Minn. Const. art. I, § 4; N.Y.Const. art. I, § 2; Wis.Const. art. I, § 5.

17. Mass.Const. art. XV.

18. For representative cases applying the historical test see: Frahm v. Briggs, 90 Cal.Rptr. 725, 12 Cal. App.3d 441 (1970); Damsky v. Zavatt, 289 F.2d 46 (2d Cir. 1961); Hallahan v. Riley, 94 N.H. 338, 53 A.2d 431 (1947); People ex rel. Lemon v. Elmore, 256 N.Y. 489, 177 N.E. 14 (1931); State v. 1920

Studebaker, 120 Or. 254, 251 P. 701 (1926).

19. Palko v. Connecticut, 302 U.S. 319, 58 S.Ct. 149, 82 L.Ed. 288 (1937).

20. Williams v. Florida, 399 U.S. 78, 90 S.Ct. 1893, 26 L.Ed.2d 446 (1970). The distinction between civil and criminal cases is usually obvious but in cases involving contempt of court there has been some confusion since the same act may constitute both a civil and a criminal contempt. The Supreme Court has held that, in the case of a criminal contempt, no jury is required if the sentence does not exceed six months, Cheff v. Schnackenberg, 384 U.S. 373, 86 S.Ct. 1523,

antees jury trial in civil cases, is still regarded as applicable only to federal court cases.[21] Thus, in civil cases in the federal courts, the constitutional definition of jury trial must be found in federal law, and in civil cases in state courts, the constitutional definition of jury trial must be found in state law.

The leading case on the definition of jury trial in civil cases in the federal courts is Capital Traction Co. v. Hof [22] which defined it as "a trial by a jury of 12 men in the presence and under the superintendence of a judge empowered to instruct them on the law and to advise them on the facts, and (except on acquittal of a criminal charge) to set aside their verdict, if, in his opinion, it is against the law or the evidence." The definition is incomplete in omitting mention of two other elements: the jury must be impartially selected and their verdict must be unanimous. In Patton v. United States [23] the Supreme Court held that a constitutional jury means a jury of twelve. On this point Patton was overruled by the recent case of Williams v. Florida.[24] The case involved the constitutionality of a Florida statute providing for juries of six in criminal cases. In upholding the validity of the statute the court said:

> We conclude, in short, as we began: the fact that the jury at common law was composed of precisely 12 is an historical accident, unnecessary to effect the purposes of the jury system and wholly without significance "except to mystics". . . . To read the Sixth Amendment as forever codifying a feature so incidental to the real purpose of the Amendment is to ascribe a blind formalism to the Framers which would require considerably more evidence than we have been able to discover in the history and language of the Constitution or in the meaning of our past decisions.

The logic of the Williams case, a criminal case, would also apply to civil cases, but the court left the matter open. However, in March of 1971 the Judicial Conference of the United States voted to reduce the size of juries in federal civil trials. In

16 L.Ed.2d 629 (1966); and that in the case of a civil contempt there is no constitutional right to a jury trial, Shillitani v. United States, 384 U.S. 364, 86 S.Ct. 1531, 16 L.Ed.2d 622 (1966). The Cheff principle was extended to the state courts in Bloom v. Illinois, 391 U.S. 194, 88 S.Ct. 1444, 20 L.Ed.2d 522 (1968).

21. Minneapolis & St. Louis Ry. v. Bombolis, 241 U.S. 211, 36 S.Ct. 595, 60 L.Ed. 961 (1916).

22. 174 U.S. 1, 13, 19 S.Ct. 580, 585, 43 L.Ed. 873, 877 (1899).

23. 281 U.S. 276, 50 S.Ct. 253, 74 L.Ed. 854 (1930).

24. 399 U.S. 78, 102, 90 S.Ct. 1893, 1907, 26 L.Ed.2d 446, 461 (1970).

announcing the decision Chief Justice Burger said the details would be worked out later. Following this announcement the district courts of at least six districts promulgated local rules reducing the size of juries in civil cases to six.[25]

If the limitations of the Seventh Amendment do not apply to the states (the general assumption) then a state is free to adopt its own definition of jury trial. In addition to "preserving" the right to trial by jury, some state constitutions authorize the legislatures to provide for juries of less than twelve,[26] or for majority verdicts.[27] If, pursuant to such provisions, a state legislature provided for juries less than twelve, or for majority verdicts, there could be no federal constitutional objection. Such was, indeed, the holding in the case of Minneapolis and St. Louis Railway Co. v. Bombolis.[28] This was a suit brought by the plaintiff in a Minnesota state court under the Federal Employers Liability Act. Under the Constitution and statutes of Minnesota, after a case has been under submission to a jury for a period of twelve hours without a unanimous verdict, five-sixths of the jury are authorized to reach a verdict. The plaintiff won a verdict under this procedure and the defendant took the case to the Supreme Court on the ground this was a violation of the Seventh Amendment. The court held that it was not, stating "That the first ten Amendments, including, of course, the 7th, are not concerned with state action, and deal only with Federal action." The authority of Bombolis was weakened by the later case of Dice v. Akron, Canton & Youngstown Railroad Co.,[29] another Federal Employers Liability Act case which had been brought in an Ohio court. The defendant pleaded a release as a defense, to which the plaintiff replied that it had been obtained by fraud. A jury awarded the plaintiff a $25,000 verdict which the court set aside on the ground there was no fraud in obtaining the release. Under Ohio law factual issues as to fraud in the execution of the release were properly decided by the judge rather than the jury. The United States Supreme Court reversed, holding that trial by jury was an important part of the remedy af-

---

25. I.J.A. Report, Vol. 3, No. 3, April 1971. See Devitt, Six-Member Civil Juries Gain Backing, 57 A.B. A.J. 1111 (1971) in which the Chief Judge of the United States District Court for Minnesota gives a glowing account of the experience with the six-man jury.

26. Cal.Const. art. I, § 7; Idaho Const. art. I, § 7; Missouri Const. art. 2, § 28; Ohio Const. art. 1,

§ 5; Nevada Const. art. 1, § 3; Utah Const. art. 1, § 10.

27. Cal.Const. art. I, § 7; Wis.Const. art. I, § 5.

28. 241 U.S. 211, 217, 36 S.Ct. 595, 596, 60 L.Ed. 961, 963 (1916).

29. 342 U.S. 359, 72 S.Ct. 312, 96 L.Ed. 398 (1952).

forded by the Federal Employers Liability Act which a local rule in Ohio could not override. The majority opinion did not overrule Bombolis, but the dissenting opinion by Mr. Justice Frankfurter said "the Bombolis case should be overruled explicitly instead of left as a derelict bound to occasion collisions on the waters of the law." [30] Dice and Bombolis, taken together, indicate that where there is a strong federal interest, as there is in the case of an Employers Liability Act suit, where plaintiff's right is derived from an act of Congress, that federal standards may control, even when the case is brought in a state court. The apparent conflict between the two cases may be reconciled on the basis that while Dice requires a trial by jury in Federal Employers Liability Act cases, including all issues, that under Bombolis the details of that trial by jury may be regulated by state law as long as the substance of the right is preserved. This rationale is fortified by the recent Williams case which sanctioned the 6-man Florida jury in a State court criminal case.[31]

The diversity jurisdiction of the federal courts presents another situation in which the Supreme Court has resolved a conflict in federal and state notions of jury trial. In Erie Railroad Co. v. Tompkins [32] the Supreme Court held that when a federal court is exercising jurisdiction on the basis of diversity of citizenship it must apply the substantive law of the state in which it sits. The reason for the rule is that where a court is enforcing state-created rights the decision should be the same whether the case is in a state court or, through the fortuitous circumstance of diverse citizenship, in a federal court. Although applying state substantive law, the court in such a case applies federal procedure. It is sometimes difficult to draw the line between substance and procedure. In Guaranty Trust Co. v. York [33] the court held that if, on a particular issue, there is a difference in state and federal procedure and the difference is one which may determine the outcome of the case then the federal court should apply state law. Again, the rationale is that the result of the case should not depend upon the accident of diversity of citizenship. In Byrd v. Blue Ridge Electric Cooperative [34] the outcome-determinative test was modified because of a strong countervailing federal interest. The case was a personal injury suit by a plaintiff against his employer, brought in a fed-

---

30. Id. at 368, 72 S.Ct. at 318, 96 L.Ed. at 407.

31. Supra n. 20.

32. 304 U.S. 64, 58 S.Ct. 817, 82 L.Ed. 1188 (1938).

33. 326 U.S. 99, 65 S.Ct. 1464, 89 L.Ed. 2079 (1945).

34. 356 U.S. 525, 537, 78 S.Ct. 893, 901, 2 L.Ed.2d 953, 962 (1958).

eral court because of diversity of citizenship. The defense was that the workmen's compensation law provided the exclusive remedy. Under state law this issue would have been decided by the judge, but the trial court submitted it to the jury and the plaintiff got a verdict. On appeal the defendant alleged that this was error because the mode of trial (judge or jury) could be outcome-determinative. The Supreme Court upheld the decision of the trial court, stating that even if it be conceded that the mode of trial on this issue might be outcome-determinative, there were "countervailing considerations at work here" which dictated the application of federal law. Said the court, "The policy of uniform enforcement of state-created rights and obligations . . . cannot in every case exact compliance with a state rule —not bound up with rights and obligations—which disrupts the federal system of allocating functions between judge and jury." Simler v. Conner [35] was another diversity case in which a lawyer was suing for his fee. Under Oklahoma law the matter would be tried by the judge because the suit was "equitable" in character, but the Supreme Court held the matter was for the jury. It stated that "In diversity cases, of course, the substantive dimension of the claim asserted finds its source in state law . . . but the characterization of that state-created claim as legal or equitable for purposes of whether a right to jury trial is indicated must be made by recourse to federal law."

The constitutional provisions regarding jury trial were intended to preserve the right as it then existed which, generally speaking, was in regard to common law actions. There are few constitutional provisions preserving the right to trial by a judge in equitable matters.[36] In the absence of such it is generally held that there is no constitutional impediment for a legislature to extend the right to trial by jury. In one instance, at least, an extension of the right to jury trial was made by the court, and not the legislature. In Fitzgerald v. United States Lines Co.[37] the suit was by an injured seaman for damages under the Jones Act, plus a claim for maintenance and cure under traditional admiralty jurisdiction. The plaintiff demanded a jury trial on all issues but the trial court granted it only on the Jones Act claim. The Supreme Court reversed. Mr. Justice Black, speaking for the court, noted that the Jones Act required a jury trial, that traditional admiralty jurisdiction did not, but said "Requiring a seaman to split up his lawsuit, submitting part of it to a jury and

---

35. 372 U.S. 221, 222, 83 S.Ct. 609, 610, 9 L.Ed.2d 691, 692 (1963).

36. James, Civil Procedure (1965) 339.

37. 374 U.S. 16, 18, 83 S.Ct. 1646, 1649, 10 L.Ed.2d 720, 723 (1963).

part to a judge, unduly complicates and confuses a trial, creates difficulties in applying the doctrine of res judicata and collateral estoppel, and can easily result in too much or too little recovery . . .. In the absence of some statutory or constitutional obstacle, an end should be put to such unfortunate, outdated, and wasteful manner of trying these cases." Finding no such barriers in the way he held that both branches of the case should be tried by a jury. In a dissenting opinion Mr. Justice Harlan said he thought that "the appropriate way to achieve what in this instance is obviously a desirable procedural reform is to deal with the matter through the Judicial Conference of the United States." [38]

The constitutional right to jury trials in criminal cases is beyond the scope of the present discussion. However, the sanction of criminal contempt of court is sometimes applied in civil cases. The Supreme Court has established the rule that where the sentence for criminal contempt does not exceed six months a jury trial is not required.[39] Citations for civil contempt do not require a jury trial even though the sentence exceeds six months because the person cited can always purge the contempt by complying with the court order.[40]

Occasionally a legislature will expand the jurisdiction of an inferior court or provide a summary remedy for the disposition of claims involving less than a certain amount. Do such legislative acts violate the constitutional right to trial by jury? The courts have answered the question in the negative provided that a jury trial may be obtained by appealing to a higher court, and provided further that the conditions for obtaining the appeal are not so onerous as to make the right practically unavailable.[41]

Complications resulting from the merger of law and equity. The merger of law and equity by the codes and the federal rules has been hailed as a great stride forward in the simplification of procedure. At the pleading level this is certainly true. In the same suit the plaintiff may seek both legal and equitable relief,[42] a defendant may interpose equitable defenses or counter-

---

38. 374 U.S. 16, 22, 83 S.Ct. 1646, 1651, 10 L.Ed.2d 720, 725 (1963).

39. Cheff v. Schnackenberg, supra n. 20.

40. Shillitani v. United States, supra n. 20.

41. Capital Traction Co. v. Hof, 174 U.S. 1, 19 S.Ct. 580, 43 L.Ed. 873 (1899); Application of Smith, 381 Pa. 223, 112 A.2d 625 (1955).

42. Bruckman v. Hollzer, 152 F.2d 730 (9th Cir. 1946); Berlin v. Club 100, Inc., 12 F.R.D. 129 (D.Mass. 1951); Bellavance v. Plastic-Craft Novelty Co., 30 F.Supp. 37 (D.Mass. 1939).

claims to a legal action,[43] or legal defenses or counterclaims to an equitable action.[44] At the trial level complications appear. What becomes of the constitutional right to trial by jury? Under the historical test, which is generally used, the right is "preserved" as it existed at the time of the adoption of the constitution. There was no "merged" procedure at that time. Common law actions were tried by juries; equity cases were not. Under the new procedure there is no serious problem if the legal and equitable claims in the same suit are independent and unrelated. In such case the judge may separate them for trial, allowing a jury in the one but not in the other.[45] Where, however, common issues of fact run through both types of claims there is no easy solution. There cannot be two trials on the same issue of fact, and whichever method is used will preclude trial by the other. Faced with this dilemma, different courts have arrived at different solutions. (1) The claim for legal relief, before a jury, should be tried first.[46] If equitable claims remain they can be tried later before the judge. This preserves the right to jury trial but it concludes the judge regarding facts found by the jury. (2) The equity claim should be tried first, before the judge.[47] If legal claims remain they can be tried before a jury. This method may eliminate any trial by jury. For example, if an insurance company sues to cancel a policy on the ground it was obtained by fraud (historically an equitable action) and the defendant counterclaims on the policy (historically legal), a finding for the plaintiff on the first claim will eliminate the second, and the defendant will never get his jury trial.[48] (3) Which claim should be tried first is a matter of discretion to be determined by the court.[49] (4) The entire case should be assessed to see if it is basically legal or equitable, and this should determine the right to jury trial.[50] (5) There should be no jury trial.[51] The theory

43. American Life Ins. Co. v. Stewart, 300 U.S. 203, 57 S.Ct. 377, 81 L.Ed. 605 (1937).

44. Union Cent. Life Ins. Co. v. Burger, 27 F.Supp. 554 (S.D.N.Y. 1939); Steiner v. Stein, 2 N.J. 367, 66 A.2d 719 (1949).

45. Fed.Rules Civ.Proc. 42(b).

46. Bruckman v. Hollzer, supra n. 42; Berlin v. Club 100, Inc., supra n. 42.

47. Union Cent. Life Ins. Co. v. Burger, supra n. 44.

48. Supra n. 43.

49. Ralph Blechman, Inc. v. I. B. Kleinert Rubber Co., 98 F.Supp. 1005 (S.D.N.Y.1951).

50. Ring v. Spina, 166 F.2d 546 (2d Cir. 1948).

51. Fitzpatrick v. Sun Life Assur. Co. of Canada, 1 F.R.D. 713 (D.N. J.1941); Fraser v. Geist, 1 F.R.D. 267 (E.D.Pa.1940); Bellavance v. Plastic-Craft Novelty Co., supra n. 42; Croucer v. Boice, 51 Cal.App. 2d 198, 124 P.2d 358 (1942); Steiner v. Stein, supra n. 44; DiMenna v. Cooper & Evans Co., 220 N.Y. 391, 115 N.E. 993 (1917).

behind this view is that, historically, a court of equity could grant incidental legal relief in order to do complete justice and avoid a multiplicity of suits. The fallacy in this view is that, historically, when a court of equity found there were no grounds for equitable relief it dismissed the case, relegating the plaintiff to his remedy at law.[52] The fallacy of all of the views is the assumption that issues may be characterized as strictly legal or equitable. This is not true. Issues involve facts. The same facts may be involved in a case seeking legal relief, or equitable relief, or both. The basic question is who is to determine these facts, a judge or a jury? In the confused state of the authorities on this question the Beacon case came as a welcome ray of light.

Beacon Theatres, Inc. v. Westover[53] was a suit in a United States district court in which the plaintiff sought equitable relief and the defendant filed a legal counterclaim. The common issue of fact involved in both was the validity of a contract (under the Sherman Antitrust Act) which gave the plaintiff exclusive rights to show "first run" movies in the San Bernardino area. The Supreme Court held that the lower court erred in holding that the equitable issues in the complaint should be tried first by the judge before the jury trial of the counterclaim. It stated that only "under the most imperative circumstances, circumstances which in view of the flexible procedure of the Federal Rules we cannot now anticipate, can the right to a jury trial of legal issues be lost through prior determination of equitable claims." Beacon was followed shortly by Dairy Queen, Inc. v. Wood[54] which involved a licensing agreement for the use of the trademark "Dairy Queen." Plaintiff sued for breach of contract seeking (1) injunctions restraining the defendant from further use of the name, and (2) an accounting to determine the exact sum owed the plaintiff. The trial court struck the defendant's demand for jury trial, but the Supreme Court reversed, holding that, although only equitable relief was asked, the basic claim was cognizable at law, and that to sue in equity the plaintiff must show that the legal remedy was inadequate. It continued: "In view of the powers given to District Courts by Federal Rule . . . 53(b) to appoint masters to assist the jury in those exceptional cases where the legal issues are too complicated for the jury adequately to handle alone, the burden of such a showing is considerably increased and it will indeed be a rare case in which it can be met." The "rare case" appeared in the form of Katchen

---

52. Croucer v. Boice, supra n. 51.

53. 359 U.S. 500, 510, 79 S.Ct. 948, 957, 3 L.Ed.2d 988, 997 (1959).

54. 369 U.S. 469, 478, 82 S.Ct. 894, 900, 8 L.Ed.2d 44, 51 (1962).

v. Landy,[55] a bankruptcy case, in which the petitioner had filed a claim with the district court. The trustee in bankruptcy sought to recoup moneys which the bankrupt had paid to the petitioner on the ground they constituted "voidable preferences." This was in effect a counterclaim. The petitioner argued he was entitled to a jury trial because, had he not filed a claim, the trustee would have had to sue him in a plenary suit in which he would have been entitled to a jury trial. The Supreme Court overruled his contention on the ground that it would frustrate the summary procedure established by the Bankruptcy Act. Said the court:

> Thus petitioner's argument would require that in every case where a § 57g objection is interposed and a jury trial is demanded the proceedings on allowance of claims must be suspended and a plenary suit initiated, with all the delay and expense that course would entail. Such a result is not consistent with the equitable purposes of the Bankruptcy Act nor with the rule of Beacon Theatres and Dairy Queen. . . . In neither Beacon Theatres nor Dairy Queen was there involved a specific statutory scheme contemplating the prompt trial of a disputed claim without the intervention of a jury.

In 1970, in the case of Ross v. Bernhard,[56] the Supreme Court extended the Beacon-Dairy Queen doctrine to stockholders' derivative suits, which traditionally had been the exclusive province of equity. This feat was accomplished by breaking the suit down into two parts: the plaintiff's right to sue on behalf of the corporation, and the merits of the corporation claim itself. Mr. Justice White, speaking for the majority, said:

> We hold that the right of jury trial attaches to those issues in derivative actions as to which the corporation, if it had been suing in its own right, would have been entitled to a jury . . . The heart of the action is the corporation claim. If it presents a legal issue, one entitling the corporation to a jury trial under the Seventh Amendment, the right to a jury trial is not forfeited merely because the stockholder's right to sue must first be adjudicated as an equitable issue triable to the court. Beacon and Dairy Queen require no less.[57]

---

55. 382 U.S. 323, 339, 86 S.Ct. 467, 478, 15 L.Ed.2d 391, 402 (1966).

56. 396 U.S. 531, 90 S.Ct. 733, 24 L.Ed.2d 729 (1970), noted in 84 Harv.L.Rev. 172 (1970).

57. Id. at 532, 539, 90 S.Ct. at 735, 738, 24 L.Ed.2d at 733, 736. Mr. Justice Stewart wrote a vigorous dissent in which he says: "Today the Court tosses aside history, logic and over 100 years of firm prece-

Since the limitations of the Seventh Amendment are not applicable to state courts they are not bound by the Beacon-Dairy Queen doctrine. However, a case which was brought in a state court but was removed to a federal court would then be subject to the Beacon-Dairy Queen doctrine.[58]

SECTION 3.　SELECTING THE JURY

Asserting the right. Under the federal rules, one who is entitled to trial by jury must assert his right to it by a demand in writing "not later than 10 days after the service of the last pleading" or he will be deemed to have waived his right to it.[59] Most states have similar provisions under which jury trial is waived if not claimed within a specified time.[60] Such automatic waiver provisions have been held constitutional.[61] Under the federal rules a judge may, in his discretion, grant a jury trial even though not demanded within the specified time,[62] but such discretion is seldom exercised.[63] There is a special rule covering cases removed from a state court to a federal court which provides that a party who has demanded a jury trial in the state court before removal need not do so again after removal, and that where state law does not require a demand none is needed in the

fed.

---

dent to hold that the plaintiff in a shareholder's derivative suit does indeed have a constitutional right to a trial by jury." Id. at 544–45, 90 S.Ct. at 741, 24 L.Ed.2d at 739–40. His concluding paragraph: "The Court's decision today can perhaps be explained as a reflection of an unarticulated but apparently overpowering bias in favor of jury trials in civil actions. It certainly cannot be explained in terms of either the Federal Rules or the Constitution." Id. at 551, 90 S.Ct. at 745, 24 L.Ed.2d at 743.

58. Simler v. Conner, 372 U.S. 221, 83 S.Ct. 609, 9 L.Ed.2d 691 (1963). There is an excellent and comprehensive review of the Beacon-Dairy Queen problem in United States v. Williams, 441 F.2d 637 (5th Cir. 1971).

59. Fed.Rules Civ.Proc. 38(b). The rule is strictly enforced; see Groome v. Steward, 79 U.S.App. D.C. 50, 142 F.2d 756 (1944).

60. Clark, Code Pleading (2d ed. 1947) 113. In Wisconsin, as in some states, an express waiver of jury trial was required, but this was changed in 1944 when the state adopted the federal rule. The new rule was not popular and, pursuant to a petition of the bar, the Wisconsin Supreme Court reinstated the old rule. In re Petition of Doar, 248 Wis. 113, 21 N.W.2d 1 (1945).

61. Wilson v. Corning Glass Co., 195 F.2d 825 (9th Cir. 1952).

62. Fed.Rules Civ.Proc. 39(b).

63. Wilson v. Corning Glass Co., supra n. 61; Washington County Ins. Co. v. Wilkinson, 19 F.R.D. 177 (D.Md.1956); Beckstrom v. Coastwise Line, 13 F.R.D. 480, 483 (D.Alas.1953), in which the court says "For more than two years past, the Court has uniformly denied such requests by reason of the volume of litigation."

federal court.[64]   The cases are divided on the question whether a party who has failed to demand a jury in time may have his right to make a demand extended by an amendment to the complaint which introduces a new issue.[65]   In view of the waiver provisions, a party who desires a jury trial will be well advised to endorse a demand therefore on his complaint or answer.[66]

The jury panel.   The trial jury, whether of twelve or less, is selected from a much larger panel of prospective jurors who have been summoned to the courthouse for jury service.   This panel is supposed to be "selected at random from a fair cross section of the community," [67] but it is open to challenge on the ground that (1) the selection was not at random, or (2) exclusion of certain segments of the community prevented it from being a fair cross section.

Challenges   The first type of challenge deals with the question of whether the statutory procedure for selecting the jury was followed.   In Moore v. Navassa Guano Co.[68] the code provided that the county commissioners should cause the names of 36 persons to be drawn from the box by a child of not more than 10 years.   The evidence showed that as the names were drawn the commissioners would discuss them and decide whether they should be put back in the box.   This was held to vitiate the entire panel.   In Roche Fruit Co. v. Northern Pacific Railway Co.[69] there was an advertisement in the newspaper for women jurors in view of the fact that facilities for women jurors had been installed in the new courthouse; this was held not a violation of the statute in view of the fact that under the statute the judge could add names to the list compiled by the county assessor.   The court held that substantial compliance with the statute was sufficient in the absence of a showing of real prejudice.

The second type of challenge deals with whether the exclusion of certain segments of the community prevented the panel from

---

64. Fed.Rules Civ.Proc. 81(c).   For a case interpreting this rule see Segal v. American Cas. Co., 250 F.Supp. 936 (D.Md.1966).

65. Bereslavsky v. Caffey, 161 F.2d 499 (2d Cir. 1947), holding the amendment gave the plaintiff an additional 10 days to demand a jury; accord, Cataldo v. E. I. DuPont de Nemours & Co., 39 F.R.D. 305 (S.D.N.Y.1966).   Alcoa S. S. Co. v. Ryan, 211 F.2d 576 (2d Cir. 1954), holding the demand time was not extended.

66. This practice is specifically authorized by Fed.Rules Civ.Proc. 38(b).

67. 28 U.S.C.A. § 1861 which is a declaration of the policy established by the courts in previous generations.

68. 130 N.C. 229, 41 S.E. 293 (1902).

69. 18 Wash.2d 484, 139 P.2d 714 (1943).

being a fair cross section. In Thiel v. Southern Pacific Co.[70] the court excluded all daily wage earners on the ground that such employees would be excused on the ground of hardship. The Supreme Court reversed because the elimination of such a class would be to establish a jury as the instrument of the socially privileged. It held that the excuse of a juror for hardship was permissible for individual reasons, but that exclusion of a class was impermissible. In Ballard v. United States [71] the Supreme Court held that the systematic exclusion of women from the jury panel was reversible error. In Preston v. Mandeville [72] the United States Court of Appeals for the fifth circuit held that a showing that 29.3% of residents of the county were negroes, but that only 15% were on the master jury roll made out a case of prima facie discrimination based on race. In Dennis v. United States [73] the Supreme Court upheld an act of Congress qualifying for jury service employees of the government in cases in which the United States was a party and in Fay v. New York [74] the Supreme Court, by a divided vote of 5 to 4, upheld New York's "blue ribbon" jury which, ostensibly, sought to exclude from the panel all those who would claim an exemption from service, those who had been convicted of a crime, those who had scruples against the death penalty, and those who doubt their ability to lay aside prior opinions of guilt or innocence.

The qualifications for jury service, and the methods prescribing the manner in which the panel is drawn are established by statute in both the state [75] and the federal courts.[76] The 1968 revision of the judicial code is a substantial amendment to the federal procedure.

The voir dire examination. There are local variations in the details of jury selection but the basic pattern is the same. When a case is assigned to a courtroom for trial the judge will request the presence of a group of prospective jurors. Their names will be written on slips of paper which will be placed in the jury wheel or similar device so that they can be thoroughly shuffled. The clerk will then draw a sufficient number of names from the wheel

70. 328 U.S. 217, 66 S.Ct. 984, 90 L.Ed. 1181 (1946).

71. 329 U.S. 187, 67 S.Ct. 261, 91 L.Ed. 181 (1946).

72. 428 F.2d 1392 (5th Cir. 1970).

73. 339 U.S. 162, 70 S.Ct. 519, 94 L.Ed. 734 (1950).

74. 332 U.S. 261, 67 S.Ct. 1613, 91 L.Ed. 2043 (1947).

75. See Knox, Jury Selection, 22 N.Y.U.L.Rev. 433 (1947); Note, Jury Selection in California, 5 Stan. L.Rev. 247 (1953).

76. See 28 U.S.C.A. § 1861 et seq. (revised in 1968).

to make up the panel.[77] As the names are called the individuals take their places in the jury box. When the panel is assembled the members are sworn to give true answers to all questions propounded to them touching their qualifications to serve as jurors. The voir dire examination will then begin. Its purpose is to elicit information about the prospective jurors (1) to determine whether they meet the statutory qualifications for jury service, (2) to determine whether any grounds exist for a challenge for cause, and (3) to provide the parties with information so that they may more intelligently exercise their peremptory challenges.[78] The federal rule provides that "The court may permit the parties or their attorneys to conduct the examination of prospective jurors or may itself conduct the examination." [79] Many judges begin the examination by asking general questions of the entire panel such as "Do any of you know the parties or the attorneys involved in this litigation? If so raise your hand." If hands are raised the judge will continue with inquiries of the individuals. When the judge has finished he will then tell counsel they may inquire. The rule provides that if the judge himself conducts the examination he must afford counsel an opportunity to supplement it. The scope of the examination rests largely within the discretion of the trial judge.[80] Some judges confine the voir dire within rather

77. The panel will consist of the number of jurors to be used in the trial. This is usually 12, although the parties may stipulate for a lesser number. Fed. Rules Civ.Proc. 48. If alternate jurors are used, the panel will be increased by the number of alternates. The federal rule provides that "The court may direct that not more than six jurors in addition to the regular jury be called and impanelled to sit as alternate jurors." Fed.Rules Civ. Proc. 47(b).

78. It is not considered proper for counsel to use the voir dire examination as a vehicle for indoctrinating the jury on the merits of the case. Rousseau v. West Coast House Movers, 256 Cal.App.2d 878, 64 Cal.Rptr. 655 (1967). This is sometimes attempted, and it is frequently difficult to draw the line between the proper and the improper. The personal injury suits resulting from automobile accidents serve as an illustration. If the defendant carries automobile li-

ability insurance, the plaintiff will want to know whether any of the prospective jurors is employed by the insurance company or carries insurance with it, because that fact would bear on his impartiality. Most courts agree that guarded inquiries along these lines are legitimate, although the court may require a prior showing (out of the presence of the jury) that the defendant was in fact insured. See Kiernan v. VanSchaik, 347 F.2d 775 (3d Cir. 1965); Wheeler v. Rudek, 397 Ill. 438, 74 N.E.2d 601 (1947).

79. Fed.Rules Civ.Proc. 47(a).

80. Eisenhauer v. Burger, 431 F.2d 833 (6th Cir. 1970); People v. Lobb, 17 Ill.2d 287, 161 N.E.2d 325 (1959); Casey v. Roman Catholic Bishop, 217 Md. 595, 143 A.2d 627 (1958). For different points of view on the scope of the voir dire see Maxwell, The Case of the Rebellious Juror, 56 A.B.A.J. 838 (1970) and Youtt, Voir Dire Has its Proper Uses, 57 A.B.A.J. 38 (1971).

narrow limits in order to expedite the trial, and others allow counsel great latitude.

Challenges to individual jurors. There are two types of challenges to individual jurors. A challenge for cause, as the name suggests, raises the question of the competency of the juror to sit in the particular case. The causes which will disqualify him are (1) lack of the statutory qualifications,[81] (2) relationship to a party or his attorney by blood, marriage, or business ties from which partiality may be presumed,[82] and (3) bias or prejudice concerning the merits of the case before the court.[83] The grounds for a challenge are developed by the juror's answers on voir dire examination. Frequently a juror will admit to some past or present connection with a party, or to having read newspaper accounts of the case or having formed some opinion about it. He may then be asked whether he can disregard the prior experience and decide the case according to the law and the evidence. Notwithstanding an affirmative answer to such a question he may still be challenged. Whether or not to sustain the challenge rests within the sound discretion of the judge, which will not be reversed save for abuse.[84] If the challenge is sustained the juror is excused and replaced by another prospective juror who is subject to voir dire examination. In the nature of things there is no limit to the number of challenges for cause, since the goal is to secure an impartial jury. In cases which have received a great deal of publicity the process of jury selection may become greatly protracted.

In addition to challenges for cause, which are unlimited, each party is given a limited number of peremptory challenges which he may exercise for any or no reason. The number is fixed by statute or court rule and generally ranges from two to six. In the federal courts in civil cases each party is entitled to three peremptory challenges.[85] The mechanics of exercising peremptory challenges vary in different jurisdictions.

If a challenge for cause is overruled the juror may hold some resentment against counsel for challenging him. To guard

81. Sutton v. Fox, 55 Wis. 531, 13 N.W. 477 (1882).

82. In Chestnut v. Ford Motor Co., 445 F.2d 967 (4th Cir. 1971), a products liability case, the appellate court reversed because the trial court overruled a challenge for cause to a prospective juror who owned 100 shares of the capital stock of the defendant.

83. Kumli v. Southern Pac. Co., 21 Or. 505, 28 P. 637 (1892).

84. Flowers v. Flowers, 397 S.W.2d 121 (Tex.Ct.Civ.App.1965); Fitts v. Southern Pac. Co., 149 Cal. 310, 86 P. 710 (1906).

85. 28 U.S.C.A. § 1870.

against this possible resentment finding its way into the verdict, counsel may be well advised to spend one of his peremptory challenges by removing the juror. If the challenge for cause was erroneously overruled counsel is being forced to correct the error by using one of his precious peremptories and thus diluting the value of the others. If he loses the case may he get a reversal on appeal? The cases go both ways. One line says the error was not prejudicial since all he was entitled to was an impartial jury and he got that.[86] The other holds that the error was not cured because the value of the remaining peremptory challenges was lessened.[87]

SECTION 4. THE PROVINCE OF JUDGE AND JURY

In general. There is substantial agreement upon the proposition that all issues of law are to be decided by the judge and all issues of fact are to be decided by the jury.[88] During the course of the litigation many questions of law may arise, such as the sufficiency of a complaint to withstand a demurrer, or the scope of pretrial discovery, or the competency of a witness to testify, or the admissibility of evidence. There is no doubt that it is the province of the judge to rule on such questions. Nor is there any doubt that it is the province of the jury to decide questions of fact where there is a direct conflict in the testimony.[89] Where, however, there is no direct evidence concerning a crucial fact a difficult question is presented. Some courts take the position that where proven facts give equal support to each of two inconsistent inferences neither is proved and judgment must, as a matter of law, go against the party having the burden of proof.[90]

---

86. Pearce v. Quincy Mining Co., 149 Mich. 112, 112 N.W. 739 (1907).

87. Francone v. Southern Pac. Co., 145 F.2d 732 (5th Cir. 1945); Theobald v. St. Louis Transit Co., 191 Mo. 395, 90 S.W. 354 (1905).

88. The leading case is Sparf & Hansen v. United States, 156 U.S. 51, 15 S.Ct. 273, 39 L.Ed. 343 (1895).

89. In Pennsylvania R. R. v. Chamberlain, 288 U.S. 333, 338, 53 S.Ct. 391, 393, 77 L.Ed. 819, 822 (1933) the court said: "It . . . is true, generally, that where there is a direct conflict of testimony upon a matter of fact, the question must be left to the jury to determine, without regard to the number of witnesses upon either side." Where there is a conflict in the testimony, the credibility of the witnesses is for the jury: Elzig v. Gudwangen, 91 F.2d 434 (8th Cir. 1937).

90. Pennsylvania R. R. v. Chamberlain, 288 U.S. 333, 53 S.Ct. 391, 77 L.Ed. 819 (1933); Reid v. San Pedro, Los Angeles & Salt Lake R. R., 39 Utah 617, 621, 118 P. 1009, 1010 (1911): "It is a familiar rule that where the undisputed evidence of the plaintiff, from which the existence of an essential fact is sought to be inferred, points with equal force to two things, one of which renders the defendant liable and the other not, the plaintiff must fail."

Other courts take the position that it is within the province of the jury to draw the inference which it deems most reasonable.[91] The Supreme Court applied this rule in Lavender v. Kurn,[92] a wrongful death action. The decedent, a switchman, was found dying in the railroad yards one dark night, suffering from a head wound inflicted by a blunt instrument. There was evidence from which it could be inferred (1) that he was murdered, or (2) that he was struck by a protruding mail hook on a passing train. In holding the matter was for the jury the court said

> Whenever facts are in dispute or the evidence is such that fair-minded men may draw different inferences, a measure of speculation and conjecture is required on the part of those whose duty it is to settle the dispute by choosing what seems to them to be the most reasonable inference.[93]

In cases such as Lavender a jury is permitted a choice of inferences as to what actually happened. From proved facts it is inferring the existence of other facts. There is another type of case in which the jury is permitted even wider scope. These are the negligence cases in which there is no dispute as to what happened, the question being whether the conduct of the defendant could be characterized as negligent. Did the defendant's behavior fall below the standard of the reasonably prudent man under the same or similar circumstances? Since, by hypothesis, there is no dispute as to what happened, if the jury is permitted to decide the issue, what it is actually doing is drawing the line between liability and nonliability or, in other words, setting a standard of conduct. Nevertheless, the courts have held that if reasonable men could come to different conclusions on the admitted facts, the question is for the jury.[94]

91. Equitable Life Assurance Soc'y of the United States v. Fry, 386 F.2d 239 (5th Cir. 1967); Blank v. Coffin, 20 Cal.2d 457, 126 P.2d 868 (1942).

92. 327 U.S. 645, 66 S.Ct. 740, 90 L.Ed. 916 (1946).

93. Id. at 653, 66 S.Ct. at 744, 90 L.Ed. at 923.

94. One of the leading cases is Sioux City & Pac. R. R. v. Stout, 84 U.S. (17 Wall.) 657, 664, 21 L.Ed. 745, 749 (1873), in which the plaintiff, a child of 6, had his foot crushed while playing on the defendant's turntable. The facts were not in dispute and the court held that whether the defendant was negligent was a jury question. It said that in some cases the inference of negligence is so clear that it becomes a matter of law for the judge, in others the inference of no negligence is so clear it is also a question of law, but in between it is for the jury to determine. "It is assumed that twelve men know more of the common affairs of life than does one man, that they can draw wiser and safer conclusions from admitted facts thus occurring, than can a single judge." See also Pokora v. Wabash Ry., 292 U.S. 98, 54 S.Ct. 580, 78 L.Ed. 1149 (1934), holding the question

The contract cases present an interesting study in defining the province of judge and jury. The existence or nonexistence of a contract raises an issue of fact for the jury.[95] The meaning of the contract, if proved, presents a question for the judge unless the contract is ambiguous.[96] Whether or not the contract is ambiguous is a question for the judge.[97] If he rules it is ambiguous, the parties may then introduce their conflicting evidence as to its meaning, which raises an issue of fact to be decided by the jury.[98] Logically the same rules should apply to both oral and written contracts, but there is authority that the meaning of an oral contract presents a jury question.[99] The meaning of a statute is a question for the judge.[100]

Instructions. The function of the jury is an important and complicated one. Its first task is to resolve the issues of fact. This means that from the mass of conflicting evidence, it must determine what actually happened. It must "find the facts." Secondly, it must apply the law to those facts in order to determine who won. Lastly, it must record the result in its verdict. The law which it applies to the facts is, not its own conception of what the law should be, but the law as laid down by the trial judge in his instructions or charge to the jury. The ritual of

of negligence in a railroad grade crossing accident was for the jury, and distinguishing the earlier case of Baltimore & O. R. R. v. Goodman, 275 U.S. 66, 48 S.Ct. 24, 72 L.Ed. 167 (1927).

95. Rankin v. Fidelity Trust and Safe Deposit Co., 189 U.S. 242, 23 S.Ct. 553, 47 L.Ed. 792 (1903).

96. Hoyt v. Tapley, 121 Me. 239, 116 A. 559 (1922). Professor Thayer, explaining the rule, says that there is no doubt that the interpretation of written instruments is for the judge, not because it is a question of law, but because the court is better trained to do the job. "Such questions are addressed to the trained faculties of an educated man, acquainted with the use and the rules of language, and with the sort of business to which the writing relates, and may be settled merely by a critical reading of the paper." Thayer, A Preliminary Treatise on Evidence at the Common Law, (Little, Brown & Co., 1898) 202–04. In Fidelity & Deposit Co. of Md. v. Courtney, 186

U.S. 342, 22 S.Ct. 833, 46 L.Ed. 1193 (1902), the suit was on a fidelity bond which provided that notice of default must be given immediately. The notice was given between 10 and 17 days after the default was discovered. The court held it was a question for the jury whether the notice was given on time. The case may be analyzed as follows: "immediately" as used in the bond means "within a reasonable time"—the judge decides this; what is a reasonable time is a question on which reasonable men might differ, which therefore presents a jury question.

97. Jones v. Chaney & James Constr. Co., 399 F.2d 84 (5th Cir. 1968).

98. Hoyt v. Tapley, supra n. 96; Jones v. Chaney & James Constr. Co., supra n. 97.

99. Dobson v. Masonite Corp., 359 F.2d 921 (5th Cir. 1966).

100. Savannah, F. & W. Ry. v. Daniels, 90 Ga. 608, 17 S.E. 647 (1892).

instructing the jury has developed some rather definite rules over the centuries. Violations of those rules is one of the chief causes of reversals by appellate courts.

The judge may give some instructions to the jurors as to their duties at the beginning of the trial,[101] but his instructions on the law are given at the conclusion of the presentation of all of the evidence in the case, and generally after the closing arguments of counsel.[102] Practice differs as to whether the instructions must be in writing, and read to the jury, or whether the judge may instruct orally, with the majority of jurisdictions adopting the latter practice.[103] It is conceivable that a judge could assume sole responsibility for the instructions which he gives to the jury, but as a matter of fact the judge is practically always aided by counsel in the form of requested instructions which they tendered to him.[104] Counsel for each party will normally prepare a set of requests covering his legal theory of the case. Opportunity will be given to each side to argue in support of his requests and to object to the requests of his opponent. This usually occurs in a conference in the judge's chambers, outside of the presence of the jury. The judge may commit reversible error in his instructions to the jury by (1) failing to include matter contained in a proper request,[105] (2) including matter in an improper request to which proper objection had been made,[106] and (3) including erroneous statements of law not covered by either of the foregoing.[107] Errors in instructions do not, ordinarily, constitute

---

101. Prettyman, Jury Instructions— First or Last? 46 A.B.A.J. 1066 (1960).

102. For the practice in the several states see Vanderbilt, Minimum Standards of Judicial Administration, 233–34 (1949).

103. The federal rule contains no mandate, but the practice generally is to instruct orally: Fed.Rules Civ. Proc. 51; California policy favors reducing the instructions to writing and reading them to the jury: West's Ann.Cal.Code Civ.Proc., § 608, Martin v. Los Angeles Turf Club, 39 Cal.App.2d 338, 103 P.2d 188 (1940); in Nebraska the instructions must be reduced to writing if either party requests it: Neb. Rev.Stat. 25–1107 (Re-issue of 1964).

104. Fed.Rules Civ.Proc. 51 provides "At the close of the evidence or at such earlier time during the trial as the court reasonably directs, any party may file written requests that the court instruct the jury on the law as set forth in the requests . . . ."

105. Christian v. Bolls, 7 Cal.App.3d 408, 86 Cal.Rptr. 545 (1970); Griffin v. City of Cincinnati, 92 Ohio App. 492, 111 N.E.2d 31 (1952); Montgomery v. Virginia Stage Lines, Inc., 89 U.S.App.D.C. 213, 191 F.2d 770 (1951).

106. Domeracki v. Humble Oil & Ref. Co., 443 F.2d 1245 (3d Cir. 1971); McWeeney v. New York, N. H. & H. R. R., 282 F.2d 34 (2d Cir. 1960).

107. Freifield v. Hennessy, 353 F.2d 97 (3d Cir. 1965); People v. Kelly, 302 N.Y. 512, 99 N.E.2d 552 (1951).

grounds for reversal unless proper objections were made by counsel.[108] The reason for this rule is that the error may have been inadvertent and, if called to the judge's attention, would have been corrected by him. Under the old federal practice, in order to lay a proper foundation for appeal, counsel was required to object to the court's erroneous charge at the time it was made. This meant interrupting the judge which, as a matter of practical psychology, no lawyer relished doing unless he thought the matter was crucial. The present rule still requires the objection to be made "before the jury retires to consider its verdict" but it saves counsel the embarrassment of objecting in open court by providing: "Opportunity shall be given to make the objection out of the hearing of the jury." [109]

The court's instructions should cover both procedure and substance. In the first category are such matters as who has the burden of proof on the various issues, what is meant by a preponderance of the evidence, what is the effect of impeaching evidence, and what weight may, or must, be given to the testimony of a witness whom the jury believes to have testified falsely to certain matters. In the second category are the legal elements of plaintiff's cause of action and of defendant's defenses. For instance, in a personal injury action, the instructions should contain definitions of negligence, proximate cause, contributory negligence, possibly last clear chance, and the elements which may properly be considered in assessing plaintiff's damages, should the verdict be in his favor. In the federal courts, as an aid to the jury, the court may analyze the evidence and even comment upon it if he makes it clear that the jury is not bound by his opinion.[110] Most state courts take a contrary view, holding that for the judge to comment upon or give his opinion on the evidence constitutes an invasion of the province of the jury.[111] Under either state or

judge's comment

108. Pridgin v. Wilkinson, 296 F.2d 74 (10th Cir. 1961); Alexander v. Kramer Bros. Freight Lines, 273 F.2d 373 (2d Cir. 1959); O'Connell v. Naess, 176 F.2d 138 (2d Cir. 1949); Rogers v. Long Island R. R., 55 Misc.2d 507, 285 N.Y.S.2d 803 (1967). In rare cases, where the appellate court considers the error very serious, it may consider it in the absence of a proper objection, Freifield v. Hennessy, supra n. 107.

109. Fed.Rules Civ.Proc. 51.

110. Trezza v. Dame, 370 F.2d 1006 (5th Cir. 1967). For cases holding the court went too far in its comment see Nunley v. Pettway Oil Co., 346 F.2d 95 (6th Cir. 1965); Quercia v. United States, 289 U.S. 466, 53 S.Ct. 698, 77 L.Ed. 1321 (1933).

111. Cahalane v. Poust, 333 Mass. 689, 132 N.E.2d 660 (1956); Withers v. Lane, 144 N.C. 184, 56 S.E. 855 (1907). See Wright, Adequacy of Instructions to Jury, 53 Mich.L. Rev. 505 (1955); Wright, Instructions to the Jury: Summary Without Comment, 1954 Wash.U.L.Q. 177; Wright, The Invasion of Jury: Temperature of the War, 27 Temp. L.Q. 137 (1953).

federal practice it is error for the judge, in his instructions, to assume the existence of facts which are in issue.[112]   It is also error to instruct on issues which are not involved in the case.[113] Gaps or ambiguities in some instructions may be cured by others, since the instructions are to be considered as a whole, but an instruction which is affirmatively erroneous is not cured by a contradictory one.[114]   In some cases, after a jury has been out for several hours without being able to agree upon a verdict, the judge is tempted to call them back and encourage them to try harder for an agreement.   This is what is sometimes referred to as a "dynamite" instruction, and has been held permissible as long as it is made in such a way as to convey the idea of encouragement, but not coercion.[115]   The line between the two may be thin.

The common law tradition was to tailor the instructions to fit the individual case.   Many appeals were taken on the ground of alleged errors in instructions and, in the course of generations, the books became full of opinions approving or disapproving instructions on particular points of law.   These would serve as precedents in similar cases.   Inevitably the idea was born that the approved instructions could be collected, classified and published as a service to the bar.   California was a pioneer in publishing standardized instructions for juries; the success of which stimulated similar endeavors in other states.[116]   Standardized instructions do not afford a complete answer since nearly every case will have some unique features calling for special treatment. However there is no doubt that such compilations have been a boon to the practicing lawyer and have reduced the waste involved in appellate reversals because of erroneous instructions.

Taking the case from the jury.   There are situations in which the judge will relieve the jury of its function by directing it to return a verdict for one party or the other.   The leading modern case on the subject is Galloway v. United States.[117]   It involved a suit on a government G.I. insurance policy, brought many years after it had lapsed for nonpayment of premiums.   The theory of

112. Griffin v. City of Cincinnati, supra n. 105.

113. Freifield v. Hennessy, supra n. 107.

114. People v. Kelly, supra n. 107. In considering whether reversible error has been committed, the instructions must be considered as a whole: Marshall v. Ford Motor Co., 446 F.2d 712 (10th Cir. 1971).

115. Railway Express Agency, Inc. v. Mackay, 181 F.2d 257 (8th Cir. 1950).

116. Note, Standard Jury Instructions, 98 U.Pa.L.Rev. 223 (1949).

117. 319 U.S. 372, 63 S.Ct. 1077, 87 L.Ed. 1458 (1943).

the plaintiff, who was the wife and guardian of her incompetent husband, was that he had been permanently and totally disabled from a period prior to the lapse. It was conceded that he was permanently insane at the time of the trial, but the evidence of insanity during the whole period was very meager. There was a gap of five years not covered by any evidence, but the plaintiff attempted to bridge it by the testimony of a doctor who, in answer to a hypothetical question, stated that it was his opinion the condition could have existed during those years. At the conclusion of plaintiff's evidence the trial court directed a verdict for the defendant. This was affirmed by the United States Supreme Court by a 6–3 vote. Mr. Justice Rutledge, for the majority, held that she had failed to prove an essential element of her case. Concerning the gap in the evidence he said: "Insanity so long and continuously sustained does not hide itself from the eyes and ears of witnesses." [118] Regarding the testimony of the doctor he said: "Expert medical inference rightly can do much. But we think the feat attempted here too large for its accomplishment." [119] Mr. Justice Black, dissenting, accused the majority of weighing the credibility of the witness, traditionally a jury function. He goes on to say: "The fact that there was no direct testimony for a period of five years, while it might be the basis of fair argument to the jury by the government, does not, as the Court seems to believe, create a presumption against the petitioner so strong that his case must be excluded from the jury entirely." [120]

The case is important because of the historical background it furnishes concerning the constitutional power of a judge to take the case from the jury. In Galloway the plaintiff argued that the device of the directed verdict, which was unknown at the time of the adoption of the Seventh Amendment, was therefore unconstitutional. Justice Rutledge answered this by recalling that it was firmly established, when the amendment was adopted, there were two procedures by which the judge could control the verdict. One was the demurrer to the evidence, which he said served the same purpose as a directed verdict, and the other was the granting of a motion for a new trial on the ground the verdict was not supported by the evidence. Mr. Justice Black, in his dissent, distinguished both. The demurrer to the evidence was a written document which required a formal admission of the facts which the plaintiff's evidence tended to prove, and if overruled the judgment went for the plaintiff. In other words, it was

118. Id. at 385, 63 S.Ct. at 1084, 87 L.Ed. at 1468.

119. Id. at 388, 63 S.Ct. at 1086, 87 L.Ed. at 1469.

120. Id. at 410, 63 S.Ct. at 1097, 87 L.Ed. at 1482.

a risky business. As Mr. Justice Black said: "Under the directed verdict practice the moving party takes no such chance, for if his motion is denied, instead of suffering a directed verdict against him, his case merely continues into the hands of the jury." [121] It differs from the motion for a new trial because a granted motion for directed verdict ends the case while a granted motion for a new trial merely means a trial before another jury. Viewing the new device with alarm, Mr. Justice Black says it is "a long step toward the determination of fact by judges instead of by juries." [122]

A motion for a directed verdict resembles a demurrer. The *directed verdict* difference lies in the fact that a demurrer is addressed to the allegations of a pleading while a motion for a directed verdict is addressed to the evidence. The thrust is, however, the same. A demurrer by a defendant challenges the sufficiency of the complaint *to state* a cause of action. A motion for a directed verdict challenges the sufficiency of the plaintiff's evidence *to prove* a cause of action. There is another difference: the demurrer is addressed to allegations of ultimate, or operative facts; the motion for directed verdict is addressed to evidence, which is much more amorphous and inconclusive. When such a motion is made, the trial judge must assess the evidence to determine whether it tends to prove the allegations of the plaintiff's complaint. If a plaintiff fails to introduce any evidence whatever on a crucial element of his cause of action, there is no problem. The difficulty arises in the borderline cases, especially where various inferences may be drawn from circumstantial evidence. What standards or tests must the court employ in passing on the sufficiency of the evidence to go to the jury? There is general agreement that (1) the court must view the evidence in the light most favorable to the party whose case is attacked, and (2) all reasonable inferences must be drawn in his favor.[123] This still leaves the question: how strong must the evidence be? What is the test, or *split* standard? On this question the authorities are in anything but agreement. In the federal courts the early cases employed what later came to be known as the scintilla rule: a verdict could not be directed if there was any evidence, even a sliver or scintilla, to support the opponent's claim. This test soon gave way to the

---

121. Id. at 403, 63 S.Ct., at 1093, 87 L.Ed. at 1478.

122. Id. at 401, 63 S.Ct. at 1093, 87 L.Ed. at 1477.

123. Galloway v. United States, supra n. 117; Wilkerson v. McCarthy, 336 U.S. 53, 69 S.Ct. 413, 93 L.Ed. 497 (1949); Gunning v. Cooley, 281 U.S. 90, 50 S.Ct. 231, 74 L.Ed. 720 (1930); Aetna Cas. & Sur. Co. v. Yeatts, 122 F.2d 350 (4th Cir. 1941); Agen v. Metropolitan Life Ins. Co., 105 Wis. 217, 80 N.W. 1020 (1899).

substantial evidence rule: to avoid a directed verdict there must be substantial evidence. At other times the federal courts have given lip service to three other standards: (1) a verdict may be directed where the overwhelming evidence favors the moving party, (2) a verdict may be directed if the moving party would be entitled to a new trial if an adverse verdict were rendered, and (3) a verdict may not be directed where fair-minded or reasonable men could draw different inferences from the evidence.[124] There has been similar confusion and vacillation in the state courts.[125] The matter is further complicated when the case is in a federal court on the basis of diversity of citizenship. Under the doctrine of Erie Railroad Co. v. Tompkins [126] a federal court in a diversity

124. The history of the evolution of federal tests is described by Mr. Justice Black in his dissent in Galloway v. United States, supra n. 117 at 403–05, 63 S.Ct. at 1094, 87 L.Ed. at 1478–79: "The substantial evidence rule did not spring into existence immediately upon the adoption of the directed verdict device. For a few more years federal judges held to the traditional rule that juries might pass finally on facts if there was 'any evidence' to support a party's contention. The rule that a case must go to the jury unless there was 'no evidence' was completely repudiated in Schuylkill & Dauphin Improvement Co. v. Munson, 1871, 14 Wall. 442, 447, 448, 20 L.Ed. 867, upon which the Court today relies in part. There the Court declared that 'some' evidence was not enough—there must be evidence sufficiently persuasive to the judge so that he thinks 'a jury can properly proceed.' The traditional rule was given an ugly name, 'the scintilla rule,' to hasten its demise. For a time traces of the old formula remained . . . but the new spirit prevailed. . . . Later cases permitted the development of added judicial control. New and totally unwarranted formulas, which should surely be eradicated from the law at the first opportunity, were added as recently as 1929 in Gunning v. Cooley, 281 U.S. 90, 50 S.Ct. 231, 74 L.Ed. 720, which, by sheerest dictum, made new encroachments on the jury's constitutional functions. There it was announced that a judge might weigh the evidence to determine whether he, and not the jury, thought it was 'overwhelming' for either party, and then direct a verdict." For the reasonable man test see Wilkerson v. McCarthy, supra n. 123; Ferguson v. Moore-McCormack Lines, 352 U.S. 521, 77 S.Ct. 457, 1 L.Ed.2d 511 (1957). Cooper, Directions for Directed Verdicts: A Compass for Federal Courts, 55 Minn.L.Rev. 903 (1971).

125. In Pedrick v. Peoria & E. R. R., 37 Ill.2d 494, 504–05, 229 N.E.2d 504, 510 (1967) the court re-examines the test to be used in Illinois and in so doing writes a very scholarly opinion in which it analyzes and tabulates the tests being used in all of the states. The following gem occurs in Justice Underwood's discussion of the substantial evidence test: "As the light from a lighted candle in a dark room seems substantial but disappears when the lights are turned on, so may weak evidence fade when the proof is viewed as a whole. Constitutional guaranties are not impaired by direction of a verdict despite the presence of some slight evidence to the contrary . . . for the right to a jury trial includes the right to a jury verdict only if there are factual disptues of some substance."

126. Supra n. 32. See the discussion of the Erie doctrine in Chap. I.

case may apply its own rules of procedure but must apply the substantive law of the state in which it sits. If the state standard for determining the sufficiency of the evidence differs from the federal standard, which must the court use? There is no direct holding on the point by the Supreme Court of the United States,[127] but some of its decisions in closely related areas indicate that the court would hold that the federal test must be applied.[128] There are conficting decisions in the federal circuits with the majority in favor of the federal test.[129] The cases are exhaustively discussed in an en banc opinion in Boeing Co. v. Shipman.[130] The present federal test, according to the court, is the "reasonable man" test which it defines as follows:

> If the facts and inferences point so strongly and overwhelmingly in favor of one party that the Court believes that reasonable men could not arrive at a contrary ver-

127. In Dick v. New York Life Ins. Co., 359 U.S. 437, 444–45, 79 S.Ct. 921, 926, 3 L.Ed.2d 935, 941 (1959) the Court expressly left the question open. In the course of his opinion, Chief Justice Warren said: "Lurking in this case is the question whether it is proper to apply a state or federal test of sufficiency of the evidence to support a jury verdict where federal jurisdiction is rested on diversity of citizenship. On this question, the lower courts are not in agreement. [Citations.] But the question is not properly here for decision because, in the briefs and arguments in this Court, both parties assumed that the North Dakota standard applied. Moreover, although the Court of Appeals appears to have applied the state standard, that court did not discuss the issue. Under these circumstances, we will not reach out to decide this important question particularly where, in the context of this case, the two standards are substantially the same. A decision as to which standard should be applied can well be left to another case where the question is briefed and argued . . .."

128. In Byrd v. Blue Ridge Elec. Coop., 356 U.S. 525, 78 S.Ct. 893, 2 L.Ed.2d 953 (1958), a diversity case, the plaintiff sued his employer for personal injuries and the latter defended on the ground the state workmen's compensation law gave the exclusive remedy. Under state law the factual issue of whether the employment was covered by the act (the employer's immunity from a tort action) was to be decided by the judge. The Supreme Court held the issue should be submitted to the jury because of the strong federal interest in the operation of the jury system in the federal courts. In Herron v. Southern Pac. Co., 283 U.S. 91, 51 S.Ct. 383, 75 L.Ed. 857 (1931), another diversity case, the Court held that a federal court was not precluded from directing a verdict by a provision in a state constitution which provided that negligence and contributory negligence shall, in all cases, be questions of fact for the jury.

129. See authorities cited in Chief Justice Warren's opinion in the Dick case, supra n. 127. For later cases applying the federal standard see: Hommel v. Jackson-Atlantic, Inc., 438 F.2d 307 (5th Cir. 1971); Falcon v. Auto Busses Internacionales, 418 F.2d 673 (5th Cir. 1969). For later cases applying the state standard see: Illinois State Trust Co. v. Terminal R. R. Ass'n, 440 F.2d 497 (7th Cir. 1971); Rumsey v. Great A. & P. Tea Co., 408 F.2d 89 (3d Cir. 1969); Sleek v. J. C. Penney Co., 324 F.2d 467 (3d Cir. 1963).

130. 411 F.2d 365 (5th Cir. 1969).

dict, granting the motions is proper. On the other hand, if there is substantial evidence opposed to the motions, that is, evidence of such quality and weight that reasonable and fair-minded men in the exercise of impartial judgment might reach different conclusions, the motions should be denied, and the case submitted to the jury.[131]

It is one thing to decide upon a test for determining the sufficiency of the evidence, and it is quite another thing to apply it. A few cases will illustrate the point. Inman v. Baltimore & Ohio Railroad Co.[132] involved a suit by a night watchman at a complicated railroad crossing, who was struck and injured by a drunken driver. He sued his employer under the Federal Employers Liability Act on the theory the company was negligent in failing to provide a reasonably safe place to work. In the Ohio courts, where the case was tried, he received a $25,000 verdict which was reversed by the Ohio appellate courts because of a complete failure of the evidence to show negligence. In a 6–3 opinion the Supreme Court affirmed. The court was applying the "reasonable man" test. In his concurring opinion Mr. Justice Whittaker said: "I simply cannot see any substantial evidence—or even a scintilla or an iota of evidence—of negligence on the part of the respondent that caused, or directly contributed in any degree to cause, the petitioner's unfortunate injury." [133] He further said: "I regard my Brothers who dissent as reasonable men." [134] In Agen v. Metropolitan Life Insurance Co.[135] a widow sued to collect on a life insurance policy. The defense was suicide. All of the evidence was circumstantial. The trial court overruled a motion for directed verdict, and on the appeal the question was whether the evidence supported the verdict. The state supreme court, applying the reasonable man test, reversed, holding that the only reasonable inference from the evidence was that the deceased had committed suicide. In a dissenting opinion Judge Winslow points out that two members of the state supreme court (a seven man court) as well as the trial judge and the jury (twelve men) reached a different conclusion. The score 15 to 5. He concludes his opinion with the question: "Is it not an extreme statement to say, as is said in the opinion, that 'different minds cannot

131. Id. at 374. See also McCullough v. United States, 442 F.2d 1011 (5th Cir. 1971); Cheek v. Agricultural Ins. Co., 432 F.2d 1267 (5th Cir. 1970).

132. 361 U.S. 138, 80 S.Ct. 242, 4 L.Ed.2d 198 (1959).

133. Id. at 142, 80 S.Ct. at 244, 4 L. Ed.2d at 202.

134. Id.

135. 105 Wis. 217, 80 N.W. 1020 (1899).

reasonably come to different conclusions from the evidence'?" [136]
In Louisville & Nashville Railroad Co. v. Chambers [137] the plaintiff testified she was thrown over the foot of the bed in which
she was sleeping when a train of defendant's got off a spur track
and crashed into the house. All of the other evidence was to the
effect that the train crashed into the fence but stopped a few feet
short of the house. The Kentucky Court of Appeals reversed a
verdict for the plaintiff, even though the state applied the scintilla rule. The reason the court disregarded the plaintiff's sworn
testimony was that it was impeached by incontrovertible physical
facts. Perhaps the case should be paired with Berry v. Chaplin [138]
in which a California appellate court upheld a verdict for the
plaintiff in a bastardy proceeding against Charles Chaplin in
spite of the evidence of three doctors who had performed a blood
grouping test on the blood of Chaplin, the plaintiff and the child,
the results of which conclusively showed that Chaplin could not
have been the father.[139] All of which has led some judges to remark that the verbalization of the test is relatively unimportant.
In Galloway, Mr. Justice Rutledge said: "Whatever may be the
general formulation, the essential requirement is that mere specu-
lation be not allowed to do duty for probative facts, after making
due allowance for all reasonably possible inferences favoring the
party whose case is being attacked." [140] Judge Learned Hand put
it this way: "The most that has been said—probably all that can
be—is that there comes a point where the evidence no longer jus-
tifies any verdict but one." [141]

There is some authority to the effect that it is error to direct
a verdict in favor of a party having the burden of proof.[142] The
theory behind this variant of the rule is that the credibility of the
witnesses is always a question for the jury. Most courts have

136. Id. at 230–31, 80 N.W. at 1025.

137. 165 Ky. 703, 178 S.W. 1041
(1915).

138. 74 Cal.App.2d 652, 169 P.2d 442
(1946), noted in 39 Cal.L.Rev. 277
(1951).

139. Contra: Houghton v. Houghton, 179 Neb. 275, 137 N.W.2d 861
(1965); Jordan v. Mace, 144 Me.
351, 354, 69 A.2d 670, 672 (1949)
in which the court said: "We are
not disposed to close our minds to
conclusions which science tells us
are established. Nor do we propose to lay down as a rule of law
that the triers of fact may reject

what science says is true; for to
do so would be to invite at some
future time a conflict between
scientific truth and stare decisis
and in that contest the result
could never be in doubt."

140. Supra n. 117 at 395, 63 S.Ct.
at 1089, 87 L.Ed. at 1473.

141. Chamberlain v. Pennsylvania R.
R., 59 F.2d 986, 987 (2d Cir. 1932).

142. Ferdinand v. Agricultural Ins.
Co., 22 N.J. 482, 126 A.2d 323
(1956); Globe Indem. Co. v. Da-
viess, 243 Ky. 356, 47 S.W.2d 990
(1932).

refused to recognize such autocratic power in the jury and have held that verdicts may be directed for or against either party, in proper cases, regardless of the burden of proof.[143]

A motion for a directed verdict is usually made at the close of the plaintiff's evidence. The motion should be made and argued out of the presence of the jury so that it will not be prejudiced by the motion, argument, or ruling thereon. The motion should specify the grounds upon which it is based.[144] If the motion is overruled, and the defendant proceeds to introduce evidence, a new motion must be made at the conclusion of the entire evidence in order to lay a proper foundation for an appeal.[145] The reason for this is that, in ruling on the motion, the court must consider all of the evidence, and the nature and quality of the evidence at the conclusion of the entire case may differ radically from the evidence as it existed at the close of the plaintiff's case.[146] In rare instances a verdict may be directed against the plaintiff immediately following his opening statement.[147] This will only be proper when, taking his opening statement at face value, and assuming he can prove all he claims, there is no basis in law for a recovery.[148]

Even after the jury has returned its verdict it is not too late to challenge the sufficiency of the evidence. This is done by a motion for judgment non obstante veredicto. The basic question raised by such a motion is the same as that raised by a motion for a directed verdict, i. e., the legal sufficiency of the evidence. Consequently the test, or standard, which the court employs for passing on the sufficiency of the evidence should be the same as that employed in ruling on a motion for a directed verdict.[149] In the federal courts a party is not entitled to make a motion for

143. Chesapeake & O. Ry. v. Martin, 283 U.S. 209, 51 S.Ct. 453, 75 L. Ed. 983 (1931); Davis Frozen Foods, Inc. v. Norfolk S. Ry., 204 F.2d 839 (4th Cir. 1953); Walters v. Bank of Amer., 9 Cal.2d 46, 69 P. 2d 839 (1937).

144. Arkwright Mut. Ins. Co. v. Philadelphia Elec. Co., 427 F.2d 1273 (3d Cir. 1970).

145. Beebe v. Highland Tank & Mfg. Co., 373 F.2d 886 (3d Cir. 1967); Gagnon v. Dana, 69 N.H. 264, 39 A. 982 (1898); Harrison v. Dickerson, 87 N.J.L. 92, 93 A. 718 (1915); Spencer v. State of New York, 187 N.Y. 484, 80 N.E. 375 (1907).

146. Johnson v. Aetna Life Ins. Co., 158 Wis. 56, 147 N.W. 32 (1914).

147. Knapp v. Wabash R. R., 375 F. 2d 983 (8th Cir. 1967); Oscanyan v. Winchester Arms Co., 103 U.S. 261, 26 L.Ed. 539 (1880).

148. Winter v. Unaitis, 123 Vt. 372, 189 A.2d 547 (1963); Pomeroy v. Pennsylvania R. R., 96 U.S.App.D. C. 128, 223 F.2d 593 (1955).

149. Juhnke v. EIG Corp., 444 F.2d 1323 (9th Cir. 1971); Pedrick v. Peoria & E. R. R., 37 Ill.2d 494, 229 N.E.2d 504 (1967); Denman v. Spain, 242 Miss. 431, 135 So.2d 195 (1961).

judgment non obstante veredicto unless he has previously moved for a directed verdict.[150]

Where a trial court denies a defendant's motion for directed verdict or motion for judgment non obstante, and the appellate court holds that the ruling was erroneous, may it reverse the case with directions to enter judgment for the defendant? The Supreme Court has struggled with this question in an interesting series of cases. In Slocum v. New York Life Insurance Co.[151] it was held that the appellate court had no such right; to permit it to do so would be a violation of the constitutional right to jury trial since, at common law, the only way to reexamine the facts, after verdict, was to grant a new trial. In Baltimore & Carolina Line v. Redman [152] the trial judge reserved his ruling on a motion for directed verdict, the jury found a verdict for the plaintiff, the court overruled the reserved motion, and the defendant appealed. The Court of Appeals held the evidence was insufficient but, feeling itself bound by Slocum, reversed for a new trial. The Supreme Court distinguished Slocum on the basis that there was a well recognized practice of reserving ruling on a motion at common law, and it reversed with directions to enter judgment for the defendant. When, a few years later, the Court promulgated its Rules of Civil Procedure, it included a provision that whenever a motion for directed verdict is denied or not granted the court is deemed to have "submitted the action to the jury subject to a later determination of the legal questions raised by the motion." [153] The rule also provided that a party who had moved for a directed verdict could, within 10 days from the entry of judgment, move for judgment non obstante and could join with it an alternative motion for a new trial. The purpose of this provision was to take care of the situation in which either the trial or appellate court found that the party was not entitled to a directed verdict but that the evidence was so weak that, in the interest of justice, he was entitled to a new trial. The rule got its first severe test in Montgomery Ward & Co. v. Duncan.[154] In that case the defendant complied with the rule by first moving for a directed verdict, and, after verdict, filing an alternative motion for judgment non obstante or for a new trial. The trial court held the evidence was insufficient and entered judgment for the defendant. On appeal by the plaintiff the Court of Ap-

---

150. Fed.Rules Civ.Proc. 50(b).

151. 228 U.S. 364, 33 S.Ct. 523, 57 L.Ed. 879 (1913).

152. 295 U.S. 654, 55 S.Ct. 890, 79 L.Ed. 1636 (1935).

153. Fed.Rules Civ.Proc. 50(b).

154. 311 U.S. 243, 61 S.Ct. 189, 85 L.Ed. 147 (1940).

peals held the evidence was sufficient, and it reversed with directions to enter judgment on the verdict for the plaintiff. It did not pass on the motion for a new trial on the theory that the trial court had never passed on it. The Supreme Court held the trial court should have made a ruling on both motions, and reversed with directions for him to rule on the motion for a new trial. There followed a series of three cases,[155] involving slightly different fact patterns, in which the Supreme Court held that even though a party had made a proper motion for directed verdict, the ruling on which would be deemed reserved under the rule, if he did not file a timely motion for judgment non obstante, the appellate court was powerless to reverse with instructions to grant the motion. Following these cases the rule was amended to spell out in detail the duties of the trial court and the authority of the appellate court.[156] As amended the rule provides that where a party files an alternative motion for a new trial in conjunction with his motion for judgment non obstante the trial court must rule on both motions and, if a verdict has been returned, it may (1) allow it to stand, (2) order a new trial, or (3) enter judgment non obstante; if no verdict has been returned it may (1) order a new trial or (2) enter the judgment requested by the motion for directed verdict. The rule also gives the appellate court flexible powers under which, if it reverses for error, it may (1) order judgment in accordance with the motion for directed verdict, (2) order a new trial, or (3) direct the trial court to determine whether to grant a new trial. The amended rule came before the Court in Neely v. Martin K. Eby Co.[157] which upheld the power of the Court of Appeals to reverse with instructions to dismiss because the trial court had erroneously denied the motion for directed verdict.

SECTION 5. VOLUNTARY DISMISSAL

If a plaintiff is disappointed in the strength of his evidence and fears that a verdict may be directed against him he may wish to dismiss his suit and wait until he is better prepared to begin it again. May he do so? At common law the answer would have been yes.[158] Because of the technical rules of pleading and prac-

155. Cone v. West Va. Pulp & Paper Co., 330 U.S. 212, 67 S.Ct. 752, 91 L.Ed. 849 (1947); Globe Liquor Co. v. San Roman, 332 U.S. 571, 68 S.Ct. 246, 92 L.Ed. 177 (1948); Johnson v. New York, N. H. & H. R. R., 344 U.S. 48, 73 S.Ct. 125, 97 L.Ed. 77 (1952).

156. Fed.Rules Civ.Proc. 50(c) & (d).

157. 386 U.S. 317, 87 S.Ct. 1072, 18 L.Ed.2d 75 (1967).

158. Toulmin v. Industrial Metal Protectives, Inc., 135 F.Supp. 925 (D.Del.1955); Koffler & Reppy, Common Law Pleading (1969) 548.

tice, because of the very real danger of surprise at the trial, and because so many errors could be fatal, the common law was generous in allowing a dismissal without prejudice at any time before verdict. The situation is quite different today, when pleading is less technical, when amendments are freely given, and when use of the discovery machinery makes surprise unlikely. We are also living in an age which regards judicial economy as a virtue. Consequently it is not surprising to find that the right of a plaintiff to take a voluntary dismissal without prejudice has been sharply curtailed.

Under the federal rules a plaintiff may dismiss as a matter of right "any time before service by the adverse party of an answer or of a motion for summary judgment, whichever first occurs." [159] Thereafter his right to dismiss is lost unless he secures the consent of his opponent or the consent of the court. There is another restriction: a voluntary dismissal will operate as an adjudication on the merits (and thus be res judicata) if the plaintiff has "once dismissed in any court of the United States or of any state an action based on or including the same claim." [160] The rules are to protect defendants from harassment by incompetent or vacillating plaintiffs. Notwithstanding their rigor, a court may always, in its discretion, grant a plaintiff leave to dismiss without prejudice upon a showing of good cause.[161] The court may, however, impose reasonable conditions, such as the payment of costs and attorney fees.[162]

SECTION 6. THE VERDICT

Arriving at a verdict. The materials which a jury uses in fashioning its verdict should come to it in open court. They are of two kinds: the evidence and the law. The evidence it receives from the witnesses who testify, together with the documents and other things which are identified, authenticated and introduced in evidence. The law it receives from the judge in the form of his instructions or charge to the jury.

The jury is not supposed to consider evidence which has not been presented and admitted in open court, and if it can be proved that it has done so, its verdict will be set aside. For instance, if in an automobile accident case some of the jurors take an un-

---

159. Fed.Rules Civ.Proc. 41(a) (1).

160. Id.

161. Fed.Rules Civ.Proc. 41(a) (2).

162. American Cyanamid Co. v. McGhee, 317 F.2d 295 (5th Cir. 1963); Pathe Lab. v. Technicolor Motion Picture Corp., 19 F.R.D. 211 (S.D. N.Y.1955); Eaddy v. Little, 234 F. Supp. 377 (E.D.S.C.1964).

authorized view of the scene of the accident,[163] or, contrary to the admonition of the judge, read newspaper accounts of the facts of the case,[164] or rely upon the personal knowledge or expertise of one of the jurors,[165] the verdict will not be allowed to stand. The reason for the rule is that where one party introduces evidence in open court, his opponent has the opportunity to test it by cross examination or to introduce other evidence to refute it, but he has no such opportunity when the evidence is furnished to the jury without his knowledge. In the automobile accident cases it is quite possible that the jurors inspecting the scene on their own volition have mistaken the true location, or that there have been physical changes in the area since the accident.

The verdict is supposed to represent the agreement of the individual jurors after a rational process of discussion, analysis, and reasoned decision. If the jurors cannot agree upon a verdict, a mistrial should be declared. It is improper for a jury to break a deadlock by cutting cards, rolling dice, or flipping a coin.[166] It is likewise improper for a jury to render a "quotient" verdict, but care must be taken in defining the term. It frequently happens in personal injury cases that the jurors are in agreement that the plaintiff should recover but differ widely as to amount. In this situation the foreman may propose that each juror write on a slip of paper the amount he thinks is proper, that the figures be added, and the sum divided by twelve. This is not objectionable if the jurors thereafter agree upon the figure. If, however, they agree in advance to be bound by the quotient, the verdict is bad.[167] This is because it gives a single juror the power to dominate the verdict by putting a wholly unreasonable figure on his slip which will result in a quotient figure to which none would otherwise have agreed. Other problems of mechanics

---

163. Skinitzero v. City of New York, 299 N.Y. 570, 86 N.E.2d 102 (1949).

164. People v. Hryciuk, 5 Ill.2d 176, 125 N.E.2d 61 (1954).

165. Texas Employers' Ins. Ass'n v. Price, 336 S.W.2d 304 (Tex.Civ. App.1960); Solberg v. Robbins Lumber Co., 147 Wis. 259, 133 N. W. 28 (1911).

166. The invalidity of such "chance" verdicts seems obvious, but even here there is room for the borderline case. Vogt v. Curtis, 200 Wash. 692, 94 P.2d 761 (1939) was a personal injury suit in Washington where 10 out of 12 jurors may

return a verdict. After several hours of deliberation 9 jurors were for plaintiff and 3 for defendant. The three agreed that one of them would change his vote so that there would be a verdict. They cut cards to see who it would be. The one who "lost" changed his vote to the plaintiff. The Washington Supreme Court held the verdict was bad as a chance verdict, but the decision was criticized in 15 Wash. L.Rev. 124 (1940).

167. Bardessono v. Michels, 3 Cal. 3d 780, 91 Cal.Rptr. 760, 478 P.2d 480 (1970); Hukle v. Kimble, 172 Kan. 630, 243 P.2d 225 (1952).

sometimes occur, especially in states which permit majority verdicts. For instance, in Kentucky, where nine jurors may agree on a verdict, if the nine jurors who signed the verdict fixing damages were not the same nine who found liability, the verdict would be void.[168]

Returning the verdict. The jury arrives at its verdict in the seclusion of the jury room. The foreman then reduces it to writing, the bailiff is notified, and the jury is conducted back to the courtroom where the verdict is delivered to the clerk or judge. Where it is anticipated that the jury may not be able to agree upon a verdict during the normal hours when court is in session, the court may give instructions for a "sealed verdict." This means that the verdict, when agreed upon, may be placed in a sealed envelope and given to the bailiff so that the jurors can separate and go home for the night. They must, however, all appear in court the next morning when their verdict will be presented to the court.[169] The verdict will not be legally effective unless agreed to by all of the jurors in open court. Hence, in the case of a sealed verdict, if one of the jurors dies during the night,[170] or if a juror changes his mind during the night [171] the verdict is legally ineffective. When a verdict is returned to court, it is quite common for the clerk, or the judge, to "poll the jury," which means asking each individual juror whether the verdict as read to him is his verdict. This is a safeguard to prevent error or misunderstanding, and it does give the juror a chance to express a last minute dissent.[172]

Impeaching the verdict. After a verdict has been returned, accepted and recorded, the jury is discharged. Is it then too late for members of the jury to give evidence to show that the verdict was erroneous or was arrived at by improper means? The common law rule was that the affidavits of jurors were admissible to correct a purely clerical error,[173] but not to prove misconduct

---

168. Baxter v. Tankersley, 416 S.W. 2d 737 (Ky.App.Ct.1967).

169. Porrett v. City of New York, 252 N.Y. 208, 169 N.E. 280 (1929).

170. Rich v. Finley, 325 Mass. 99, 89 N.E.2d 213 (1949).

171. Kramer v. Kister, 187 Pa. 227, 40 A. 1008 (1898).

172. Weeks v. Hart, 31 Hun 181 (1881).

173. Dalrymple v. Williams, 63 N.Y. 361 (1875). Cf. Shears v. Metropolitan Transit Auth., 324 Mass. 358, 86 N.E.2d 437 (1949) where, in a personal injury action, verdicts of $3500 were rendered against the two defendants; affidavits of jurors that they intended the plaintiff to get a total of $7000 were held inadmissible since this was not a clerical error but an error of law in misapplying the plain instructions of the judge. See Robb v. John C. Hickey, Inc., 19

on the part of the jury or to overthrow its verdict.[174]   The ancient reasons given for the rule were that the jurors had taken an oath to well and truly try the case, and they would not later be permitted to "stultify" themselves by showing that they did not do their duty.   There is a very practical reason that, were the rule otherwise, one corrupt juror might undo the work of all, thus undermining the stability of the jury system.   On the other hand, if the jurors were guilty of misconduct, albeit unwittingly, by using the quotient method of assessing damages, or taking an unauthorized view of the premises, unless their affidavits are admissible the misconduct could rarely be shown.   The trend of the modern cases is to modify the strict common law rule by drawing a distinction between matters which "inhere" in the verdict and those which do not.[175]   Putting it another way, affidavits of jurors are not admissible to show subjective misconduct, such as that the juror did not assent to the verdict or that he did not understand or misconstrued the court's instructions or that he was unduly influenced by his colleagues.   However, affidavits as to objective misconduct are admissible, such as taking an unauthorized view, or conversing with a witness, or participating in a chance or quotient verdict.   In other words, the affidavits would be admissible regarding matters which do not rest alone in the juror's breast but are capable of corroboration.

Types of verdict.   There are two types of verdict: general and special.[176]   A general verdict is one in which the jury makes a general finding for one party or the other, and if for the plaintiff, assessing the amount of his damages.   Most verdicts are of this type.   In form they are simple, but their use imposes upon the jury the difficult task of (1) ascertaining the facts from the conflicting evidence, (2) comprehending all the rules of law involved in the case which have been given to it in the court's instructions, and (3) applying the rules of law to the facts of the case.   The jury may fall into error in any one or more of

N.J.Misc. 455, 20 A.2d 707 (1941), to the effect that a judge may correct a verdict by striking mere surplusage, but not correct it in regard to an error of law.

174. Domeracki v. Humble Oil & Ref. Co., 443 F.2d 1245 (3d Cir. 1971); Complete Auto Transit, Inc. v. Wayne Broyles Eng. Corp., 351 F.2d 478 (5th Cir. 1965); Kollert v. Cundiff, 50 Cal.2d 768, 329 P.2d 897 (1958) (but California has two exceptions: one, by statute, regarding chance verdicts, and the

other by judicial decision, where bias or disqualification of a juror was concealed by false answers on the voir dire examination).

175. One of the best early discussions of what has become the "modern" rule is found in Wright v. Illinois & Miss. Tel. Co., 20 Iowa 195 (1866). See also Jorgensen v. York Ice Mach. Corp., 160 F.2d 432 (2d Cir. 1947).

176. Sunderland, Verdicts, General and Special, 29 Yale L.J. 253 (1920).

these three functions, or it may render a verdict based neither on the law or the facts but on its own ideas of law and justice. From the general verdict itself there is no way of telling whether the jury has performed its function properly.[177] The second type of verdict, the special verdict, is designed to simplify the task of the jury and to eliminate most of the sources of jury-error. Instead of a general finding for one party or the other the special verdict requires the jury to make a specific finding on each ultimate fact put in issue by the pleadings.[178] That is all it has to do. The court will then apply the law to those found facts.[179] In theory the special verdict is much superior, but it was seldom used, perhaps because of the difficulty in framing specific questions to be answered by the jury, and perhaps because if the jury failed to find on any issue, the verdict was a nullity.[180] The federal rules eliminated the latter pitfall by providing that if, in submitting the case:

> the court omits any issue of fact raised by the pleadings or by the evidence, each party waives his right to a trial by jury on the issue so omitted unless before the jury retires he demands its submission to the jury. As to an issue omitted without such demand the court may make a finding; or, if it fails to do so, it shall be deemed to have made a finding in accord with the judgment on the special verdict.[181]

177. In Skidmore v. Baltimore & O. R. R., 167 F.2d 54 (2d Cir. 1948) Judge Frank's opinion contains a brilliant, penetrating and scathing criticism of the general verdict and a eulogy of the special verdict. Sahr v. Bierd, 354 Mich. 353, 92 N.W.2d 467 (1958) should be read in connection with Skidmore. It is practically a law review article by Judge Smith on the history and functions of the jury system. For an appraisal of the jury system in civil cases see Green, Juries and Justice—The Jury's Role in Personal Injury Cases, 1962 U.Ill.L.F. 152. The article contains an extensive bibliography on the jury system.

178. It is the ultimate or operative facts upon which findings must be made, and not the evidentiary facts. Baxter v. Chicago & N. W. R. R., 104 Wis. 307, 80 N.W. 644 (1899).

179. Id. No instructions on the law are given to the jury, but the court may define legal terms.

180. Even under the old practice it was difficult to be sure that every issue made by the pleadings was submitted to the jury. Under modern practice the difficulty is enhanced because of rules such as Fed.Rules Civ.Proc. 15(b) which provides that "When issues not raised by the pleadings are tried by express or implied consent of the parties, they shall be treated in all respects as if they had been raised in the pleadings."

181. Fed.Rules Civ.Proc. 49(a). For interesting applications of this rule see Columbia Horse & Mule Comm'n Co. v. American Ins. Co., 173 F.2d 773 (6th Cir. 1949); Brenham v. Southern Pac. Co., 328 F.Supp. 119 (W.D.La.1971). See generally Lipscomb, Special Verdicts under the Federal Rules, 25 Wash.U.L.Q. 185 (1940).

The fact that special verdicts are rarely used, plus the inscrutability of the general verdict, led to a statutory procedure by which special interrogatories could be submitted to the jury regarding key facts, to be answered in connection with the general verdict. In this way, it was thought, the reliability of the general verdict could be tested by the answers to the special interrogatories. It should be emphasized that these special interrogatories are not a special verdict because they do not purport to cover all the issues in the case. They are merely a testing device to be used with the general verdict.[182] The jury will be instructed to return a general verdict and, in addition, answers to the special interrogatories. If the answers to the interrogatories are harmonious or consistent with the general verdict, then the judge will enter judgment for the party who wins in accordance with the general verdict. If the answers are consistent with each other but one or more is inconsistent with the general verdict, the court may (1) enter judgment in accordance with the answers notwithstanding the general verdict, (2) return the jury for further deliberation, or (3) grant a new trial. When the answers are inconsistent with each other and one or more are likewise inconsistent with the general verdict, this indicates a confused jury so the court may (1) send them back for further deliberation, or (2) grant a new trial.[183]

Special interrogatories must call for answers regarding ultimate or operative facts since a mere evidentiary fact could not be in irreconcilable conflict with a general verdict.[184] Since the effect of an answer to a special interrogatory may be to destroy the general verdict, the courts make every effort to harmonize them.[185] For instance, in a personal injury action where the jury returned a general verdict for the plaintiff, it also answered "No" to a special interrogatory which asked "Did the plaintiff use ordinary care and caution for his own safety on the occasion in question?" The Court of Appeals held it was error for the District Court to enter a judgment for the defendant on the basis of the answer since the jury might have thought the plain-

182. The use and form of special interrogatories by a federal court in a diversity case is governed by the federal rules and not by state law, and is a matter within the discretion of the trial judge. Elston v. Morgan, 440 F.2d 47 (7th Cir. 1971).

183. Fed.Rules Civ.Proc. 49(b).

184. Although an answer involving merely an evidentiary fact could not serve to justify a judgment notwithstanding the verdict, it might be the basis for awarding a new trial.

185. Marley v. Wichita Transp. Corp., 150 Kan. 818, 96 P.2d 877 (1939).

tiff's negligence was not the proximate cause of the accident,[186] or it might have thought that the defendant had the last clear chance to avoid the injury.[187]　Occasionally a jury will return a general verdict and report that it is unable to agree upon answers to the interrogatories.　In such a situation there is a split of authority whether the court may withdraw the interrogatories and thus ease the way for the verdict.[188]　Occasionally a court will confuse the general verdict plus interrogatories device with a special verdict.[189]

SECTION 7.　NON–JURY TRIALS

Cases are tried to the judge sitting without a jury (1) where there is no constitutional or statutory right to a jury, as in equity and admiralty cases, and (2) where the right to a jury trial is waived by failure to make a seasonable demand for one,[190] and (3) where the parties stipulate or consent to a trial to the court.[191]

The conduct of a trial in a non-jury case is essentially the same as in a jury case with the one important difference that the judge takes over the functions of the jury.　He becomes the fact-finder as well as the law-giver.　Instructions on the law become superfluous, but for the record the judge must set forth his conclusions of law and separately state his findings of fact.[192]　As in the case of a jury trial counsel for the parties are permitted to argue the law to the court and they may request specific findings of fact.　It is the duty of the judge to prepare the findings

186. Mayer v. Petzelt, 311 F.2d 601 (7th Cir. 1962).

187. Some cases hold that in order to justify giving judgment on the special interrogatories, the inconsistency with the general verdict must be such that it is incapable of being removed by any evidence admissible under the issues, Chicago & N. W. Ry. v. Dunleavy, 129 Ill. 132, 22 N.E. 15 (1889), and the court will treat the case as though the evidence had been introduced, Evansville & S. Traction Co. v. Spiegel, 49 Ind.App. 412, 94 N.E. 718 (1911).

188. Diniero v. United States Lines, 288 F.2d 595 (2d Cir. 1961), noted in 14 Stan.L.Rev. 395 (1962); 47 Va.L.Rev. 1439 (1961).

189. Gallick v. Baltimore & O. R. R., 372 U.S. 108, 83 S.Ct. 659, 9 L.Ed. 2d 618 (1963); Nollenberger v. United Air Lines, Inc., 216 F.Supp. 734 (S.D.Cal.1963), reversed sub nom United Air Lines, Inc. v. Wiener, 335 F.2d 379 (9th Cir. 1964); Halprin v. Mora & Davis, 231 F.2d 197 (3d Cir. 1956).

190. Fed.Rules Civ.Proc. 38(d), 39 (b).

191. Fed.Rules Civ.Proc. 39(a).

192. Fed.Rules Civ.Proc. 52(a) provides: "In all actions tried upon the facts without a jury or with an advisory jury, the court shall find the facts specially and state separately its conclusions of law thereon, and judgment shall be entered pursuant to Rule 58."

and conclusions but it is not uncommon for him to invite counsel to submit proposed findings which he may adopt or modify.[193]

In a jury trial, at the conclusion of the plaintiff's evidence, the defendant may move for a directed verdict. In a non-jury trial the defendant may move for an involuntary dismissal, which raises the same basic issue: the insufficiency of plaintiff's evidence to support a recovery. There is an important difference in the two situations. When passing on a motion for a directed verdict the judge must view the evidence in the light most favorable to the plaintiff because he is deciding whether there is enough evidence to carry the case to the jury. But in a non-jury case he is in effect the jury, which means he may weigh the evidence and pass upon the credibility of the witnesses.[194]

193. In Roberts v. Ross, 344 F.2d 747, 751 (3d Cir. 1965) the court chastises the lower court for its practice of announcing a decision and then directing counsel for the prevailing party to prepare findings and conclusions. Said the court: "We strongly disapprove this practice. For it not only imposes a well-nigh impossible task upon counsel but also flies in the face of the spirit and purpose, if not the letter, of Rule 52(a). The purpose of that rule is to require the trial judge to formulate and articulate his findings of fact and conclusions of law in the course of his consideration and determination of the case and as a part of his decision making process, so that he may himself be satisfied that he has dealt fully and properly with all the issues in the case before he decides it and so that the parties involved and this court on appeal may be fully informed as to the bases of his decision when it is made. Findings and conclusions prepared ex post facto by counsel, even though signed by the judge, do not serve adequately the function contemplated by the rule. At most they provide the judge with an opportunity to reconsider the bases of his original decision but without affording the parties any information as to what those issues were or which of them are being reconsidered. At worst they are likely to convict the judge of error because, as here, they are inadequate to support his decision

or because, as we have observed in other cases, they are loaded down with argumentative over-detailed partisan matter much of which is likely to be of doubtful validity or even wholly without support in the record." The second circuit inserted a similar admonition in a footnote to Montgomery v. Goodyear Aircraft Co., 392 F.2d 777, 782 (2d Cir. 1968).

194. Fed.Rules Civ.Proc. 41(b) provides: "After the plaintiff, in an action tried by the court without a jury, has completed the presentation of his evidence, the defendant . . . may move for a dismissal on the ground that upon the facts and the law the plaintiff has shown no right to relief. The court as trier of the facts may then determine them and render judgment against the plaintiff or may decline to render any judgment until the close of the evidence. If the court renders judgment on the merits against the plaintiff, the court shall make findings as provided in Rule 52(a)." See Emerson Elec. Co. v. Farmer, 427 F.2d 1082 (5th Cir. 1970) which says that prior to the amendment of the rule in 1948, the circuits were split on whether the court could weigh the evidence on such a motion, but that since the amendment, the rule is clear that the court may do so. Accord, with the federal rule: Mabey v. Hansen, 60 N.J.Super. 272, 158 A.2d 831 (1960); Richards v. Kuppinger, 46 Wash.2d 62, 278 P.2d 395 (1955).

SECTION 8. NEW TRIALS

In any trial it is possible that errors or irregularities occurred along the way or that the verdict, for some reason, was not responsive to the law, the facts, or the merits of the case, resulting in a miscarriage of justice, at least from the point of view of the losing party. In such circumstances an appeal would be possible, but perhaps not necessary, because the judge who tried the case has the power to grant a motion for a new trial. Such a motion must be filed in apt time, usually specified by statute or ~~motion~~ court rule,[195] and a proper foundation for the motion must have been laid by proper objections to those rulings of the court which are deemed erroneous.[196] The grounds for which a new trial may be granted are sometimes specifically enumerated in a statute,[197] and sometimes are to be found in the common law.[198] Where the grounds are enumerated in a statute there is a split of authority as to whether the statutory grounds are exclusive.[199] The discussion which follows will be limited to the most common grounds.

Weight of the evidence. Probably the most frequent ground for the granting of a new trial is that the verdict is against the

---

195. Under the federal rules a motion for a new trial must be *served* within 10 days from the entry of judgment, Fed.Rules Civ.Proc. 59 (b), unless it is joined with a motion for judgment notwithstanding the verdict, Fed.Rules Civ.Proc. 50(b). On certain grounds the motion must be filed "within a reasonable time," Fed.Rules Civ.Proc. 60(b). See Hulson v. Atchison, T. & S. F. Ry., 289 F.2d 726 (7th Cir. 1961) to the effect that the time limits are mandatory and cannot be extended. But see Thompson v. Immigration & Naturalization Serv., 375 U.S. 384, 84 S.Ct. 397, 11 L.Ed.2d 404 (1964) holding that the appellate court would not go behind a specific finding by the trial judge that the motion was made "in ample time."

196. Everett v. Southern Pac. Co., 181 F.2d 58 (9th Cir. 1950).

197. For example, the West's Ann. Cal.Code Civ.Proc., § 657 lists seven grounds.

198. The federal rule merely provides: "A new trial may be granted to all or any of the parties on all or part of the issues (1) in an action in which there has been a trial by jury, for any of the reasons for which new trials have heretofore been granted in actions at law in the courts of the United States; and (2) in an action tried without a jury, for any of the reasons for which rehearings have heretofore been granted in suits in equity in the courts of the United States." Fed.Rules Civ.Proc. 59(a).

199. Holding the statutory grounds are exclusive: St. Louis & S. F. Ry. v. Werner, 70 Kan. 190, 78 P. 410 (1904); Ginsberg v. Williams, 270 Minn. 474, 135 N.W.2d 213 (1965). Holding the statutory grounds not exclusive: Bottineau Land Co. v. Hintze, 150 Iowa 646, 125 N.W. 842 (1910); Corley v. New York & H. R. R., 12 App.Div. 409, 42 N.Y.S. 941 (1896). See note, New Trial— Exclusiveness of Statutory Grounds —Loss of Reporter's Notes, 5 Minn. L.Rev. 564 (1921).

weight of the evidence. In passing upon such a motion the trial court employs a different test than it does in passing on a motion for a directed verdict.[200] In either case the judge is reviewing the evidence, but in the case of the directed verdict his concern is to determine whether there was enough evidence to send the case to the jury, and he is obliged to view the evidence in the light most favorable to the party opposing the motion. In passing on a motion for a new trial he is assuming there is enough evidence to prevent a directed verdict, but is concerned with whether the verdict is against the weight of the evidence. Since the judge was present at the trial and observed the witnesses, he is vested with a wide discretion in granting or denying a new trial on this ground, and will not be reversed except for a clear abuse of discretion.[201]

One of the frequent instances in which a verdict is attacked for being against the weight of the evidence is the personal injury case where the damages awarded appear to be excessive or inadequate. Either would be ground for a new trial, but new trials are expensive and time consuming. Is there a better way? May the judge, if he believes the verdict to be grossly excessive, give the plaintiff the option of remitting part of it, in lieu of submitting to a new trial? This practice is known as remittitur and has long been recognized as proper.[202] The theory is that,

200. Hampton v. Magnolia Towing Co., 338 F.2d 303 (5th Cir. 1964); Snead v. New York Cent. R. R., 216 F.2d 169 (4th Cir. 1954); Aetna Cas. & Sur. Co. v. Yeatts, supra n. 123.

201. United States v. Bucon Constr. Co., 430 F.2d 420 (5th Cir. 1970); Aetna Cas. & Sur. Co. v. Yeatts, supra n. 123; In re Green's Estate, 25 Cal.2d 535, 154 P.2d 692 (1944); In re Goretska's Estate, 234 Iowa 1080, 13 N.W.2d 432 (1944); Walters v. DeFelice & Son, 381 Pa. 433, 113 A.2d 218 (1955) (where the trial court granted the new trial on his own motion). In Lind v. Schenley Ind., Inc., 278 F.2d 79 (3d Cir. 1960), a case which seems contrary to the general view, the court says the trial court has a wider discretion where the ground of the motion is error of law than it does when the ground is that the verdict is against the weight of the evidence. There are a few cases, such as Dyer v. Hastings, 87 Ohio App.

147, 94 N.E.2d 213 (1950), which hold that the trial court has no discretion to set aside a verdict which is supported by "competent, substantial and apparently credible evidence."

202. Gila Valley, Globe & North Ry. v. Hall, 232 U.S. 94, 34 S.Ct. 229, 58 L.Ed. 521 (1914) (case coming up from the territorial courts of Arizona, in which the Supreme Court upheld the practice); Gruenthal v. Long Island R. R., 393 U.S. 156, 89 S.Ct. 331, 21 L.Ed.2d 309 (1968) (FELA case in which the jury rendered a verdict for $305,000 which the District Court sustained when D moved for a new trial; the Court of Appeals ordered a new trial unless plaintiff would remit $105,000; the Supreme Court, two dissenting, did not reach the constitutional question, but reversed to uphold the District Court in refusing a new trial); Powers v. Allstate Ins. Co., 10 Wis.2d 78, 102 N.W.2d 393 (1960) (holding that

because the judge has discretion to grant or refuse a new trial he may exercise the discretion by refusing on condition the plaintiff consent to cutting down the verdict to a figure the judge deems reasonable. The plaintiff cannot complain because he has consented, and the defendant cannot because the jury has already fixed his liability at a larger figure which the judge, in his discretion, could let stand. Is the converse true? May the judge, in the case of a grossly inadequate verdict, deny a motion for a new trial on the condition that the defendant consent to raise the amount to a figure which the judge deems reasonable? This is known as additur. In the leading case of Dimick v. Schiedt,[203] in a 5–4 decision, the Supreme Court held that additur violated the plaintiff's right to a jury trial as guaranteed by the Seventh Amendment. Remittitur was distinguished: there all the court was doing was trimming down to reasonable size a verdict that had already been rendered by a jury. In the case of additur, on the other hand, what the court was doing was to add to the verdict and thus was usurping the function of the jury. Mr. Justice Stone wrote a vigorous dissent in which he said:

> It is difficult to see upon what principle the denial of a motion for a new trial, which for centuries has been regarded as so much a matter of discretion that it is not disturbed when its only support may be a bad or inadequate reason, may nevertheless be set aside on appeal when it is supported by a good one: That the defendant has bound himself to pay an increased amount of damages which the court judicially knows is within the limits of a proper verdict.[204]

Since the Seventh Amendment has never been held to be a restriction on the state courts, Dimick is not binding on them and, indeed, several have upheld additur.[205]

Partial new trials. There is another device to avoid the time and expense of an entire new trial when the only vice in the verdict seems to be the amount of damages awarded: the partial new trial, restricted to the issue of damages alone. The diffi-

---

the standard to be used in determining the amount of the remittitur is the amount which the court deems reasonable, rather than the lowest amount a reasonable jury could have awarded).

203. 293 U.S. 474, 55 S.Ct. 296, 79 L.Ed. 603 (1935).

204. Id. at 497, 55 S.Ct. at 305, 79 L. Ed. at 617.

205. Jehl v. Southern Pac. Co., 66 Cal.2d 821, 427 P.2d 988 (1967), overruling Dorsey v. Barba, 38 Cal. 2d 350, 240 P.2d 604 (1952), which is noted in 40 Cal.L.Rev. 276 (1952); Fisch v. Manger, 24 N.J. 66, 130 A.2d 815 (1957). The Washington courts permit additur only when there is no conflict as to the amount of special damages which can be computed from the record with certainty: Cox v.

culty with this device is that, where there is a sharp conflict on the issue of liability, the verdict may reflect a compromise not only on the issue of damages but also of liability.[206] Consequently, although the practice of awarding partial new trials has been approved as not violative of the constitution, it should not be used except in clear cases. In the leading case of Gasoline Products Co. v. Champlin Refining Co.[207] the Supreme Court stated:

> Where the practice permits a partial new trial, it may not properly be resorted to unless it clearly appears that the issue to be retried is so distinct and separable from the others that a trial of it alone may be had without injustice. . . . Here the question of damages . . . is so interwoven with that of liability that the former cannot be submitted to the jury independently of the latter without confusion and uncertainty, which would amount to a denial of a fair trial.[208]

At common law the verdict of the jury was regarded as indivisible, which stood or fell as a unit. Hence, partial new trials were impossible.[209] The modern rule, more sensitive to the needs of judicial economy, is otherwise. The federal rule provides that "A new trial may be granted to all or any of the parties and on all or part of the issues." [210]

A comparable time-saving device is the split trial which tries the issue of liability first, and only if the jury finding is in favor of liability does the trial proceed into the second stage of damages. Such a device, it is thought by some, would be a corrective for excessive delay in personal injury suits. Such a rule for bifurcated trials was promulgated for the United States District Court for the Northern District of Illinois in 1959. Its constitutionality was upheld in Hosie v. Chicago & Northwestern Railway.[211]

Charles Wright Academy, 70 Wash.2d 173, 422 P.2d 515 (1967).

206. Hatch v. Lewis, 274 Cal.App.2d 150, 78 Cal.Rptr. 794 (1969).

207. 283 U.S. 494, 51 S.Ct. 513, 75 L.Ed. 1188 (1931).

208. Id. at 500, 51 S.Ct. at 515, 75 L.Ed. at 1191. In Williams v. Slade, 431 F.2d 605 (5th Cir. 1970) the court holds that, in a proper case (where the issue to be retried could not have affected the other issues) an appellate court also has power to order a retrial as to one defendant and not the other. In Devine v. Patteson, 242 F.2d 828 (6th Cir. 1957) the court, one judge dissenting, holds the lower court erred in not granting a partial new trial on the issue of damages alone.

209. James, Civil Procedure (1965) § 7.21(5).

210. Fed.Rules Civ.Proc. 59(a). Modern state procedure is in accord: Doutre v. Niec, 2 Mich.App. 88, 138 N.W.2d 501 (1965).

211. 282 F.2d 639 (7th Cir. 1960). For contrary views on the value

Newly discovered evidence. In the days before pretrial discovery was available it was not uncommon for new evidence to turn up after the trial was over. Such newly discovered evidence was a ground for granting a new trial if the following conditions were met: (1) the evidence must have come to light after the trial was over, (2) the party seeking the new trial was not negligent in failing to discover it in time for presentation at the trial, (3) the evidence must be material, (4) it must not be merely cumulative, and (5) it must be such that it is reasonably probable that it would change the result of the trial.[212] The time for filing a motion for a new trial on this ground was necessarily longer than for the usual grounds since, obviously, the motion could not be filed until the evidence was discovered. Under the *fed.* federal rule such motion must be filed within a reasonable time but not later than one year after judgment.[213] Under modern *modern* practice, with extensive pretrial discovery available, it will be more difficult for a party to prove he was not negligent in failing to unearth the "newly discovered evidence."

Miscellaneous grounds. Any prejudicial error of law which would be ground for a reversal on appeal will also be a ground *I !* for a motion for a new trial. Such errors may occur at any stage of the trial. For instance, an erroneous ruling denying the defendant the right to open and close when he had admitted the plaintiff's case and all that remained in issue was the counterclaim,[214] erroneous rulings admitting or excluding evidence,[215] erroneous instructions to the jury,[216] errors in the form of the verdict,[217] and verdicts which are contrary to the law or the

---

of split trials see Zeisel & Callahan, Split Trials and Time-Saving: A Statistical Analysis, 76 Harv.L. Rev. 1606 (1963); Weinstein, Routine Bifurcation of Jury Negligence Trials: An Example of the Questionable Use of Rule Making Power, 14 Vand.L.Rev. 831 (1961).

212. Patrick v. Sedwick, 413 P.2d 169 (Alas.1966); Mickoleski v. Becker, 252 Wis. 307, 31 N.W.2d 508 (1948). In the latter case the court said that such motions are regarded with suspicion and disfavor and that the presumption is that with proper effort and diligence the evidence could have been produced; to rebut that presumption the moveant must make out a case free from delinquency.

213. Fed.Rules Civ.Proc. 60(b).

214. Carmody v. Kolocheski, supra n. 1.

215. Doutre v. Niec, supra n. 210.

216. Virginian Ry. v. Armentrout, 166 F.2d 400 (4th Cir. 1948).

217. Magnani v. Trogi, 70 Ill.App. 2d 216, 218 N.E.2d 21 (1966). In this case, Count I was a wrongful death case, where the recovery would be apportioned between the widow and a minor son, and Count II was under the family expense statute (funeral expenses) which would all go to the widow. Unfortunately neither party requested forms for separate verdicts, and

evidence.[218] Misconduct of opposing counsel is a frequent ground for a new trial,[219] but incompetence of one's own counsel is seldom recognized as a ground in civil cases, although it sometimes is in criminal cases.[220]

the verdict was merely a general one for $19,000. The lower court granted a new trial, which was affirmed on appeal.

218. Jenkins v. Gerber, 336 Ill.App. 469, 84 N.E.2d 699 (1949). Here the suit was for property damage; the uncontradicted evidence was that the damage amounted to $527.16, but the jury brought in a verdict of only $200. The court granted a new trial since the verdict could not be supported on any theory advanced by either party.

219. Maggio v. City of Cleveland, supra n. 4 (attempting to influence jury by reciting facts in opening statement which were inadmissible in evidence); Fitzpatrick v. St. Louis-San Francisco Ry., 327 S.W. 2d 801 (Mo.1959) (in suit for loss of eye, improperly attempting to influence jury by having a blind man led in to sit in the front row); In re Bruener, 159 Wash. 504, 294

P. 254 (1930) (during weekend recess, lawyer went on picnic with a woman juror); Klotz v. Sears, Roebuck & Co., 267 F.2d 53 (7th Cir. 1959); Conn v. Seaboard Air Line Ry., 201 N.C. 157, 159 S.E. 331 (1931); New York Cent. R. R. v. Johnson, supra n. 10 (going beyond fair comment on the evidence in closing argument); Gutzman v. Clancy, supra n. 11.

220. Everett v. Everett, 319 Mich. 475, 29 N.W.2d 919 (1947) (the dubious ground advanced for the rule is that the lawyer is the agent of the client and therefore the neglect of the lawyer is the neglect of the client). Compare Barber v. Tuberville, 94 U.S.App.D.C. 335, 218 F.2d 34 (1954) where the trial court was reversed for refusing to relieve the defendant of a default judgment which was obtained because of the neglect of her counsel to file an answer.

CHAPTER VIII.   JUDGMENTS

SECTION 1.   IN GENERAL

The judgment is the final determination of the rights of the parties.[1] It is pronounced by the judge, orally or in writing as local practice dictates,[2] and is entered in the records of the court by the clerk.[3] The judgment comes at the end of the litigation, which may be terminated in various ways. Thus we may have a judgment by default, when the defendant fails to appear;[4] or a

1. West's Ann.Cal.Code Civ.Proc., § 577. Restatement of Judgments, (1942) Intro., p. 3: "In the Restatement of this Subject the term 'judgment' is used in this broad sense to include the final determination of a court, whether the proceeding is at law or in equity." Fed.Rules Civ.Proc. 54(a) defines "judgment" to include "a decree and any order from which an appeal lies." In Ferrara v. Jordan, 134 Cal.App.2d 917, 286 P.2d 589 (1955) the court dismissed as improvident an appeal from a purported judgment which merely awarded costs on the ground that costs were incidental and that the judgment should show that the plaintiff was entitled to an award or that he take nothing.

2. In Goldreyer v. Cronan, 76 Conn. 113, 117, 55 A. 594, 596 (1903), the court said, "A judgment, speaking generally, is the determination or sentence of the law, speaking through the court; and it does not exist, as a legal entity, until pronounced, expressed, or made known in some appropriate way. It may be expressed orally or in writing, or in both of these ways, in accordance with the customs and usages of the court in which the judgment is rendered."

3. In Los Angeles County Bank v. Raynor, 61 Cal. 145, 147 (1882) the court said, "The enforcement of a judgment does not depend upon its entry or docketing. These are merely ministerial acts, the first of which is required to be

done for putting in motion the right of appeal from the judgment itself, and of limiting the time within which the right may be exercised . . . or in which the judgment may be enforced."

Nunc pro tunc judgments. Under certain circumstances a court will order that a judgment be entered as of a prior date. This will be done when there has been a delay in pronouncing or entering the judgment, when the delay is not due to the fault of the parties, and when prejudice would result if the judgment were not entered as of a prior date. For example, in a trial to the court, where the judge takes the case under advisement and does not render his judgment until after one of the parties has died, the judgment may be entered as of a date prior to the death to keep the action from abating. Such a case was Fox v. Hale & Norcross Silver Mining Co., 108 Cal. 478, 480, 41 P. 328, 329 (1895), in which the court said, "A court will always exercise this authority when it is apparent that the delay in rendering the judgment, or a failure to enter it after its rendition, is the result of some act or delay of the court, and is not owing to any fault of the party making the application." See also Young v. Gardner-Denver Co., 244 Cal.App. 2d 915, 53 Cal.Rptr. 522 (1966); Cox v. Hagan, 125 Va. 656, 100 S. E. 666 (1919).

4. When the defendant fails to appear within the time specified in the summons, the plaintiff may

judgment following the ruling on a demurrer [5] or motion to dismiss; [6] or a judgment by consent when the parties settle the case; [7] or a judgment following the sustaining of a motion for nonsuit or directed verdict; or a judgment based upon the verdict of a jury, or the findings of the court where the trial was without a jury.

have the clerk enter his default. This will preclude the defendant from filing a late pleading without making application to the court to remove the default. After a default has been entered the plaintiff may then proceed to obtain judgment. Where the damages are unliquidated he will have to introduce evidence to prove them. Usually it is the judge who renders the judgment by default. However, "when the plaintiff's claim against a defendant is for a sum certain or for a sum which can by computation be made certain, the clerk upon request of the plaintiff and upon affidavit of the amount due shall enter judgment for that amount and costs against the defendant, if he has been defaulted for failure to appear and if he is not an infant or incompetent person." Fed.Rules Civ.Proc. 55(b) (1). See also West's Ann. Cal.Code Civ.Proc. § 585. Some cases hold that a judgment by default may not be taken against a defendant who has appeared and pleaded in the case: Bass v. Hoagland, 172 F.2d 205 (5th Cir. 1949); Wilson v. Goldman, 274 Cal.App. 2d 573, 79 Cal.Rptr. 309 (1969). Others hold that a default may be entered against a defendant who fails to appear at the trial or who fails to take any step required by the rules of procedure, Hutchinson v. Manchester St. Ry., 73 N.H. 271, 60 A. 1011 (1905).

5. The order sustaining or overruling the demurrer is not a judgment, but it may be followed by a judgment, especially if the party against whom the ruling was made is given the opportunity to amend or replead and refuses to do so. Elfman v. Glaser, 313 Mass. 370, 47 N.E.2d 925 (1943); H. Christiansen & Sons v. Duluth, 225 Minn. 486, 31 N.W.2d 277 (1948); Powell v. Chastain, 359 P.2d 336 (Okl.1961).

6. A motion to dismiss for failure to state a claim is the federal counterpart of a demurrer. However, failure to comply with a discovery order or other court order may also ground a motion to dismiss, resulting in a judgment on the merits. Nasser v. Isthmian Lines, 331 F.2d 124 (2d Cir. 1964); Anguiano v. Transcontinental Bus Sys., 76 Ariz. 246, 263 P.2d 305 (1963).

7. Securities & Exch. Comm'n. v. Thermodynamics, Inc., 319 F.Supp. 1380 (D.Colo.1970); Avery v. Avery, 10 Cal.App.3d 525, 89 Cal. Rptr. 195 (1970). Where the parties consent to judgment in open court or by stipulation, there is no problem. However, where consent to judgment is given in advance of suit, as in the case of a judgment note, the matter is not free from doubt. Such notes contain a provision that upon default in payment the maker appoints any attorney as his attorney to confess judgment in favor of the payee. They were held valid in some states, Egley v. Bennett & Co., 196 Ind. 50, 145 N.E. 830 (1924), noted in 38 Harv.L.Rev. 110 (1924); but serious doubt was cast upon their validity, where actual notice was not given to the defendant, in the case of National Equip. Rental, Ltd. v. Szukhent, 375 U.S. 311, 84 S.Ct. 411, 11 L.Ed.2d 354 (1964). In Atlas Credit Corp. v. Ezrine, 25 N.Y.2d 219, 250 N.E.2d 474, 303 N.Y.S.2d 382 (1969) the court refused to recognize a Pennsylvania judgment based on such a clause on the ground that, without notice to the defendant, there could be no valid judgment.

Unlike the situation at common law, where joinder of parties and causes of actions in one lawsuit was strictly limited, modern procedure encourages, or at least permits, the inclusion of multiple parties and multiple claims in one suit.   In this situation it may be that a hardship would result if the final judgment were postponed until all claims against all parties were decided.   Consequently, the federal rule gives the judge authority to "direct the entry of a final judgment as to one or more but fewer than all of the claims or parties but only upon an express determination that there is no just reason for delay . . . ." [8]   In the absence of such determination the usual rule applies, i. e., that there can be but one final judgment in the case, and it must determine the rights of all of the parties as to all of the issues.[9]

The same federal rule likewise modifies the common law rule that the relief awarded in the judgment must not depart from that demanded in the pleadings.[10]   As to default judgments the traditional rule is retained, but in every other case the rule provides that the judgment shall grant the relief to which the party is entitled even though he has not demanded it in his pleadings. The distinction is a sound one.   Where the defendant has not appeared, it would be unfair to grant relief greater than that demanded in the papers which were served on him, and therefore would be a violation of due process.[11]   However, where the defendant appeared and the matter was litigated, he could not be legally aggrieved,[12] for under the rules the pleadings may be amended to conform to the evidence, even after judgment.[13]

Occasionally the only relief a plaintiff wants is a declaration of his legal rights.   Such a remedy was unknown to the common law but is now available in the federal courts [14] and in a majority of the states under declaratory judgment statutes.[15]   In interpreting such statutes the courts have drawn a thin line between

---

8.   Fed.Rules Civ.Proc. 54(b).

9.   Donovan v. Hayden Stone, Inc., 434 F.2d 619 (6th Cir. 1970); Miles v. City of Chandler, 297 F.2d 690 (9th Cir. 1961).

10.   Fed.Rules Civ.Proc. 54(c).

11.   Reynolds v. Stockton, 140 U.S. 254, 11 S.Ct. 773, 35 L.Ed. 464 (1891).

12.   Riggs, Ferris & Geer v. Lillibridge, 316 F.2d 60 (2d Cir. 1963); Garland v. Garland, 165 F.2d 131 (10th Cir. 1948); compare Olwell

v. Nye & Nissen Co., 26 Wash.2d 282, 173 P.2d 652 (1947).

13.   Fed.Rules Civ.Proc. 15(b).

14.   The federal statute is found in 28 U.S.C.A. § 2201.

15.   The commissioners on Uniform State Laws proposed a Uniform Declaratory Judgments Act which has been adopted in a majority of the states, Puerto Rico, and the Virgin Islands.   Rosenberg, Weinstein & Smit, Elements of Civil Procedure (2d ed. 1970), p. 106.

the proper judicial function of deciding "cases and controversies," [16] and the improper function of giving legal advice. One of the leading cases is Aetna Life Insurance Co. v. Haworth [17] in which the plaintiff company sued for a judicial declaration that five life insurance policies which it had issued on the life of the defendant had lapsed. This would have been a defense had the defendant sued on the policies (for permanent disability benefits) but no action had been brought. The allegations of the complaint indicated that the defendant would attempt to avoid the lapse by a waiver of premium provision in the policies. In this instance, what the declaratory statute did was to give the initiative to one who would normally be the defendant. The court held that this was proper and, quoting from an earlier case, said the Constitution "did not crystallize into changeless form the procedure of 1789 as the only possible means for presenting a case or controversy otherwise cognizable by the federal courts." [18] The courts are, however, vigilant in insisting on a genuine controversy. For example, where a union sought a declaratory judgment that the new immigration statute did not apply to aliens domiciled in the United States, who go to Alaska for temporary summer work, the court dismissed for want of a controversy, holding that the union was posing a hypothetical question.[19] Mr. Justice Black dissented on the ground the aliens faced a real risk, as the country can exclude aliens for reasons which would not be grounds for deportation.[20]

Enforcement of judgments. A plaintiff who has obtained a money judgment against a defendant has won his case but has not yet been paid. If, upon demand, the defendant refuses to pay, the plaintiff must take the necessary legal steps to enforce the judgment. The first step is for him to obtain from the clerk

16. U.S.Const. art. III, § 2 limits the judicial power of the United States to "cases" and "controversies." In Muskrat v. United States, 219 U.S. 346, 31 S.Ct. 250, 55 L. Ed. 246 (1911) the court held the judicial power did not extend to giving advisory opinions.

17. 300 U.S. 227, 57 S.Ct. 461, 81 L.Ed. 617 (1937).

18. Id. at 240, 57 S.Ct. at 464, 81 L. Ed. at 621.

19. Local 37, International Longshoremen & Warehousemen v. Boyd, 347 U.S. 222, 74 S.Ct. 447, 98 L.Ed. 650 (1954).

20. Id. at 224, 74 S.Ct. at 448, 98 L.Ed. at 650. For illustrative cases granting declaratory relief see American Mach. & Metals, Inc. v. DeBothezat Impeller Co., 166 F.2d 535 (2d Cir. 1948); Reservists Committee to Stop the War v. Laird, 323 F.Supp. 833 (D.D.C. 1971); Thiokol Chem. Corp. v. Burlington Indus., Inc., 319 F. Supp. 218 (D.Del.1970). For recent cases denying it see Firemen's Ins. Co. v. Riley, 322 F.Supp. 349 (W.D.Ky.1971); Nebraska State AFL–CIO v. State of Nebraska, 319 F.Supp. 239 (D.Neb.1970).

of the court a writ of execution which is a routine court order addressed to the sheriff directing him to attach and sell so much of the defendant's property as is necessary to pay it.[21] The plaintiff will next take this writ of execution to the sheriff and give him the description and location of the property of the defendant he wishes attached. The sheriff will then levy on the property, and if the defendant still does not pay, he will hold a public sheriff's sale, deliver the proceeds to the plaintiff, or enough to pay his judgment, and remit the balance, if any, to the court for the use of the defendant. Upon payment of the judgment the plaintiff must execute a satisfaction of the same to be filed in the clerk's office. Every state has statutes exempting from execution certain property of judgment debtors.[22] Statutes also commonly provide that upon the entry, docketing, or filing of a judgment, it becomes a lien upon all property of the judgment debtor.[23] Such liens become extremely important in cases in which the judgment debtor has some property but not enough to satisfy all of his creditors. In that situation priority in liens (determined by priority in time) may make all the difference in one having his judgment paid in full or receiving nothing.[24] Sometimes a plaintiff is unable to find property subject to execution but is convinced that the defendant can afford to pay. If he can make a reasonable showing to the court that such is the case the judge may order the defendant to appear for supplementary proceedings at which time he may be cross-examined by the plaintiff as to his assets and financial position. In such proceedings, if warranted by the facts, the judge may order the defendant to make weekly or monthly payments on the judgment, may cite him for contempt if he disobeys the order, and even order him to jail. Such a proceeding has been attacked as unconstitutional imprisonment for debt, but has been upheld on the same ground that jail sentences for civil contempt have been upheld—the defendant may effect his own release at any time

---

21. An execution is not leviable on all of the property of the defendant but only so much as is necessary to pay the judgment, plus interest and costs. In Griggs v. Miller, 374 S.W.2d 119 (Mo.1963) the court set aside an execution sale because the value of the property levied on so greatly exceeded the amount of the judgment.

22. Exemption statutes routinely include a percentage of the judgment debtor's wages, varying in amount from state to state. Abrahams & Feldman, The Exemption of Wages from Garnishment: Some Comparisons and Comments, 3 DePaul L.Rev. 153 (1954); Brunn, Wage Garnishment in California: A Study and Recommendations, 53 Cal.L.Rev. 1214 (1965).

23. Burroughs, The Choate Lien Doctrine, 1963 Duke L.J. 449; Comment, Priorities of Creditors Under Judgment Creditor's Bills, 42 Yale L.J. 919 (1933).

24. Matter of Fornabai, 227 F.Supp. 928 (D.N.J.1964).

by complying with the order.[25] Such an order would probably be invalid if it were beyond the means of the defendant to comply with it, or if by complying he would be deprived of the ability to care for his family.[26] If the plaintiff discovers that the judgment debtor has property in another state, he may reach it but only by bringing a suit in the other state, based on the judgment, and securing a new judgment in the other state. The reason for this cumbersome procedure is that the sheriff of one state has no authority to execute the judgments of another state. Until 1948, in the federal system, the federal districts occupied the same position as states regarding the enforcement of judgments, but in that year Congress greatly simplified the process by providing for the registration in any federal district court of a judgment rendered in any other district, which gives it the same effect as if it were rendered in that district.[27] A final word about enforcement: a defendant against whom a judgment has been rendered may wish to appeal. If he does so, the appeal will not automatically suspend the operation of the judgment. In order to have that effect the defendant must post a supersedeas bond, in an amount to be approved by the judge, by which he and his sureties guarantee to pay the judgment if it is affirmed by the higher court.[28]

Relief from judgments. It is generally agreed that a void judgment may be vacated at any time by the trial judge,[29] that a mere clerical error in a judgment may be corrected by him at any time,[30] but that a judicial error can ordinarily be corrected only on appeal.[31] There are situations, however, in which the trial judge may relieve a party from a judgment even though it does not fall into one of the above categories. In the days before the merger of law and equity, a court of chancery would relieve a party of a judgment obtained by fraud or under circumstances which made it unconscionable to enforce it. The old

25. Reeves v. Crownshield, 274 N.Y. 74, 8 N.E.2d 283 (1937).

26. Id. On supplementary proceedings in general see Cohen, Collection of Money Judgments in New York: Supplementary Proceedings, 35 Colum.L.Rev. 1007 (1935); Cohen, Collection of Money Judgments: Experimentation with Supplementary Proceedings, 36 Colum.L.Rev. 1061 (1936); Note, Present Status of Execution Against the Body of the Judgment Debtor, 42 Iowa L.Rev. 306 (1957).

27. 28 U.S.C.A. § 1963.

28. Fed.Rules Civ.Proc. 62(d).

29. Woods Bros. Const. Co. v. Yankton County, 54 F.2d 304 (8th Cir. 1931); City of Salinas v. Lake Kow Lee, 217 Cal. 252, 18 P.2d 335 (1933).

30. Denton v. Denton, 18 Cal.App. 3d 708, 96 Cal.Rptr. 136 (1971); Packard v. Kinzie Ave. Heights Co., 105 Wis. 323, 81 N.W. 488 (1900); Fed.Rules Civ.Proc. 60(a).

31. Hansen v. City of New York, 274 App.Div. 196, 80 N.Y.S.2d 249 (1948).

equitable grounds for relief against judgments still exist under the modern merged procedure, but they are frequently codified by statute or rule.[32] The two most common grounds today are excusable neglect and fraud. Excusable neglect is the ground generally asserted when a defendant moves to set aside a default judgment. A good example is the case of Butner v. Neustadter,[33] in which the defendant, a business man from Little Rock, Arkansas, was served with process when he was temporarily in Los Angeles; he mailed the papers to his Little Rock attorney, suggesting that he employ a Los Angeles attorney; the Little Rock attorney sent the papers to a Los Angeles attorney who was, as it happened, away on a trip, with the result that no answer was filed and a $20,000 default judgment was rendered against the defendant. The trial court denied a motion to set aside the default, but the appellate court reversed because it thought the facts showed excusable neglect. In so doing it cited a California case in which the court said, "It is also well settled that it is the policy of the law to bring about a trial on the merits wherever possible, so that any doubts which may exist should be resolved in favor of the application, to the end of securing a trial upon the merits." [34] In Rierson v. York [35] a default judgment was set aside on the ground of excusable neglect where the sudden illness of the defendant's attorney prevented the timely filing of an answer. The second most common ground of setting aside a judgment is probably fraud. In the leading case of United States v. Throckmorton,[36] the Supreme Court distinguished between intrinsic and extrinsic fraud, holding that only the latter would justify setting aside a judgment. The distinction is a subtle one which has logical validity but is difficult to apply. Intrinsic fraud is that which occurred during the course of the trial, i. e.,

32. Fed.Rules Civ.Proc. 60(b) lists the following grounds: "(1) mistake, inadvertence, surprise or excusable neglect; (2) newly discovered evidence which by due diligence could not have been discovered in time to move for a new trial under Rule 59(b); (3) fraud (whether heretofor denominated intrinsic or extrinsic), misrepresentation, or other misconduct of an adverse party; (4) the judgment is void; (5) the judgment has been satisfied, released or discharged, or a prior judgment upon which it is based has been reversed or otherwise vacated, or it is no longer equitable that the judgment should have prospective application; or (6) any other reason justifying relief from the operation of the judgment."

The courts are inclined to give a narrow interpretation to category (6) in Rule 60(b); Ackermann v. United States, 340 U.S. 193, 71 S. Ct. 209, 95 L.Ed. 207 (1950); Rinieri v. News Syndicate Co., 385 F.2d 818 (2d Cir. 1967).

33. 324 F.2d 783 (9th Cir. 1963).

34. Brill v. Fox, 211 Cal. 739, 743–44, 297 P. 25, 26 (1931).

35. 227 N.C. 575, 42 S.E.2d 902 (1947).

36. 98 U.S. 61, 25 L.Ed. 93 (1878).

perjury or false evidence. The theory is that such fraud could have been detected by diligent cross-examination and that, in any event, if perjury would suffice, the stability of judgments would be impaired. Extrinsic fraud, on the other hand, is fraud which prevents a party from having his day in court. The Supreme Court gave the following illustrations of extrinsic fraud:

> Where the unsuccessful party has been prevented from exhibiting fully his case, by fraud or deception practiced on him by his opponent, as by keeping him away from court, a false promise or compromise; or where the defendant never had knowledge of the suit, being kept in ignorance by the acts of the plaintiff; or where an attorney fraudulently or without authority assumes to represent a party and connives at his defeat; or where the attorney regularly employed corruptly sells out his client's interest to the other side,—these, and similar cases which show that there never has been a real contest in the trial or hearing of the case, are reasons for which a new suit may be sustained to set aside and annul the former judgment or decree, and open the case for a new and fair hearing.[37]

In a later case,[38] which cited the Throckmorton case with approval, the Supreme Court held that what really amounted to intrinsic fraud justified a lower court in enjoining a judgment. This confusion in the cases has never been satisfactorily explained, and the cases are in conflict as to whether intrinsic fraud is enough to justify setting aside a judgment,[39] but the federal rule lists as a ground for relief "fraud (whether heretofore denominated intrinsic or extrinsic)." [40]

Newly discovered evidence is also a ground for setting aside a judgment and granting a new trial.[41] This is discussed in Chapter VII, § 8.

---

37. Id. at 65–66, 25 L.Ed. at 95.

38. Marshall v. Holmes, 141 U.S. 589, 12 S.Ct. 62, 35 L.Ed. 870 (1891).

39. Following Throckmorton: New York Life Ins. Co. v. Nashville Trust Co., 200 Tenn. 513, 292 S.W. 2d 749 (1956); Chermak v. Chermak, 227 Ind. 625, 88 N.E.2d 250 (1949); Gale v. Witt, 31 Cal.2d 362, 188 P.2d 755 (1948). Holding

intrinsic fraud sufficient if proved by clear and convincing evidence: Peacock Records, Inc. v. Checker Records, Inc., 365 F.2d 145 (7th Cir. 1966); Atchison, T. & S. F. Ry., v. Barrett, 246 F.2d 846 (9th Cir. 1957).

40. Fed.Rules Civ.Proc. 60(b).

41. Stilwell v. Travelers Ins. Co., 327 F.2d 931 (5th Cir. 1964).

SECTION 2.   RES JUDICATA

According to Anglo-American tradition every man is entitled to his day in court—a competent court with jurisdiction over the subject matter and the parties—and he is entitled to appeal from any adverse judgment to a higher court. But, when a final decision has been reached, that should be the end of it.[42] This is the heart of the doctrine of res judicata: a final judgment by a court of competent jurisdiction is conclusive upon the parties in any subsequent litigation involving the same cause of action. The sizeable body of law on the subject involves an attempt to define and explain the elements comprising this succinct definition.

In order to be conclusive, the judgment must have been rendered by a court which had jurisdiction over the subject matter and over the parties.[43] If the judgment was rendered by default, the jurisdiction of the court which rendered it may be attacked in any court in which the judgment subsequently comes in question, because unless the court had jurisdiction the alleged judgment is a nullity.[44] However, if the jurisdiction was litigated in the court which rendered the judgment, its decision on that point will be conclusive just as it is on any other question in the case.[45]

The policy underlying the doctrine of res judicata is one of repose, the same policy which is reflected in the statute of limitations which outlaws stale claims. The theoretical basis of the doctrine is more sophisticated. When a plaintiff sues a defendant, he is seeking to establish and enforce a cause of action. He may or may not be able to prove it, and he may be stopped by an affirmative defense. Before judgment the matter is in doubt. The judgment resolves that doubt. "If the judgment is for the defendant and is on the merits, the cause of action is extinguished; that is, the judgment operates as a *bar*. If the judgment is

42. As to what constitutes a final judgment see Restatement, Judgments (1942) § 41 and Comments.

43. See Chapter II.

44. Restatement, Judgments (1942) § 11. This is known as a collateral attack which the Restatement (Comment a) defines as follows: "Where a judgment is attacked in other ways than by proceedings in the original action to have it vacated or reversed or modified or by a proceeding in equity to prevent its enforcement, the attack is a 'collateral attack.'"

45. This is true whether the point involved is jurisdiction over the parties, Baldwin v. Iowa State Traveling Men's Ass'n, 283 U.S. 522, 51 S.Ct. 517, 75 L.Ed. 1244 (1931), or jurisdiction over the subject matter, Durfee v. Duke, 375 U.S. 106, 84 S.Ct. 242, 11 L.Ed.2d 186 (1963). Generally, see Dobbs, The Validation of Void Judgments: The Bootstrap Principle, 53 Va.L. Rev. 1003, 1241 (1967).

for the plaintiff, the cause of action is extinguished but something new is added, namely, rights based on the judgment; there is *merger* of the cause of action in the judgment." [46] Since the judgment has the effect of extinguishing the cause of action, it is conclusive in any later suit, not only on those matters which actually were litigated, but on all matters which could have been litigated in that action.[47] For example, a plaintiff who is dissatisfied with the amount of the judgment cannot sue for more since he has used up his cause of action in the first suit, and the policy of repose which underlies the doctrine precludes him from splitting his cause of action and suing on it piecemeal.[48] Likewise, in a later suit on the judgment, the defendant cannot interpose additional defenses which were not presented in the first action. He cannot split his defenses.[49]

The authorities are in general agreement that a plaintiff may not split his cause of action,[50] but they differ sharply on a proper definition of "cause of action." [51] For example, where a person sustains injuries to his person and to his property by the same wrongful act of the defendant, does he have one or two causes of action? One line of cases holds that the defendant's wrongful

---

46. Scott, Collateral Estoppel by Judgment, 56 Harv.L.Rev. 1, 2 (1942).

47. Harrison v. Bloomfield Bldg. Indus., 435 F.2d 1192 (6th Cir. 1970).

48. Le John Mfg. Co. v. Webb, 91 A.2d 332 (D.C.Mun.App.1952); Jacobson v. Mutual Benefit Health & Acc. Ass'n, 73 N.D. 108, 11 N.W. 2d 442 (1943).

49. Mitchell v. Federal Intermediate Credit Bank, 165 S.C. 457, 164 S.E. 136, 83 A.L.R. 629 (1932). In this case the court held that where the defendant has matter which he could set up as a defense, or a counterclaim, or both, that if he uses it only defensively he is precluded from later using it as a basis for suit against the plaintiff. Accord: Derderian v. Union Mkt. Nat. Bank, 326 Mass. 538, 95 N.E. 2d 552 (1950). Where a defendant fails to assert a compulsory counterclaim (see Fed.Rules Civ. Proc. 13a) he is precluded from later using it as a basis for an independent suit: Kennedy v. Jones, 44 F.R.D. 52 (E.D.Va.1968); Newton v. Mitchell, 42 So.2d 53 (Fla.

1949); Horne v. Woolever, 170 Ohio St. 178, 163 N.E.2d 378 (1959). There is some authority that this rule does not apply where an insurer is defending a personal injury suit and under its policy there is no obligation to represent the policyholder on a counterclaim: Reynolds v. Hartford Accident & Indem. Co., 278 F.Supp. 331 (S.D.N.Y.1967). See also Manning v. Wymer, 273 Cal.App.2d 519, 78 Cal.Rptr. 600 (1969) (a two car accident in which each owner brought a separate suit against the other and one case was settled and dismissed before an answer was due; held, not a bar, since the case was settled before an answer or counterclaim was due).

50. McConnell v. Travelers Indem. Co., 346 F.2d 219 (5th Cir. 1965); Sutcliffe Storage & Warehouse Co. v. United States, 162 F.2d 849 (1st Cir. 1947).

51. The judicial differences in definitions of "cause of action" which plagued the courts in pleading (See Ch. V, supra) carry over into the area of res judicata and collateral estoppel.

act gives rise to two causes of action because two rights of the plaintiff were invaded, one, his right to personal security, and the other his property right.[52] The other line of cases, representing the majority view, holds that the single wrongful act of the defendant gives rise to but one cause of action which the plaintiff cannot split.[53] Under this view a plaintiff who has recovered a judgment for damage to his car is precluded from later suing for his personal injuries.[54] In some cases the result seems harsh, but the rule does prevent a multiplicity of suits and serves the policy of repose. The problem of splitting also arises in contract cases. Where a contract provides for payments in installments, it is generally held that a cause of action arises for the non-payment of each installment as it falls due but that a plaintiff must include all installments that are due at the time of the bringing of the suit. In other words, he could sue for each installment as it came due and not be held guilty of splitting, but if he sued for only one of several past due installments he would be guilty of splitting and the judgment in that case would be a bar to suits for the other installments which were due when the first suit was brought.[55]

Up to this point we have been considering only the situation in which the judgment was in favor of the plaintiff. If the judgment is in favor of the defendant, that the plaintiff take nothing, obviously there has been no merger since the effect of the judgment is either (1) that the plaintiff did not have a cause of action, or (2) that the defendant had a defense to it. Nevertheless, the judgment is conclusive, not because there has been a merger, but because the judgment establishes a bar to the plaintiff's suit. This bar will be effective to preclude the plaintiff from ever again collecting on that cause of action.[56] Again, we have the problem of what constitutes a "cause of action." In the illustrations given above, if plaintiff had lost the personal property suit, the judg-

52. Clancey v. McBride, 338 Ill. 35, 169 N.E. 729 (1929); Reilly v. Sicilian Asphalt Paving Co., 170 N.Y. 40, 62 N.E. 772 (1902).

53. Holmes v. David H. Bricker, Inc., 70 Cal.2d 786, 452 P.2d 647 (1969); McConnell v. Travelers Indemn. Co., supra n. 50; Dearden v. Hey, 304 Mass. 659, 24 N.E.2d 644 (1939); Rush v. City of Maple Heights, 167 Ohio St. 221, 147 N.E. 2d 599 (1958).

54. Id.

55. Kruce v. Lakeside Biscuit Co., 198 Mich. 736, 165 N.W. 609 (1917); Jones v. Morris Plan Bank of Portsmouth, 168 Va. 284, 191 S.E. 608 (1937); Sutcliffe Storage & Warehouse Co. v. United States, supra n. 50 (applying the same rule to a running account for quantum meruit for the occupancy of land not covered by a lease but occupied by defendant).

56. Williamson v. Columbia Gas & Elec. Corp., 186 F.2d 464 (3d Cir. 1950); Thompson v. Washington Nat'l Bank, 68 Wash. 42, 122 P. 606 (1912).

ment would have been a bar to the personal injury suit growing out of the defendant's single wrongful act, in those jurisdictions holding that only one cause of action was created.

It sometimes happens that the same set of facts, if proved, will give rise to more than one remedy. For instance, a breach of contract may give the plaintiff a choice between an action for damages and a suit for specific performance.[57] In these situations the courts are not in agreement as to whether there are several causes of action or merely several remedies for one cause of action.[58] Under modern rules of civil procedure, which merge law and equity, which encourage joinder of claims, and which emphasize the economies of sound judicial administration by cutting down multiplicity of suits, there will be less excuse for a plaintiff to split his causes of action.[59]

---

57. Restatement, Judgments (1942) § 64.

58. The authorities are divided on whether a plaintiff, who has lost a suit on an express contract, is precluded from suing on quantum meruit: Samuel Blanken & Co. v. Goldblatt, 371 F.2d 949 (D.C.Cir. 1966) (holding he is precluded); Smith v. Kirkpatrick, 305 N.Y. 66, 111 N.E.2d 209 (1953) (holding he is not). See annotation in 35 A.L. R.3d 874 (1970).

Before the merger of law and equity a court of law could not grant equitable relief, and a court of equity rarely granted legal relief. Hence a judgment of dismissal in one such forum was not res judicata to a suit seeking different relief in the other. Restatement, Judgments (1942) § 65(2): "Where a judgment is rendered in favor of the defendant because the plaintiff seeks a form of remedy which is not available to him, the plaintiff is not precluded from subsequently maintaining an action in which he seeks an available remedy." See Adams v. Pearson, 411 Ill. 431, 104 N.E.2d 267 (1952). Under the reformed procedure, where one court may give both forms of relief, a second suit seeking relief which was available in the first forum will be barred: Hennepin Paper Co. v. Fort Wayne Corrugated Paper Co., 153 F.2d 822 (7th Cir. 1946); Massari v. Einsiedler,

6 N.J. 303, 78 A.2d 572 (1951); Hahl v. Sugo, 169 N.Y. 109, 62 N. E. 135 (1901).

59. See the opinion of Judge Goodrich in Williamson v. Columbia Gas & Elec. Corp., supra n. 56.

Courts sometimes bend the doctrine of res judicata to achieve results which they feel will implement important public policies. In Woodbury v. Porter, 158 F.2d 194 (8th Cir. 1946) the plaintiff, the OPA Administrator, sued for treble damages, alleging that the defendant had overcharged tenants during a certain period. The defendant pleaded in bar the judgment in a former suit in which plaintiff had obtained an injunction against defendant for noncompliance with the federal law. The court held the plea was bad on the rather questionable ground that the evidence to prove the two causes of action was not identical. The true reason was probably that a contrary holding would have interfered with the government's program of emergency rent controls. In White v. Adler, 289 N.Y. 34, 43 N.E.2d 798 (1942) the defendant owned 326 shares of stock in a bank, and presented 325 of them for transfer on 12/10/30, but the transfer was not registered until a few days later. On 12/11/30 the plaintiff, Supt. of Banks, took over the bank as insolvent. To enforce a stockholders statutory liability

In order for a judgment to be accorded conclusive effect, it must be "on the merits." [60] Where the judgment is in favor of the plaintiff and awards him affirmative relief, there is no question,[61] but where the judgment is in favor of the defendant, it may or may not be upon the merits. At common law a judgment of dismissal on a ground not going to the merits of the case was not a bar.[62] This has been modified by the federal rules which provide that the court may dismiss "for failure of the plaintiff to prosecute or to comply with these rules or any order of court" or "on the ground that upon the facts and the law the plaintiff has shown no right to relief." The rule goes on to say "Unless the court in its order for dismissal otherwise specifies, a dismissal under this subdivision and any dismissal not provided for in this rule, other than a dismissal for lack of jurisdiction, for improper venue, or for failure to join a party under Rule 19, operates as an adjudication on the merits." [63] A literal reading of this rule greatly extends the doctrine of res judicata.[64] However, since the rule derogates from the common law, most courts have given it a strict construction and have strained to avoid precluding a plaintiff whose substantive rights have never been adjudicated. The case of Costello v. United States,[65] decided by the Supreme Court

he sued defendant on the one share and got a judgment. Later there was a court decision that a shareholder remained liable until the transfer was recorded. The plaintiff sued on the other 325 shares, and defendant pleaded the first judgment in bar. The court held the plea bad on the ground that the rule against splitting was to prevent vexatious suits, or at least to estop a plaintiff who had been negligent, and that neither of these applied in the instant case. The inarticulate premise was probably that a contrary holding would have frustrated, pro tanto, a statutory policy of protecting the bank's creditors.

60. Haldeman v. United States, 91 U.S. 584, 23 L.Ed. 433 (1875); Thomas v. Consolidation Coal Co., 380 F.2d 69 (4th Cir. 1967).

61. This is true even if the judgment was rendered by default. See extensive Annotation in 77 A. L.R.2d 1410 (1961).

62. Costello v. United States, 365 U.S. 265, 81 S.Ct. 534, 5 L.Ed.2d

551 (1961); Haldeman v. United States, supra n. 60.

63. Fed.Rules Civ.Proc. 41(b).

64. Anguiano v. Transcontinental Bus Sys., 76 Ariz. 246, 250, 263 P. 2d 305, 308 (1953) involved Arizona's rule which was identical with 41(b). In that case the court refused to go into the question of whether the dismissal was on the merits. It applied the rule literally, stating: "While dismissals may be entered at varying times and for varying reasons, still all dismissals may be dichotomized as voluntary or involuntary. The Rules have adopted this latter classification, and if we were to depart from this and begin classifying dismissals according to the time and reasons for which they were granted, we should conjure up a hydra-headed monster in the field of procedure." This was before the decision in Costello. See following note.

65. 365 U.S. 265, 81 S.Ct. 534, 5 L.Ed.2d 551 (1961).

in 1961, has indicated how it thinks the rule should be interpreted, and, after all, it is the Court's own rule that is in question. Costello was naturalized in 1925. In 1952 the government brought a denaturalization proceeding against him which was dismissed because the government failed to file an affidavit of good cause. In 1958 it brought another proceeding to denaturalize, and Costello pleaded the first judgment in bar. In holding the plea bad the Court said "We hold that a dismissal for failure to file the affidavit of good cause is a dismissal 'for lack of jurisdiction,' within the meaning of the exception under Rule 41(b)." [66] This was a broad interpretation of the meaning of "jurisdiction" which was all that was necessary to decide the case. The Court went on, however, to expound upon the meaning of the rule. It said:

> All the dismissals enumerated in Rule 41(b) which operate as adjudications on the merits—failure of the plaintiff to prosecute, or to comply with the Rules of Civil Procedure, or to comply with an order of the Court, or to present evidence showing a right to the relief on the facts and the law—primarily involve situations in which the defendant must incur the inconvenience of preparing to meet the merits because there is no initial bar to the Court's reaching them. It is therefore logical that a dismissal on one of these grounds should, unless the Court otherwise specifies, bar a subsequent action. In defining the situations where dismissals "not provided for in this rule" also operate as adjudications on the merits, and are not to be deemed jurisdictional, it seems reasonable to confine them to those situations where the policy behind the enumerated grounds is equally applicable.[67]

There is some confusion in the cases as to whether a judgment for the defendant following the sustaining of his demurrer to the

---

66. Id. at 285, 81 S.Ct. at 544, 5 L. Ed.2d at 564.

67. Id. at 286, 81 S.Ct. at 545, 5 L.Ed.2d at 565. In Saylor v. Lindsley, 391 F.2d 965, 969 (2d Cir. 1968) the first suit, a stockholders derivative suit, was dismissed for failure to comply with an order requiring plaintiff to post a security-for-costs bond. The court held the case came within the Costello doctrine and did not bar a second action. It said: "The present defendants make no claim that they were put to the inconvenience of preparing a defense . . ." In Nasser v. Isthmian Lines, supra n. 6, the first suit was dismissed under Rule 37 for failure of the plaintiff to answer interrogatories. Years later he sued again and was met by a plea of res judicata. The court said Rule 37 must be read with Rule 41(b), it acknowledged the Costello doctrine, but held the plea was good because of the history of the case which showed the plaintiff had "countless opportunities" to challenge the validity of the dismissal order. Generally see Annotation in 5 A.L.R.Fed. 897 (1970).

complaint is conclusive in a later suit on the same cause of action. Some courts hold that the first judgment is conclusive only as to the facts alleged in the first complaint.[68] If the demurrer was sustained on the ground the complaint did not state sufficient facts to constitute a cause of action because of the omission of an essential fact, the judgment is not conclusive in a second suit wherein the complaint corrects the error by alleging the fact.[69] If the demurrer was sustained on several grounds, going both to form and substance, some courts hold the judgment is not conclusive.[70] Occasionally the matter will be governed by a code provision which makes the judgment conclusive.[71] Where, after the sustaining of the demurrer, the plaintiff is given leave to amend and refuses to do so, the judgment is conclusive.[72] This is sound. Where the second suit is on the same cause of action, the policy underlying the doctrine of res judicata dictates that the first judgment should be conclusive, not only on all matters actually litigated, but on all matters which could have been litigated.

SECTION 3.   COLLATERAL ESTOPPEL

Collateral estoppel is sometimes regarded as a branch of res judicata. The two doctrines are, however, quite different. Both involve the conclusive effect of judgments in subsequent actions. The difference lies in the fact that in res judicata the subsequent suit involves the same cause of action, while in collateral estoppel the subsequent suit involves a different cause of action. In res judicata the first judgment is conclusive, not only on all matters which were actually litigated, but on all matters which could have been litigated. This is because the effect of the first judgment was to extinguish the cause of action. Where the subsequent suit is on a different cause of action, these principles cannot operate. If any conclusive effect is given to the first judgment it can only be in regard to issues that were actually litigated and which are pertinent to the cause of action in the subsequent suit.[73]

---

68. Keidatz v. Albany, 39 Cal.2d 826, 249 P.2d 264 (1952).

69. Rost v. Kroke, 195 Minn. 219, 262 N.W. 450 (1935).

70. Hacker v. Beck, 325 Mass. 594, 91 N.E.2d 832 (1950).

71. Northern Assur. Co. v. Almand, 210 Ga. 243, 78 S.E.2d 788 (1953).

72. Elfman v. Glaser, supra n. 5; Powell v. Chastain, supra n. 5.

73. Donald v. J. J. White Lumber Co., 68 F.2d 441 (5th Cir. 1934); Lea v. Shank, 5 Cal.App.3d 964, 85 Cal.Rptr. 709 (1970); Jacobson v. Miller, 41 Mich. 90, 1 N.W. 1013 (1879); Mansker v. Dealers Transp. Co., 160 Ohio St. 255, 116 N.E.2d 3 (1953).

The leading case on the subject is Cromwell v. County of Sac.[74] The first suit was on a bond issued by the county in which judgment went for the defendant on the ground that the county had been induced to issue the bonds by fraud, and that they were therefore void in the hands of one who did not acquire them before maturity for value and without notice. The second suit was on a different bond, but one of the same series. The plaintiff offered evidence that he received this bond before maturity for value and without notice. The trial court excluded the evidence and gave judgment for the defendant on the ground that the prior judgment was conclusive. The Supreme Court reversed, holding that each bond constituted a separate cause of action and that the first judgment was conclusive only on issues which were actually litigated. In explaining the reason for the rule the Court said:

> Various considerations, other than the actual merits, may govern a party in bringing forward grounds of recovery or defense in one action, which may not exist in another action upon a different demand, such as the smallness of the amount or the value of the property in controversy, the difficulty of obtaining the necessary evidence, the expense of the litigation, and his own situation at the time. A party acting upon considerations like these ought not to be precluded from contesting in a subsequent action other demands arising out of the same transaction.[75]

Collateral estoppel is not operative to conclude a party in a second suit on any point unless the point was actually litigated in the prior case,[76] and was necessary to the decision.[77] For example, where several persons were injured in an intersection accident, a general verdict in favor of the defendant in one case is not conclusive in another because the verdict may have been based on the contributory negligence of the injured party, rather than on the lack of negligence upon the part of the defendant.[78] Another example is a taxpayer's suit to declare certain realty exempt from taxation because it is being used for charitable and religious purposes; a prior judgment adverse to the taxpayer for

74. 94 U.S. 351, 24 L.Ed. 195 (1876).

75. Id. at 356, 24 L.Ed. at 199.

76. Note, Collateral Estoppel in Default Judgments: The Case for Abolition, 70 Colum.L.Rev. 523 (1970).

77. James Talcott, Inc. v. Allahabad Bank, Ltd., 444 F.2d 451 (5th Cir. 1971); Ingalls Iron Works Co. v. Fehlhaber Corp., 327 F.Supp. 272 (S.D.N.Y.1971); Cambria v. Jeffery, 307 Mass. 49, 29 N.E.2d 555 (1940); Ressequie v. Byers, 52 Wis. 650, 9 N.W. 779 (1881).

78. Banas v. Jensen, 350 Ill.App. 582, 113 N.E.2d 590 (1953).

another year is not conclusive because the land use in one year is not conclusive on what it is in another.[79] In order to have conclusive effect in a subsequent suit the issue decided in the first suit must also have been on an ultimate or operative fact and not merely on an evidentiary one.[80] If this condition is met the first judgment will, as to that issue, be conclusive and not merely prima facie.[81] It therefore becomes very important to ascertain exactly what was decided in the first case and, if the matter is not apparent from the record, resort may be had to extrinsic evidence.[82]

Because of the difference in the burden of proof in civil cases (a mere preponderance of the evidence) and in criminal cases (beyond a reasonable doubt) an acquittal in a criminal case can have no collateral estoppel effect in a civil case.[83] Sometimes, however, facts decided in a criminal case will be conclusive in a later civil case. In Teitelbaum Furs, Inc. v. Dominion Insurance Co.,[84] a conviction of staging a fake robbery to collect the insurance was held conclusive in a later civil action to recover the insurance. In United States v. Bower [85] a conviction under the federal false claims act was held conclusive in a later civil suit to recover civil penalties.

The conclusive effect of judgments is not dependent upon the type of court which renders them as long as the court was a competent one with jurisdiction over the subject matter and the parties. A state court will give conclusive effect to a federal court judgment,[86] and a federal court will give conclusive effect to a state court judgment.[87] As a matter of fact, the full faith and credit clause of the constitution requires this.[88] There is no

---

79. People ex rel. Watchtower Bible & Tract Soc. v. Haring, 286 App. Div. 676, 146 N.Y.S.2d 151 (1955).

80. The Evergreens v. Nunan, 141 F.2d 927 (2d Cir. 1944); nor does collateral estoppel apply to questions of law, but a mixed question of law and fact, such as status, is subject to the doctrine: United States v. Moser, 266 U.S. 236, 45 S.Ct. 66, 69 L.Ed. 262 (1924).

81. King, Adm'r v. Chase, 15 N.H. 9 (1844).

82. Russell v. Place, 94 U.S. 606, 24 L.Ed. 214 (1876); Waterhouse v. Levine, 182 Mass. 407, 65 N.E. 822 (1903).

83. Lee v. United States, 323 F. Supp. 658 (N.D.Miss.1971).

84. 58 Cal.2d 601, 375 P.2d 439 (1962).

85. 95 F.Supp. 19 (E.D.Tenn.1951).

86. Shell Oil Co. v. Texas Gas Transmission Corp., 176 So.2d 692 (La.Ct.App.1965).

87. Vernitron Corp. v. Benjamin, 440 F.2d 105 (2d Cir. 1971); Roth v. McAllister Bros., 316 F.2d 143 (2d Cir. 1963).

88. Actually, the full faith and credit clause (Art. IV § 1) is obligatory only on the states: Baldwin v.

such constitutional compulsion in regard to the judgments of courts of foreign nations, but they will usually be given conclusive effect by comity.[89]

There are certain situations in which courts have refused to apply the doctrine of collateral estoppel. In Commissioner of Internal Revenue v. Sunnen [90] the Supreme Court held the doctrine inapplicable in an income tax case. The taxpayer, an inventor, had several contracts with a corporation under which he licensed it to use his patents in exchange for royalties. Some of these contracts he assigned to his wife. In a 1935 case it was decided that the taxpayer was not liable for taxes on the income received by the wife. In a later proceeding, for another year, the government sought to collect taxes on the income received by the wife under these contracts. The taxpayer pleaded the former decision as a defense. The court admitted that there was a complete identity of facts, issues and parties, but overruled the defense because, since the time of the first decision the cases had been contrary to the taxpayer's position and, to use the language of the court, there had been "a sufficient change in the legal climate to render inapplicable in the instant proceeding, the doctrine of collateral estoppel." [91] The court said that collateral estoppel does apply in the income tax field but, to avoid undue disparity of tax liability "it must be confined to situations where the matter raised in the second suit is identical in all respects with that decided in the first proceeding and where the controlling facts and applicable legal rules remain unchanged." [92] In City of Pittsburgh v. United States [93] a pedestrian sued the city in a state court and recovered a judgment for injuries he received when he fell due to a defective sidewalk adjoining federal proper-

---

Iowa State Traveling Men's Ass'n, supra n. 45; Fauntleroy v. Lum, 210 U.S. 230, 28 S.Ct. 641, 52 L. Ed. 1039 (1908). However, by statute and judicial decision, the state and federal courts are under reciprocal obligations to honor the judgments of each other: American Sur. Co. v. Baldwin, 287 U.S. 156, 53 S.Ct. 98, 77 L.Ed. 231 (1932).

89. Cowans v. Ticonderoga Pulp & Paper Co., 219 App.Div. 120, 219 N.Y.S. 284 (1927). In Hilton v. Guyot, 159 U.S. 113, 16 S.Ct. 139, 40 L.Ed. 95 (1895) the Supreme Court applied a reciprocity doctrine: it refused to give conclusive effect to a French judgment because France would not give con-

clusive effect to ours. On the same day, in Ritchie v. McMullen, 159 U.S. 235, 16 S.Ct. 171, 40 L.Ed. 133 (1895) it gave conclusive effect to a Canadian judgment because Canada would give conclusive effect to one of ours.

90. 333 U.S. 591, 68 S.Ct. 715, 92 L.Ed. 898 (1948).

91. Id. at 606, 68 S.Ct. at 723, 92 L.Ed. at 911.

92. Id. at 599, 68 S.Ct. at 720, 92 L.Ed. at 907. See Griswold, Res Judicata in Federal Tax Cases, 46 Yale L.J. 1320 (1937).

93. 359 F.2d 564 (3rd Cir. 1966).

ty. The city paid the judgment and then sued the United States for indemnity under the federal tort claims act. The trial court held the state court judgment was conclusive on the issue of liability, but the appellate court reversed because, under the federal tort claims act the government had waived its sovereign immunity but only when sued in a federal court without a jury; hence it could not be bound by the findings of a state court jury. In Lyons v. Westinghouse Electric Corp.[94] the company sued one of its agents in a state court for an accounting. He defended on the ground the agency contract was illegal under the antitrust acts, and he also brought an antitrust suit for damages in a federal court. In the state case there was a finding of no violation of the antitrust act and the question was whether this would be conclusive in the federal case. Judge Learned Hand, writing for the court, held that were it not for § 15 of the antitrust act the state court judgment would be conclusive, but that when Congress gave the federal courts exclusive jurisdiction to try treble damage suits it intended to confer unfettered jurisdiction, and that uniformity in the administration of the act dictates that the federal courts should not be concluded by state court decisions. "For these reasons we think the situation is one where the delay and expense of a double trial of the same issue do not balance the importance of an uncommitted enforcement of the remedy provided by Section 15." [95] In each of these three cases there was a strong governmental interest which the court considered more important than the policy of repose represented by the doctrine of collateral estoppel. Such cases are rare, but they do occur, even where a governmental interest is not involved.[96] In Spilker v. Hankin [97] the defendant gave the plaintiff a series of notes in payment for attorney fees. When sued on the first note the defendant pleaded that the fee was exorbitant, but judgment went for the plaintiff. In a later suit on the other notes the court refused to apply the doctrine of collateral estoppel, holding it must yield because of the fiduciary relationship.

Closely allied to res judicata and collateral estoppel is a doctrine known as the law of the case. Unlike the former two, which involve successive suits, it involves successive stages of the same suit. The same policy of repose, however, underlies all. An issue which has been litigated and decided in one stage of a case should not be relitigated in a later stage.[98] Such issues are

94. 222 F.2d 184 (2d Cir. 1955).

95. Id. at 190.

96. Cleary, Res Judicata Re-examined, 57 Yale L.J. 339, 349 (1948).

97. 188 F.2d 35 (D.C.Cir. 1951).

98. "[T]he doctrine operates only to preclude a reconsideration of substantially similar, if not identical, issues." Consumers Union of

usually points of law which, according to the doctrine, become the law of the case, and are conclusive in later stages of the litigation.[99] The doctrine is not, however, applied with the same rigor as res judicata and collateral estoppel.[100]

SECTION 4. PARTIES, PRIVIES AND MUTUALITY

The general rule is that a judgment has no binding effect upon anyone who was not a party to the action.[101] A stranger cannot take advantage of a judgment, nor can it be enforced against him. Consequently, as a general proposition, the rules of res judicata and collateral estoppel do not apply unless the parties in the subsequent suit are identical with the parties in the first suit. The reason for the rule is one of basic fairness; every man is entitled to his day in court. There is an exception to the rule in the case of a non-party whose interests were in fact represented and protected in the litigation although he was not a formal party to the proceedings. Our sense of fair play and sub-

United States, Inc. v. Veterans Adm'r, 436 F.2d 1363 (2d Cir. 1971).

99. Vestal, Law of the Case: Single-Suit Preclusion, 1967 Utah L.Rev. 1.

100. The problem becomes acute when the later stage of the litigation falls before a different judge than the one who decided the issue in the first place. An illustrative case is Lincoln Nat. Life Ins. Co. v. Roosth, 306 F.2d 110 (5th Cir. 1962). There the trial court had granted the defendant's motion for judgment non obstante veredicto. A three-judge panel of the Court of Appeals reversed for a new trial on the ground the evidence was sufficient to take the case to the jury. Plaintiff won a verdict on the second trial, and the defendant appealed. The case fell before a different panel of the Court of Appeals, and the question arose whether it was bound by the finding of the earlier panel that the evidence was sufficient, a legal question. The case was thrown en banc, and the decision was by a divided court. Brown, J., for the majority, held that the law of the case doctrine should be applied,

stating: "We think that in a multi-judge court it is most essential that it acquire an institutional stability . . . that the decision on identical questions, once made, will not be re-examined and redecided merely because of a change in the composition of the Court or of the new panel hearing the case." Id. at 114. Hutcheson, J., for the dissenters, while agreeing with the desirability of stability and predictability, questioned whether these goals were advanced by the rule of the majority, especially in view of the fact that "we do not have the infallibility of finality . . . .. 'Our law of the case is not the Supreme Court's law of the case. Our judgment on the second appeal stands or falls on its merits and has no improved standing before the Supreme Court from the fact that it resulted from an application of our law of the case. This being so, it would seem that if on second appeal we thought our earlier opinion was erroneous, we ought sensibly to set ourselves right, rather than to invite reversal above.'" Id. at 117.

101. Neenan v. Woodside Astoria Transp. Co., 261 N.Y. 159, 184 N. E. 744 (1933).

stantial justice is not offended if such a person is concluded by the judgment, but we should carefully restrict the situations in which the exception is applicable. The law has coined a name for these non-parties who are bound by judgments; they are called privies. The Restatement breaks them down into three classes: "those who control an action although not parties to it (see § 84); those whose interests are represented by a party to the action (see §§ 85–88); successors in interest to those having derivative claims (§§ 89–92)." [102]

It sometimes happens that a defendant who is sued may have a right to be indemnified by another if he is held liable. A retailer who is held liable in damages for the sale of defective goods may sue his supplier for indemnity; an employer who is held liable vicariously for the negligence of his employee may sue the latter for indemnity. In such cases if the person primarily liable, although not a party, takes over control of the suit, the judgment will be conclusive against him in a later suit.[103] The fact that the non-party's participation in the first suit was not open and avowed will not prevent the judgment from being conclusive against him. In disposing of such an argument Judge Goodrich, of the Third Circuit Court of Appeals, said, "The defendant here is in the position of asking for two days in court if he successfully masked his participation upon his first appearance." [104]

The Restatement's second category of privy, those whose interests are represented by a party, is illustrated by actions by personal representatives in their fiduciary capacity, by wrongful death actions, where the nominal plaintiff is suing on behalf of statutory beneficiaries, and by class actions.

The third category, successors in interest, is illustrated by the cases in which a judgment has been rendered for or against a claimant to real property; in such cases the judgment will bind subsequent grantees.[105] It is also illustrated by cases where a party to a suit dies and is replaced by his personal representative. In Little v. Blue Goose Motor Coach Co.[106] the decedent's car collided with a Blue Goose bus. The Bus Company sued him and recovered a judgment for the property damage to the bus. He

---

102. Restatement, Judgments (1942) § 83, Comment a.

103. Freeman, Judgments §§ 447–50 (5th ed. 1925).

104. Caterpillar Tractor Co. v. International Harvester Co., 120 F. 2d 82, 84 (3d Cir. 1941).

105. Restatement, Judgments (1942) § 89.

106. 346 Ill. 266, 178 N.E. 496 (1931).

then sued the company for his personal injuries but died while the suit was pending. His administrator was substituted and the case was converted into a wrongful death claim. The court held that the decedent's negligence had been determined in the first suit and was conclusive against his administrator, barring recovery.

The factual variation in cases is so great that it is impossible to compress them into neat categories. In determining whether a judgment in a prior action will be conclusive on a non-party in a later action, although the court may say it is seeking to determine whether there was privity, what it is actually doing is deciding whether, under the particular circumstances, it would be fair to hold the judgment conclusive. Thus "privity" is not a tool for deciding cases, but a shorthand expression to describe the result reached. A few illustrations may prove the point. Where a passenger in a vehicle is injured in an intersection collision with another vehicle and sues the owners of both and recovers a judgment against both, is that judgment conclusive on the question of negligence in a later suit by one of the defendants against the other? The parties in the second suit were both defendants in the first suit but not necessarily adversaries, and their negligence inter se may not have been litigated. The cases go both ways.[107] One commentator has said, "In final analysis much of the difference between the several rules announced is a matter of semantics, the essence of all of them being that such a prior judgment is not conclusive in the subsequent action unless the codefendants occupied adversary positions in the prior action and actually litigated therein the issue of their liability inter se as well as the issue of their liability to the injured party." [108] Another situation in which the courts are divided is whether or not a judgment for a wife in a personal injury action is conclusive in a later suit by the husband (a non-party to the first suit) for loss of consortium, medical expenses and similar resulting damage, with the majority holding that the mere marital relationship does not necessarily establish privity.[109] Nor does a

---

107. Holding the first judgment conclusive: Schwartz v. Public Adm'r of County of Bronx, 24 N. Y.2d 65, 246 N.E.2d 725 (1969); Pack v. McCoy, 251 N.C. 590, 112 S.E.2d 118 (1960) (there was a dissent on two grounds, (1) the first judgment was by consent, and (2) the defendants in the first suit were not adversaries inter se). Holding the first judgment was not conclusive: Brown Hotel Co. v. Pittsburgh Fuel Co., 311 Ky. 396, 224 S.W.2d 165 (1949); Rios v. Davis, 373 S.W.2d 386 (Tex.Civ. App.1963).

108. Annotation in 24 A.L.R.3d 318, 323 (1969).

109. Smith v. Bishop, 26 Ill.2d 434, 187 N.E.2d 217 (1963); Gilman v. Gilman, 115 Vt. 49, 51 A.2d 46 (1947); Annotation in 12 A.L.R.3d 933 (1967).

contractual relationship between a party and a non-party necessarily make the latter a privy. This is illustrated in the case of Ralph Wolff & Sons v. New Zealand Insurance Co.[110] in which the plaintiff suffered a fire loss on his factory which was covered by 12 insurance policies in different companies, each of which limited its liability to a pro rata share of the damage. In a consolidated suit against nine of the companies the plaintiff recovered a judgment based upon a figure fixed by the jury. This judgment was held nonconclusive in a later suit against the other companies on the ground the pro rata clauses in the policies did not make them privies.

The courts have struggled with the cases involving vicarious or derivative liability. For instance, if a plaintiff is run over by a truck belonging to a company and being driven by its employee in the scope of his employment, the plaintiff may have an action against the company, the driver, or both. If he sues the driver first and loses, and later sues the company, may the latter use the first judgment as a bar?[111] If the company's liability is based solely on the doctrine of respondeat superior, the negligence of its employee, then it seems the first judgment should be a bar as that issue was decided in the first case. If the plaintiff sued the company first and lost, would that judgment be conclusive in a later suit against the employee[112] or, if the plaintiff had won in the first suit would the judgment be conclusive in a later action by the company against its employee for reimbursement?[113] The questions posed by these and similar situations have led the courts to develop the so-called doctrine of the mutuality of estoppel.

In the leading case of Bigelow v. Old Dominion Copper Mining & Smelting Co.[114] the Supreme Court said that "it is a principle of general elementary law that the estoppel of a judgment must be mutual." Literally this means that both parties to a judgment are estopped or concluded by it. This seems to make sense. Both parties have had their day in court, so both should be concluded, whatever the outcome of the litigation. Otherwise the doctrine

110. 248 Ky. 304, 58 S.W.2d 623 (1933).

111. It is unlikely that a plaintiff would sue the employee driver instead of the company, but see the analogous situation in City of Anderson v. Fleming, 160 Ind. 597, 67 N.E. 443 (1903), in which plaintiff was injured when she fell into an excavation in the street, sued the contractor and lost, and then sued the city, but lost again when the first judgment was held to be conclusive.

112. Held conclusive in Giedrewicz v. Donovan, 277 Mass. 563, 179 N.E. 246 (1932).

113. Held conclusive in Schimke v. Earley, 173 Ohio St. 521, 184 N.E. 2d 209 (1962).

114. 225 U.S. 111, 127, 32 S.Ct. 641, 642, 56 L.Ed. 1009, 1021 (1912).

of res judicata would mean very little. If in a subsequent suit the parties are identical, there is no problem. It is only when the first judgment is given conclusive effect as to someone who was not a party to the first suit, that the doctrine of mutuality comes into play. Since one who was not a party to the first suit would ordinarily not be bound by an adverse judgment, since he did not have his day in court, it would be unfair to permit him to take the benefits of a favorable judgment. Hence the rule is that, in order to take advantage of a judgment one must have been so related to the case that he would have been bound by it if the judgment had gone the other way.[115] The effect of the mutuality rule was to restrict res judicata and collateral estoppel to a comparatively narrow scope: it applied only to parties and privies. Situations arose, however, in which a strict application of the mutuality rule would result in expensive and time consuming litigation of an issue which had been thoroughly tried in a previous case and in which it did not seem unfair to hold the first judgment conclusive, even against one who was not a party or privy to the original suit. One such situation, discussed above, was the subsequent suit against an employer, on the basis of respondeat superior, whose employee had been exonerated in the prior suit. A court could handle this situation in one of three ways: (1) apply the traditional mutuality rule and hold the first judgment was not conclusive, regardless of the duplicated effort and waste of a second trial, (2) expand the concept of privity to include the employer-employee relationship, which courts were loath to do, or (3) create an exception to the mutuality rule. The latter is the course which most courts pursued, making ad hoc exceptions where fairness seemed to demand it.[116]

Then came the Bernhard case in 1942,[117] in which Mr. Justice Traynor, of the California Supreme Court, blazed a new trail. In an opinion which broke with precedent and jettisoned the mutuality rule he said, "No satisfactory rationalization has been advanced for requirement of mutuality. Just why a party who

---

115. There is a comprehensive note on the mutuality doctrine in 31 A. L.R.3d 1044 (1970).

116. The New York courts have taken the lead in creating exceptions to the mutuality doctrine. Good Health Dairy Prods. Co. v. Emery, 275 N.Y. 14, 9 N.E.2d 758 (1937) (an exception exists in the case of derivative liability dependent upon the culpability of one exonerated in the prior suit); Elder v. New York & Pa. Motor Express, 284 N.Y. 350, 31 N.E.2d 188 (1940) (for the exception to apply the judgment in the first suit must be in favor of the agent or servant); Israel v. Wood Dolson Co., 1 N.Y. 2d 116, 134 N.E.2d 97 (1956) (in this case the court is seeking the "underlying principle" of the exceptions, which it finds to be "identity of issues").

117. Bernhard v. Bank of America Nat'l Trust & Sav. Ass'n, 19 Cal. 2d 807, 122 P.2d 892 (1942).

was not bound by a previous action should be precluded from asserting it as res judicata against a party who was bound by it is difficult to comprehend." [118] The facts in Bernhard were simple: Mrs. Sather, an elderly and ailing lady, gave money to Mr. Cook, her business advisor, who deposited it in a bank account in their two names. Later he changed the account to one in his own name. When Mrs. Sather died, Cook became her executor. He did not include the account in the estate inventory, and the heirs objected. In the probate court the issue of the ownership of the account was litigated, and the court found that it belonged to Cook, having been a gift from Mrs. Sather. In a later suit by the heirs against the Bank, the court held that the first judgment was conclusive. The Bank was not a party to the first suit and would not have been concluded, had the judgment gone the other way. Nevertheless, the California Supreme Court held the Bank could take advantage of that judgment. In explaining the theory behind the decision the court said:

> The criteria for determining who may assert a plea of res judicata differ fundamentally from the criteria for determining against whom a plea of res judicata may be asserted. The requirements of due process of law forbid the assertion of a plea of res judicata against a party unless he was bound by the earlier litigation in which the matter was decided. . . . He is bound by that litigation only if he has been a party thereto or in privity with a party thereto. . . . There is no compelling reason, however, for requiring that a party asserting the plea of res judicata must have been a party, or in privity with a party, to the earlier litigation.[119]

Having thus eliminated the necessity for mutuality Mr. Justice Traynor goes on to define the new criteria:

> In determining the validity of a plea of res judicata three questions are pertinent: Was the issue decided in the prior adjudication identical with the one presented in the action in question? Was there a final judgment on the merits? Was the party against whom the plea was asserted a party or in privity with a party to the prior adjudication? [120]

If affirmative answers may be given to all three questions, the plea of res judicata is valid and the former judgment is conclusive. In Bernhard the answers were affirmative, and the prior judgment was held conclusive. Note that the one as-

---

118. Id. at 812, 122 P.2d at 895.   **120.** Id. at 813, 122 P.2d at 895.

119. Id. at 811–12, 122 P.2d at 894.

serting the plea, the Bank, was using the prior judgment defensively. Twenty years later Mr. Justice Traynor had the opportunity to reaffirm the Bernhard doctrine in a case in which a conviction in a criminal case was held conclusive in a later civil case.[121] The president of a fur company was convicted of staging a fake robbery for the purpose of presenting a fraudulent insurance claim. In a later civil case by the company against the insurance company the latter was permitted to use the conviction defensively since the Bernhard criteria were met: the issues in the two cases were identical, the first judgment was final, and the person against whom the plea was asserted was a party to the prior action.[122] Between the two dates the Bernhard doctrine had become one of the most widely discussed subjects in the literature of the law.[123]

The Bernhard doctrine has a ring of fairness about it. If one has litigated an issue in one case, and the identical issue arises in another case, why should he not be bound? Why should he be given the luxury of relitigation? Answers to these questions were forthcoming, by courts and commentators. Viewed critically, the Bernhard doctrine was a rather startling one. It was offered as a substitute for the deeply entrenched rule of mutuality which itself was developed as a safeguard to an over-liberal use of the res judicata principle. Did the Bernhard doctrine mean that once a party had litigated an issue in court that the decision of that issue could be used against him in any later case under any circumstances by anyone, be he party, privy, or complete stranger? What if the decision in the first case had been by a jury verdict which was, as many verdicts are, a compromise between liability and damages? What if the amount involved in the first suit were too small to warrant an appeal? What if, under the circumstances, the party had no opportunity to appeal? In Bernhard the plea of res judicata was interposed

---

121. Teitelbaum Furs, Inc. v. Dominion Ins. Co., supra n. 84.

122. In the civil case the plaintiff corporation conceded that it was merely the alter ego of its president who was convicted in the criminal action.

123. B. Currie, Mutuality of Collateral Estoppel—Limits of the Bernhard Doctrine, 9 Stan.L.Rev. 281 (1957); Moore & Currier, Mutuality and Conclusiveness of Judgments, 35 Tul.L.Rev. 301 (1961); Polasky, Collateral Estoppel—Effects of Prior Litigation, 39 Iowa L.Rev. 217 (1954). Subsequent to 1962, but carrying on the discussion are: B. Currie, Civil Procedure: The Tempest Brews, 53 Cal. L.Rev. 25 (1965), which contains an Appendix digesting the cases which have involved the Bernhard doctrine; Semmel, Collateral Estoppel, Mutuality and Joinder of Parties, 68 Colum.L.Rev. 1457 (1968); Note, Collateral Estoppel: The Demise of Mutuality, 52 Corn. L.Q. 724 (1967); Note, The Impacts of Defensive and Offensive Assertion of Collateral Estoppel by a Nonparty, 35 Geo.Wash.L.Rev. 1010 (1967).

defensively, as a shield against liability. Did Bernhard also mean that one not a party to the original suit could use the doctrine offensively? The approach to answers to these questions by the courts has been gingerly, on a case to case basis, and the answers have not been uniform.

The trend of the courts has been to accept the defensive use of the Bernhard doctrine. In Nickerson v. Pep Boys—Manny, Moe and Jack [124] it was applied in a patent infringement suit, which constitutes a clean break with tradition. The plaintiff had sued the defendant for patent infringement, and the defendant pleaded the invalidity of the patent which had been decided in another suit between the plaintiff and a third party. The court held the plea was good. In so doing it based its decision on fairness under the circumstances. In the prior suit the plaintiff had selected the defendant it wished to sue, and had chosen the forum. Consequently, it was not unfair to hold it was concluded by the prior holding. In its opinion the court admitted that a hard case might arise requiring a different decision. After adverting to the fact that patent ownership, unlike many rights which the law protects, possesses the inherent possibility of multiple law suits, the court said;

> because of this, a situation may be imagined which might make it unfair to hold a patentee bound by an adverse decision as to validity when he sues a different defendant. Suppose, for instance, a patentee had sued successively a large number of infringers and in each instance his patent had been sustained. Suppose further, that in his next suit the patent is adjudged invalid. To hold that the last decision is a bar to the patentee suing other infringers might be unjust, for the holding of invalidity, in view of repeated prior decisions to the contrary, would at least suggest that something was amiss with the decision which held the patent invalid. The present case is not the 'hard case' such as that hypothesized . . .. If a case comparable to that postulated should ever arise it is not to be expected that the estoppel rule would be applied to bring about an unjust result.[125]

---

124.   247 F.Supp. 221 (D.Del.1965).

125.   Id. at 224. In the recent case of Blonder-Tongue Lab., Inc. v. University of Ill. Foundation, 402 U.S. 313, 91 S.Ct. 1434, 28 L.Ed. 2d 788 (1971) the Supreme Court followed the Bernhard doctrine and held that the patentee is estopped by the first judgment of invalidity.

In Coca-Cola Co. v. Pepsi-Cola Co.,[126] in upholding a plea of res judicata, the court said:

> But assuming the identity of the issues, we are of the opinion that a plaintiff who deliberately selects his forum and there unsuccessfully presents his proofs, is bound by such adverse judgment in a second suit involving all of the identical issues already decided. The requirement of mutuality must yield to public policy.

In Eisel v. Columbia Packing Co.,[127] Judge Wyzanski notes the growing tendency to apply the Bernhard doctrine defensively against a plaintiff.

The arguments against applying the Bernhard doctrine offensively are more cogent. Perhaps the severest test of the doctrine is encountered in the case of the mass tort, in which dozens or hundreds of persons are killed or injured in the same disaster. Let us suppose a bus accident in which twenty passengers are killed. If the representative of one passenger brings a wrongful death action against the bus company, and a jury finds for the company, the judgment based on that verdict is not conclusive on the other passengers because they were not parties to the suit. If the representative of a second passenger sues and loses, the judgment in that case will likewise not be conclusive. And so it would go as long as the company kept winning. It would have to relitigate its liability in each suit. But if, in the tenth suit, there was a verdict and judgment for the plaintiff, that judgment, on the issue of liability, would be conclusive on the bus company in every later suit—that is, if the Bernhard doctrine were applied. Such an "anomalous" result has led some courts, along with other reasons, to reject the Bernhard doctrine in such situations.[128] Other courts, relying on other arguments, have not boggled at applying the doctrine offensively in the case of mass torts.

The leading case is probably United States v. United Air Lines, Inc.[129] On April 21, 1958, a United Air Lines plane collided with a government jet over Nevada, and all passengers on the United craft were killed. Suits involving 24 passengers were consolidated for trial in the United States District Court for the Southern

---

126. 36 Del. 124, 132–33, 172 A. 260, 263 (1934).

127. 181 F.Supp. 298 (D.Mass.1960).

128. Berner v. British Commonwealth Pac. Airlines, 346 F.2d 532 (2d Cir. 1965).

129. 216 F.Supp. 709 (E.D.Wash. & D.Nev.1962), affirmed sub nom United Air Lines, Inc. v. Wiener, 335 F.2d 379, 404 (9th Cir. 1964), in which the court said "We affirm and adopt herein as our own the district court's treatment of the issue of mutuality of collateral estoppel."

District of California. There was a bifurcated trial on the issue of liability which resulted in a judgment against United. Suits involving the other passengers were brought in federal courts in Nevada and Washington. In those cases (consolidated) the plaintiffs moved to have the finding of liability in the earlier case given conclusive effect. In granting the motion the court said:

> The issue of liability of United Air Lines to the passengers on the plane was litigated to the hilt, by lawyers of the highest competence in their fields, in the trial of the 24 cases in Los Angeles. The trial of that issue before a jury consumed the better part of 15 weeks . . . . Throughout the Federal Rules of Civil Procedure, the Judicial Code and other Statutes of the United States, the recurrent phrase is found "in the interest of justice." It would be a travesty upon that concept to now require these plaintiffs who are the survivors of passengers for hire on the United Air Lines plane to again relitigate the issue of liability after it has been so thoroughly and consummately litigated in the trial court in the 24 consolidated cases tried at Los Angeles.[130]

There was a similar holding in the case of State of Maryland for the Use of Gliedman v. Capital Airlines, Inc.,[131] a case involving a mid-air collision of a Capital Airlines plane with a National Guard training jet over Maryland on May 20, 1958. Two groups of wrongful death cases were brought on behalf of the passengers, one group in the District of Columbia and the other in Pennsylvania. The present case, involving a passenger in the plane, was brought in the United States District Court in Maryland. The question was whether a finding of negligence on the part of the government (being sued under the Federal Tort Claims Act) could be held conclusive. The court held that it could, but in so doing it added another element to the Bernhard criteria: "Was the party against whom the plea was asserted given a fair opportunity to be heard on the issue?"[132] The court also made the following comment in regard to mutuality: "In view of the crowded dockets of the courts today, ancient principles must give way to principles based on today's realities so long as these new principles do not deprive a litigant of his day in court."[133]

---

130. 216 F.Supp. at 728.

131. 267 F.Supp. 298 (D.Md.1967).

132. Id. at 304.

133. Id. In Blonder-Tongue Lab., Inc. v. University of Ill. Foundation, 402 U.S. 313, 328, 91 S.Ct. 1434, 1442, 28 L.Ed.2d 788, 799 (1971) the court said "more than

The offensive use of the Bernhard doctrine has not been limited to disaster cases. Zdanok v. Glidden Co.[134] involved a labor dispute. Glidden, whose principal plant was in New York, opened a new plant in Pennsylvania. Zdanok and four other employees sued to establish seniority in opportunity for working in the new plant. The case was removed to the federal court and litigated all the way to the United States Supreme Court, where the plaintiffs prevailed. While the case was pending, other employees brought another suit in the state court seeking the same relief. After the plaintiffs' victory in the first case the second set of employees dropped the state court suit, filed a new action in the federal court, and asked for summary judgment, based on the Zdanok judgment. The trial court held the former judgment was conclusive, and the appellate court affirmed, holding the case was a proper one for the offensive application of the Bernhard doctrine since Glidden knew the case was "lurking in the wings," since its opportunity to litigate the issue in the first suit was "full and fair," and, as a matter of fact, was litigated "with the utmost vigor." [135]

It must not be assumed that the court which decided Zdanok would necessarily apply the Bernhard doctrine offensively in another situation. As a matter of fact, the year following Zdanok it refused to do so in an airplane wrongful death case.[136] It said, "Even if the Zdanok approach were thought applicable to this prior judgment, mutuality should not so quickly be discarded in multiple accident cases like this." [137] It distinguished the United Air Lines case as one in which the question of liability had been litigated to the hilt in the first action, whereas in the present case there was substantial doubt on that score.

Even in California, where the Bernhard doctrine originated, it is applied with caution. In two multi-injury accident cases the courts refused to apply it offensively,[138] and in another case [139] the California Supreme Court, in an opinion by Mr. Justice Traynor, refused to apply it where his criteria were met, but where

crowded dockets is involved. The broader question is whether it is any longer tenable to afford a litigant more than one full and fair opportunity for judicial resolution of the same issue."

134. 327 F.2d 944 (2d Cir. 1964).

135. Id. at 956.

136. Berner v. British Commonwealth Pac. Airlines, Ltd., 346 F. 2d 532 (2d Cir. 1965).

137. Id. at 541.

138. Nevarov v. Caldwell, 161 Cal. App.2d 762, 327 P.2d 111 (1958); Price v. Atchison, T. & S. F. Ry., 164 Cal.App.2d 400, 330 P.2d 933 (1958).

139. Taylor v. Hawkinson, 47 Cal. 2d 893, 306 P.2d 797 (1957).

there was internal evidence in the record that the first judgment was based on a compromise verdict.

As noted earlier, the New York cases adopted the practice of creating exceptions to the mutuality doctrine, but in 1967, in B. R. DeWitt v. Hall,[140] the Court of Appeals reviewed its prior cases, Bernhard, and cases from other jurisdictions following Bernhard, and concluded, "To recapitulate, we are saying that the 'doctrine of mutuality' is a dead letter."[141] In DeWitt the court was applying the Bernhard doctrine offensively. The plaintiff's truck, driven by one Farnum, collided with defendant's jeep. Farnum sued the defendant for personal injuries and recovered a $5,000 judgment. Plaintiff then sued the defendant for $8,000 damages to his truck. The court held the first judgment was conclusive on the issue of liability. Breitel, J., dissented on the offensive use of the doctrine:

> "To say of a plaintiff that he has had his day in court in a litigation of his own choosing is not as aptly said of a defendant."[142]

The above does not purport to be an exhaustive discussion of the cases dealing with the demise of mutuality. Their number is legion.[143] What can be said, in summary, is that the doctrine of mutuality is on its way out. The trend is definitely in that direction. It is being replaced by the Bernhard doctrine, or something like it.[144] To recapitulate that doctrine: "In determining the validity of a plea of res judicata three questions are pertinent: Was the issue decided in the prior adjudication identical with the one presented in the action in question? Was there a final judgment on the merits? Was the party against whom the plea was asserted a party or in privity with a party to the prior adjudication?"[145] Some would add a fourth question: "Was the party against whom the plea was asserted given a fair opportunity to be heard on the issue?"[146] Even if all four ques-

---

140. 19 N.Y.2d 141, 225 N.E.2d 195 (1967).

141. Id. at 147, 225 N.E.2d at 198.

142. Id. at 148, 225 N.E.2d at 199.

143. B. Currie, Civil Procedure: The Tempest Brews, 53 Cal.L.Rev. 25 (1965), Appendix (containing digest of cases); Comprehensive annotation in 31 A.L.R.3d 1044 (1970).

144. Later cases following Bernhard: Bahler v. Fletcher, 474 P.2d 329 (Or.1970); Pennington v. Snow, 471 P.2d 370 (Alas.1970); Ellis v. Crockett, 451 P.2d 814 (Hawaii 1969).

145. Bernhard v. Bank of America Nat'l Trust & Sav. Ass'n, 19 Cal. 2d 807, 813, 122 P.2d 892, 895 (1942).

146. State of Maryland for the use of Gliedman v. Capital Airlines, Inc., 267 F.Supp. 298, 304 (D.Md. 1967).

tions are answered in the affirmative, the cases indicate that the doctrine must be applied with discretion, and must not be used when, under the circumstances of the instant case, it would produce an unfair result.[147]

147. A striking illustration is found in the case of Rachal v. Hill, 435 F.2d 59, 63 (5th Cir. 1970). The Securities & Exchange Commission sued the defendant for violations of the Securities & Exchange Acts of 1933 and 1934 and, after a trial, obtained an injunction against further violations. In a later civil suit by defendant's customers the court held that the findings of violations in the prior suit, although the issues were identical, could not be used as a collateral estoppel because, to permit this, would be to deprive the defendant of his constitutional right to jury trial, since that right was not available to him in the previous injunction suit. The court posed the question as follows: "whether a litigant can lose his constitutional right to a trial by jury by estoppel when the issue to be decided has been adjudicated adversely to him in a prior proceeding at which there was no right to a trial by jury and his present adversary was not a party." The court found no case directly in point, but relied heavily by analogy on Beacon Theatres v. Westover, 359 U.S. 500, 79 S.Ct. 948, 3 L.Ed.2d 988 (1959), discussed in Chapt. VII. Compare Vernitron Corp. v. Benjamin, 440 F.2d 105 (2d Cir. 1971).

CHAPTER IX. APPEALS

SECTION 1. IN GENERAL

An appellate court is a court of review: its purpose is not to retry the case but to scrutinize the record of the trial court to determine whether reversible error has been committed. This is the traditional view although, as we shall see, the ambit of appellate power is not always so limited.

In order to understand the appellate process in the United States today, it is necessary to bear in mind a bit of historical background. Again, the dual system of law and equity which we inherited from England, has left its mark on our procedure. Appellate review of an action at law was quite different from a suit in equity.[1]

Review of a common law action was begun by a writ of error issuing out of the appellate court and served on the trial judge ordering him to send up the record in the case. The one who sought the review, whether plaintiff or defendant in the trial court, was designated as the plaintiff in error. His opponent was the defendant in error, and a copy of the writ was also served upon him. After the writ was served, the plaintiff in error was required to file a document called the Assignments of Error, which was the counterpart of the complaint in the trial court. It set forth, in detail, the alleged errors committed by the trial judge. Thus the only function of the appellate court was to review alleged errors of law,[2] and in so doing it was confined to the common law record which consisted of the writ (summons), the return, pleadings, verdict and judgment.[3] The court could not review the facts since they were the sole province of the jury, and furthermore no record of the testimony was kept. Consequently the scope of review was very narrow, at least until the year 1285 when Parliament passed the famous Statute of Westminster II[4] which, among other things, provided for Bills of Exceptions.

The purpose of a Bill of Exceptions was to bring before the appellate court for review matters which otherwise would not appear on the common law record due to the fact that there were

---

1. Clark & Stone, Review of Findings of Fact, 4 U.Chi.L.Rev. 190 (1937).

2. Dower v. Richards, 151 U.S. 658, 14 S.Ct. 452 (1894).

3. State ex rel. Summerson v. Goodrich, 257 Mo. 40, 165 S.W. 707 (1914); Prindle v. Anderson, 19 Wend. (N.Y.) 391 (1838).

4. 13 Edw. I, ch. 31, 1 Stat. at Large 78 (1285).

no court reporters to record the testimony and the proceedings at the trial. This was before the days of shorthand and recording devices. After the Statute of Westminster II if a litigant believed the court had erred in a ruling, he could make it a matter of record by "saving his exception." For example, if counsel had objected to a question asked of a witness and the court had overruled the objection and counsel thought the ruling was erroneous, he could say, "If the court please, I desire to save an exception to your honor's ruling." The judge was then obliged to stop the trial and call the scriviner who, with his quill pen, would make a record on parchment which would read something like the following: (after giving the caption of the case) "Elmer Zilch, a witness sworn in the above entitled case, was asked the following question, 'Have you stopped beating your wife?' to which counsel for the defendant objected on the ground the question was improper because an answer either way would incriminate him; whereupon, after argument the court overruled the objection, to which ruling the defendant duly saved his exception." When this document was completed, it would be signed by the judge. During the course of the trial numerous exceptions might be "saved." At the conclusion of the trial they would be bound together and certified by the trial judge as the Bill of Exceptions in the case, and they would be attached to and become a part of the record on appeal. Today, with modern methods of court reporting, this antiquated method of preserving a record has become obsolete and court rules make "exceptions" unnecessary.[5]

Appellate review of an equity case was quite different. This was primarily due to the difference in the manner of taking testimony. Unlike the common law courts, where the witnesses testified orally before the judge and jury, in the equity courts the testimony of witnesses was taken by a Master who reduced the testimony to writing in the form of depositions. When the taking of testimony was completed, the depositions were given to the chancellor to read and make his findings of fact. He never saw the witnesses. Consequently, an appellate court, with the same materials before it, felt equally competent to come to its own conclusions on issues of fact as well as issues of law.[6] The review of an equity case was not to discover mere error, but was a review de novo, and was considered merely a continuation of the suit, and not a new suit as the common law considered the writ of error. The mechanics of transferring the case to the reviewing court were also different. A simple notice of appeal to the trial court would suffice since the appeal was considered merely a

---

5. Fed.Rules Civ.Proc. 46.   **6.** Clark & Stone, supra n. 1.

later stage of the case and not as a new suit which must be begun by original process.

The merger of law and equity under modern procedure has caused problems on the appellate level but none of the same magnitude as its effect on the right to jury trial.[7] Today testimony is orally taken in open court and recorded in all types of cases whether formerly denominated legal or equitable; hence there are no longer any differences in producing a record for appeal. The mechanics of review, whether by writ of error or appeal, present few problems; most states have adopted one or the other as the procedure for both types of cases. The chief problem is the scope of appellate review. Is it the same for both types of cases under the merged procedure, or is there still a difference in the power of the appellate court to review issues of fact? As we shall see, this still presents a problem.

What has been said concerning the reviewing function of appellate courts must be qualified in the case of appeals from inferior courts, such as justice of the peace courts, small claims courts, and police courts. Customarily, in those courts little or no record is kept of the myriad of cases which pass through; hence there is no record to review. Consequently, where appeals are provided from such tribunals, they are taken to trial courts of general jurisdiction where the case is tried de novo.[8]

Every state has an appellate court to which appeals may be taken from trial courts of general jurisdiction. Due to increasing population and expanding case loads a growing number of states have established intermediate appellate courts to lessen the burden on the highest court. Amazingly, the federal government operated with a single appellate court until 1891 when Congress created the Circuit Courts of Appeal.[9] In jurisdictions which have intermediate appellate courts, such courts will handle most routine appeals with a possible further review by the highest court at its discretion. In certain types of cases, which are considered of sufficient importance, a direct appeal to the highest court may be allowed, by-passing the intermediate appellate court.[10]

---

7. See supra, Ch. VII, Section 2.

8. Capital Traction Co. v. Hof, 174 U.S. 1, 19 S.Ct. 580, 43 L.Ed. 873 (1899); Comment, The California Small Claims Court, 52 Cal.L.Rev. 876 (1964).

9. 26 Stat. 826 (1891).

10. 28 U.S.C.A. § 252 provides for direct appeals to the Supreme Court from decisions of District Courts invalidating Acts of Congress; 28 U.S.C.A. § 1253 provides for direct appeals to the Supreme Court from three-judge District Courts. Such three-judge District Courts are required, under 28 U.S.

Prior to the adoption of the Federal Rules of Civil Procedure in 1938 appellate practice in the federal courts, and in most states, was "almost unbelievably technical and expensive, full of pitfalls and dangers for the unwary." [11] This was because most of the steps which were required for an appeal, such as the notice, the bond, the filing of the record, etc. were regarded as jurisdictional, and a failure to take any one of them, or a failure to take it on time, resulted in a dismissal of the appeal. When the Federal Rules were adopted, although they were directed primarily to procedure on the trial level, they also greatly simplified the appellate process and provided that the only jurisdictional step was the timely filing of a notice of appeal.[12] The rules also provided that harmless error was to be disregarded at every stage of the proceedings.[13] A party must show, not only that he was "aggrieved" by the judgment in order to appeal,[14] but must also be prepared to convince the appellate court that any errors commit-

C.A. § 2281, where the suit is to enjoin the enforcement of a state statute, and under 28 U.S.C.A. § 2282, where the suit is to enjoin the enforcement of a federal statute.

11. Parker, Improving Appellate Methods, 25 N.Y.U.L.Rev. 1, 3 (1950).

12. Fed.Rules Civ.Proc. 73, which was superseded in 1968 by Fed. Rules App.Proc. 3(a).

13. Fed.Rules Civ.Proc. 61. Harmless error statutes are also in existence in most states, but it is sometimes a debatable question as to whether error was or was not harmless. See People v. Jackson, 7 N.Y.2d 142, 164 N.E.2d 381 (1959).

14. The general rule is that only one who is "aggrieved" by a judgment has standing to appeal. Whether one is aggrieved by a judgment is sometimes a close question. In Electrical Fittings Corp. v. Thomas & Betts Co., 307 U.S. 241, 59 S.Ct. 860, 83 L.Ed. 1263 (1939) plaintiff sued for infringement of his patent. The District Court held the patent was valid but dismissed the bill for failure to prove infringement. Defendant appealed from so much of the decree as adjudged the patent valid. The Supreme Court said a party may not appeal from a judgment in his favor, and that if the court had merely dismissed the suit, this rule would have applied. However, the finding of validity of the patent was unnecessary to the decision and the defendant may appeal to have this portion of the decree eliminated. In Ferraro v. Pacific Fin. Corp., 8 Cal.App.3d 339, 87 Cal.Rptr. 226 (1970) it was held that one who moved for a new trial on all issues and was granted only a partial new trial was aggrieved. In Adair County v. Urban, 364 Mo. 746, 268 S.W.2d 801 (1954) the jury rendered a verdict of $4,000 against the defendant which the court set aside on its own motion and granted a new trial; a divided court held the defendant was "aggrieved" since the effect of the order, although temporarily favorable to the defendant, subjected him to the risk of a larger verdict. One cannot be aggrieved by a consent judgment: Hart v. State Fire Marshall, 178 Mich. 609, 146 N.W. 169 (1914). One who is not a party to the suit ordinarily is not aggrieved: Turner v. Williamson, 77 Ark. 586, 92 S. W. 867 (1906); Elliott v. Superior Court, 144 Cal. 501, 77 P. 1109 (1904).

ted were actually prejudicial to his rights. Taken together, as representing the modern philosophy of judicial administration, the newer procedure makes appeals easier and emphasizes the merits or "substantial justice" of the case,[15] but it does not make reversals easy because the trial represents a substantial investment of time, energy and money which should not be lightly set aside.

SECTION 2. LAYING A FOUNDATION FOR REVIEW

It has been said that a good lawyer will try his case with one eye on the appellate court. This means that he will lay a proper foundation for an appeal by making a proper objection to every ruling of the trial court which he believes may be erroneous.

The federal rules provide that "No party may assign as error the giving or the failure to give an instruction unless he objects thereto before the jury retires to consider its verdict, stating distinctly the matter to which he objects and the grounds of his objection." [16] The purpose of the requirement is to play fair with the trial judge. Counsel should not be permitted to lie in wait for him and convict him of error on a later appeal without specifically calling his attention to the ruling complained of and giving him a chance to correct his own error. The rule in this instance does no more than to codify existing law, and the same rule applies to rulings throughout the whole trial and not merely to the instructions to the jury.[17]

Although appellate courts usually refuse to consider an error where proper objection was not made, they sometimes make an exception where there has been an obvious miscarriage of justice. For instance, in State v. Garcia,[18] two brothers were tried for murder and convicted of manslaughter. The evidence showed that one of the brothers had been shot by the deceased and was lying unconscious on the floor when his brother killed the deceased. In affirming the conviction against both, the appellate court said that no foundation had been laid because the defendants did not challenge the sufficiency of the evidence in the lower court, and their objections to the court's instructions to the jury were not sufficiently specific. On rehearing the court reversed

---

15. See Fed.Rules Civ.Proc. 61.

16. Fed.Rules Civ.Proc. 51.

17. Sturm v. Chicago & N. W. Ry., 157 F.2d 407 (8th Cir. 1946); Williams v. Williams, 172 So.2d 488 (Fla.D.Ct.App.1965); Hewlett Arcade v. Five Towns Refrigeration Corp., 3 A.D.2d 728, 159 N.Y.S.2d 771 (1957).

18. 19 N.M. 414, 143 P. 1012 (1914).

as to the one defendant in the exercise of its inherent power to do justice where fundamental rights are involved.[19]

It is not always enough to make a specific objection, especially in regard to rulings on the admissibility of evidence. If the objection to a question propounded to a witness is overruled and the witness is permitted to answer, counsel should immediately move the court to strike the answer and instruct the jury to disregard it, or, if the matter is extremely serious, move for a mistrial. In this way it is certain that an appellate court will not hold that the objection was waived. The same procedure is suggested in objecting to unwarranted remarks of opposing counsel. If an objection is sustained to a question propounded to a witness, an immediate request should be made to the court for permission to make an offer of proof outside of the presence of the jury. The federal rules specifically authorize such procedure.[20] The purpose of such an offer is to have the record show what the witness would have said, if the question were permitted, and thus demonstrate to the appellate court the prejudicial effect of the judge's ruling.[21] As previously noted, a motion for a directed verdict is a prerequisite for a later motion for judgment non obstante veredicto, and a defendant's motion for a directed verdict made at the close of the plaintiff's case is waived if not renewed at the close of the entire evidence. In some states a motion for a new trial is a prerequisite to a review of errors occurring during the course of the trial.[22] The reasoning behind this rule is that the judge should have one last chance to correct his errors. Most states do not have such a requirement, probably on the theory that one opportunity afforded to the judge is enough.[23] In all states, however, a motion for a new trial is a necessary prerequisite to appellate reviews of matters which have not otherwise been presented to the trial court.[24] This would include such things as misconduct of the jury, discovered after it had been discharged, newly discovered evidence, or that the verdict was excessive or inadequate. One other point deserves emphasis: the fact that the federal rules dispense with the necessity of "sav-

19. See also Citron v. Aro Corp., 377 F.2d 750 (3d Cir. 1967); Keen v. Overseas Tankship Corp., 194 F.2d 515 (2d Cir. 1952).

20. Fed.Rules Civ.Proc. 43(c).

21. McCormick, Evidence (1954) § 51; Witkin, California Evidence (2d ed. 1966) §§ 1310–14.

22. Martin v. Opdyke Agency, Inc., 156 Colo. 316, 398 P.2d 971 (1965); Evans v. Wilkinson, 419 P.2d 275 (Okl.1966).

23. Kallay v. Community Nat. Life Ins. Co., 52 F.R.D. 139 (N.D.Okl. 1971).

24. Law v. Smith, 34 Utah 394, 98 P. 300 (1908).

ing exceptions" [25] does not mean that proper objections are unnecessary.

Closely allied to the above is the rule that a party cannot switch legal theories in the appellate court. For instance, in Apex Smelting Co. v. Burns,[26] the plaintiff who had sued on a negligence theory and lost could not, on appeal, be heard to argue that a recovery would be justified on a breach of contract theory. In Miller v. Avirom [27] a defendant who failed to raise the issue of the legality of an oral contract for the sale of realty in the lower court was not permitted to raise it in the appellate court. And in Curtis Publishing Co. v. Butts [28] the appealing defendant was not permitted to raise, for the first time on appeal, the constitutional issue of freedom of the press. In all of the above cases the appellant was seeking a reversal. Where an appellee seeks to use a different theory to sustain the action of the lower court, his argument falls upon more attentive ears. In Ward v. Taggart [29] the plaintiff sued on a fraud theory and obtained a large verdict. On appeal the appellate court said the evidence would not sustain a finding of fraud but permitted the plaintiff to argue unjust enrichment. Said the court, "Although this theory of recovery was not advanced by plaintiffs in the trial court, it is settled that a change in theory is permitted on appeal when 'a question of law only is presented on the facts appearing in the record.'" [30] Some matters, especially want of subject matter jurisdiction and defect of indispensable parties, are considered so fundamental that they can be raised for the first time on appeal.[31]

SECTION 3.   THE FINAL JUDGMENT RULE

The rule at common law was that there could be no appeal except from a final judgment, which was defined as one that disposed of all of the issues as to all of the parties.[32] There was a

25.   Fed.Rules Civ.Proc. 46.

26.   175 F.2d 978 (7th Cir. 1949).

27.   127 U.S.App.D.C. 367, 384 F.2d 319 (1967).

28.   351 F.2d 702 (5th Cir. 1965).

29.   51 Cal.2d 736, 336 P.2d 534 (1959).

30.   Id. at 742, 336 P.2d at 537. See also Elson v. Security State Bank, 246 Iowa 601, 67 N.W.2d 525 (1955) where the court permitted

an appellant to switch theories and reversed because a simple point of law was involved.

31.   See Lohman v. Edgewater Holding Co., 227 Minn. 40, 33 N.W. 2d 842 (1948).

32.   Collins v. Miller, 252 U.S. 364, 40 S.Ct. 347, 64 L.Ed. 616 (1920); McMillin v. Ventura Sav. & Loan Ass'n, 15 Cal.App.3d 588, 93 Cal. Rptr. 359 (1971); North East Independent School Dist. v. Aldridge, 400 S.W.2d 893 (Texas 1966); Crick, The Final Judgment as a Ba-

common sense basis for the rule. One was not really aggrieved until the final judgment. Regardless of interlocutory errors committed along the way the final decision may have been correct. Also, to permit appeals from interlocutory orders would result in delay. As observed by Mr. Justice Frankfurter, "To be effective, judicial administration must not be leaden-footed. Its momentum would be arrested by permitting separate reviews of the component elements in a unified cause." [33] At common law the rule operated satisfactorily because the typical common law action had few parties and few issues. Suits in equity, however, often involved multiple parties and more complex issues. Consequently, equity would permit appeals from some interlocutory orders, typically those in which an error could cause irreparable harm if not corrected promptly.[34] Among these would be orders granting or denying temporary injunction, and orders appointing receivers.[35] In this country the question of what orders other than final judgments are reviewable, is governed by statute. There is no general agreement among the states since the matter is essentially one of a compromise between too many and too few appeals, and on this question legislatures are bound to differ.[36] In the federal system, from the beginning, Congress has held fast to a policy against piecemeal review.[37] It has limited appeals to "final decisions" [38] and interlocutory orders falling within four rather narrow categories.[39]

The phrase "final decisions," as used in the act of Congress, may appear to be clear but, in some circumstances, it is subject to judicial interpretation. The point was made by Mr. Justice Black in Gillespie v. United States Steel Corp.,[40] when he remarked that there were "marginal cases" in a "twilight zone"

sis for Appeal, 41 Yale L.J. 539 (1932).

33. Cobbledick v. United States, 309 U.S. 323, 325, 60 S.Ct. 540, 541, 84 L.Ed. 783, 785 (1940).

34. Kasishke v. Baker, 144 F.2d 384 (10th Cir. 1944).

35. McAuslan v. McAuslan, 34 R.I. 462, 83 A. 837 (1912).

36. New York has perhaps gone to extremes in allowing interlocutory appeals. See McKinney's N.Y.C.P. L.R. § 5701; California has taken a position between this and the strict federal rule. See West's Ann.Cal.Code Civ.Proc., § 904.1.

See also Donnelly, What is a Final Order in Ohio? 19 U.Cinn.L.R. 507 (1950); Cunningham, Appealable Orders in Minnesota, 37 Minn. L.R. 309 (1953); Sherwood & Nichols, The Final Judgment Rule and Appellate Review of Discovery Orders in Nebraska, 35 Neb.L.R. 469 (1956).

37. Cobbledick v. United States, 309 U.S. 323, 60 S.Ct. 540, 84 L.Ed. 783 (1940).

38. 28 U.S.C.A. § 1291.

39. 28 U.S.C.A. § 1292.

40. 379 U.S. 148, 85 S.Ct. 308, 13 L. Ed.2d 199 (1964).

and that a "final decision" within the meaning of the Congressional Act "does not necessarily mean the last order possible to be made in a case." [41]   In Gillespie the plaintiff's son was drowned while working on the defendant's ship.   She sued under the Jones Act and also under the Ohio Wrongful Death statute in behalf of herself and the son's brothers and sisters.   The District Court held the Jones Act was exclusive and struck all references to the Ohio law.   The court, over the vigorous dissent of Mr. Justice Harlan, held that this was an appealable "final decision" since it determined the rights of the brothers and sisters. Where a plaintiff brings a class action, suing on behalf of himself and all others similarly situated and the court holds it is not a proper situation for a class action and dismisses that aspect of the case, it has been held the order is not appealable [42] unless the order virtually sounds a "death knell" to the entire case.[43] An order granting a summary judgment but retaining the case to determine the amount of the damages is not an appealable order.[44]   An order granting a motion for a new trial is not appealable even though, if erroneous, it results in the economic waste of an entire new trial.[45]

In Cohen v. Beneficial Industrial Loan Corp.[46] the Supreme Court created an exception to the final judgment rule in the small class of orders "which finally determine claims of right separable from, and collateral to, rights asserted in the action, too important to be denied review and too independent of the cause itself to require that appellate consideration be deferred until the whole case is adjudicated." [47]   The Cohen case was a stockholder's

---

41. Id. at 152, 85 S.Ct. at 311, 13 L. Ed. at 203.

42. Caceres v. International Air Transp. Ass'n, 422 F.2d 141 (2d Cir. 1970).

43. Eisen v. Carlisle & Jacquelin, 370 F.2d 119 (2d Cir. 1966).   In this case plaintiff brought a class action on behalf of himself and all other purchasers of "odd lots" of stock on the New York Stock Exchange, alleging a conspiracy to violate the antitrust laws.   The court dismissed his class action but left intact his individual claim.   In holding the order appealable the court said, "We can safely assume that no lawyer of competence is going to undertake this complex and costly case to recover $70 for Mr. Eisen .   .   .. If the appeal

is dismissed, not only will Eisen's claim never be adjudicated, but no appellate court will be given the chance to decide if this class action was proper under the newly amended Rule 23." Id. at 121.

44. Russell v. Barnes Foundation, 136 F.2d 654 (3rd Cir. 1943).

45. Conney v. Erickson, 317 F.2d 247 (7th Cir. 1963); Hoberman v. Lake of Isles, 138 Conn. 573, 87 A.2d 137 (1952).   An order granting a new trial is frequently made appealable by statute.   See the code sections cited in n. 36, supra.

46. 337 U.S. 541, 69 S.Ct. 1221, 93 L.Ed. 1528 (1949).

47. Id. at 546, 69 S.Ct. at 1225, 93 L.Ed. at 1536.

derivative action brought in the federal court because of diversity of citizenship. While the case was pending, a state statute was passed providing that in derivative suits if the suit failed, the plaintiff would be liable for costs and attorney fees and requiring him to post a bond, which in this case would be in the sum of $125,000. The district court held the statute was inapplicable in a federal case. The Supreme Court held this order was appealable, as coming within the exception above mentioned since the matter of security for costs and attorney fees was collateral to the main case but was important to be determined at the outset. Unless an immediate appeal was permitted, the whole purpose of the statute would be frustrated. The purpose of the statute was to prevent the stockholder's derivative suit from being used as a blackmailing device by a lone stockholder who brings a strike suit against the corporation in the hope of forcing a settlement.

The Cohen principle was applied in a labor dispute involving the Georgia right-to-work statute.[48] A suit had been brought in a state court to secure an injunction against peaceful picketing alleged to be in violation of the statute. The trial court denied a temporary injunction, but the Georgia Supreme Court reversed and granted it in the face of the Union's claim that the matter was within the exclusive jurisdiction of the National Labor Relations Board. Although the decision of the Georgia Supreme Court was not a "final" judgment since it sent the case back for trial, the Supreme Court granted certiorari and held the judgment appealable as coming within the Cohen principle. "What we do have here," said the court, "is a judgment of the Georgia court finally and erroneously asserting its jurisdiction to deal with a controversy which is beyond its power and instead is within the exclusive domain of the National Labor Relations Board. Whether or not the Georgia courts have power to issue an injunction is a matter wholly separate from and independent of the merits of respondents' cause." [49]

In Brown Shoe Co. v. United States,[50] an antitrust suit, the district court held there had been a violation and directed divestiture of a subsidiary but reserved ruling on a specific plan of divestiture. The Supreme Court held the order appealable since the substantive aspects of the case had been fully determined and to delay a review of the merits would chill the "careful and often

48. Local 438, Constr. & Gen. Laborers Union v. Curry, 371 U.S. 542, 83 S.Ct. 531, 9 L.Ed.2d 514 (1963).

49. Id. at 548, 83 S.Ct. at 535–36, 9 L.Ed.2d at 519.

50. 370 U.S. 294, 82 S.Ct. 1502, 8 L.Ed.2d 510 (1962).

extended, negotiation and formulation" [51] of the final divestiture order.[52]

The federal rules greatly expanded the possible scope of a lawsuit over the common law conception by providing for liberal joinder of claims [53] and parties.[54] They expanded the scope of class actions,[55] they liberalized the right of a stranger to a suit to intervene,[56] and they provided that parties to a suit could, with the court's permission, expand it by bringing in additional parties.[57] Thus, the old common law concept of a final judgment as one which decided all the issues as to all of the parties could not be utilized without danger of creating injustices. To take care of this situation the rules provided that where there were multiple claims, the court could enter a final judgment as to some and not others. As originally drafted the rule stated "The judgment shall terminate the action with respect to the claim so disposed of and the action shall proceed as to the remaining claims." [58] This was indeed an improvement,[59] but it did not eliminate the possibility of the "hardship" case, as demonstrated by Dickinson v. Petroleum Conversion Corp.[60] That was a complicated case in which the plaintiff sued the defendant to im-

---

51. Id. at 309, 82 S.Ct. at 1515, 8 L.Ed.2d at 526.

52. Other cases applying the Cohen principle: Diaz v. Southern Drilling Corp., 427 F.2d 1118 (5th Cir. 1970) (multiple party suit in which the court granted a default judgment against an intervening party for his failure to respond to notices to take his deposition); United States v. Wood, 295 F.2d 772 (5th Cir. 1961) (civil rights voter registration case; order denying a temporary restraining order held appealable due to fact the election would be over and any appeal would be effectively foreclosed if present one not allowed). Cases holding the Cohen principle inapplicable: American Express Warehousing, Ltd. v. Transamerica Ins. Co., 380 F.2d 277 (2d Cir. 1967) (Cohen not applicable to review interlocutory discovery orders); Fleischer v. Phillips, 264 F.2d 515 (2d Cir. 1959) (order denying motion to disqualify attorney from participating in case because of conflict of interest, distinguishing Harmar Drive-In Theatre, Inc. v. Warner Bros. Pictures, 239 F.2d

555 (2d Cir. 1957) which held that an order disqualifying an attorney was appealable).

53. Fed.Rules Civ.Proc. 18.

54. Fed.Rules Civ.Proc. 20.

55. Fed.Rules Civ.Proc. 23.

56. Fed.Rules Civ.Proc. 24.

57. Fed.Rules Civ.Proc. 14.

58. Fed.Rules Civ.Proc. 54(b) (1938).

59. In Reeves v. Beardall, 316 U.S. 283, 62 S.Ct. 1085, 86 L.Ed. 1478 (1942) plaintiff's complaint was in three counts, one of which was dismissed, and he appealed. The Court of Appeals dismissed because the appeal was not taken from a final judgment. The Supreme Court reversed holding that Rule 54(b), taken with the other rules indicates a definite policy to permit the entry of separate judgments where the same are entirely distinct.

60. 338 U.S. 507, 70 S.Ct. 322, 94 L. Ed. 299 (1950).

press a trust on certain shares of stock in the Petroleum company; some stockholders were allowed to intervene on a class-action basis, and then Petroleum intervened. A complicated decree was entered in 1947 which dismissed Petroleum's claims but granted relief to the intervening shareholders and reserved a decision regarding their several claims. Petroleum did not appeal then, but attempted to appeal from the "final decree" which was entered in 1948. The Supreme Court held that, under the rule, the 1947 decree was "final" as to Petroleum, that no appeal was taken from it, and that the present appeal should be dismissed. Mr. Justice Black dissented, saying, "Litigants have too often been thrown out of court because their lawyers failed to guess that an order would be held 'final' by an appellate court." [61] To remedy the situation the rule was amended to provide "The court may direct the entry of a final judgment upon one or more but less than all of the claims only upon an express determination that there is no just reason for delay and upon an express direction for the entry of judgment . . . ." [62] This again was an improvement since the judgment did not become "final" in the appealable sense unless the trial judge made the express declaration required by the rule. However, the rule was still inadequate since it dealt only with an interim final judgment as to *claims*. It was amended again to include *parties* as well. It now provides that the court may direct the entry of the final judgment "as to one or more but fewer than all of the claims or parties." [63]

Since the appellate jurisdiction of the federal courts is fixed by Congress,[64] and since Congress has from the first established a policy against piecemeal review,[65] the question arose as to the validity of Rule 54(b). Was it an unconstitutional expansion of appellate jurisdiction? The question was answered in the case of Sears Roebuck & Co. v. Mackey [66] which held that the rule does not relax the final judgment requirement as established by Congress as to individual claims, but establishes the individual claim as the unit of litigation (for appellate purposes) rather than the

---

61. Id. at 517, 70 S.Ct. at 327, 94 L.Ed. at 305.

62. Fed.Rules Civ.Proc. 54(b); Green, Federal Juris. & Practice, 1961 Ann.Survey Am.Law 481, 499.

63. Fed.Rules Civ.Proc. 54(b).

64. U.S.Const. art. III, §§ 1, 2.

65. 28 U.S.C.A. § 1291.

66. 351 U.S. 427, 76 S.Ct. 895, 100 L.Ed. 1297 (1956). Decided the same day was Cold Metal Process Co. v. United Eng'r & Foundry Co., 351 U.S. 445, 76 S.Ct. 904, 100 L.Ed. 1311 (1956). In this case the court sanctioned an appeal under 28 U.S.C.A. § 1291 and Rule 54(b) of a judgment on a main claim, leaving a counterclaim unadjudicated, and the court indicated it mattered not whether the counterclaim was compulsory or permis-

entire law suit. In other words, a district court cannot exercise discretion under the rule to treat as final that which is not final. What it may do is to release for appeal final decisions upon one or more, but less than all of the claims. In the Sears Roebuck case the complaint contained several counts, some for treble damages for antitrust violations, some for common law actions for inducing breach of contract and some for unfair competition. The district court entered judgment for the defendant on two of the counts and made the finding of "no just reason for delay." The Supreme Court split (7–2) on the proper definition of a "claim" within the ambit of the rule.[67] The courts of appeals have no jurisdiction under Rule 54(b) unless the district court has made the proper "express determination" required by the rule.[68] However, the courts of appeals are not bound by the district court's finding.[69] Moreover, district courts have been admonished not to certify cases under the rule as a routine matter or as an accommodation to counsel but only in the infrequent hardship case.[70]

SECTION 4. INTERLOCUTORY ORDERS

As previously noted, because of the harshness of the final judgment rule if rigorously applied, in all jurisdictions there are statutory exceptions to it. Under the federal judicial code there are four categories of interlocutory orders which are appealable: (1) those granting or denying injunctions, (2) those appointing or discharging receivers, (3) certain interlocutory decrees in admiralty, and (4) judgments in patent infringement cases which

---

sive, since a counterclaim is treated the same as any multiple claim.

67. The rule will continue to cause trouble, chiefly due to the fact that "claim for relief"—the federal substitute for the code "cause of action"—is no more precise than its predecessor. (For the divergent views of the proper definition of "cause of action" under the codes, and the trouble which it caused, see Clark, Code Pleading (2d ed. 1947) 127–47). Under the rules some courts adopt a broad definition to encompass several demands if they are based on the same factual situation: Audi Vision, Inc. v. Radio Corp. Amer. Mfg. Co., 136 F.2d 621 (2d Cir. 1943); Rosenblum v. Dingfelder, 111 F.2d 406 (2d Cir. 1940). Other courts narrowly define "claim" and more nearly equate it with the "right of action" theory of the code cause of action: Zarati S. S. Co. v. Park Bridge Co., 154 F.2d 377 (2d Cir. 1946); Lydick v. Fischer, 135 F.2d 983 (5th Cir. 1943).

68. Backus Plywood Corp. v. Commercial Decal, Inc., 317 F.2d 339 (2d Cir. 1963).

69. Id. See also Baca Land & Cattle Co. v. New Mexico Timber, Inc., 384 F.2d 701 (10th Cir. 1967).

70. Campbell v. Westmoreland Farm, Inc., 403 F.2d 939 (2d Cir. 1968).

are final except for accounting.[71] Until 1958 these were the only appealable interlocutory orders specifically covered by the judicial code.[72]

There has been considerable judicial controversy over the proper interpretation of the first category. Does the term "injunctions" as therein used include temporary restraining orders? Under the federal rules, in a suit for an injunction it is provided that under some circumstances the court may grant an ex parte temporary restraining order.[73] The usual interpretation is that such an order is not within the scope of the exception and is therefore not appealable.[74] There has also been judicial disagreement when a plaintiff is seeking an injunction and a motion for summary judgment is denied. In Federal Glass Co. v. Loshin [75] plaintiff sued to enjoin the defendant from copying its trade name, for an accounting and damages. After considerable pretrial discovery, plaintiff moved for summary judgment, which was denied. A divided court held the order was appealable with Judge Clark dissenting on the ground that, by adding a prayer for a preliminary injunction a plaintiff could make all of his pretrial motions appealable.[76] The controversy was settled by the Supreme Court in the case of Switzerland Cheese Ass'n v. E. Horne's Market, Inc.[77] by holding such orders nonappealable. "Unlike some state procedures," said the Court, "federal law expresses the policy against piecemeal appeals . . . .. Hence we approach this statute somewhat gingerly lest a floodgate be opened that brings into the exception many pretrial orders."[78] It said the denial of a motion for summary judgment "does not settle or even tentatively decide anything about the merits of the

---

71. 28 U.S.C.A. § 1292(a).

72. In 1958 Congress added subsection (b) to provide some flexibility.

73. Fed.Rules Civ.Proc. 65(b).

74. Richardson v. Kennedy, 418 F. 2d 235 (3d Cir. 1969). There may be cases in which denial of a temporary restraining order may be tantamount to a decision on the merits, in which case the order is appealable. In United States v. Wood, supra n. 52, the United States sued to restrain a criminal action brought against a black person allegedly for the purpose of intimidating other black persons from exercising their voting rights; a temporary restraining order was denied, but the Court of Appeals held it was appealable since, to hold otherwise, would result in the election being held and the matter would become moot. See also Graham v. Minter, 437 F.2d 427 (1st Cir. 1971); Kimball v. Commandant 12th Naval Dist., 423 F.2d 88 (9th Cir. 1970).

75. 217 F.2d 936 (2d Cir. 1954).

76. In Chappell & Co. v. Frankel, 367 F.2d 197 (2d Cir. 1966) the court, sitting en banc, reversed its position.

77. 385 U.S. 23, 87 S.Ct. 193, 17 L. Ed.2d 23 (1966).

78. Id. at 24, 87 S.Ct. at 195, 17 L. Ed.2d at 25.

claim. It is strictly a pretrial order that decides only one thing —that the case should go to trial." [79] In Goldstein v. Cox [80] the Supreme Court applied the same rule to an attempted direct appeal from an order of a three-judge district court. [81]

The courts have been confronted with a rather thorny question as to whether a court order staying future proceedings in the cause is an "injunction" within the meaning of § 1292(a) (1). In Ettelson v. Metropolitan Life Insurance Co. [82] the plaintiff sued to recover on four life insurance policies. The defendant's answer set up fraud in the procurement of the policies as a defense. Plaintiff demanded a jury trial, but the defendant moved to try the issue of fraud first. This motion was granted and the issue on appeal was whether the order (amounting to a stay of the jury trial) was appealable. The court held that it was, reasoning by analogy that before the merger of law and equity a chancery court would have enjoined the law suit until the issue of fraud was determined; [83] thus the stay order under the merged procedure was the equivalent of an injunction. In Morgantown v. Royal Insurance Co. [84] the insurance company brought suit to reform the contract and the defendant counterclaimed, seeking to enforce the contract as written. The court struck the defendant's demand for a jury and set the case for trial to the court without a jury. This order was held not appealable since it was merely an interlocutory decision as to how to try the case. The two cases were reconciled by the Supreme Court in the case of Baltimore Contractors, Inc. v. Bodinger. [85] In that case the plaintiff sought an accounting of the profits of a joint venture, and the defendant moved for a stay of the action pursuant to the federal arbitration act. The court held the order was not equivalent to an injunction and hence was not appealable. The court draws this distinction: if the main case is a law case, a stay order is equivalent to an injunction and is appealable, but if the main case is an equity case, a stay order is merely a decision of how to try

79. Id. at 25, 87 S.Ct. at 195, 17 L. Ed.2d at 25.

80. 396 U.S. 471, 90 S.Ct. 671, 24 L.Ed.2d 663 (1970).

81. Three-judge district courts are authorized by 28 U.S.C.A. § 2284, and direct appeals from them to the Supreme Court are authorized by 28 U.S.C.A. § 1253. In Mitchell v. Donovan, 398 U.S. 427, 90 S.Ct. 1763, 26 L.Ed.2d 378 (1970) it was held that an order merely granting or denying a motion for declaratory judgment was not appealable under § 1253.

82. 317 U.S. 188, 63 S.Ct. 163, 87 L.Ed. 176 (1942).

83. Enelow v. New York Life Ins. Co., 293 U.S. 379, 55 S.Ct. 310, 79 L.Ed. 440 (1935).

84. 337 U.S. 254, 69 S.Ct. 1067, 93 L.Ed. 1347 (1949).

85. 348 U.S. 176, 75 S.Ct. 249, 99 L.Ed. 233 (1955).

the case, is interlocutory, and not appealable. The result seems ridiculous but is explainable in terms of historical precedent. Said the court: "The incongruity of taking jurisdiction from a stay in a law type and denying jurisdiction in an equity type proceeding springs from the persistence of outmoded procedural differentiations." [86] The distinction has become less important since the decision in Beacon Theatres, Inc. v. Westover,[87] which held that where legal and equitable issues were combined in the same case and a jury trial is demanded, the legal issue must be tried first. Where no such combination of issues is involved a stay order is not equivalent to an injunction and is not appealable.[88]

In 1958 Congress adopted an amendment to the Judicial Code which introduced a greater degree of flexibility into the final judgment rule.[89] It provides that any interlocutory order may be reviewed by appeal if two conditions are met: (1) the district judge certifies that "such order involves a controlling question of law as to which there is substantial ground for difference of opinion and that an immediate appeal may materially advance the ultimate termination of the litigation," and (2) the appellate court, in its discretion, permits the appeal. While the procedure under § 1292(b) is similar to the procedure under Rule 54(b), there are important differences. The similarities are that in each case the district judge has discretion whether or not to release the matter for appeal, in each case a certificate of the district judge is a prerequisite for the appeal, and in each case the appellate court is not bound by the finding of the district judge on the question of appealability. The differences are that Rule 54(b) deals with final judgments (where there are multiple claims or parties) whereas § 1292(b) deals with interlocutory orders; that under Rule 54(b) the district court's discretion is more sharply limited since he can certify only judgments which pass the test of finality under § 1291; and that the appellate court's discretion is much broader under § 1292(b) than it is under Rule 54(b). The purpose of the new subsection is to af-

---

86. Id. at 184, 75 S.Ct. at 254, 99 L.Ed. at 240.

87. 359 U.S. 500, 79 S.Ct. 948, 3 L.Ed.2d 988 (1959). The Beacon case and its impact on the constitutional right to jury trial is discussed supra Ch. VII, Section 2.

88. An order granting or denying a motion to stay proceedings pending arbitration is not appealable: Greater Continental Corp. v. Schechter, 422 F.2d 1100 (2d Cir. 1970); Hart v. Orion Ins. Co., 427 F.2d 528 (10th Cir. 1970); Alexander v. Pacific Maritime Ass'n, 332 F.2d 266 (9th Cir. 1964).

89. 28 U.S.C.A. § 1292(b).

ford an immediate appeal only in the cases of real hardship, and the courts have construed it narrowly.[90]

The general rule is that an appeal from the final judgment in a case brings up for review all errors committed by the trial court at all stages in the trial, provided that a proper foundation has been laid. Does this rule apply to an interlocutory order which was appealable under the statute? In other words, if a temporary injunction is granted against a defendant in a case, must he appeal immediately, or may he await the final judgment and appeal from it without waiving any error in the granting of the injunction? In Victor Talking Machine Co. v. George [91] the court held that one did not waive his rights under the general rule by failure to take an immediate appeal from the interlocutory order. There is, however, a split of authority on the point.[92]

90. In Garner v. Wolfinbarger, 433 F.2d 117, 120 (5th Cir. 1970) the court said: "We are of the view that § 1292(b) review is inappropriate for challenges to a judge's discretion in granting or denying transfers under § 1404(a). The Congressional policy against piecemeal appeals, as expressed in the final judgment rule, 28 U.S.C. § 1291, to which § 1292(b) is a narrow exception, is eroded by permitting review of exercise of the judge's discretion under § 1404(a) as a 'controlling question of law.' Our conclusion is the same as that already reached by the Second, Third, and Sixth Circuits, and by the text writers." (Court's footnotes omitted). In Control Data Corp. v. International Business Mach. Corp., 421 F.2d 323, 325 (8th Cir. 1970), in denying permission to appeal under § 1292(b), the court said: "It has, of course, long been the policy of the courts to discourage piecemeal appeals because most often such appeals result in additional burdens to both the court and the litigants. Permission to allow interlocutory appeals should thus be granted sparingly and with discrimination . . . ." Also denying interlocutory appeals under the subsection: Atlantic City Elec. Co. v. General Elec. Co., 337 F.2d 844 (2d Cir. 1964); Atlantic City Elec. Co. v. A. B. Chance Co., 313 F.2d 431 (2d

Cir. 1963); United States v. Woodbury, 263 F.2d 784 (9th Cir. 1959). For a case permitting a § 1292(b) appeal from a discovery order see Groover, Christie & Merritt v. LoBianco, 119 U.S.App.D.C. 50, 336 F.2d 969 (1964).

91. 105 F.2d 697, 699 (3d Cir. 1939), in which the court said (referring to the statute permitting interlocutory appeals): "The statute does not, however, require an aggrieved party to take such an appeal in order to protect his rights, and, where it is not taken, does not impair or abridge in any way the previously existing right upon appeal from the final decree to challenge the validity of the prior interlocutory decree."

92. A note to the Victor Talking Machine case in 38 Mich.L.Rev. 548 (1940) states: "Decisions in the seventh and ninth circuits indicate that those courts interpret the statute as denying a party who fails to appeal from an interlocutory decree within thirty days the right to be heard on the same issue upon appeal from the final decree. The principal case and others regard appeal from an interlocutory decree under the statute as permissive, so that an aggrieved party may await final determination of the case before raising the issue. The state courts of Pennsylvania

SECTION 5.   THE GREAT WRITS ROUTE

At the time of the separation of the colonies from England, the common law courts had developed five extraordinary writs, each designed to do a particular job when no other avenue of relief was available.   (1) Mandamus would lie to compel a government officer, a corporate officer, or a court to perform a nondiscretionary duty.   (2) Prohibition would lie to prevent an inferior court or judicial tribunal from acting in excess of its authority.   (3) Certiorari would lie to review the quasijudicial actions of an administrative tribunal and also to test the legality of actions of an inferior court.   (4) Quo warranto would lie to test the title of a public officer to his office or to inquire into the misuse of a corporate franchise.   (5) Habeas corpus would lie to inquire into the legality of the detention of one held in custody.   All of these writs were "discretionary" in the sense that they were not writs of right, that a strong showing of necessity was required before they would issue, and that the normal avenues of recourse were nonexistent or inadequate.   The common law courts in this country inherited the power to issue such writs.   Lest there be any doubt about the matter Congress enacted the "all writs" statute which reads:

> (a) The Supreme Court and all courts established by Act of Congress may issue all writs necessary or appropriate in aid of their respective jurisdictions and agreeable to the usages and principles of law.

> (b) An alternative writ or rule nisi may be issued by a justice or judge of a court which has jurisdiction.[93]

Notwithstanding the general language of the statute the Supreme Court has interpreted it narrowly and has restricted the use of the writs to the extraordinary situations contemplated by the common law.   The great writs may not be used, said the Court, "merely as a substitute for the appeal procedure pre-

and New Mexico in construing statutes similar to the federal statute adopt the permissive view. In Wisconsin, a statute is interpreted as making appeal from interlocutory decrees mandatory within the time stipulated .   .   . . Statutes of California and Montana clearly require the mandatory view." The West's Ann.Cal. Code Civ. Proc., § 906, as amended in 1968, in defining the powers of the re-

viewing court, says: "The provisions of this section do not authorize the reviewing court to review any decision or order from which an appeal might have been taken." See also Durkin v. Mason & Dixon Lines, Inc., 202 F.2d 425 (6th Cir. 1953); Burgin v. Sugg, 210 Ala. 142, 97 So. 216 (1923).

93.   28 U.S.C.A. § 1651.

scribed by the statute." [94] Nor may they be used "to thwart the congressional policy against piecemeal appeals." [95] They must be "reserved for really extraordinary cases." [96] Such utterances have not completely discouraged counsel from applying for writs to review interlocutory orders, and the court has sanctioned their use where the hardship was apparent or the situation was deemed truly extraordinary.

One of the leading cases is La Buy v. Howes Leather Co.,[97] a complicated antitrust suit in which there were 93 plaintiffs and 12 defendants. There had been extensive pretrial proceedings, evidenced by the fact that the docket entries listing them occupied 27 pages. At this point the judge referred the case to a master. Thereupon all of the parties applied to the Court of Appeals for a writ of mandamus to compel him to try the case personally, since he was thoroughly familiar with it. The Court of Appeals issued the writ and a divided Supreme Court (5–4) affirmed, stating:

> Under all of the circumstances, we believe the Court of Appeals was justified in finding the orders of reference were an abuse of the petitioner's power under Rule 53 (b). They amounted to little less than an abdication of the judicial function depriving the parties of a trial before the court on the basic issues involved in the litigation.[98]

In Beacon Theatres v. Westover,[99] and again in Dairy Queen, Inc. v. Wood,[100] the Supreme Court held that mandamus was proper to correct the error of a trial court in denying a party his con-

---

94. Roche v. Evaporated Milk Ass'n, 319 U.S. 21, 26, 63 S.Ct. 938, 941, 87 L.Ed. 1185, 1190 (1943).

95. Parr v. United States, 351 U.S. 513, 520, 76 S.Ct. 912, 917, 100 L. Ed. 1377, 1385 (1956).

96. Ex parte Fahey, 332 U.S. 258, 260, 67 S.Ct. 1558, 1559, 91 L.Ed. 2041, 2043 (1947).

97. 352 U.S. 249, 77 S.Ct. 309, 1 L. Ed.2d 290 (1957).

98. Id. at 256, 77 S.Ct. at 313, 1 L. Ed.2d at 297. Mr. Justice Brennan, dissenting, said: "The issue here is not whether Judge La Buy's order was reviewable by the Court of Appeals. The sole question is whether review should have await-

ed final decision . . . . This is not a case where a court has exceeded or refused to exercise its jurisdiction . . . nor one where appellate review will be defeated if a writ does not issue . . . . Here the most that could be claimed is that the district courts have erred in ruling on matters within their jurisdiction. The extraordinary writs do not reach to such cases." Id. at 260–61, 77 S.Ct. at 315–16, 1 L.Ed.2d at 299–300.

99. Supra n. 87.

100. 369 U.S. 469, 82 S.Ct. 894, 8 L.Ed.2d 44 (1962). See also Bruce v. Bohanon, 436 F.2d 733 (10th Cir. 1971).

stitutional right to a trial by jury. In Hoffman v. Blaski [101] the Supreme Court held that an erroneous transfer of a case from a federal district court in Texas to a federal district court in Illinois was subject to immediate review by mandamus. The case involved the newly enacted change of venue statute which provided that the change could be made to any district "where it might have been brought." [102] The court held the case could not originally have been brought in Illinois and that mandamus would lie to rescind the transfer order. In the later case of Van Dusen v. Barrack [103] the Supreme Court sanctioned the use of mandamus to review and correct the error of a district court in refusing a proper change of venue under the same statute. In A. Olinick & Sons v. Dempster Bros. [104] another case involving transfer of venue under the statute, the Court of Appeals for the Second Circuit held that "Mandamus does not lie to review mere error in the disposition of § 1404(a) motions, but only to redress a clear-cut abuse of discretion."

One of the more recent cases on the use of the writs is Schlagenhauf v. Holder [105] in which the question was whether a district court had power, under Rule 35, to compel the defendant in a personal injury action to submit to a physical and mental examination. Before this time the rule had been applied only to plaintiffs who, by their suits, had placed their physical or mental condition in issue. This case, for the first time, raised the question as to whether the rule would also apply to compel the physical or mental examination of a defendant to elicit evidence as to his competence as a driver. In upholding the power of the appellate court, on mandamus, to review the propriety of the order, the court pays lip service to the rule that mandamus is no substitute for appeal, but holds that under the special circumstances of the case (a case of first impression under the rule, and a question going to the power of the court) mandamus would lie.

The great common law writs are also available in the state courts for reviewing interlocutory orders where great hardship would result if review were deferred until the final judgment. [106]

---

101. 363 U.S. 335, 80 S.Ct. 1084, 4 L.Ed.2d 1254 (1960).

102. 28 U.S.C.A. § 1404(a).

103. 376 U.S. 612, 84 S.Ct. 805, 11 L.Ed.2d 945 (1964).

104. 365 F.2d 439, 445 (2d Cir. 1966). See comprehensive note on the subject in 2 A.L.R. Fed. 573 (1969).

105. 379 U.S. 104, 85 S.Ct. 234, 13 L.Ed.2d 152 (1964).

106. For representative state court cases see: *Certiorari:* McClatchy v. Superior Court, 119 Cal. 413, 51 P. 696 (1897); Holabird v. Railroad Comm'n, 171 Cal. 691, 154 P. 831 (1916); Timonds v. Hunter, 169 Iowa 598, 151 N.W. 961 (1915); *Mandamus:* Roman Cath. Arch. of

As in the federal court system a strong showing must be made to justify the issuance of the writ, and the matter is largely discretionary with the appellate court, except where, in certain situations, there is a statutory right to the writ.[107]

SECTION 6. SCOPE OF REVIEW

As stated at the beginning of this chapter, the function of appellate courts is not to retry cases, but to check to see that the trials below were fair and free from prejudicial error. In performing this function they are limited to the record of the proceedings in the trial court, to the briefs filed by counsel, and to the oral arguments of counsel at the hearing in the appellate court. The record which has been sent up from the trial court consists of the pleadings, depositions, pretrial papers, verdict, judgment, and a transcript of so much of the testimony and proceedings in the court as the parties deem necessary for the appeal.[108] If the record is incomplete it may be supplemented by requiring the trial court to send up additional portions of it which were omitted,[109] but the appellate court may not ordinarily augment the record by taking additional testimony since to do so would be to exercise original jurisdiction.[110]

San Francisco v. Superior Court, 15 Cal.App.3d 405, 93 Cal.Rptr. 338 (1971); Crocker v. Justices of Superior Court, 208 Mass. 162, 94 N. E. 369 (1911); State ex rel. Pump Works v. Homer, 249 Mo. 58, 155 S.W. 405 (1913); State ex rel. Nash v. Superior Court, 82 Wash. 614, 144 P. 898 (1914); *Prohibition:* Quimbo Appo v. People, 20 N.Y. 531 (1860); Havemeyer v. Superior Court, 84 Cal. 327, 24 P. 121 (1890); State ex rel. Terminal R. R. v. Tracy, 237 Mo. 109, 140 S. W. 888 (1911).

107. In California there are code provisions giving a quick review by mandamus of rulings challenging jurisdiction (West's Ann.Cal. Code Civ.Proc., § 418.10) and venue (West's Ann.Cal.Code Civ. Proc., § 400). Also discovery orders are reviewable by mandamus or prohibition: Kaiser Foundation Hosps. v. Superior Court, 275 Cal. App.2d 801, 80 Cal.Rptr. 263 (1969); Burke v. Superior Court, 71 Cal.2d 276, 455 P.2d 409 (1969);

Greyhound Corp. v. Superior Court, 56 Cal.2d 355, 364 P.2d 266 (1961); McClatchy Newspapers v. Superior Court, 26 Cal.2d 386, 159 P.2d 944 (1945).

108. Fed.Rules App.Proc. 10(a), 10 (b).

109. Fed.Rules App.Proc. 10(e).

110. In Caldwell v. Modern Woodmen of America, 90 Kan. 175, 133 P. 843 (1913) the plaintiff had recovered a judgment on a life insurance policy on her husband upon the presumption of death after seven years unexplained absence; while the appeal was pending the company filed depositions containing newly discovered evidence that he was still alive; the Supreme Court rejected the evidence but reversed for a new trial on that issue. In Ballurio v. Castellini, 28 N.J.Super. 368, 373, 100 A.2d 678, 681 (1953), the court interprets a statute which permitted the record to be supplemented in the appel-

Pure errors of law present few difficulties. Whether a court erred in overruling a demurrer to a complaint depends upon the allegations of the complaint and the appropriate rule of law, both of which are readily available to the appellate court. Whether a court erred in instructing a jury that they could include damages for mental anguish in a breach of contract case presents a pure question of law which the court should be readily able to determine from the authorities. A question of different dimension is presented when the issue is whether the trial court erred in denying a motion for a directed verdict in a personal injury suit, or whether it erred in granting a motion for a new trial on the ground the verdict was grossly excessive. An answer to such questions depends upon an evaluation of the testimony presented at the trial which often revolves around the credibility of the witnesses. The crucial question, upon review, will be the extent to which the appellate court should be permitted to substitute its judgment on the facts for that of the trier of the facts in the lower court, be it judge or jury.

The answer to this question is colored by history. In common law actions the appellate court, on writ of error, could not re-examine the facts. To do so would be to invade the province of the jury. Its function was restricted to passing on alleged errors of law. The verdict of a jury which was totally without support in the evidence was invalid as a matter of law. Hence a reviewing court could examine the evidence to see if it supported the verdict—that was a question of law—but it could not weigh the evidence, because that was a matter of fact, exclusively within the province of the jury. In appeals in equity, on the other hand, the appellate court felt free to re-examine the facts as well as the law, and to substitute its judgment on the facts for that of the trial court because (1) there was no jury whose province must be respected, and (2) since the evidence was taken by deposition before a master, the appellate court was just as competent as the chancellor in reading the testimony and interpreting it. Under the merged procedure of modern times, as might be expected, the historical distinctions have been blurred, and the cases are far from unanimous in regard to the power of an appellate court to

late court by other evidence, saying it "was designed to cure technical errors in aid of affirmance of the judgment, but not to permit new evidence, however incontrovertible, for the purpose of bringing about a reversal." In Tupman v. Haberkern, 208 Cal. 256, 280 P. 970 (1929), the court gave a similar interpretation to a constitutional provision. See also West's Ann. Cal.Code Civ.Proc., § 909. Louisell & Degnan, Rehearing in American Appellate Courts, 44 Cal.L.Rev. 627 (1956); Pound, New Evidence in the Appellate Court, 56 Harv.L. Rev. 1313 (1943).

review questions of fact. It is possible, however, to make some generalizations.

In the first place, an appellate court will review the evidence to determine whether or not a trial court erred in ruling on a motion for a directed verdict or a motion for judgment non obstante veredicto. In so doing it will not weigh the evidence, it will draw every reasonable inference in favor of the party against whom the motion is made, and it will not upset a jury verdict unless the evidence does not measure up to the test which the court uses to determine whether the evidence was strong enough to take the case to the jury. As indicated previously, the courts are not in agreement upon the tests to be used, and even within the same court, the judges frequently disagree upon whether the evidence in a particular case measures up to the test which is currently being used. A case in point is Dick v. New York Life Insurance Co.,[111] a suit on a life insurance policy where the defense was suicide. The case was tried in a federal court in North Dakota where voluminous evidence was introduced to the effect that the deceased was a happily married farmer with no worries who, one cold morning, was found dead in one of the farm outbuildings, the victim of two gunshot wounds from a double-barreled shotgun which he customarily kept in the barn because of vicious dogs and foxes in the neighborhood. The trial court denied a motion for directed verdict and the jury found for the plaintiff. The Court of Appeals reviewed the evidence in detail, held the evidence showed suicide, and reversed to dismiss. It stated that "one can believe that even an experienced hunter might accidentally shoot himself once, but the asserted theory that he could accidentally shoot himself first with one barrel and then with the other stretches credulity beyond the breaking point." [112] The Supreme Court granted certiorari and, after a lengthy review of the evidence, it concluded that the Court of Appeals was wrong. That court, it said, "committed its basic error in resolving a factual dispute in favor of respondent that the shotgun would not fire unless someone or something pulled the triggers." [113] Two justices dissented, stressing the futility of the Supreme Court spending its valuable time reviewing the sufficiency of the evidence after one appellate court had already done so. "Questions of fact," said Mr. Justice Frankfurter, "have traditionally been deemed to be the kind of questions which ought not to be recan-

111. 359 U.S. 437, 79 S.Ct. 921, 3 L.Ed.2d 935 (1959).

112. Id. at 444, 79 S.Ct. at 926, 3 L.Ed.2d at 941.

113. Id. at 445, 79 S.Ct. at 926–27, 3 L.Ed.2d at 942.

vassed here unless they are entangled in the proper determination of constitutional or other important legal issues." [114]

In the second place, an appellate court will review the evidence to determine whether or not the trial court abused its discretion in ruling on a motion for a new trial on the ground that the verdict was against the weight of the evidence.[115] This situation must be distinguished from the one previously discussed. We are assuming that there was enough evidence to take the case to the jury, but the claim is made by the losing party that the verdict is against the weight of the evidence. In moving for a new trial on that ground he is asking the trial judge to exercise his discretion. In so doing the trial judge is not supposed to substitute his judgment for that of the jury but rather to set aside the verdict only if he believes a miscarriage of justice will result if he fails to do so. In exercising this discretion the trial judge must, of course, weigh the evidence and draw his own conclusions regarding the credibility of the witnesses. His ambit of discretion is quite wide. When his ruling comes up for review in the appellate court, however, the ambit of discretion of the appellate court is much narrower. It is not reviewing the verdict of the jury but the action of the trial judge in ruling on the motion, and its only function is to determine whether or not he has abused his discretion.[116] In making this decision it must review the evidence but in so doing it must resolve all reasonable doubts in favor of the trial judge since, after all, he was present at the trial and had the opportunity to observe the demeanor of the witnesses and the manner in which they testified—matters of some significance, which cannot possibly be reflected in the printed record. If the appellate court comes to the conclusion that the trial court has in fact abused its discretion in denying a motion for a new trial, the appellate court has the power to grant it.[117]

The third situation in which the appellate court will review the facts is appeal from a case tried without a jury.[118] This could be

---

114. Id. at 454, 79 S.Ct. at 931, 3 L.Ed.2d at 946. In Rogers v. Missouri Pac. R. R., 352 U.S. 500, 77 S.Ct. 443, 1 L.Ed.2d 493 (1957), Mr. Justice Frankfurter wrote a lengthy dissent in which he criticized the Supreme Court in granting certiorari in FELA cases. Mr. Justice Douglas responded in a concurring opinion in Harris v. Pennsylvania R. R., 361 U.S. 15, 80 S.Ct. 22, 4 L.Ed.2d 1 (1959).

115. Aetna Cas. & Sur. Co. v. Yeatts, 122 F.2d 350 (4th Cir. 1941).

116. In re Green's Estate, 25 Cal.2d 535, 154 P.2d 692 (1944).

117. Bryan v. United States, 338 U. S. 552, 70 S.Ct. 317, 94 L.Ed. 335 (1950); Corcoran v. City of Chicago, 373 Ill. 567, 27 N.E.2d 451 (1940).

118. See Weiner, The Civil Nonjury Trial and the Law-Fact Distinction, 55 Cal.L.Rev. 1020 (1967); Wright, The Doubtful Omniscience of Appellate Courts, 41 Minn.L.Rev. 751 (1957).

an equity case or a common law case in which a jury was waived. There is a federal rule covering this situation which states: "Findings of fact shall not be set aside unless clearly erroneous, and due regard shall be given to the opportunity of the trial court to judge of the credibility of the witnesses." [119] This rule was interpreted in Orvis v. Higgins,[120] perhaps the most frequently cited case on the subject, in which Judge Frank puts the whole matter in perspective in the following succinct summation:

> In the light of the Gypsum case, we may make approximate gradations as follows: We must sustain a general or a special verdict when there is some evidence which the jury might have believed, and when a reasonable inference from that evidence will support the verdict, regardless of whether that evidence is oral or by deposition. In the case of findings by an administrative agency, the usual rule is substantially the same as that in the case of a jury, the findings being treated like a special verdict. Where a trial judge sits without a jury, the rule varies with the character of the evidence: (a) If he decides a fact issue on written evidence alone, we are as able as he to determine credibility, and so we may disregard his finding. (b) Where the evidence is partly oral and the balance is written or deals with undisputed facts, then we may ignore the trial judge's findings and substitute our own, (1) if the written evidence or some undisputed fact renders the credibility of the oral testimony extremely doubtful, or (2) if the trial judge's findings must rest exclusively on the written evidence or the undisputed facts, so that his evaluation of credibility has no significance. (c) But where the evidence supporting his finding as to any fact issue is entirely oral testimony, we may disturb that finding only in the most unusual circumstances.[121]

As noted in earlier portions of this chapter the traditional function of an appellate court is to review the record to determine whether error has been committed. It normally confines itself to the rulings of the trial court which have been challenged below. Generally it will not permit a switch in theory but, as one court has said, "We do not feel that we are precluded from deciding on a ground not pressed by counsel. Such a course, however, is undesirable where not necessary; it is usually better, if possible, to

119. Fed.Rules Civ.Proc. 52(a).

120. 180 F.2d 537, 539 (2d Cir. 1950).

121. See also Hicks v. United States, 368 F.2d 626 (4th Cir. 1966); Lundgren v. Freeman, 307 F.2d 104 (9th Cir. 1962).

consider a case as it was presented to the lower court." [122] Sometimes a court will permit a change in theory especially if it will result in an affirmance of the judgment,[123] sometimes it will consider "plain error" even though no proper foundation has been laid,[124] and sometimes, though rarely, it will interject into the case an issue which was not in contemplation of either party.[125] These are the rare exceptions to the general rule upon which counsel have no right to rely.[126]

SECTION 7. MECHANICS

If a case has been properly prepared and tried, a great deal of the work of the appeal has already been done. Counsel should be thoroughly familiar with the facts and the law and he should have a fairly good idea of the "reversible errors" which have been committed. His task, in appealing the case, is twofold: (1) to take all of the necessary steps to transfer the case from the trial court to the appellate court, and (2) to convince a group of judges that an injustice has been done to his client by errors committed by the trial judge. The first is a task which, under today's modern procedure, any competent lawyer should be able to accomplish. It is a mere matter of meticulously following the rules. Success or failure in the second task depends upon many things, among which are the skill and persuasive power of the advocate, the state of the law in the particular jurisdiction, the degree to which the court feels bound by precedent, the quality of the judges comprising the appellate court, the current legal climate in the community, and the justice of the client's cause. The elements entering into the second task are so subtle and diverse that a treatment of them would be inappropriate in a short text on pro-

---

122. In re Barnett, 124 F.2d 1005, 1007 (2d Cir. 1942).

123. Standard Accident Ins. Co. v. Roberts, 132 F.2d 794 (8th Cir. 1942); Ward v. Taggart, supra n. 29; Parker v. Washington, 421 P. 2d 861 (Okl.1966).

124. Choy v. Bouchelle, 436 F.2d 319 (3d Cir. 1970).

125. United States v. Ohio Power Co., 353 U.S. 98, 77 S.Ct. 652, 1 L. Ed.2d 683 (1957); Rentways, Inc. v. O'Neill Milk & Cream Co., 308 N.Y. 342, 126 N.E.2d 271 (1955). Perhaps the most famous case in which the court injected an issue is Erie R. R. v. Tompkins, 304 U.S. 64, 58 S.Ct. 817, 82 L.Ed. 1188 (1938), in which Mr. Justice Brandeis begins the opinion by saying: "The question for decision is whether the oft-challenged doctrine of Swift v. Tyson .   .   . shall now be disapproved." Neither party to the case had challenged the doctrine.

126. Vestal, Sua Sponte Consideration in Appellate Review, 27 Ford. L.Rev. 477 (1958); Traynor, Some Open Questions on the Work of State Appellate Courts, 24 U.Chi.L. Rev. 211 (1957).

cedure. Hence we turn to the first task which is largely a matter of mechanics.

The precise steps which one must take to perfect an appeal probably differ in each state, except in those which have adopted verbatim copies of the federal rules. All are, however, quite definite and are readily available in the statutes or court rules of the particular jurisdiction. All are in agreement on one cardinal point and that is that the right to appeal must be taken within the prescribed time or it will be lost. Timeliness is the sine qua non of any appeal.

Until comparatively recent times, timeliness was not only a necessity in the filing of notice of appeal but also in all of the subsequent steps. The theory behind such a harsh rule was that all prescribed steps were jurisdictional, i. e., they went to the power of the appellate court to hear the appeal. This was no doubt due to the idea that appeal was a matter of grace and not of right; [127] hence anyone desiring to avail himself of the privilege must comply strictly with each and every requirement. The extent to which this barbarous rule was carried is illustrated by the case of Wheeler v. S. Birch & Sons [128] in which the appellant was late in filing the transcript of the evidence due to the fact that there was a court reporters strike. Twenty-five lawyers appeared for the appellant and fourteen more as amicus curiae arguing for a relaxation of the rule since the fault was due solely to a breakdown of the machinery of the lower court, but the Supreme Court held it had no power to relax the rule since it was jurisdictional. In Hanley's Estate [129] the appellant's notice of appeal was one day late due to the fact that he had relied upon a misrepresentation of opposing counsel. In dismissing the appeal the court said it was immaterial whether the misrepresentation was wilful or inadvertent, or whether the reliance was reasonable or unreasonable. The court assumed that the appellant had presented grounds for relief which would be sufficient if relief could be granted, but added, "In the absence of statutory authorization, neither the trial nor appellate courts may extend or shorten the time for appeal." [130]

127. Cobbledick v. United States, 309 U.S. 323, 325, 60 S.Ct. 540, 541, 84 L.Ed. 783, 785 (1940) in which Mr. Justice Frankfurter said "the right to a judgment from more than one court is a matter of grace and not a necessary ingredient of justice." But see Fins, Is The Right of Appeal Protected by The Fourteenth Amendment? 54 Judicature 296 (Feb. 1971).

128. 27 Wash.2d 325, 178 P.2d 331 (1947).

129. 23 Cal.2d 120, 142 P.2d 423 (1943).

130. Id. at 123, 142 P.2d at 424–25. See also Nu-Way Associates, Inc. v. Keefe, 15 Cal.App.2d 926, 93 Cal.Rptr. 614 (1971), holding that jurisdiction to entertain a late ap-

Although the Federal Rules of Civil Procedure of 1938 were limited to a regulation of procedure in the United States District Courts, they had an important influence on appellate practice. Certain steps must be taken in the trial court to prepare the record for appeal and to see that it is properly transferred to the appellate court. These steps were covered by the new rules [131] and, in line with the general liberal philosophy of the rules, they took a giant step in eliminating the hypertechnical practice in federal appellate procedure which, in the words of Judge Parker, was "full of pitfalls and dangers for the unwary." [132] The rules provided that the only jurisdictional step in the process was the timely filing of the notice of appeal with the district court. They further stated: "Failure of the appellant to take any of the further steps to secure the review of the judgment appealed from does not affect the validity of the appeal, but is ground only for such remedies as are specified in this rule or, when no remedy is specified, for such action as the appellate court deems appropriate, which may include dismissal of the appeal." [133] This language was carried over into the new Federal Rules of Appellate Procedure which became effective on July 1, 1968.[134]

Under the federal rules the notice of appeal must be filed with the district court within 30 days from the entry of the judgment or order appealed from, unless the United States or an officer or agent thereof is a party, in which case the time is within 60 days of such entry. Upon a showing of "excusable neglect" the district court may extend the time not to exceed 30 days.[135] Since these provisions in the new rules of appellate procedure are substantially the same as those contained in the old rules of civil procedure, the cases interpreting the old provisions should be authoritative under the new. The new appellate rules contain a provision that they "shall not be construed to extend or limit the jurisdiction of the courts of appeal as established by law." [136] Thus, notwithstanding the generally liberal interpretation that

peal cannot be conferred by consent or waiver of the parties even though the notice of appeal is filed but one day late.

131. Fed.Rules Civ.Proc. 72–76 (Abrogated 12/4/67, effective 7/1/68).

132. Parker, Improving Appellate Methods, 25 N.Y.U.L.Rev. 1, 3 (1950).

133. Fed.Rules Civ.Proc. 73(a).

134. Fed.Rules App.Proc. 3(a). In 1966 Congress amended 28 U.S.C. A. § 2072 to permit the Supreme Court to promulgate uniform rules of procedure for the courts of appeals. The court made such rules effective July 1, 1968.

135. Fed.Rules App.Proc. 4(a).

136. Fed.Rules App.Proc. 1(b).

the rules have received, the courts have been strict in holding the parties to compliance with that first jurisdictional step.[137]

It is to be noted that the time for filing the notice of appeal starts to run from the date of the *entry* of the judgment or order appealed from.[138] Under the rules it is the duty of the clerk to give the parties immediate notice of the entry of the judgment or order.[139] Suppose he does not? That happened in Hill v. Hawes [140] with the result that the time for appeal had expired before the appellant knew the judgment had been entered. He conceived an ingenious plan to save his appeal. He persuaded the district court to vacate the judgment and enter a new one as of a later date so that he could appeal from that. The Supreme Court sustained the appeal as timely but thereafter promulgated an amendment to the rules by adding the following: "Lack of notice of the entry by the clerk does not affect the time to appeal or relieve or authorize the court to relieve a party for failure to appeal within the time allowed." [141] This amendment was interpreted by a Minnesota court,[142] which had adopted the federal rules, as effectively preventing an extension of the time for appeal by the device used in the Hill case.[143] There is some authority to the effect that where counsel was misled by a statement of the district court, to which nobody objected, a two-day delay in filing the notice would not be fatal.[144] Although the rule authorizes the

---

137. Files v. City of Rockford, 440 F.2d 811 (7th Cir. 1971); Lathrop v. Oklahoma City Housing Authority, 438 F.2d 914 (10th Cir. 1971).

138. It is the duty of the clerk to make many entries in the civil docket, and it is sometimes difficult to determine exactly which entry starts the running of the time to appeal. In United States v. F. & M. Schaefer Brewing Co., 356 U.S. 227, 78 S.Ct. 674, 2 L.Ed. 2d 721 (1958) the clerk made an entry that a motion for summary judgment was granted, and six weeks later made an entry of the formal judgment; in a 7–2 decision the majority held the latter entry was the one and that the appeal was in apt time. See also Merlands Club, Inc. v. Messall, 208 A. 2d 687 (Md. 1965).

139. Fed.Rules Civ.Proc. 77(d).

140. 320 U.S. 520, 64 S.Ct. 334, 88 L.Ed. 283 (1944).

141. Fed.Rules Civ.Proc. 77(d) (as amended in 1948).

142. Tombs v. Ashworth, 255 Minn. 55, 95 N.W.2d 423 (1959).

143. "The great weight of authority is that a trial court may not permit, in any indirect manner, an extension of time for taking an appeal, particularly after the time for taking it has elapsed, so as to evade an express statutory requirement that the appeal must be taken within a certain time." Id. at 60, 95 N.W.2d at 426.

144. Thompson v. Immigration & Naturalization Serv., 375 U.S. 384, 84 S.Ct. 397, 11 L.Ed.2d 404 (1964). In this case the defendant's motion for new trial was filed 12 days after the entry of judgment (2 days late) but his lawyer was not in court when the judgment was entered. The government made no objection and the trial judge specifically stated that the motion was

district court to extend the time for filing the notice upon a show-ing of "excusable neglect," the courts take a very narrow view of that term,[145] and, in any event, the extension may not be grant-ed beyond a 30 day period.[146]

The importance of taking the first jurisdictional step—the filing of the notice of appeal in ample time—cannot be overem-phasized. It would be a mistake to assume, however, that once this is done the appellant has no further cause for worry. The road to reversal is long and tortuous, and a misstep along the way, although usually not fatal, may cause embarrassment, de-lay and expense. Fortunately these may be avoided because there is available an excellent road map and timetable in the form of the Federal Rules of Appellate Procedure.[147] If the lawyer for the appellant meticulously follows the rules, he may not achieve a victory for his client but, at the very least, he will succeed in hav-ing his case heard on the merits.

The following is a brief outline of the steps which the appellant must take to have a district court judgment reviewed by the court of appeals. *In the district court*: (1) file the notice of appeal; [148] (2) file a cost bond at the same time, usually in the amount of $250; [149] (3) file a supersedeas bond, to be approved by the dis-trict court, if he wishes the execution of the judgment to be stayed pending the appeal; [150] and (4) order the record on ap-

in apt time. The defendant appeal-ed from the denial of the motion (in apt time if the filing period was measured from the date of the denial of the motion, but not if measured from the entry of judg-ment). The Court of Appeals dis-missed the appeal but the Supreme Court reversed (5–4) on the ground the appellant could rely on the statement of the district court as to timeliness. See also Wolfsohn v. Hankin, 375 U.S. 384, 84 S.Ct. 397, 11 L.Ed.2d 404 (1964), noted in 63 Mich.L.Rev. 1288 (1965); In re Robertson's Estate, 246 Iowa 685, 68 N.W.2d 909 (1955).

145. Winchell v. Lortscher, 377 F. 2d 247 (8th Cir. 1967); Maryland Cas. Co. v. Conner, 382 F.2d 13 (10th Cir. 1967).

146. Pittsburgh Towing Co. v. Mis-sissippi Valley Barge Line Co., 385 U.S. 32, 87 S.Ct. 195, 17 L.Ed.2d 31 (1966); Dyotherm Corp. v. Turbo Mach. Co., 434 F.2d 65 (3d Cir. 1970).

147. The Federal Rules of Civil Pro-cedure brought uniformity to civil procedure in the district courts of the United States, but they did nothing for procedure in the courts of appeal. Consequently, though the steps to be taken in the dis-trict courts were simplified and standardized, the procedure in the various courts of appeals contin-ued to be complex and varied greatly from circuit to circuit. See Green, The Next Step: Uniform Rules for the Courts of Appeals, 14 Vand.L.Rev. 947 (1961). Pursu-ant to an enabling act passed by Congress in 1966 (28 U.S.C.A. § 2072) the Supreme Court promul-gated uniform rules for the courts of appeals, effective July 1, 1968.

148. Fed.Rules App.Proc. 3(a).

149. Fed.Rules App.Proc. 7.

150. At common law a writ of error, without any security, was of itself a supersedeas of execution from the time of its allowance. The

peal.[151] The original papers and certain docket entries are always included. How much of the evidence is to be included depends upon the questions which are to be raised upon the appeal. If one of the questions is whether the verdict of a jury is supported by the evidence then, obviously, all of the evidence should be included. If the questions to be raised on appeal deal only with particular rulings on the admissibility of evidence, or the correctness of certain instructions to the jury, then it may be unnecessary to incur the expense of ordering a full transcript of all of the evidence. The responsibility of determining what portions of the record must be included rests with the appellant. It may be that, inadvertently or otherwise, he may omit certain portions which are unfavorable to him. The rule therefore wisely provides: "Unless the entire transcript is to be included, the appellant shall, within the time above provided, file and serve upon the appellee a description of the parts of the transcript which he intends to include in the record and a statement of the issues he intends to present on the appeal." [152] The purpose of the rule is to give advance notice to the appellee of the points his opponent relies upon for reversal. The appellee may then insist that the record be augmented to present the full picture and also to include the parts he feels necessary to present the points he relies upon if he is alleging cross-errors. It not infrequently happens that both parties are dissatisfied with various rulings of the trial court, and each wishes a review of those rulings. In lieu of the record as defined by the rules the parties themselves may agree upon a statement of the case "showing how the issues presented by the appeal arose and were decided in the district court and setting forth only so many of the facts averred and proved or sought to be proved as are essential to a decision of the issues presented." [153] In the event the parties differ on whether the record prepared by the reporter truly discloses what occurred, the differences "shall be submitted to and settled by" the district court.[154] When the record is finally settled, in whatever manner,

rule was changed by statute as writs of error came to be used for delay. The general purpose of a supersedeas bond is to stay execution on the judgment pending appeal and to guarantee payment should the judgment be affirmed or the appeal dismissed. Kountze v. Omaha Hotel Co., 107 U.S. 378, 2 S.Ct. 911, 27 L.Ed. 609 (1882). The supersedeas bond must, in the first instance, be approved by the district court: Fed.Rules Civ.Proc. 62. But see Fed.Rules App.Proc. 8, which gives the court of appeals or a judge thereof, concurrent power.

151. Fed.Rules App.Proc. 10.

152. Fed.Rules App.Proc. 10(b). If the appellee deems more is necessary he may require it. Id.

153. Fed.Rules App.Proc. 10(d).

154. Fed.Rules App.Proc. 10(e).

it is the duty of the clerk of the court to transmit it to the clerk of the court of appeals.[155] This concludes the steps to be taken in the district court.

The case is now in the court of appeals, but the task of the appellant is far from done. The following is an outline of the steps which must be taken *in the court of appeals.* (1) Within the time prescribed by the rule, pay the clerk of the court of appeals the docket fee and see that the case is properly entered on the docket.[156] (2) Prepare and file his brief, the format,[157] contents,[158] and time of filing [159] being specified by the rules. (3) The appellee may then file his brief [160] to which the appellant may file a reply.[161] (4) The appellant must be sure to include in his brief an appendix giving a digest of the pertinent parts of the record. Prior to the new rules it was common practice, in many courts, to require the parties to print a transcript of the record, or an abstract of it, so that each appellate judge could have a copy. This was very expensive, and often unnecessary when the legal points argued involved only small portions of the record.[162] The new rules have greatly improved this procedure by requiring only that appellant, as an appendix to his brief, print so much of the proceedings as he deems necessary which, if demonstrated to be inadequate, may be augmented. The entire original record in the case is on file with the court and is available for reference if needed.[163] (5) A prehearing conference of counsel may be called by the court to simplify the issues and explore the possibilities of admissions or agreements.[164] This is similar to the pretrial conference in the trial court. (6) The oral argument before the court, the most dramatic aspect of the appeal, is usually limited to 30 minutes per side, with the appellant being accorded the privilege of opening and closing.[165] (7) The next step is taken, not by the parties, but by the court which decides the case and hands down its opinion. Normally a case is decided by a panel of three

155. Fed.Rules App.Proc. 11(b).

156. Fed.Rules App.Proc. 12.

157. Fed.Rules App.Proc. 32.

158. Fed.Rules App.Proc. 28(a).

159. Fed.Rules App.Proc. 31.

160. Fed.Rules App.Proc. 28(b).

161. Fed.Rules App.Proc. 28(c).

162. See Willcox, Karlen & Roemer, Justice Lost—By What Appellate Papers Cost, 33 N.Y.U.L.Rev. 934 (1958); Note, Cost of Appeal, 27 Mont.L.Rev. 49 (1965).

163. Fed.Rules App.Proc. 30.

164. Fed.Rules App.Proc. 33.

165. Fed.Rules App.Proc. 34. Due to the crowded condition of appellate dockets several circuits have established a screening procedure by which oral argument is eliminated in a substantial portion of the cases. In re Amendment of Rule 3, 440 F.2d 847 (9th Cir. 1970).

judges although, in unusual situations, the case may be thrown en banc in which case all judges participate in the decision.[166] (8) The losing party may file a petition for rehearing if he has grounds to believe that the court has "overlooked or misapprehended" points of law or fact.[167] Oral argument is not permitted in support of such petitions, and they are seldom granted but, as many counsel feel, there is no harm in trying.

A chapter on appellate practice, no matter how brief, should not close without some mention of the unique position of the Supreme Court of the United States. It is the highest court in the federal judicial system and may, by analogy, be likened to the highest court in a state judicial system which possesses an intermediate court of appeals. In both systems the routine appeal from the trial court will be to the intermediate court of appeals; in both systems there will be special situations in which the intermediate court may be by-passed and the appeal go directly to the highest court; and in both systems the highest court may grant a discretionary further review from the judgment of the intermediate court. Here the analogy ends. A state court has no power to review the judgment of a federal court, but the Supreme Court of the United States does have power to review certain state court judgments. The following is a brief review of the appellate jurisdiction of the Supreme Court.

Congress has provided three methods by which a decision of a court of appeals may be reviewed by the Supreme Court. The most common one is by writ of certiorari, which, unlike the common law writ, vests the court with discretionary power to issue the writ "upon the petition of any party to any civil or criminal case." [168] The power is very broad, but its exercise is very narrow. It is generally issued only in cases of great importance or in situations in which there is a conflict of authority on a legal point in the various courts of appeals. When a party petitions for a writ of certiorari, he must accompany his petition with a short record and brief, copies of which are distributed to all of the justices.[169] If four justices vote to grant the writ, the case is put on the docket for review. As Mr. Justice Frankfurter has taken pains to explain, a denial of the writ does not add any

---

166. En banc hearings "ordinarily will not be ordered except (1) when consideration by the full court is necessary to secure or maintain uniformity of its decisions, or (2) when the proceeding involves a question of exceptional importance." Fed.Rules **App.** Proc. 35(a).

167. Fed.Rules App.Proc. 40.

168. 28 U.S.C.A. § 1254(1).

169. The Certiorari practice of the court is described by Mr. Justice Frankfurter in his dissenting opinion in Rogers v. Missouri Pac. R. R., supra n. 114.

precedent value to the decision of the lower court; it merely means that the petitioner was unable to muster four votes in his favor.[170] The second method is by appeal, which will lie only in a case in which the court of appeals has held a state statute invalid as repugnant to the Constitution, treaties or laws of the United States.[171] The third method is by certification by the court of appeals of a question of law in a pending case, which question the Supreme Court may, in its discretion, answer and give binding instructions to the court of appeals.[172]

There are four situations in which it is possible to obtain a direct review of a district court decision by the Supreme Court. (1) Under the Expediting Act of 1903,[173] as amended, the United States is given a direct appeal to the Supreme Court in certain actions under the antitrust laws, the Interstate Commerce Act, and the Communications Act. (2) The Criminal Appeals Act of 1907,[174] as amended, gives the United States a direct appeal to the Supreme Court in certain cases in which the defendant has not been put in jeopardy. (3) A direct appeal lies from the district court to the Supreme Court from a decision "holding an Act of Congress unconstitutional in any civil action, suit, or proceeding to which the United States or any of its agencies, or any officer or employee thereof . . . is a party." [175] (4) A direct appeal lies to the Supreme Court from a district court order granting or denying an injunction in any civil suit which, by act of Congress, must be heard by a three-judge district court.[176] All of these represent extraordinary situations in which (1) the implementation of an important federal policy is at stake and expedition is desirable, or (2) the delicate problem of separation of powers of government is involved, or (3) the equally sensitive problem of federal-state relationships is presented.

A unique aspect of the jurisdiction of the United States Supreme Court is that it is also vested with the power to review the decisions of the courts of the several states. There is nothing in the constitution which explicitly gives it this power. As a matter of fact, although the original jurisdiction of the Supreme Court is defined by the constitution, its appellate jurisdiction is

---

170. Agoston v. Pennsylvania, 340 U.S. 844, 71 S.Ct. 9, 95 L.Ed. 619 (1950).

171. 28 U.S.C.A. § 1254(2).

172. 28 U.S.C.A. § 1254(3).

173. Act of Feb. 11, 1903, ch. 544, 32 Stat. 823.

174. Act of Mar. 2, 1907, ch. 2564, 34 Stat. 1246; 18 U.S.C.A. § 3731.

175. 28 U.S.C.A. § 1252.

176. 28 U.S.C.A. § 1253. Three-judge courts are required to enjoin the enforcement of State statutes: 28 U.S.C.A. § 2281; and to enjoin the enforcement of federal statutes: 28 U.S.C.A. § 2282.

left to be defined by Congress.[177] In exercising that authority Congress has provided that the Supreme Court may review the judgments of state courts in certain situations.[178] It has carefully restricted this power of review to federal questions which come clearly within the judicial power which the constitution grants to the United States. In order for a state court decision to be reviewable by the United States Supreme Court, it must meet certain criteria. (1) It must be a final judgment, and this means "final" in the sense the term is usually employed in appellate practice. (2) It must have been rendered "by the highest court of a State in which a decision could be had." [179] This means that the appellant must have exhausted the judicial remedies available in his state. It does not mean that review lies only from the highest court in the state; only that he must go as high as possible in the state system. In Thompson v. City of Louisville [180] the Supreme Court took jurisdiction to review a decision of the Police Court of Louisville where the fines imposed were so small that no review was available in any Kentucky court. (3) The case must involve a "substantial" federal question.[181] (4) The decision of the federal question must have been crucial to the case. If the decision can be supported on an adequate and independent state ground, the Supreme Court will not review the case. The reason for this criterion was concisely stated by Mr. Justice Jackson in Herb v. Pitcairn: [182]

> Our only power over state judgments is to correct them to the extent that they incorrectly adjudge federal rights. And our power is to correct wrong judgments, not to revise opinions. We are not permitted to render an advisory opinion, and if the same judgment would be rendered by the state court after we corrected its views of federal laws, our review could amount to nothing more than an advisory opinion.

It is often not clear whether a state court judgment was based on a federal ground, an independent state ground, or both. Two similar cases emphasize the difficulty. In Lynch v. New York [183]

---

177. U.S.Const. art. III, § 2.

178. 28 U.S.C.A. § 1257.

179. 28 U.S.C.A. § 1257.

180. 362 U.S. 199, 80 S.Ct. 624, 4 L.Ed.2d 654 (1960).

181. Angel v. Bullington, 330 U.S. 183, 67 S.Ct. 657, 91 L.Ed. 832 (1947). See Ulman & Spears, Dis-missal for Want of a Substantial Federal Question, 20 B.U.L.Rev. 501 (1940); Note, The Insubstantial Federal Question, 62 Harv.L. Rev. 488 (1949).

182. 324 U.S. 117, 125–26, 65 S.Ct. 459, 463, 89 L.Ed. 789, 794 (1945).

183. 293 U.S. 52, 55 S.Ct. 16, 79 L.Ed. 191 (1934).

the petitioner attacked the constitutionality of an income tax on the rentals from his Ohio land, claiming it violated both the state and federal constitutions. The New York courts annulled the tax but the United States Supreme Court refused to review the case, stating that for jurisdiction to exist the record must affirmatively show that the decision rested on the federal ground. In Department of Mental Hygiene of California v. Kirchner,[184] the California Supreme Court held that a statute upon which petitioner relied "violates the basic constitutional guaranty of equal protection of the law." [185] On appeal to the United States Supreme Court it declared the opinion of the California court was ambiguous, leaving it in doubt as to whether it relied on the Equal Protection clause of the Fourteenth Amendment or to a corresponding clause in the California constitution.[186] Instead of refusing jurisdiction, however, it reversed and remanded to the California court for a clarification of its holding.

A lawyer has a duty to his client to pursue every legitimate avenue open to him where there is any reasonable hope of success. The possibility of appeal should not be lightly discarded. A law professor, who later became a federal judge, described the Supreme Court as "the Court of Last Conjecture and Final Error." A member of that court once said: "There is no doubt that if there were a super-Supreme Court, a substantial proportion of our reversals of state courts would also be reversed. We are not final because we are infallible, but we are infallible only because we are final." [187]

---

184. 380 U.S. 194, 85 S.Ct. 871, 13 L.Ed.2d 753 (1965).

185. Id. at 196, 85 S.Ct. at 873, 13 L.Ed.2d at 757.

186. "This Court is always wary of assuming jurisdiction of a case from a state court unless it is plain that a federal question is necessarily presented, and the party seeking review here must show that we have jurisdiction of the case. Were we to assume that the federal question was the basis for the decision below, it is clear that the California Supreme Court, either on remand or in another case presenting the same issues, could inform us that its opinion was in fact based, at least in part, on the California Constitution, thus leaving the result untouched by whatever conclusions this Court might have reached on the merits of the federal question. For reasons that follow we conclude that further clarifying proceedings in the California Supreme Court are called for . . ." Id. at 197, 85 S. Ct. at 873, 13 L.Ed.2d at 756.

187. Mr. Justice Jackson, concurring, in Brown v. Allen, 344 U.S. 443, 540, 73 S.Ct. 397, 427, 97 L. Ed. 469, 533 (1953).

TABLE OF CASES

References are to Pages

TABLE OF COURT RULES

References are to Pages

FEDERAL RULES OF CIVIL PROCEDURE

FEDERAL RULES OF CIVIL PROCEDURE—Continued

FEDERAL RULES OF CIVIL PROCEDURE—Continued

FEDERAL RULES OF APPELLATE PROCEDURE

*

INDEX

END OF VOLUME